Computational Models of Language Evolution

Editors: Luc Steels, Remi van Trijp

In this series:

1. Steels, Luc. The Talking Heads experiment: Origins of words and meanings.

2. Vogt, Paul. How mobile robots can self-organize a vocabulary.

3. Bleys, Joris. Language strategies for the domain of colour.

4. van Trijp, Remi. The evolution of case grammar.

5. Spranger, Michael. The evolution of grounded spatial language.

The Talking Heads experiment

Origins of words and meanings

Luc Steels

Luc Steels. 2015. *The Talking Heads experiment: Origins of words and meanings* (Computational Models of Language Evolution 1). Berlin: Language Science Press.

This title can be downloaded at:
http://langsci-press.org/catalog/book/49
© 2015, Luc Steels
Published under the Creative Commons Attribution 4.0 Licence (CC BY 4.0):
http://creativecommons.org/licenses/by/4.0/
ISBN: 978-3-944675-42-8

Cover and concept of design: Ulrike Harbort
Typesetting: Felix Kopecky, Sebastian Nordhoff
Proofreading: Martin Hilpert, Felix Kopecky, Peter Petré, Daniela Schröder
Fonts: Linux Libertine, Arimo
Typesetting software: X∃LATEX

Language Science Press
Habelschwerdter Allee 45
14195 Berlin, Germany
langsci-press.org

Storage and cataloguing done by FU Berlin

Language Science Press has no responsibility for the persistence or accuracy of URLs for external or third-party Internet websites referred to in this publication, and does not guarantee that any content on such websites is, or will remain, accurate or appropriate. Information regarding prices, travel timetables and other factual information given in this work are correct at the time of first publication but Language Science Press does not guarantee the accuracy of such information thereafter.

For my daughter Lenie

Preface

I set up the Talking Heads experiment with a group of brilliant students and collaborators at the end of the nineteen nineties. It was intended to be the first large-scale, open-ended experiment in the emergence of a shared set of grounded concepts and a vocabulary for expressing these concepts by a population of autonomous agents. Inspired by Ludwig Wittgenstein, the experiment took the form of a series of language games, more concretely games of reference about a "world" made up of geometric figures pasted on a white board and observable by the agents through pan-tilt cameras. I wanted to demonstrate with this experiment earlier breakthroughs in the study of language origins and test whether they would hold for large-scale populations and open-ended environments. I also wanted to find out how humans would interact with these agents. So we made it such that human users, after logging in through the Internet, could teach new words to agents or use the words they learned from the agents to play their own language games.

In 1999, the experiment went live in the context of an exhibition called Laboratorium organised in Antwerp (Belgium) by Hans-Ulrich Obrist and Barbara Vanderlinden. After a first experimental run from 27 June 1999 to 3 October 1999, the experiment was repeated as part of a new exhibition called N01SE organised in Cambridge and London (UK) by Adam Lowe and Simon Schaffer from 22 January to 26 March 2000, with additional installations at the Palais de la Découverte in Paris and several other places.

At the occasion of the 1999 Laboratorium exhibition, the draft of a book was published that described the experiment and the underlying theoretical assumptions in considerable detail. For many reasons, not at least that work continued at great speed on other exciting experiments, the original "pre-edition" of the book never made it to a fully finished officially published work, and circulated only as an "underground" edition. This was disappointing because the Talking Heads experiment was an important breakthrough. Moreover the experiment contained the first inklings of mechanisms that since then have been worked out, enhanced and tested in many experiments which replicated the original results and further enhanced them. The present volume is intended to fill this gap.

Part I of this book contains the original Talking Heads volume which has been only slightly edited to correct for minor mistakes. It is a miracle that the original source files survived and that the figures could be reconstructed. Part II of this book contains additional unpublished background material, reports on different aspects of the experiment, including its scientific results, and a brief overview of further developments in language evolution research that took place on the basis of the experiment.

Dozens of people worked on the Talking Heads. The initial research started in 1997 at the Artificial Intelligence Laboratory of the Free University of Brussels (VUB) funded by a "Geconcentreerde onderzoeks actie" (GOA) of the Belgian government. Joris Van Looveren worked closely with me on a first prototype that was demonstrated in 1997, using an active vision system custom-built by Tony Belpaeme and segmentation algorithms implemented by Danny van Tieghem. Edwin de Jong did the first theoretical investigations of the underlying semiotic dynamics. Once the initiative for a public installation was taken, the main hub became the Sony Computer Science Laboratory in Paris, where I worked together intensely with Frédéric Kaplan and Angus McIntyre, with additional contributions for the teleportation infrastructure by Silvère Tajan and Alexis Agahi. The AI Laboratory of the VUB remained a second hub where important contributions were made most notably by Joris Van Looveren, Tony Belpaeme, Holger Kenn and Mario Campanella. To all of them I am grateful that we were able to create such an extremely exciting experiment that stimulated many thousands of people to think about language and its origins in new ways.

I also thank the curators of the Laboratorium Exhibition in Antwerp (Hans-Ulrich Obrist and Barbara Vanderlinden) and the members of its curating board (Bruno Latour and Carsten Höller), the curators of the N01SE exhibition in London (Adam Lowe and Simon Schaffer), artist Olafur Eliasson, with whom I collaborated on the Look into the Box piece at the Musé d'art Moderne in Paris, artist Anne-Mie Van Kerckhoven for collaborations for the Chromosophy laboratory in Aachen and the many organisers and helping hands who made the other installations possible. Sylvia Spruck Wrigley has helped to improve the 1999 pre-edition (now Part I of the book) under considerable time pressure and Marleen Wynants was crucial in the last phases of this publication with comments, professional advice, photographs, and support.

Part II of the book discusses what happened after the Talking Heads experiment. Our research went through various boom and bust cycles. In the good years there was money to hire new people and push the research forwards, but then bad years would come and the team disintegrated again due to lack of resources. This made progress less substantial than it could have been but had the advantages that waves of new young people were given a chance to contribute. The first wave started working after the Talking Heads experiments were finished. At Sony CSL there was first exciting work by Pierre-Yves Oudeyer and Frederic Kaplan pursuing the origins of turn taking and symbol usage with the AIBO robots, thus exploring even earlier stages in the origins of language.

Thanks to the FP6 ECAgents project and the FP7 ALEAR projects of the European Commission, a new team could be formed around 2004, which included Joris Bleys, Joachim De Beule, Bart de Vylder, and Jelle Zuidema at the VUB in Brussels. Meanwhile, we got access through the Sony Computer Science Laboratory to the QRIO humanoid robots thanks to Masahiro Fujita and Hideki Shimomura. A new team formed in Paris which included Nancy Chang, Katya Gerasimova, Martin Loetzsch, Vanessa Micelli, Michael Spranger, Simon Pauw and Remi Van Trijp. I thank them all for major contributions to the experiments reported in the second part of the book. I also thank Stefano Nolfi for coordinating the ECAgents project with a firm hand and Manfred Hild and his team for creating the new humanoid MYON robot that we used in later experiments.

In 2008/2009 I was a fellow at the Wissenschaftskolleg in Berlin, which was an ideal environment to reflect on our research program and how we could proceed. Many new ideas came out of that year, in particular, a realisation that for several of the key puzzles we were trying to solve, inspiration could be found in evolutionary biology, and this led to a new path which only now is beginning to be explored. It is good to know that after a major collapse in funding around 2009, there is again a team of young people assembling to push research on language games further. They include Emilia Garcia Casademont in Barcelona, Miquel Cornudella and Paul Van Eecke in Paris, and Yana Knight in Brussels. Financing remains precarious but the future is in their hands!

The present new edition is not only special because of the historical significance of the Talking Heads experiment but also because it is the first one in a new series "Computational Models of Language Evolution" published by the Language Science Press. The intention of this series is to make available through Open Access in-depth models of language evolution that have been validated using agent-based computational simulations. I am grateful to Martin Haspelmath and Stefan Müller (the editors of the Language Science Press) for making it possible to publish in Open Access research results which do not quite fit in the standard mode. I thank Maria Ferrer Bonnet for help in the final stage of adapting bibliographies. And I am grateful to ICREA for time to create a revised and extended version of the Talking Heads Book and to the Institut de Biologia Evolutiva in Barcelona for providing such an excellent working environment. I thank in addition Remi van Trijp for his help in making this series a reality and Annemie Maes for her encouragement in the final stretches to finish this book.

Barcelona, October 2014.

Contents

Preface   iv

I   The 1999 Talking Heads book   1

1   Introduction   5
- 1.1   The Talking Heads experiment   5
- 1.2   The main hypotheses   7
- 1.3   A bottom-up approach to artificial intelligence   9
- 1.4   History of the project   10
- 1.5   Beyond Turing   15
- 1.6   The book   17

2   Preview   19
- 2.1   The main components   19
  - 2.1.1   Teleporting   19
  - 2.1.2   The robots   21
  - 2.1.3   The agents   23
  - 2.1.4   Interactivity   24
- 2.2   The Guessing Game   26
  - 2.2.1   Rules of the game   26
  - 2.2.2   Nature of the game   27
  - 2.2.3   The semiotic square   28
  - 2.2.4   Processes involved in language communication   30
  - 2.2.5   Knowledge sources and competences   31
- 2.3   Perception and categorisation   32
  - 2.3.1   Scene and topic selection   32
  - 2.3.2   Sensory channels   34
  - 2.3.3   Making distinctions   35
- 2.4   Lexicalisation   37
  - 2.4.1   Same meaning, same referent   37
  - 2.4.2   A new word   38
  - 2.4.3   Competition between words   39
  - 2.4.4   Disambiguation   40
  - 2.4.5   Same meaning, different referent   42
  - 2.4.6   Situated grounded semantics   43

	2.5	The origins of grammar	45
	2.6	Conclusions	47

3 Perception — 49
- 3.1 What sensors sense — 50
  - 3.1.1 Artificial sensors and actuators — 50
  - 3.1.2 Natural sensing — 51
  - 3.1.3 Behaviours — 51
- 3.2 Segmentation — 53
  - 3.2.1 Feature extraction — 54
  - 3.2.2 Divergent perception — 56
  - 3.2.3 The sieve architecture — 56
- 3.3 Sensory channels — 58
  - 3.3.1 Example channels — 58
  - 3.3.2 Conceptual spaces — 59
  - 3.3.3 Perceptual constancy — 60
  - 3.3.4 Transformations — 61
  - 3.3.5 Scaling — 61
  - 3.3.6 Saliency — 62
- 3.4 Methodology — 65
  - 3.4.1 Putting up scaffolds — 66
  - 3.4.2 Idealisation and realism — 67
- 3.5 The GEOM world — 70
- 3.6 Conclusions — 72

4 The Discrimination Game — 75
- 4.1 The paradoxes of meaning — 76
  - 4.1.1 The empiricist's stance — 77
  - 4.1.2 The rationalist's stance — 78
  - 4.1.3 Arguments for and against rationalism — 78
  - 4.1.4 Arguments for and against empiricism — 80
- 4.2 Selectionism — 81
  - 4.2.1 Principles of selectionism — 81
  - 4.2.2 Selectionist cognitive systems — 82
  - 4.2.3 The tree metaphor — 83
  - 4.2.4 Deriving new sensory channels — 84
  - 4.2.5 Comparing approaches — 84
- 4.3 Discrimination trees — 85
  - 4.3.1 Making distinctions — 85
  - 4.3.2 Categorisers — 86
  - 4.3.3 The Discrimination Game — 88
  - 4.3.4 The Pachinko machine — 89
  - 4.3.5 Competition between categories — 90
  - 4.3.6 Variations on discrimination — 91

		4.3.7	The Discrimination Game in action	91
		4.3.8	The importance of scaling and saliency	94
		4.3.9	Combinations of categories	95
		4.3.10	A real world scene	95
	4.4	An ecology of distinctions	97
		4.4.1	Growth dynamics	97
		4.4.2	Pruning dynamics	98
		4.4.3	Average discriminatory success and repertoire size	98
		4.4.4	Adaptivity in categorisation	100
		4.4.5	Real world scenes	102
	4.5	Conclusions	102

5 The Naming Game — 105

	5.1	Inventing a lexicon	106
		5.1.1	Representing lexical associations	107
		5.1.2	Updating the score	108
		5.1.3	Constructing and acquiring words	109
		5.1.4	The Naming Game in action	110
		5.1.5	Characterising the lexicon	111
		5.1.6	Monitoring	113
		5.1.7	Measuring lexical coherence	115
	5.2	Scaling up	116
		5.2.1	Coping with new meanings	116
		5.2.2	Lexicon acquisition by virgin agents	119
		5.2.3	Preservation in changing populations	120
	5.3	Self-organisation	122
		5.3.1	Winner-take-all processes	123
		5.3.2	Collective behaviour and self-organisation	123
		5.3.3	Increasing-returns economics	125
		5.3.4	Lessons from nature	126
	5.4	Lexical dynamics	126
		5.4.1	Spatially distributed naming games	127
		5.4.2	Language contact	129
	5.5	Conclusions	131

6 The Guessing Game — 133

	6.1	Defining the Guessing Game	134
		6.1.1	Example of a coupled game	135
		6.1.2	Input-output coupling	140
		6.1.3	Updating the scores	141
		6.1.4	Repair processes	143
	6.2	Synonymy	144
	6.3	Ambiguity	149
		6.3.1	How words may still get the same meaning	150

		6.3.2	How words get different meanings	151
		6.3.3	Competition between word meanings	155
		6.3.4	Lexical and ontological development	157
	6.4	Scaling up		159
		6.4.1	Increasing the population size	159
		6.4.2	Lexicon acquisition by new agents	163
	6.5	Conclusions		165

7 Grounding — 167

	7.1	A first grounding experiment		168
		7.1.1	Integrating perception and action	168
		7.1.2	Concept acquisition	170
		7.1.3	Generalisation without learning	172
		7.1.4	The influence of the environment	174
		7.1.5	Coping with perceptual anomalies	179
	7.2	Semiotic dynamics		183
		7.2.1	Tracking language evolution	183
		7.2.2	Semiotic landscapes	183
		7.2.3	Competition diagrams	185
		7.2.4	RMF coherence	186
	7.3	The ideal language		187
		7.3.1	Total coherence	187
		7.3.2	Communicative success despite incoherence	188
	7.4	Damping synonymy and ambiguity		189
		7.4.1	The story of *fepi*	190
		7.4.2	The story of *xu*	192
		7.4.3	The entry of *O3*	194
	7.5	Rousseau's paradox		195
		7.5.1	Universality versus relativism	195
		7.5.2	Ontological coherence	197
	7.6	Conclusions		198

II Installations and experiments — 201

8 The first series (1999) — 203

	8.1	The Laboratorium exhibition	203
	8.2	The installation	205
	8.3	Start up of the experiment	208
	8.4	Results of the experiment	222
	8.5	Conclusions	224

9 The second series (2000–2001)   231
- 9.1 The N01SE exhibition 231
  - 9.1.1 The exhibition 231
  - 9.1.2 Installation at Kettle's Yard in Cambridge 234
  - 9.1.3 Installation at the Wellcome Gallery in London 238
- 9.2 Iconoclasm 242
- 9.3 Installation at the Palais de la Découverte in Paris 258
- 9.4 The portable Talking Heads 258
- 9.5 Look into the Box 260
- 9.6 Conclusions 264

III Beyond the Talking Heads   267

10 Beyond the Talking Heads experiment   269
- 10.1 Experiments with the AIBO robots 269
  - 10.1.1 AIBO's first words 270
  - 10.1.2 The Perspective Reversal experiment 273
- 10.2 Scaling up to grammar 278
  - 10.2.1 Early syntax experiments 278
  - 10.2.2 The Case Grammar experiments 282
- 10.3 Conclusions 294

11 Language strategies for humanoid robots   295
- 11.1 The Proper Naming Game 296
  - 11.1.1 Challenges 297
  - 11.1.2 Semiotic networks 300
- 11.2 Action Games 304
- 11.3 The Colour Description Game 306
  - 11.3.1 Compositional procedural semantics with IRL 311
  - 11.3.2 Building blocks for natural language semantics 313
  - 11.3.3 Strategies for colour 314
  - 11.3.4 Translation to grammar 316
  - 11.3.5 Influence of embodiment 320
- 11.4 Conclusion 321

12 Language evolution   323
- 12.1 Culture-driven language evolution 323
- 12.2 Fitness landscapes 329
  - 12.2.1 Fitness landscapes of language systems 330
  - 12.2.2 The fitness landscape of language strategies 335
- 12.3 Selection and alignment of language strategies 338
- 12.4 Generation of new strategies 343
  - 12.4.1 A meta-strategy for generating new conceptualisation strategies 344

         12.4.2   Meta-strategies for generating new lexicogrammatical strategies   347
    12.5   Conclusions 354

Bibliography   **357**

Index   **369**
    Name index 369
    Subject index 373

Part I

The 1999 Talking Heads book

The Talking Heads
Experiment

Volume I. Words and Meanings

Luc Steels

Special pre-edition for
LABORATORIUM, Antwerpen 1999

Original cover of the Talking Heads book published in 1999 on the occasion of the Laboratorium exhibition in Antwerp.

1 Introduction

Inquiring about the origins of a phenomenon, as opposed to merely describing its present state, often leads to profound new discoveries. Biology provides a wealth of examples. Darwin asked the question of the origins of species diversity and thus discovered evolution by natural selection. Pasteur wondered about the origins of life and thus discovered the role of bacteria in human diseases. My approach in this book is going to be similar. In order to advance our understanding of human language and cognition, I propose to address the fundamental question how language and meaning might ever have originated. I will not do this by a historical reconstruction, nor by an empirical investigation of child language acquisition or by examining data from the birth of new languages.[1] Rather, I will pose the question in a completely general way: how can a physically embodied autonomous agent arrive at a repertoire of categories for conceptualising his world and how can a group of such agents ever develop a shared communication system with the same complexity as human natural languages?

1.1 The Talking Heads experiment

For centuries, philosophers, linguists, psychologists and neuroscientists have been groping with the amazing capacities of the mind. By necessity, they have been doing this through thought experiments or by observing human behaviour and brain anatomy. Although this has generated a wealth of insights,[2] everyone involved in this research must surely agree that we are still lacking adequate models, particularly for higher order cognitive functions like language processing, and definitely for understanding how such functions may have arisen. To discover or test such models, it therefore remains useful to do experiments with artificial systems. We can build robots that receive sensory inputs through a camera or other sensors, give them computational power and memory, and empower them for action in the world by adding actuators. Given such a set-up, we

---

[1] There has been a renewed interest the last five years in the question of the origins of language from these various perspectives. Hurford, Studdert-Kennedy & Knight (1998) contains a representative sample of the most recent work. Other samples of recent research can be found in Hawkins (1992) and Velichkovsky & Rumbaugh (1996).

[2] Attempts are made to bring together the insights from various disciplines to establish a true "cognitive science". Osherton (1995) contains an introduction into some of the main research trends in this very diverse scientific field. See also Luger (1994). The work reported in the present book can be classified as theoretical cognitive science because I try to formulate and test the operational adequacy of possible models for the origins of language and meaning but do not claim nor give any evidence that these models are also valid for human cognition, just as the study of aerodynamics and aircraft design may help to understand how birds can fly but is more generic than its biological implementations.

1 Introduction

can precisely examine the operational adequacy of a hypothesis. For example, if someone proposes a process for segmenting images, we can test this process by capturing streams of images through a camera and see whether the process is indeed capable of performing segmentation. When someone proposes a process for parsing sentences, we can implement this process and confront it with a series of example sentences to measure success and failure. How else can we test the operational adequacy of a proposed cognitive model, given the enormous complexity involved? Of course, building an artificial system in no way proves that the principles that were used to construct it are valid for natural systems. But it is an enormously valuable source of insight for approaching the extraordinarily complex phenomena observed in human cognition.

Figure 1.1: Two Talking Heads are shown **a1** and **a2** each seeing the scene on the white board from a slightly different viewpoint.

The Talking Heads experiment follows this research strategy. It features an enormously challenging experimental infrastructure to explore how a cognitive system, like the one underlying human language, might be able to bootstrap itself into interaction with other cognitive systems and driven by increasing challenges from the environment. The experiment involves a set of robotic "Talking Heads" engaged in language games, with each other or with human interlocutors, about real world scenes they perceive through their sensors (see Figures 1.1 and 1.2). The robots use vision as major sensory source. They are located in different places in the world and connected through the Internet. Two robotic agents can only engage in an interaction when they are instantiated in robot bodies in a shared physical environment. After an exchange, an agent can teleport himself to another body in another location and engage in interactions there.

The agents' categorisations of the world and their language is *not* programmed but emerges. It is constructed and learned by the agents themselves. The more interactions they have with other humans the more they adopt our concepts and language. Interacting with the Talking Heads is a bit like interacting with two year old twins; they play

1.2 The main hypotheses

Figure 1.2: A single "Talking Head". There is a camera oriented towards a white board. The bottom screen shows what the camera observes. The top right screen shows the result of processing. A loudspeaker reproduces the utterances of the agent.

most of the time with each other and develop their own language in the process, but the more humans engage in interaction with them, the more the language resembles existing human languages.[3]

Although the agents invent their own language and conceptualisations of the world, we had to program a basic cognitive architecture into the agents. This architecture is based on a set of relatively simple, biologically plausible mechanisms, which nevertheless gives rise to enormous complexity. The goal of the experiment is to examine the explanatory power of these mechanisms: What phenomena do they cause and hence explain?

1.2 The main hypotheses

The Talking Heads experiment is first and foremost a scientific experiment. It subjects four radical ideas to experimental scrutiny. The first idea is that language emerges through self-organisation out of local interactions of language users. It spontaneously becomes more complex to increase reliability and optimise transmission across generations of users, without a central designer. I call this THE SELFISH LANGUAGE HYPOTHESIS:

---

[3] Often twins develop a private language, particularly if they do not interact much with adults. Compared to other children, twins are usually 6 months behind in their language development but that delay and also the private languages that go with it disappear by the age of 8.

1 Introduction

Language colonises brains and recruits available cognitive capacities to satisfy its appetite for expressing ever more complex meaning with minimal effort and maximum effectiveness.[4] Language is not a uniform abstract system of rules (and definitely not an innate system of rules) but a creative open-ended complex adaptive system, like a natural ecology, in which certain solutions to relate forms with meanings become temporarily conventionalised in the community, even though new creative solutions emerge almost any time someone speaks. Language is in constant flux because new meanings continuously arise and existing forms undergo change beyond the control of any individual language user.

The second radical idea is that meaning is built up slowly by each individual in a cumulative growth process. Meaning is not innate, as rationalists in the footprints of Plato have been arguing for centuries, nor learned through stepwise induction from examples and counterexamples, as empiricists have been saying. Meaning is at first very concrete and strongly situated in the environment and bodily experiences. I will take the suggestions made by Wittgenstein one step further, namely that meaning (and language) is constructed and practised as part of language games.[5] I will introduce a selectionist approach to the acquisition of meaning, introducing models to show that conceptual distinctions can "grow" in the brain like the leaves and branches on a tree and be pruned to fit the demands and characteristics of the environment in which an agent finds itself. Even though non-verbal activities, like predicting the future based on a model or deciding what to do in specific circumstances, stimulates the growth of distinctions, language use is probably one of the greatest stimulators of conceptual growth. It provides feedback about which distinctions were successful in linguistic communication and thus whether or not they should be preserved. Thus language and cognition co-evolve. Each one pushes the other up towards more complexity and they become tightly co-ordinated with neither a central co-ordinator nor prior innate design.

A third idea concerns the characteristics of cognitive architectures. For centuries, the human cognitive system has been likened to a machine, most recently to the computer as an information processing machine.[6] Although there is a lot to say for adopting such a viewpoint, I will instead emphasise biological metaphors. Specifically, I will defend the idea that a living ecology is a better metaphor for a realistic cognitive system. In an ecology, there is constant change as the individual organisms adapt themselves to the physical environment and to other organisms sharing the same environment. There is evolution by selection so that successful adaptations survive and others disappear. There are failures but also repair processes happening at all levels of the ecological hierarchy. These various characteristics inspired the artificial architectures used in the experiments.

A fourth radical idea concerns the nature and origins of grammar. Rather than invoking the need of a highly specialised genetically determined language organ,[7] I believe

---

[4] See Deacon (1997) for a discussion of co-evolution between cognitive and linguistic capacities and brain structures.

[5] Wittgenstein (1953) emphasises the relativity of concepts and the role of language and hence meaning in social interactions.

[6] See Newell & Simon (1976).

[7] As strongly argued by Chomsky in various writings, for example Chomsky (1986). Even though Chomsky

that grammar spontaneously arises when generic capabilities to categorise reality, store past events in terms of abstract schemas, remember associations between events, etc., reach a critical level and are applied to language itself. These capabilities are relevant across many different cognitive domains. In order to store linguistic experiences, human memories spontaneously structure them, thus introducing abstract schemas, internal categories, and roles that substructures can play in schemas. These organisational elements then become externalised. Categories are marked by enriching the form of words, schema boundaries are marked by imposing patterns on the expression of a schema, roles are marked by assigning them to specific positions in a pattern. This externalisation increases the reliability in communication because it reduces ambiguities and supplies additional context. It also aids the stable transmission of the language from one generation to the next because the language learner gets additional hints to guess the meaning and function of unknown words and constructions. Once such structuring devices are in place, they help to increase the expressive power of the language. The complexity of possible language interactions can increase, and words or word groups which had multiple usages can become specialised for particular semantic functions.

The various language construction processes gradually shaping a full-blown language are not under the conscious control of individuals but instead constitute a collective enterprise. Language users structure and restructure their language and thus increase its systematicity, but there are also forces causing a breakdown of systematicity, such as erosion of a form through sloppiness of pronunciation, in turn causing a grammatical regularity to break down. The interplay between these constructive and destructive forces helps to explain the constant evolution of language and the growing diversity among languages emanating from the same source, such as French, Italian, and Spanish from Latin.

1.3 A bottom-up approach to artificial intelligence

My daughter Lenie grew up surrounded by computers and robots which her obsessed father was trying to infuse with artificial intelligence. When she was twelve, I asked her whether she thought any of the machines or programs she had seen were intelligent. She said no, someone had programmed them, so they were not intelligent themselves. The programmer was intelligent, not the machine. Indeed, this is true.

In 1996, a computer program called Deep Blue defeated the reigning world champion Kasparov in a game of chess (Newborn 1996). Kasparov was astonished and depressed, and claimed this was a defeat of humans in the race against machines. But was he actually beaten by ARTIFICIAL intelligence? Not really. A team of engineers and scientists from Carnegie Mellon University and from the IBM Watson Research Center had been working for ten years to program vast amounts of chess knowledge, invented by human experts, into Deep Blue. They had built extremely sophisticated dedicated computing

---

argues for an innate language acquisition device he has expressed scepticism about evolution by natural selection as an explanation for the origin of this device (and therefore of language). A genetic theory of language evolution has been suggested by Pinker (1994).

hardware to apply this knowledge at a blinding speed. So, in beating Kasparov, other humans were the clever ones, not machines.

Recently, the whole world looked on in fascination for several weeks as a small robot, the Rover Sojourner, ventured out on Mars, navigating through the rocky landscape, collecting samples, taking pictures and performing experiments.[8] Was this a first sign of artificial life? Even though the behaviour of the robot has some apparent characteristics of living systems, people more familiar with the project would say no. The robot was hardly autonomous; it continuously had to rely on signals coming from human engineers in order to set its next targets, or to deal with unforeseen circumstances. The robot's behaviours were all human designed and carefully programmed. The robot itself was in no way adaptive. It did not learn new behaviours nor new interaction modes, as a living system would do. It was critically dependent on human engineers whenever its functionality needed to be extended or modified.

This in no way diminishes the achievement in building these artificial devices, on the contrary, it does show we have to be careful in ascribing mental or biological qualities to machines. Despite the hype generated by the media and the occasional researcher taking his dreams for reality, intelligence and life remain very much the property of natural rather than artificial systems. In a way, our powerful engineering methodologies make it too easy to succumb to a strategy of programming directly the human or animal behaviours we observe and interpret as being intelligent. But doing this, we keep simulating the end products of intelligence rather than getting at the heart of intelligence itself. We put our own human concepts explicitly in the machine instead of implementing the mechanisms that enable an artificial agent to acquire new categories itself, implementing by hand a fixed set of predetermined behaviours which we believe the agent should have, rather than supplying mechanisms that allow the agent to acquire new behaviours when faced with unforeseen circumstances, and so on. Things are done this way because we simply do not know how to do them otherwise.

The goal of the fundamental research reported in this book is not only to raise some profound fascinating questions about language, but also to lay the groundwork for an alternative bottom-up approach towards artificial intelligence. In this approach, the human designer does not put his or her language and concepts into the computer, but tries to set up systems that autonomously generate their own. Indeed, if we have scientific models which explain how language originates, both in a language community and in new individuals born into a community, we should be able to operationalise these models and show that they work on autonomous robotic agents. This is exactly what the Talking Heads experiment tries to accomplish.

1.4 History of the project

The Talking Heads experiment is the culmination of one of the most exciting scientific and engineering projects I have ever been involved in. It has required the creative efforts

---

[8] See Wunsch (1998) (a book for children!).

of a dozen excellent researchers over many years. The story started in 1985. Instead of continuing to design and program intelligence explicitly based on formalising human cognitive capacities, as most of my colleagues in artificial intelligence research labs were doing,[9] I started to focus on the question of how intelligence might originate and evolve in physical agents as they interact autonomously with their environment or with other humans, and I encouraged my students at the Artificial Intelligence Laboratory of the University of Brussels (VUB) to experiment in the same direction. We initially developed a bottom-up, behaviour-oriented approach to sensori-motor intelligence, which was also being explored around the same time by Rodney Brooks at the MIT Artificial Intelligence Laboratory. The behaviour-oriented, bottom-up approach was a counter reaction to the symbolic, top-down approach of earlier AI research. See Steels & Brooks (1995) and Arkin (1998). We built robots of various sizes and shapes, using simple electronic circuits, Lego bricks, small motors, rechargeable batteries, self-made sensors, single board computers, and everything else that appeared useful (Figure 1.3).

Figure 1.3: Example of a *Lego vehicle* built by Tim Smithers based on Lego bricks, a sensori-motor processing board, and a variety of sensors and actuators. We developed these robots in the early nineties for exploring a behaviour-oriented approach to robotics.

Most robots drove around on wheels, but we also used balloons and propellers to build flying robots and experimented with a fish-shaped robot which swam in the university swimming pool by wagging its tail (see Figure 1.4).

To investigate the role of the environment in shaping the evolving sensori-motor capacities of these robots, we built various robotic ecosystems in which robots could recharge themselves but also had to work for their living by dimming lights that took away energy from the total energy flowing in their ecosystem (see Figure 1.5). Visitors

---

[9] Some recent overviews of this "classical" approach to artificial intelligence can be found in: Nilsson (1998) and Russell & Norvig (2003).

1 Introduction

Figure 1.4: "Artificial fish" built by Miles Pebody to explore influence of robot bodies on behaviour. The fish could swim around by wagging its tail and avoid obstacles based on infrared sensing.

to our lab could see robots helping each other or engaging in fierce competition for the resources available for survival. In all of this research, we tried to see how far behaviours would autonomously evolve, in other words we tried to find mechanisms by which the robots would bootstrap themselves towards greater sensori-motor complexity. One of the main lessons from these experiments was that explanations for cognition lie partly outside the brain of the individual agent: The environment, the body, the sensori-motor apparatus and the behaviour of the other agents all partly shaped their capacities and further development.[10]

Many fascinating tales can be told about this research but the intelligence being exhibited by these autonomous robots hardly seemed worthy of the name. Yes, they learned by themselves how to avoid obstacles, how to recharge themselves in a charging station, or how to co-ordinate efforts to exploit the resources in the ecosystems we had built for them. But critical observers did not see much more than rat intelligence and they were right. The original goal of reaching human cognitive levels, as observable for instance in expert problem solving or conversations in natural language, remained elusive. The traditional artificial intelligence approach of explicitly programming symbolic intelligence still gave far superior performance in tasks requiring cognition. Clearly, essential theoretical concepts were missing for a truly bottom-up approach to succeed.

In the summer of 1995, a clear breakthrough occurred. I was working as a visiting researcher in the Sony Computer Science Laboratory in Tokyo, invited by its director Mario Tokoro. Reflecting on our experiments from a distance, two new ideas occurred to me. First of all, language may have been the missing key in the initial experiments. Language may be a necessary route by which the human cognitive system bootstraps itself autonomously, in tight interaction with the environment and aided by a community of other language speakers. This suggested that if we wanted to have emergent forms of cognitive intelligence, we needed to go the same route. Second, the principles and mechanisms that had been pouring out of the study of complexity had to be relevant to understanding the origins and evolution of language, because they provided generic

---

[10] This approach is also known as *situated cognition*. Clancey (1997), see also: Varela, Thomson & Rosch (1991).

1.4 History of the project

Figure 1.5: This ecosystem was designed together with David McFarland (Oxford University) to explore emergent cooperation and competition. The robots in the form of lego vehicles could recharge themselves in the charging station (shown in the right top corner). But they had to ensure that there was enough energy in the charging station by dimming a light in black cylinders by pushing against them.

explanations for how complexity may emerge. These principles include self-organisation, structural coupling, selectionism, level formation, and many others (Nicolis & Prigogine 1989). The field of ARTIFICIAL LIFE brings together researchers exploring the insights of complex systems with computational and robotic experiments (see: Langton 1995).

Together with other researchers interested in the then-arising field of "artificial life", I had already been simulating path formation in ant societies and other biological phenomena exhibiting an emergence of complexity. It dawned on me that the importance of these mechanisms for bootstrapping intelligence and language might be much greater than thought so far.[11]

---

[11] The following reference provides a general survey of similar work in the area of lexicon formation: Steels (1997b). A representative sample of work on syntax is Briscoe (1999).

1 Introduction

Back in Brussels, an extremely exciting but very intense period of research started as I tried to apply these principles to language and subject them to experimental scrutiny.[12] We very quickly built a first prototype of a TALKING HEAD with our own hardware and low-level software (see Figure 1.6) and experimented with language games on mobile robotic agents.[13] New fundamental insights and discoveries emerged almost daily. The first experiments, particularly in grounding language on real robots, were extremely difficult but we were clearly making steady progress.

Figure 1.6: First prototype of a *Talking Head* camera with associated electronics built by Tony Belpaeme. The camera is capable to track moving images.

As my research programme grew more radical, it became more and more difficult to get funding. European research and development programmes were increasingly demanding short-term projects that targeted information technology products already available on the American or Japanese market. Increasingly, my research proposals were being rejected and running projects were cut off, as reviewers could not see direct short-term commercial benefits. All this was endangering the further existence of my Brussels laboratory, whereas I, paradoxically, thought that our research had never been more promising. Fortunately at this critical moment Mario Tokoro helped me again in a crucial way. He understood what I was hoping to achieve and ensured secure and stable resources from the Sony Corporation. At the end of 1996, I consequently set up a new research structure in Paris, a spin-off from the Sony Computer Science Laboratory in

---

[12] The earliest papers on these mechanisms are in: Steels (1995) and Steels (1997a).

[13] The electronics and tracking software for this active camera were built by Tony Belpaeme. The mobile robot experiments were conducted with Paul Vogt. Other early work on the grounding and autonomous acquisition of language-like communication systems by robotic systems is described in Steels & Vogt (1997). See also: Billard & Dautenhahn (1999).

Tokyo, where the bulk of the research reported in this book could be done in almost ideal circumstances. The Paris research was complemented with many important contributions from my graduate students at the VUB AI Laboratory in Brussels.

1.5 Beyond Turing

A scientific experiment creates, in a controlled and repeatable way, phenomena which shed light on similar phenomena observed in the natural world. Initially there is always some discussion about the relation between the artificially created phenomena and the natural phenomena. Galileo dropped cannon balls from the tower of Pisa and claimed that these experiments validated a general theory of falling bodies; but his contemporaries objected that birds gracefully landing on a roof can also be seen as falling bodies, so how general was his theory really?

When dealing with cognitive phenomena such as language and meaning, the same problem arises. To what extent do the languages constructed by the Talking Heads count as languages? Does it make any sense to say that these robotic agents categorise their world? Do the Talking Heads learn? Do they genuinely understand each other? Do they understand us? To what extent is there a real increase in syntactic complexity? Intense discussions about whether cognitive phenomena can be recreated in artificial systems have raged since researchers have been exploring this route, and they have been shown extremely difficult to resolve to everyone's satisfaction.

It seems unavoidable that there is disagreement because judgements about cognitive capabilities are to some extent subjective. Most people ascribe more intelligence to their pets than a casual observer is willing to admit. In any case, judgements should clearly rest with humans, and definitely *not* with the designers who are all too keen to call their systems intelligent. This was clearly recognised by Turing when he devised his famous Turing test.[14] Turing started from a popular societal game of his time, where an observer had to tell through a dialog whether he was talking to a man or a woman. He proposed to call a computer program intelligent when it was capable of playing the role of a man or woman so well that the observer could no longer tell whether a person or a computer program was playing the game. The Turing test has rightfully been criticised as being on the one hand too difficult, because it is completely open-ended, and on the other hand too narrow, because it does not incorporate important aspects of intelligence such as learning or sensori-motor intelligence. The only way to have a decent showing in the Turing test is to cheat, i. e. to let the computer mimic intelligence by manipulating symbolic patterns without any notion of what they mean. It is therefore desirable to have an alternative set up which still preserves some of Turing's original ideas.

The goal of the Talking Heads experiment is not to demonstrate an artificial intelligence with the same capacities as human intelligence, but to perform scientific experiments so as to examine aspects of a theory of the origins of language and meaning. However, as in Turing's proposal, the public should be the ultimate judge whether cognitive

---

[14] The Turing test is originally described in Turing (1950).

phenomena are taking place, and the artificial agents should be able to play their role in interaction with humans. Sound scientific methodology requires that the experimental apparatus is a white box which can be fully probed by anyone who wants, that the experiments are repeatable, and that the phenomena that are generated (for example, the complexity of the lexicons or grammars) can be compared by anyone to human cognitive phenomena in order to gage their similarity and thus their relevance for understanding human cognition.

In 1999, a golden opportunity presented itself to expose our theories and systems to public scrutiny and thus solicit judgements from a wide range of human observers. Barbara Vanderlinden and Hans-Ulrich Obrist, two internationally renowned young curators, had been put in charge of an important art event in the city of Antwerp (Belgium) and made the brilliant decision to organise a confrontation/co-operation between art and science.[15] They invited artists and scientists to set up a public laboratory in the city and conduct experiments from the viewpoint of their discipline. This is how the Talking Heads experiment came to be installed in a public space in Antwerp and how thousands of people, some more bewildered than others, took part in the first ever large-scale public experiment in artificial intelligence. Everybody was encouraged to interact with the robots and to try and understand what was going on. This was not an obvious thing to do because the Talking Heads construct their own language and their own conceptualisation of the world. Understanding what they are talking about resembles the work of an anthropologist who is studying the language and conceptualisations of a newly discovered tribe living secluded in the rainforest.

The *Laboratory for cognitive robots and teleportation* that housed the Talking Heads experiment also contained a documentation room in which the audience could get additional background information and provide feedback and commentary on the experiment. We created a website that was accessible worldwide through the Internet. This allowed viewers from anywhere in the world to follow the dialogs, inspect the lexicons and ontologies (sets of perceptually grounded concepts) of the robots, and even interact remotely with the physical robots, playing language games and doing their own experiments. We also added other physical sites in Tokyo, Brussels, Paris, Amsterdam, San Jose (US) and other places, to increase the environmental complexity that the agents could experience.

The massive response and thoughtful judgements of the public were crucial to validate many aspects of the theories put forward in this book. But the interactions with a broad public and the intense discussions that it generated also added new dimensions to the research. First of all, a whole new type of interface between man and machine was taking shape under our very eyes. In contrast to pre-programmed computer interfaces, which more often than not make it difficult to do what one wants, the Talking Heads demonstrated for the first time the concept of NEGOTIATED USER INTERFACES. The interaction was based on mutual respect and adaptation of man *and* machine. Communicative failure was not fatal but an opportunity to fine-tune and negotiate the way communication would take place in the future.

---

[15] The catalogue of this event (Obrist & Vanderlinden 1999) gives an idea of the other laboratories and the coming together of art and science.

Secondly, the Talking Heads experiment turned out to be an ideal learning environment for raising philosophical issues. Children and adults alike started to ask questions about the nature of meaning, the relation between language and reality, the mind-body problem, the origins and evolution of language, consciousness, social identity, and so on. They started to play language games among themselves and some of them reported profound changes in the way they think about language. If these reflections create greater tolerance towards other languages and the conceptualisations of the world they implicitly embody, then I consider the Talking Heads experiment of great societal value, irrespective of the scientific and engineering breakthroughs the project has generated.

1.6 The book

This book describes in detail the rationale behind the Talking Heads experiment, the mechanisms that make it all work, the ontologies and languages the agents develop, and what happened when the Talking Heads were exposed to public scrutiny. It studies processes which must already be active in the very first stages of language use in the child, and must also have been present in the early phases of human language genesis.

The main text contains the principled line of the argument in a form which is intended to be generally accessible without compromising exactness. The notes after each chapter contain references to other work, as well as details or additional material of relevance to the specialist. Each chapter also contains a set of references to literature on the same topic.

This book starts with a preview of the experiment and a brief illustration of the core ideas (Chapter 2). I then cover the different tasks step-by-step that speakers and hearers must carry out: perception (Chapter 3), conceptualisation (Chapter 4), and lexicalisation (Chapter 5). Each chapter discusses the architectural components with which the Talking Heads have been endowed and the kinds of cognitive structures that the agents generate in interaction with the environment and the other agents. Chapter 6 and Chapter 7 then bring all these results together and tests the rich complex semiotic dynamics that arise when the Talking Heads effectively interact with real world environments.

The research discussed in this book is far from finished. It is still science in the making. Many cognitive structures and capabilities, even very elementary ones arising during the first years of human life, are still unveiled. Many language issues have not been covered yet. The current set-up shows only inklings of what future forms of man-machine interaction might be like. Nevertheless, I believe that the hypotheses proposed in this book, and the methodology of experimentation that has been used to explore these hypotheses, open new venues for a scientific understanding of the human mind. Building artificial systems that exhibit cognitive capabilities does not de-humanise the mind, in the same way as the telescope does not demystify the cosmos. We see much more and what we see is infinitely more beautiful and impressive.

2 Preview

When people see the Talking Heads for the first time, they are stunned. It takes a while before one gets used to the self-generated movements of each robot, the strange dialogues in an incomprehensible language, the graphs plotting the evolution of their internal states, and the colourful environment which is the subject of their language games. But after some time, almost everyone gets involved in the game and attempts to figure out the language the robots have developed or to teach them his own. Some people come back day after day to follow the progression of the language and conceptualisations that the Talking Heads build in collaboration with interacting observers. Children are the first ones to start playing with neither fear nor preconception.

This chapter explains the general setup of the experiment and gives a rough idea of what is going on. The various principles and mechanisms at work will be discussed in more detail later and I will also give many more examples taken from concrete interactions.

2.1 The main components

Clearly in the development of language and meaning, the group and the environment matter. A child who grows up without a caring community or without sufficient environmental stimuli never develops the rich cognitive capacities normal adults have. From attempts to educate *wolf children* who grow up in isolation from a human community, or impaired children for whom the intensity of early interactions are limited, we know that there are critical periods where a community and a challenging environment must be present otherwise the child's capacities for language are damaged for the rest of his or her life.[1]

But how can we sufficiently recreate these social conditions in experiments with artificial systems? Building colonies of physical autonomous robots roaming the world in search of stimulating environments and rich interactions with other robots is not feasible today. So how can we ever test seriously situated and socially embedded approaches to cognition?

2.1.1 Teleporting

Let me make a distinction between the physical aspects of a cognitive agent and the mental aspects. The physical aspects include the agent's body, the sensors and articulators, the physical location, the objects in this location, and the other agents physically

---

[1] See Tager-Flusberg (1994).

present in the environment. The mental aspects include the agent's repertoire of behaviours, the brain structures and processes performing categorisations of reality, his memory, lexicon, grammar, and so on. In the case of humans, these two aspects are intimately connected and indivisible. We cannot teleport our mental faculties into another body, or into another copy of our body, even though there have been speculations that we could in the future record human brain states,[2] I believe that this will still not enable teleportation because in human brains there is no distinction between hardware and software. The architecture of a human brain, the physical connections between cells, and the biochemical processes in each cell determine the brain's behaviour. There is no separation between a BRAIN PROGRAM and an interpreter that reads brain programs and executes them. The brain is a special-purpose hardware device which is unique to each individual. To copy such a device we would have to rebuild it physically, atom by atom, and integrate it in an exact copy of the same body.

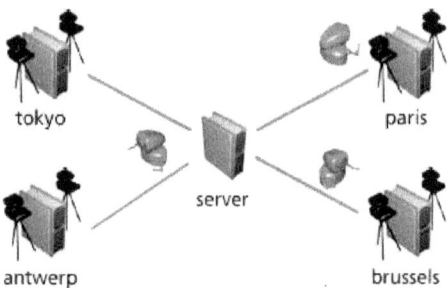

Figure 2.1: The Talking Heads agents are implemented as software entities that can travel over the internet. To play a game, they get downloaded in a local server that drives the cameras and orchestrates a game. After a game, the software state is uploaded again to travel towards another location.

However, in the case of computer-based artificial agents, we *can* make the distinction. It is possible to capture the mental state of an agent in software, load this into a physical body, and then operate the agent. Afterwards the agent can extract himself again from the body, teleport himself to another physical location through a data transmission network like the Internet, get instantiated there in another body, and experience another reality and physically meet other agents. This is exactly how we have implemented the Talking Heads experiment.[3] There are on the one hand the physical structures, which I

---

[2] Such visions of the future have been put forward by Moravec (1995). Neither current artificial intelligence technology nor the state of the art in brain state recording are anywhere near to realising these visions.

[3] The agent teleportation infrastructure is in itself a fascinating non-trivial engineering project. Contributions from Angus McIntyre, Alexis Agahi, Sylvere Tajan and Frederic Kaplan are gratefully acknowledged (McIntyre, Steels & Kaplan 1999). The fact that agents can teleport proves that we are dealing with a truly distributed multi-agent system. It also introduces physical parallelism in the agent-agent and agent-environment interactions. For a general introduction into multi-agent system technologies and design methodologies, see Ferber (1998).

will refer to as the ROBOT BODIES. They are installed in different physical locations somewhere in the world and connected with each other through the Internet. Then there is a population of software structures that are occasionally loaded and instantiated in specific robots. I will call these software structures VIRTUAL AGENTS. A REAL AGENT (a Talking Head) only exists when the virtual agent is loaded in a physical robot body.

Virtual agents cannot interact and an interaction between two "real" agents can only take place when they are both physically present in the same location. Thus an agent can travel from Paris to Tokyo at the blink of an eye, rather than having to take a plane, but two agents can only interact when they are instantiated in the same physical environment. It is in principle possible that agents in different physical locations describe to each other the environment that they see (but which the other one does not see), just as we would do in a telephone conversation. This is only possible, however, after the agents have had sufficient interactions with each other in a shared physical world to have developed and learned a grounded shared language.

The teleporting setup enables fascinating experiments, engulfing the whole globe. The same agent can look at a scene from different points of view or at scenes in different physical locations in the world by teleporting himself in different bodies. He can develop categories in one location and enrich his learning experience by moving to a new location which has different objects and thus poses new categorial challenges. There can be populations of varying sizes with new agents being born and older agents dying, just like in natural human populations, so that we can study the transmission of language from one generation to the next or the resilience of a language against an influx and outflux of agents. We can also let agents develop in different parts of the world and have them migrate to study intercultural exchange and language contact.

2.1.2 The robots

A blind person who receives sight after the critical period for acquiring visual categorisation undergoes a traumatic experience, see Zeki (1993). We could in principle build robot bodies through which agents can experience their world with tactile sensing and other robot bodies which support visual sensing, or both. But then an agent which had only access to tactile sensing might suddenly find himself in a body equipped with vision. This pathological complication will be avoided by using the same robotic infrastructure in every location, even though it would be fascinating and technically possible to study multi-modality in its own right. We also decided to make the robots vision-based, because visual sensing is one of the major sources of meaning in human natural languages.

Concretely, each robot consists of five building blocks (see Figure 1.2):

- A camera mounted on pan/tilt motors so that it can move up or down and left or right.

- A loudspeaker (for voice output) and a microphone (for voice input). Each agent has a particular quality of voice output with male and female voices, so that it is possible to keep them apart in the dialogue.

- A computer that can house an agent's cognitive architecture as well as peripheral control software to steer the movements of the camera, receive and preprocess images, or synthesise and analyse sound. This computer is connected to the Internet to allow virtual agents to be loaded and instantiated.
- A television screen that shows *us* what the agent instantiated in a body currently sees through the camera.
- A computer screen that shows *us* what is going on inside the brain of the agent currently installed in the robot (Figure 2.2)

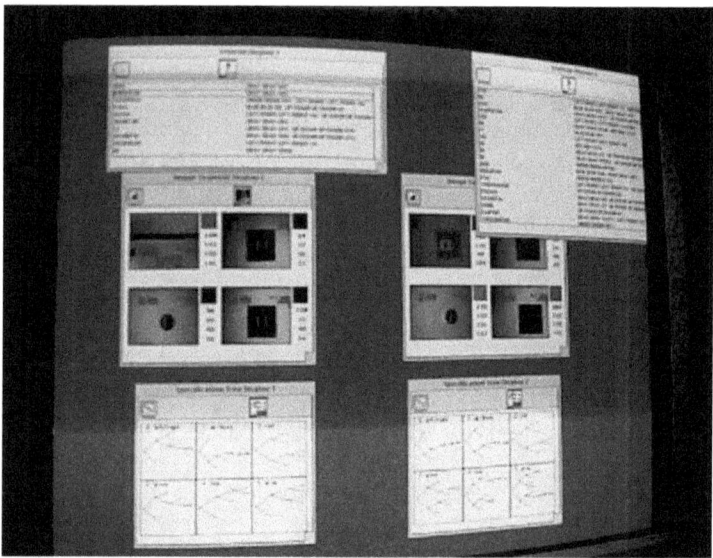

Figure 2.2: Interface through which the internal states of agents can be inspected. Two agents are shown. The top windows show the state of an agent, the middle windows the camera inputs that the agent sees and the bottom windows show their discrimination trees.

In constructing the robot bodies, we have used as much as possible off-the-shelf standard components so that we could focus almost completely on issues directly relevant to language and meaning. Each robot's low-level vision system (integrated in the camera) is already very sophisticated.[4] It can focus automatically to get a sharper image and autonomously track a moving object. The speech signal is produced with a standard text-to-speech system so that we did not have to worry about building complex audio modules ourselves. The computer hardware is powerful, but not specialised nor in the supercomputer range. All programs have been written in the standard symbolic

---

[4] The camera is a Sony EVI-D31. The main computer is a Power Macintosh from Apple, Inc. The agent servers run under the Linux operating system.

programming language of artificial intelligence research, namely LISP.[5] What makes the Talking Heads experiment special is not the hardware or software tools but what we have done with it.

2.1.3 The agents

Agents can only engage in interactions with other agents when they are physically instantiated in a robot. Each agent has a basic brain architecture with different layers performing the cognitive functions relevant for playing language games:

- A perceptual layer which performs low-level signal processing to segment the image and collect data about each segment such as the colour, size, position or shape of a segment.

- A conceptual layer which categorises and conceptualises the segmented and processed image. It is based on a self-generated and evolving repertoire of categorial distinctions, such as red versus green, or small versus large. Such a repertoire is referred to as the agent's ontology in this book.

- A lexical layer which maintains an evolving repertoire of associations between meanings and words, which I will refer to as the lexicon, and performs lexical lookup while parsing or producing utterances.

- A syntactic layer which uses grammatical schemata for organising words in larger structures or for recognising these structures and reconstructing complex meanings.

- A pragmatic layer which carries out the scripts for playing language games and maintains the machinery for engaging in interactions with other agents in a shared environment.

Each of these layers is described in more detail later. The internals of the layers are not static but constantly evolving and adapting. They are not strictly modular but coupled in various ways to each other. Each verbal interaction in effect changes the agent's internal state and thus influences future behaviour. A new, virgin agent starts without any built-in ontology, lexicon, or grammar. This is one of the crucial points of the whole experiment, because we want to test possible theories on how language and meaning can evolve and be acquired *ab initio*.

Agents are part of populations which determine the probability with which they encounter each other. This generates a dynamic process at two levels: There is the dynamics of the evolving cognitive competence of each agent (the ontologies, the lexicon, the

---

[5] The construction of the programs underlying the Talking Heads experiment has required advanced artificial intelligence programming techniques, such as discussed by Norvig (1992). A general toolkit for the systematic execution of simulation and physical experiments, called BABEL, has been designed and implemented by Angus McIntyre. The toolkit allows the definition and modular composition of cognitive architectures, the design of experiments, and the monitoring and displaying of results, see McIntyre (1998).

grammar), and there are the evolving macroscopic structures which arise in a population of agents, such as the common lexicons or shared grammars. We will see that the mental characteristics of agents, even in a single population, are never identical because each agent has his own history of interactions with the environment and with other agents. This is another crucial aspect of the experiment. We want to investigate in how far communication is possible without complete ontological or linguistic coherence.

2.1.4 Interactivity

To qualify as a sound scientific experiment, anybody who wishes to challenge the claims should be given the tools "to see for him- or herself". There are three ways in which we have empowered observers to do so.

First, each physical Talking Heads site has a complex infrastructure to organise the interactions between agents operating in that location, and to support the arrival and teleporting of agents. This infrastructure also houses a *commentator*, a computer program that monitors the dialogues, inspects the internal states of each agent, and displays useful statistics such as the degree of sharing of the lexicon, the competition between different words to express a particular meaning, the stability of certain syntactic constructions, etc. The commentator produces spoken or written comments and displays measurement results on an additional computer screen.

Second, the teleporting infrastructure makes it possible to implement interactions between humans and artificial agents, either directly in the shared physical environment or through the Internet. At any time, a human experimenter can pretend to be one of the agents: seize a robot, partly control the camera to set the context of an interaction, and type in expressions playing the role of speaker or hearer in a language game. The human experimenter can create a new, virgin agent, track in detail how this agent acquires the categories and language in an existing group, or try to influence the currently dominating language by introducing new words or constructs and following their propagation (see Figure 2.3).

Finally, the environment has been restricted to increase the transparency of experimental results. It consists in all locations of a magnetic white board mounted on the wall in front of the robots (see Figure 2.4). On this board, the human experimenter can paste various figures, typically stylised geometric figures like rectangles, circles, and squares, in various sizes, shapes and colours. By changing the environment, the experimenter can try to find out what visual categories the agents employ and force the expansion of categorial repertoires, for example by pasting new types of figures on the board. He can probe the adaptivity of the agents by setting up situations that destabilise an existing lexicon and see how long it takes before a new, perhaps more abstract lexicon emerges. All these tools generate unprecedented opportunities to apply the most rigid scientific evaluation criteria to the theories of language and cognition that I will propose in this book.

2.1 The main components

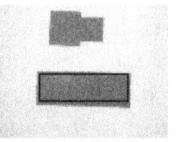

Figure 2.3: Internet interface through which users can access the state of games on remote sites and follow the experiment.

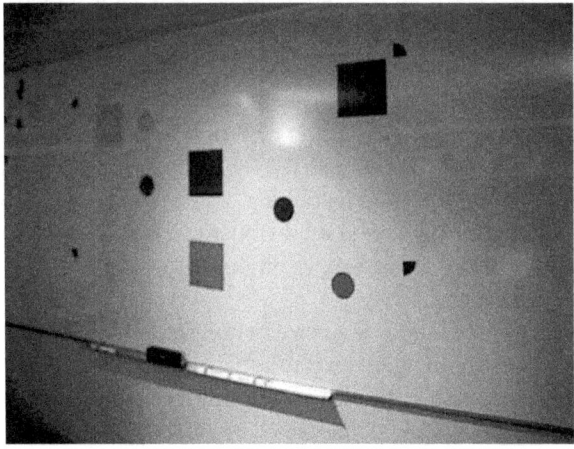

Figure 2.4: The physical environment of the Talking Heads consists of a white board on which various geometric figures can be pasted. The light conditions were not under the control of the experimenters in most locations.

2.2 The Guessing Game

Given this rich computational and robotic infrastructure, many specific experiments are possible. Each experiment could explore a particular interaction between the robots, the environment, and human observers. In this book, I explore only one type of interaction, which I call the *Guessing Game*.[6] The Talking Heads play this game either among themselves or with a human experimenter.

2.2.1 Rules of the game

The Guessing Game is played between two physically instantiated agents. Agents in a virtual state must queue up to have access to one of the robot bodies installed in a particular site before they can play the game. One agent plays the role of SPEAKER and the other then plays the role of HEARER. Agents take turn playing games so that all of them develop the capacity to be speaker or hearer. A human experimenter can pick one of these roles and play the game instead of an artificial agent.

The speaker first looks at one area of the white board and directs the attention of the hearer to the same area.[7] The objects located in this area constitute the CONTEXT. The speaker then chooses one object from the context, which I will call the TOPIC, and gives a verbal hint to the hearer. The VERBAL HINT is an expression that identifies the topic with respect to the other objects in the context. For example, if the context contains a red square, a blue triangle, and a green circle, then the speaker may say something like *the red one* to identify the red square as the topic. If the context contains also a red triangle, he has to be more precise and say something like *the red square* to delineate the topic from the red triangle as well as from the blue square. Of course, the Talking Heads do not say *the red square* but use their own language and concepts which are not necessarily the same as those used in English. For example, they may say *malewina* to mean [UPPER EXTREME-LEFT LOW-REDNESS].

Based on the verbal hint, the hearer tries to guess what topic the speaker has chosen, and communicates his choice to the speaker by pointing to the object. Given that the robots do not have arms, pointing is realised by focusing on an object. One robot can "see" in which direction another one is looking, and thus know where he is "pointing". The game succeeds if the topic guessed by the hearer is equal to the topic chosen by the speaker. The game fails if the guess was wrong or if the speaker or the hearer failed at some earlier point in the game.

In case of a failure, the speaker gives an extra non-verbal hint to the hearer by himself pointing to the topic, and both agents try to repair their internal structures to be more successful in future games: The speaker weakens his hypothesis that the words and con-

---

[6] A very similar game has been called the original language game by Brown (1973) in the context of research on child language acquisition. See also the thoughtful analysis in Halliday (1987). Research on child language has inspired the agent architectures and behaviours but they should not be seen as a realistic model of child language acquisition.

[7] I will explain later how exactly agents decide on a particular scene and how they are able to draw each other's attention to specific areas of the white board.

structions he used were correct, in the sense of shared by other agents. The hearer tries to guess what meanings the speaker might have used and deduce what form-meaning relations or syntactic constructions he is missing. Pointing by gesturing is always vague, and the repair actions are far from guaranteed to succeed. Nevertheless, they gradually lead (as we will see) to a sufficiently shared communication system meaning that success in guessing the topic purely based on language communication increases to reach almost 100%.

2.2.2 Nature of the game

The Guessing Game is one of the common things we do with language. For example, I play a similar game when I sit with a friend at the dining table and say *could you give me the salt*. If she guesses correctly what I mean and hands me the salt, the game has succeeded. If she looks at me with a puzzled face (maybe she does not speak English) or hands me the salmon instead of the salt, the game has failed. In that case, I can gesture in the direction of the salt and say *no, no, the SALT please*, and then she hopefully realises and gives the salt to me. Failure is common in natural language dialogues and may be caused by many factors. For example, the salmon could indeed be close to the salt and my pronunciation of the word *salt* may have sounded a bit like *salmon*, perhaps because there was loud music playing in the background or perhaps my friend does not understand English. A failure is often an opportunity to negotiate how something will be expressed in the future. For example, the hearer may pick up a new word or the speaker may realise that a certain word is not appropriate in this particular context.

The Guessing Game is not a game of winners and losers because both agents win or both agents lose at the same time. But it is a game nevertheless, because it is played with clear rules, with a clear outcome and strict limitations on how success can be achieved. An agent can not look inside another agent's brain state. Agents can only interact through the external environment. There is no global control center that is monitoring the behaviour and internal states of all agents and setting the way they should speak or perceive their world. The artificial agents are autonomous and fully distributed, just like human beings.

The game is different from a closed world game like chess, because the environment is open. The human experimenter may introduce new objects at any time, any one agent can extend the language (for example invent a new word), possibly requiring the other agents to adopt it as well, or the human experimenter may inject new language forms in the dialogues. Agents try to maximise their communicative success by cooperating to the fullest and update or change their internal structures and processes to improve their chances in the game.[8]

---

[8] The Guessing Game is a cooperative game, because both the agents win or loose at the same time and have the highest gain if they develop co-ordinated behaviour. The agent who manages to have the most success in the game is the global winner. Because the commentator requires to know from the speaker which topic he wants to communicate before he is allowed to speak, no cheating is possible. Game theory, originally founded by John von Neumann and Oskar Morgenstern, can be applied to study the language game mathematically. We are dealing with an evolutionary game in which the players optimise their internal states to become better in the game, see Maynard Smith (1982).

In the Talking Heads experiment, it is assumed that agents want to cooperate and that they use communication as part of their cooperation. The evolution of cooperative games has been studied extensively by artificial life researchers often in the context of Robert Axelrod's prisoners dilemma game, see for example Ikegami (1994). For a general introduction how communication can evolve in the context of cooperation, see Hauser (1996). Computer simulations showing the evolution of cooperation and communication have been reported in the artificial life literature. See for example MacLennan & Burghardt (1993). Most of these computer simulations are closer to animal signaling systems than to human lexicons both in size and in terms of the complexity of meaning.

The Guessing Game is clearly not the only thing we do with language. Humans are capable of playing a whole range of language games and inventing new ones when the circumstances require it; however, to do controlled experiments we need to limit ourselves. The objective of the Talking Heads experiment is not to cover the full range and complexity of human natural language interaction but to examine with objective precision a limited number of issues concerning the nature of language and meaning.

2.2.3 The semiotic square

The environment of the Talking Heads is not fixed. The human experimenter may change the position of objects, add new kinds of objects, or eliminate others. Consequently a strategy of naming individual objects will not work. It would lead to a proliferation of proper names and it would require the Talking Heads to recognise objects, which is very difficult to do.[9] Indeed, humans don't exclusively use proper names in natural language conversations either. We say *could you give me the red small square* as opposed to *could you give me O_143*. Natural language words like *red* or *small* name perceptually grounded categories and syntactic structures indicate how they should be combined and used to find the topic. The relation between a language expression and its referent is therefore always indirect. This is summarised in the semiotic square (Figure 2.5), which I will use throughout this book to help understand and analyse the nature of language communication. The semiotic square relates the four entities involved in a verbal interaction:

- An UTTERANCE, such as *small red square*, which is transmitted as a physical signal from one agent to another one through the external environment. It is written between double quotes.

- A MEANING, which consists of categories like [RED], [SMALL], or combinations of categories, like {[RED] [SMALL]}. Labels of categories are written in capital letters between square brackets.

---

[9] For a thorough exposition of the difficulties of object recognition, see Ullman (1996). Object constancy comes fairly late in the acquisition of a child's ontology, as Piaget's conservation experiments have shown. Language probably plays an important role in forming the notion of an object.

- An IMAGE SEGMENT, denoted as *S143*, which is a segment of the image perceived through the camera.
- A REFERENT, like object *O143*, which is an entity in the real world.

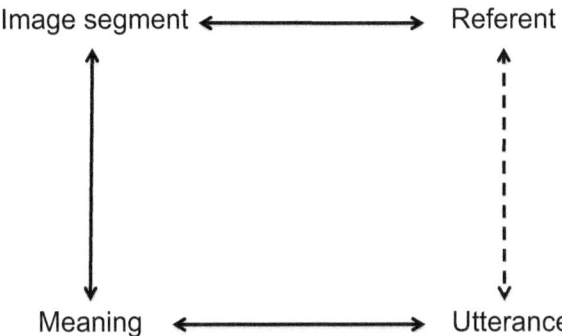

Figure 2.5: Any verbal interaction involves four entities here grouped in the *semiotic square*. The relation between utterance and referent always needs to be established indirectly by passing through perception and meaning.

The systematic relation between meaning and referent is usually studied under the heading of semantics, and the systematic relation between meaning and utterance as grammar (including syntax, morphology and lexicon).[10]

Many tricky philosophical issues are raised in the unavoidable distinction between the sensed image of an object (which is local to the agent) and the object itself (which is external to the agent). Some philosophers even doubt that objects have an existence outside our perception of them! We need to make the distinction because agents always have different internal images even if they look at the same object seen from our viewpoint as an external observer. However, for simplifying the explanations, I will sometimes assume that perceived image and external object are the same, so that the semiotic square becomes a semiotic triangle.[11]

---

[10] For a general introduction to the contemporary linguistic viewpoint on the processes involved, see Van Valin jr & LaPolla (1997). In a logical approach to language, as exemplified by Montague grammar (Montague 1974), meanings are represented using a logical formalism, i.e. a variant of intensional logic. Natural language expressions are systematically related to expressions in this logic, and a formal semantics system defines how expressions in the logic are mapped onto their denotations. Because this is a formal framework, the denotations consist of formal models. To make the Talking Heads experiment work, we needed to develop a grounded semantics system, which details how an agent may go from physical reality to meaning using a perceptual apparatus, and from meaning to physical reality. The logical structure of the meanings we will investigate are very simple (unary predicates and conjunctions). But once we know how to set up a grounded semantics for simple meaning structures we can scale it up to the more complex meaning structures typically studied in logic.

[11] The notion of a semiotic triangle was first introduced in a classic of the semiotic literature, see Ogden & Richards (1935).

When we put together the semiotic squares of two agents (Figure 2.6), we see more clearly that agents are trying to agree about a common object in the external word, but they never have any direct access and hence confirmation whether they are really referring to the same object. Only through pointing or other cooperative actions can speaker and hearer co-ordinate whether they indeed refer to the same object in the external reality.

The utterance is not the same for both agents, because it needs to be articulated, transmitted, and perceived through a physical medium. Errors in transmission or perception may and do occur and have an important impact on the evolution of language. To remain focused, I will not treat this issue in depth in this book but will instead assume that there is direct, error-free transmission of the utterance.

2.2.4 Processes involved in language communication

I will use the following terms for denoting the processes speakers and hearers go through while traversing the relations in the semiotic square as they play a language game (Figure 2.6). A similar framework, but emphasising the language production side, has been described in great detail by Levelt (1989). This book also provides a wealth of psychological evidence that these processes must be going on and expands the phonetic and phonological side. An example of a detailed architecture inspired by generative grammar is discussed in: Jackendoff (1997). Generative approaches to language attempt to define a language by generating its set of possible utterances. Interpretations are constructed from the syntactic structure derived by the generative grammar. In this book, we are interested in the mapping from communicative intent in a perceived reality to an utterance and back. The knowledge and skill needed to solve this problem is different from that need to systematically generate the set of sentences in a language and their possible interpretations.

1. The speaker as well as the hearer PERCEIVE reality by capturing an image through the camera, segmenting the image into coherent units, and deriving various sensory characteristics about each image segment, such as the colour, size, movement.

2. The speaker must then CONCEPTUALISE the scene on the basis of this perception. He must find a set of categories or a conjunctive combination of categories that distinguishes the referent from the other objects in the context, and which will act as the meaning of his communication. For example, he might choose [BLUE] if the topic has a blue colour and all the other objects in the context are not blue.

3. The speaker must then VERBALISE this conceptualisation. He must use his language system to find words and syntactic constructions expressing this meaning. For example, he might choose *blauw* (if he speaks Dutch), or *bleu* (if he speaks French), to convey the category [BLUE].

4. The hearer must engage in similar tasks but now going in the reverse direction. He must INTERPRET the utterance to find out which conceptualisation constitutes the meaning.

2.2 The Guessing Game

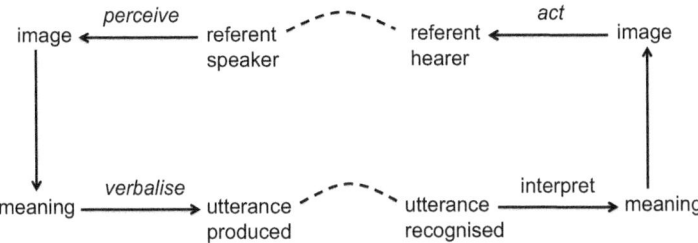

Figure 2.6: Left: processes carried out by the speaker. Right: processes carried out by the hearer. There are also feedback processes moving in alternate directions until the agents settle on coherent choices for all the items in their semiotic squares.

5. Then the hearer must APPLY this meaning to see what referent was intended. The hearer has also perceived the scene in terms of a set of segments and now uses the meaning to identify the segment that could have been the one intended by the speaker.

6. Finally the hearer ACTS upon the outcome of meaning application. He points to the topic he has identified. This is the step where both agents co-ordinate their behaviour through the external world.

2.2.5 Knowledge sources and competences

Each of these activities requires knowledge and/or skill (summarised in the table below). Perceiving requires visual processes capable of segmenting images and deriving image segments. Conceptualisation requires an ontology, a repertoire of perceptually grounded distinctions that can be applied to a segmented image to yield distinctive categories or category combinations that may constitute the meaning of the utterance. Verbalising a conceptualisation requires a LEXICON that maps parts of the meaning to words and a SYNTAX that specifies how to organise individual words into a larger complex. The hearer must use similar knowledge sources in the other direction. He must use his lexicon and syntax to reconstruct the meanings expressed by the utterance, and then use the ontology again to apply the meaning to the present context to find the referent (see Table 2.1).

There is no simple linear flow from perception to utterance or from utterance to perception. Instead, we must imagine a dynamic process involving forward and backward propagation of information until coherent choices for all the nodes in the two semiotic squares have been established by the speaker and the hearer. Many different choices are initially possible (many segmentations, conceptualisations, verbalisations, interpretations), but the dynamic process gradually settles into a single coherent attractor, so that speaker and hearer agree upon a common referent. The co-ordination between cho-

Table 2.1: Activities and knowledge soruces

Activity	From	To	Knowledge source
Perceive	Object	Image segments	Visual processes
Conceptualise	Topic	Meaning	Ontology
Verbalise	Meaning	Utterance	Lexicon + syntax
Interpret	Utterance	Meaning	Lexicon + syntax
Apply	Meaning	Topic	Ontology
Act	Topic	Object	Behavioural process

sen topic and identified referent is done through the real world (pointing, handing an object, performing an action).

I deliberately left an important aspect of language out. In the case of physical agents, the form cannot be transmitted directly but needs to be articulated in speech sounds, written signs, or gestures, to create a true utterance. This additional complexity will not be discussed further in this book – even though it is a fascinating topic in its own right.[12] To make a verbal interaction nevertheless complete, agents are given a repertoire of consonants and vowels with which they can make random syllables and syllable combinations, like *wabido*, *bimaku*, etc. The articulation and recognition of these syllables is assumed to be acquired already and transmission is engineered to be error-free. This way, our attention can be focused on how ontologies, lexicons, and grammars may emerge.

2.3 Perception and categorisation

I will now discuss in some more detail each of the processes the Talking Heads go through when they play a complete language game, leaving a more detailed discussion to subsequent chapters.

2.3.1 Scene and topic selection

Every physical Talking Heads set-up features a WAITING ROOM in which agents are stored, ready to be loaded into the robotic infrastructure or to be teleported to another physical site. A game starts when two agents are chosen at random from this waiting room and loaded into the two physical robots. The internal architecture of each agent is connected with the sensori-motor apparatus of the robot so that they can receive the sensory data

---

[12] See for a state of the art review: Clark & Yallop (1995). We have already been conducting quite extensive research in our group on the origin of sound systems using similar principles as the ones discussed in this book for the origins of word semantics. See de Boer (2000). The complex adaptive systems approach underlying this phonetics work was already foreshadowed in work of phoneticians like Liljencrants & Lindblom (1972).

2.3 Perception and categorisation

streams recorded by the camera and control the movements of the robots. Then the general control system assigns randomly the role of speaker and hearer to each of the agents and the game can begin.

Next the speaker randomly moves around its camera, halts at a particular location, and captures the image. The speaker then attempts to segment this image. If the scene is interesting, which means that there are at least two clear segments, it is chosen for playing a language game. Otherwise the agent makes another random movement and repeats the process. An example of an interesting scene with its subsequent segmentation by the speaker is shown in Figure 2.7 (top image on the right). The scene has two circles as main objects. Segments which are too small are ignored.

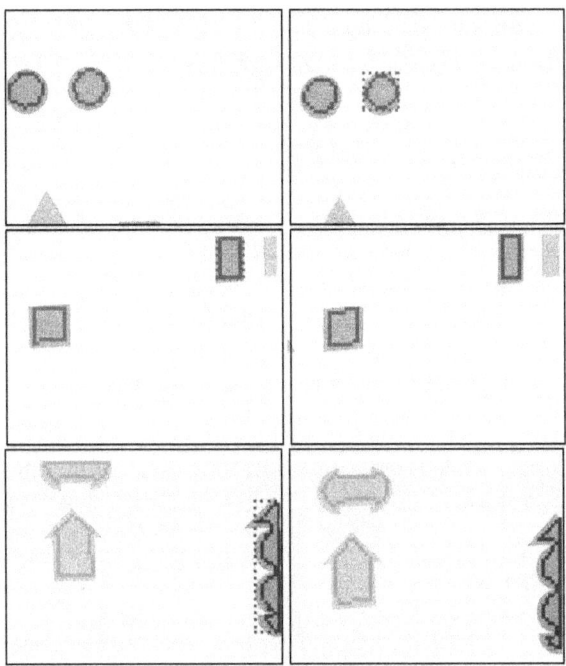

Figure 2.7: Three examples of segmented images (from top to bottom). Left and right images show the perceived and segmented images for two agents respectively. These images are always different because they are dependent on the position of the agent. The topic is indicated by a dashed bounding box in the image of the speaker (on the right for the first case and on the left for the others). Segments which are too small are ignored. The topics have all been conceptualised as being to the right and so the same word *gofubo* has been used to successfully refer to them.

Segmentation can happen according to several criteria. For example, patches with similar colour can be grouped into a single patch, edges can be identified and then linked with each other to form line segments circumscribing the contours of an object, or consecutive images can be compared to extract the parts that changed and hence moved as a single object. There is now a solid body of techniques from decades of machine vision research to efficiently segment scenes according to these and other methods. The Talking Heads use several methods in parallel and combine their output to get a clearly segmented picture.[13]

The hearer must be able to sense in which direction the speaker is looking. This facility is at the moment implemented by having the speaker indicate to the hearer the point on the white board at which its camera is focused. The hearer then moves the camera to this point and records an image as well. The hearer segments this image (see Figure 2.7, top image on the left) so that now both the speaker and the hearer have a set of segments and can start playing a language game. Note that the speaker and hearer never get exactly the same image because they are standing about one metre apart from each other before the white board. Also the calibration is never entirely accurate so that perceptual differences are unavoidable.

2.3.2 Sensory channels

Next low-level visual processes gather information about each segment, such as its average colour, size, shape, the position with respect to horizontal or vertical axes. Each process outputs its information on a SENSORY CHANNEL scaled between 0.0 and 1.0. The mechanisms from the conceptualisation layer that subsequently use this information can operate on any kind of sensory channel. I will assume for the rest of this chapter that the low-level routines produce each only three types of information, sent on the following sensory channels:

- The first channel is called HPOS (horizontal position). It contains the x-midposition of a segmented object within the field of view of the robot.

- The second channel is called VPOS (vertical position). It specifies the y-midposition of the segmented object.

- The third channel is called GRAY and contains the average gray-scale of the object.

Later on additional channels will be introduced.

Consider the two objects in Figure 2.8. The triangular object has the (scaled) values HPOS=0.35, VPOS=0.40, GRAY=0.33, and the rectangular object has the values HPOS=0.70, VPOS=0.85, GRAY=0.33. The agents can already visually distinguish millions of possible scenes with these three sensory channels. The number of scenes quickly grows when the set of sensory channels increases.

The low-level visual processes outputting values on the various sensory channels are already quite complicated in themselves. I will discuss them further in Chapter 3. I will then argue that the agent's repertoire of visual processes does not have to be static and programmed in advance but evolves and adapts through a selectionist process. New processes may "grow" by the random combination of primitive operations and are pruned

---

[13] For general introductions to these areas, see Ballard & Brown (1982) and Fischler & Firchein (1987).

2.3 Perception and categorisation

when they fail to yield useful information or information which is irrelevant in the environment in which the agent finds himself.

2.3.3 Making distinctions

The data on sensory channels are values from a continuous domain (between 0.0 and 1.0). To be the basis of natural language communication, these values must be transformed into a discrete domain. This is precisely the task of the conceptual layer. It performs massive data reduction to make infinitely rich environments manageable. One means of categorisation is to divide up each domain of values on a particular sensory channel into regions and simply assign a category to each region, thus creating a discrimination tree. For example, the HPOS-channel can be cut in two halves leading to a distinction between [LEFT] ($0.0 \leq q$HPOS < 0.5) and [RIGHT] ($0.5 \leq q$HPOS$\leq q1.0$). The triangular object in Figure 2.8 has the value HPOS=0.35 and would therefore be categorised as [LEFT]. Similarly, the VPOS-channel can be divided in two halves yielding the categories [LOWER] and [UPPER], and likewise the GRAY-channel yielding the categories [LIGHT] and [DARK]. Given these categories, the rectangular object in the scene of Figure 2.8 would be categorised as [RIGHT UPPER LIGHT]. Of course, light, dark, left, lower, etc. are labels that I have given to these categories. The Talking Heads create categories by partitioning sensory channels but do not use these labels internally.

It is always possible to refine a distinction by further subdividing its region. Thus an agent could further divide the bottom region of the HPOS-channel (categorised as [LEFT]) into two subregions [TOTALLY-LEFT] ($0.0 \leq$HPOS < 0.25), and [MID-LEFT] ($0.25 \leq$HPOS < 0.5). The triangular object can now be categorised as [MID-LEFT], if simply categorising it as [LEFT] is not distinctive enough. Each of these categories can still be further refined. The categorisation networks resulting from these consecutive binary subdivisions form discrimination trees (Figure 2.9). It is not at all assumed that all agents have the same trees; due to different developmental histories, divergence is inevitable.

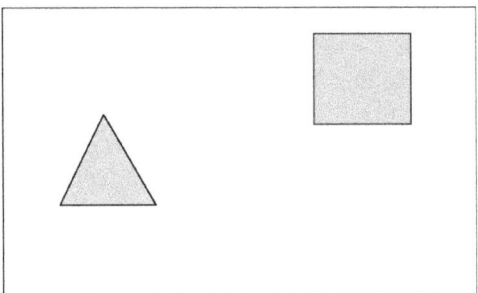

Figure 2.8: The scene contains two objects: a triangular object and a rectangular object with the same gray levels. Each one is characterised by values on three sensory channels: HPOS, VPOS, and GRAY.

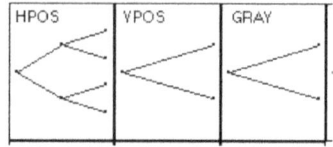

Figure 2.9: A discrimination tree displays the divisions of the total range of values on a sensory channel into finer and finer subregions. Categories are assigned to each region at different levels of the tree.

There are obviously other ways to move from the continuous domain of sensory channels to the discrete domain of categories.[14] For example, it is not really necessary to have a binary division, we could just as well split each region into three or more subregions. Or we could introduce focal (prototypical) values and associate a category with each of them. In the latter case, the categorisation process consists in identifying the prototype that is closest to an object's value. For the current experiment, I will stick however to a binary categorisation strategy because that is the simplest to understand and formally investigate.

We will see that agents build hundreds, even thousands, of categories as they play their language games, and in addition they make combinations of categories. To bring some order in this profusion of categories, I will label them using the sensory channel from which a category operates, followed by the upper and lower bound of the region they carve out. Thus [TOTALLY-LEFT] is labeled as [HPOS 0.0–0.25], because it carves out a region between 0.0 and 0.25 on the HPOS-channel. When it must be emphasised that a category belongs to a particular agent, for example a1, we write [HPOS 0.0–0.25]$_{a1}$. The same category in agent a2 is labeled as [HPOS 0.0–0.25]$_{a2}$. If I want to talk about this category in the abstract, I will not mention any agent and simply write [HPOS 0.0–0.25]. We will also allow conjunctive combinations of categories which will be written as a set, as in {[HPOS 0.0–0.25], [VPOS 0.0–0.25]}, which could be paraphrased as totally-left *and* totally-down.

Where do an agent's discrimination trees, and hence categories, come from? This is one of the main puzzles to be addressed in this book and it will occupy most of Chapter 4. Very briefly, I propose again a selectionist approach, as for the formation of low-level visual routines. I hypothesise that the nodes and branches of the discrimination trees grow more or less randomly in all directions. The use and success of categories is monitored and categories which are not sufficiently useful or successful in the environments encountered by the agent are pruned. I will argue in Chapter 4 that this mechanism indeed leads to a repertoire of distinctions that is adequate for playing language games, and that categories therefore need not be innate nor learned by induction from a large series of examples.

---

[14] See Taylor (1995).

2.4 Lexicalisation

Verbalisation (mapping meaning to form) involves two distinguishable activities. The first one relies on a lexicon to map components of meaning to individual words. The second one relies on syntactic rules to provide supra-word structuring and additional syntactic marking to express additional aspects of meaning, particularly how component meanings are combined into a complex whole. Both types of activities also take place in interpretation (mapping form to meaning): the individual words are mapped back to their meanings and the meaning of the whole is reconstructed from the meaning of the parts.

In the early origins of language, there must have been an initial phase in which no complex syntax was in place yet. Utterances then must have consisted of single words or multiple words without further syntax. Such syntax-less languages have been called *proto-languages*.[15]

Children acquire their first words around the first year of life.[16] Most people believe that they do this as a result of hearing a particular word repeated several times in a certain context and gradually abstracting an association between a word and a meaning. But how is it that they know which meaning to associate with a particular word? How is it that word acquisition goes so rapid? We will follow a different approach, which leaves an open question whether this applies to human word acquisition as well. The approach will be selectionist. The agents CONSTRUCT hypotheses, either on the basis of one specific case where they guess through a non-verbal strategy what the meaning of an unknown word might be, or they have simply invented a new word because they do not have one yet. The hypotheses are then tried out in subsequent games and either receive confirmation or are falsified. As a side effect of this local behaviour, a global self-organising dynamic process arises leading gradually to coherence.

Here are a few example games to give a general flavor of this selectionist approach to word acquisition. Let us assume that there are only two agents, **a1** and **a2**, and they use only the three sensory channels introduced earlier: VPOS for vertical position, HPOS for horizontal position, and GRAY for grayscale.

2.4.1 Same meaning, same referent

Here is the simplest possible instance of a language game, based on the scene in Figure 2.8. The speaker, **a1**, has picked the triangle as the topic. To give a verbal hint, he needs to conceptualise this topic, which means in this specific case, to find a category

---

[15] See Bickerton (1999) as well as Thomason & Kaufman (1988). Children similarly go through a single word phase (even though a single word for them might be multiple words for us), and then slowly start to bootstrap their grammar. See Tomasello (1992) and Bates, Bretherton & Snyder (1988). They are still observed in the very first phases of child language acquisition or in pidgins that spontaneously form when two communities with widely diverging languages need to interact. Out of proto-languages, languages with a fully-fledged syntax must have emerged at some point. How this occurred is still a heavily debated mystery. In this volume I only treat the origins of proto-languages.

[16] Representative work in the study of child language learning focuses mostly on the acquisition of specific meanings. See Gleitman & Landau (1994), Clark (1993), Bowerman (1996).

(or set of categories) which distinguishes the topic from the other objects in the context. Here the context contains only one additional object, namely the rectangle. The category [VPOS 0.0–0.5]$_{a1}$ (lower) fits the criteria. [VPOS 0.0–0.5] is valid when VPOS< 0.5 which is the case for the triangle but not for the rectangle. **a1** has an association in his lexicon relating [VPOS 0.0–0.5]$_{a1}$ with the word *lu*, **a1** retrieves this word and transmits it to the hearer, which is agent **a2**.

a2 has stored in his lexicon an association between *lu* and [VPOS 0.0–0.5]$_{a2}$, and so hypothesises that [VPOS 0.0–0.5]$_{a2}$ must be the meaning of *lu*. When this category is applied to the present scene, in other words, when **a2** filters out the objects whose value for VPOS do not fall in the region [0.0–0.5], only one remaining object is obtained, the triangle. Hence **a2** concludes that this must be the topic and points to it.

The speaker recognises that the hearer has pointed to the right object and so the game succeeds. The complete dialogue is reported by the commentator as follows:

```
Game 125.
  a1 is the speaker. a2 is the hearer.
  a1 segments the context into 2 objects
  a1 categorises the topic as [VPOS 0.0-0.5]
  a1 says:   "lu"
  a2 interprets "lu" as [VPOS 0.0-0.5]
  a2 points to the topic
  a1 says: "OK"
```

This game illustrates a situation where the speaker and the hearer associate the same meaning with the same form and where the meaning picks out the same referent for both agents. No wonder the game succeeds. Unfortunately things are seldom that simple.

2.4.2 A new word

There are (at least) two ways in which a game similar to game 125, but played earlier might have failed. First of all it can be that the speaker does not have a word yet for the meaning he wants to convey. The speaker then invokes a strategy to repair this failure. The simplest strategy is to create a new word for the present meaning. This is how **a1** might have created the word *lu*, and associated it with [VPOS 0.0–0.5] in his lexicon. Such simple constructive steps cause new words to enter the lexicon.

Second, it can be that the hearer does not know the word. The game then fails and the speaker points to the topic so that the hearer can make an educated guess what the meaning might have been: If the hearer is able to recover a possible topic from the non-verbal hint given by the speaker, he himself can seek a distinctive category or set of categories that delineates this topic from the other objects in the context just as the speaker has done. It is possible (although not necessary as we will see) that the hearer **a2** arrives at his own version of the same category, namely [VPOS 0.0–0.5]$_{a2}$. The hearer now stores in his lexicon a new association between the form heard, *lu*, and the guessed meaning [VPOS 0.0–0.5]$_{a2}$. Based on this extended lexicon, he will succeed in the same

2.4 Lexicalisation

game in the future and he can use *lu* himself to verbalise [VPOS 0.0–0.5]$_{a2}$ when talking to other agents. This is the way new words spread in the population.

A game where these two repair activities have taken place is reported by the commentator as follows:

```
Game 25.
  a1 is the speaker. a2 is the hearer.
  a1 segments the context into 2 objects
  a1 categorises the topic as [VPOS 0.0-0.5]
  a1 creates a new word: "lu"
  a2 does not know "lu"
  a2 says: "lu?"
  a1 points to the topic
  a2 categorises the topic as [VPOS 0.0-0.5]
  a2 stores "lu" as [VPOS 0.0-0.5]
```

2.4.3 Competition between words

The observant reader will have noticed immediately that I have swept some important difficulties under the carpet. First, it could very well be that unknown to the speaker another agent had already used the word *lu* for another meaning, so that there are now two alternative meanings for *lu* in the lexicon. *lu* has become ambiguous. Second, it may be the hearer a2 already had a word for [VPOS 0.0–0.5]$_{a2}$, for example *bomida*, so that there are now two synonyms for [VPOS 0.0–0.5] in the lexicon. Synonymy and ambiguity are very common in natural languages and unavoidable when a group of distributed autonomous agents creates a language without a central co-ordinator. This implies that the agents' lexicon must be sophisticated enough to support multiple associations. An agent must be able to store the different meanings being used for the same word, and the different words being used for the same meaning.

Will this process not lead to a proliferation of words and massive, inefficient lexicons, particularly in large populations? No. As I will discuss extensively in Chapter 5, a positive feedback loop between use and success can be set up causing progressive convergence towards an efficient lexicon. The agents keep track of the use and success of each form-meaning pair and prefer the forms that have had the most success in past use. The more success a form has, the more it will be chosen and consequently the more success it will have in the future. This positive feedback loop creates a winner-take-all situation because as soon as one form is slightly preferred, its success grows and overtakes its competitors to eventually dominate (Figure 2.10). Particularly in open environments, the dominance may only be temporary after which a new struggle develops and another word becomes the winner.

2 Preview

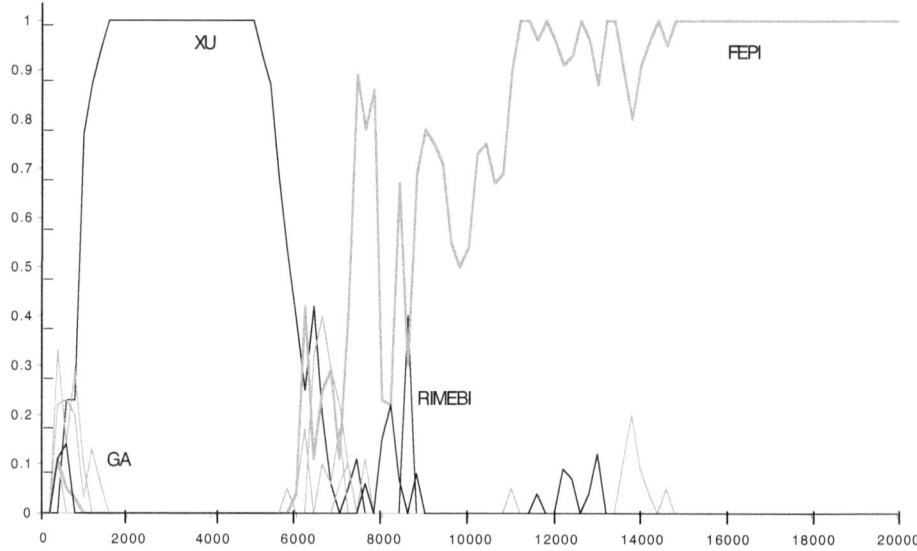

Figure 2.10: The graph shows the competition between different forms for expressing one meaning in a population of 20 agents. The graph plots the frequency of each form in the population, more precisely the percentage of agents that prefer a particular word. A complex dynamic process unfolds with periods where one word (first *xu* and then *fepi*) dominates.

2.4.4 Disambiguation

Another difficulty which I did not deal with when discussing Game 25 above, is that the hearer may conceptualise the scene differently from the speaker. For example, the triangular object is not only located at the lower half of the scene and the rectangle at the upper half, but it is also to the left, i.e. with HPOS < 0.5, whereas the rectangle is to the right. It follows that the hearer could just as well have hypothesised that *lu* means [HPOS 0.0–0.5] (left) and not [VPOS 0.0–0.5] (lower).

Is this bad? It depends on the situations being encountered in the future. When the game is played again for the same scene with **a1** saying *lu* to mean [VPOS 0.0–0.5], and a2 interpreting *lu* as [HPOS 0.0–0.5], the game would succeed! Communicative success is achieved whenever the hearer recovers the referent chosen by the speaker; it is not required that they use exactly the same meaning. In fact, the hearer can never know for sure what meaning was initially conceptualised by the speaker and neither can the speaker know which meaning was understood by the hearer because they cannot look inside each other's head. The meaning can be quite different, as we have just seen, as long as it is compatible.

2.4 Lexicalisation

Even more remarkably, if a topic which is at the lower portion of the scene, is always on the left side and vice-versa, there would always be success despite the different meanings of *lu*, and the players would never discover that each means something else by *lu*.

Similar situations arise in human natural language communication as well, particularly for words which are not stabilised yet or whose interpretation depends strongly on the non-verbal information provided by the context. They also arise when the speaker or hearer have different sensory modalities or sensibilities. For example, a colour-blind person (unable to make the distinction between red and green) will recognise the red traffic light by its position. For that person, *stop for the red light* does not mean stop for the light that has the colour red but stop when the upper-most light is lit.

These examples show clearly that shared language and meaning arise from the efforts of agents to co-ordinate their conceptualisations and lexicalisations with respect to the environments they encounter and the games they play, but that these co-ordinations cannot be perfect nor totally uniform because the agents have limited rationality. In general, we can *not* assume that different agents have exactly the same conceptualisation of reality and that they mean the same thing by the same words. As we will see in later experiments, the Talking Heads hardly agree on the meaning of a word, particularly in the early phases of language development, but they nevertheless manage to have a surprisingly high communicative success rate. There is no guarantee that a particular form maps onto the same meaning, even in the same language community. Despite these shaky foundations, communication is generally successful because there is sufficient coherence among the members of a community and sufficient constraints from the context.

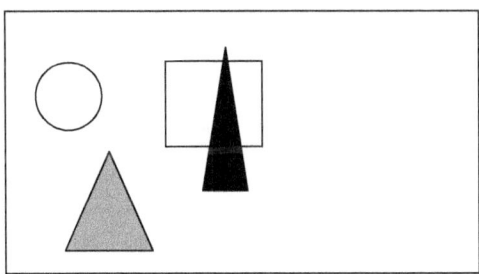

Figure 2.11: A second scene which can be used to disambiguate *lu*.

Consider now another scene (Figure 2.11). The speaker is again **a1** and categorises the bottom triangle as [VPOS 0.0–0.5]$_{a1}$, meaning the object at the lower half of the scene. Assuming that the hearer **a2** has associated *lu* with [HPOS 0.0–0.5]$_{a2}$, he would interpret *lu* as [HPOS 0.0–0.5]$_{a2}$ (to the left). But this does not yield a single referent and therefore the game fails. This failure is an opportunity for the hearer to repair his hypotheses about the possible meanings of *lu*. When he conceptualises the scene himself, he finds that [VPOS 0.0–0.5]$_{a2}$ distinguishes the triangle from the circle. A new association between *lu* and [VPOS 0.0–0.5]$_{a2}$ is stored. The old association is not removed but enters in competition with the new one, and gradually one meaning will come to dominate by the winner-take-all mechanism discussed earlier on.

The commentator reports this kind of interaction as follows:

```
Game 137.
  a1 is the speaker. a2 is the hearer.
  a1 segments the context into 4 objects
  a1 categorises the topic as [VPOS 0.0-0.5]
  a1 says:   "lu"
  a2 interprets "lu" as [HPOS 0.0-0.5]
  There is more than one such object
  a2 says: "lu?"
  a1 points to the topic
  a2 categorises the topic as [VPOS 0.0-0.5]
  a2 stores "lu" as [VPOS 0.0-0.5]
```

Through such disambiguating situations, meanings of words get clarified and the lexicons of the agents become more similar. Note that the dominating meaning of *lu* can still go in two directions. For example, **a2** could have used *lu* with **a1** in a situation where its only possible meaning is [HPOS 0.0–0.5] (left). Then **a1**, now playing the role of hearer, would have stored the association between *lu* and [HPOS 0.0–0.5]. If this happened often enough [HPOS 0.0–0.5] (left) might have become the dominant meaning of *lu*, instead of [VPOS 0.0–0.5] (lower). This shows clearly that the evolution of language will never be predictable. At a critical bifurcation, small preferential differences between the agents or the chance occurrence of certain situations may tilt the competition in one direction or the other.[17] There is no right or wrong solution in the language game and no one has any more rights than anyone else.

2.4.5 Same meaning, different referent

When agents have the same meaning for the same form, it is likely that they pick out the same referent from the context. When agents have a different meaning for the same form, it is less likely although it may still happen that they pick out the same referent, as we have seen. But there is an even more problematic situation: When agents have the same meaning for the same form but nevertheless pick out different referents!

For example, suppose that two Talking Heads have developed the concept of [LEFT] and [RIGHT] with respect to their own position in front of the scene. In terms of the sensory channels we have been using, anything to the left of their field of vision (0.0 ≤ HPOS < 0.5) is categorised as left, i.e. [HPOS 0.0 0.5], and everything right (0.5 < HPOS ≤ 1.0) is categorised as right, i.e. [HPOS 0.0 0.5]. But because the agents stand next to each other and have therefore slightly different positions with respect to the scene in front

---

[17] This high sensitivity to initial conditions is one of the characteristics of a chaotic dynamic system, see Lorenz (1993). Indeed, as I will explore in more detail later, evolving languages have all the characteristics of complex adaptive systems, including the potential for punctuated equilibria.

of them, there is an area which will be categorised as right for one head and left for the other (Figure 2.12).

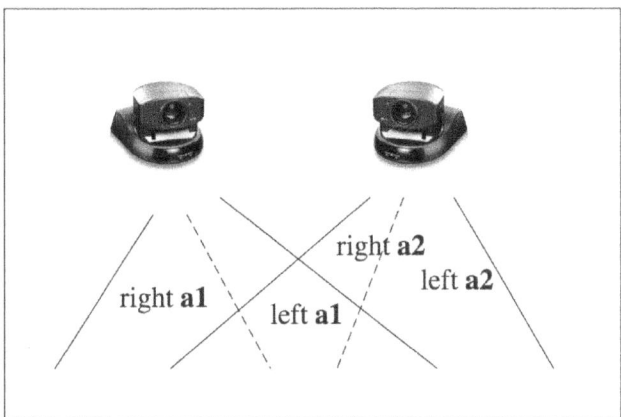

Figure 2.12: Two Talking Heads are shown a1 and a2 each seeing the scene from a slightly different viewpoint.

When this occurs in real dialogues, the form-meaning pairs lexicalising the distinctions left and right destabilise, because sometimes it gets positive feedback as it succeeds in the game, and at other times it gets negative feedback. This is one of the reasons why human categories are often relative and scaled with respect to a context. For example, we say *the triangle to the left of the square*, in other words left with respect to the square, to avoid the uncertainty inherent in the absolute use of *left*. Humans scale the size of objects with respect to the scene, so that small objects are small compared to the others in the scene and not small in an absolute sense.

2.4.6 Situated grounded semantics

These various examples, and I am clearly only scratching the surface, already illustrate the major thrust of the approach explored in the remainder of this book. There are dynamic processes at two levels. (1) There is the evolution of a lexicon in a single agent: new words are invented or adopted from another agent and the scores of form-meaning pairs in the lexicon go up and down depending on success or failure in the game. At any point in time, an agent will have a preferred form to express a particular meaning, but he has also stored the alternative words floating around in the population, and his preference will change depending on feedback in further language games. (2) There is also lexicon evolution at the level of the group. A coherent global lexicon emerges because the lexicons of the individual agents become more and more similar. This is due to the positive feedback loop between the outcome of using a certain form-meaning pair and the probability that this pair will be used again in the future. The group lexicon will however seldom be exactly uniform because new meanings constantly pop up and agents may arrive from other language communities, bringing in new words. I will study this two level dynamic process in much more detail in Chapter 7. It explains many of the mysteries of language, for example why there is ambiguity.

The *semantic theory* required to make the Talking Heads experiment work is very different from the classical textbook approaches to the subject, which tend to assume that categories can be defined in the abstract, independent of their context of use. Grounded processes of conceptualisation and interpretation are necessarily strongly situated and context-dependent. Whether 'blue triangle' is going to be effective in picking out the intended topic depends on what else is in the scene. If all other objects in the context are also blue triangles, the game will fail. If there is only one triangle, it was not really necessary to say that it is blue. This situatedness and context-dependence, together with the non-verbal hints given by the speaker, are crucial keys for restricting the possible meanings of a form and they therefore help the hearer disambiguate utterances or figure out the meaning of an unknown form. But situatedness and context-dependence are also major sources of difficulty, because the same categories may refer to different things for different agents in different contexts. Even if both agents agree that a particular form names a certain category, they may still fail in the game if the category picks out a different referent, for example because they see the context from a slightly different vantage point.

Another major difference with classical theories of meaning and reference is that the repertoire of meanings and form-meaning pairs is open-ended and subject to change at any time. Logicians would say that the truth conditions of the forms are non-monotonic. Non-monotonicity is unavoidable in the case of grounded situated agents with limited rationality.[18] Agents should always be allowed to introduce new forms or recruit existing forms to express new meanings, simply because the set of meanings must expand to cope with novel contexts and new communicative situations. After enough interactions among the members of the same group in a relatively stable environment, we expect there to be a stable set of conventionalised form-meaning relations, but it cannot be expected that everything anyone ever wants to say is already conventionalised, and so there will always be turbulence at the fringes. The idea that the lexicon and the syntax of a language are static entities is completely false. Both are in constant flux. Non-monotonicity is consequently one of the big topics in logic-based approaches to artificial intelligence.

A theory of language must try to capture the strategies by which language users shape and reshape their language and by which some solutions may become conventionalised and spread in the rest of the population, rather than focus on describing the end results of this process. This open-ended adaptive character of language systems is explored extensively in Chapter 7.

This section probably raised many questions in the mind of the critical reader: Will the agents really reach a sufficiently similar lexicon to have successful communication,

---

[18] Examples of these processes are described in: Bybee, Perkins & Pagliuca (1994), Traugott & Heine (1991). For attempts to explain these "grammaticalisation" processes in terms of general cognitive operations, see Heine (1997).

despite the fact that no one has a complete overview nor controls globally what the others can say? Are the unclear situations, i.e. those where more than one possible meaning is possible, not going to destabilise existing lexicons? Will all this scale up both for the size of the agent set and for the size of the meaning set? Is a new, virgin agent going to be able to catch up with a lexicon already existing in a population? What happens when two populations each with their own entrenched lexicon meet? These are exactly the kinds of questions that I will address later. They can all be posed in a precise way within the context of the Talking Heads experiment.

2.5 The origins of grammar

The self-organisation of a shared lexicon in a population of agents already represents a formidable challenge. We need to find models that work in principle *and* we have to make them operational on physically instantiated autonomous robots. But many linguists would claim that this does not yet represent true language, they would want to see the emergence of a genuine syntax. How that might happen is one of the ultimate remaining scientific mysteries of our time but let me sketch a possible approach.

Basically, I hypothesise that the agents must first of all have the capability to generate much more complex semantic and pragmatic strategies for conceptualising reality or applying a conceptualisation to retrieve a referent.

For example, a phrase like 'the two red triangles to the left of the smallest green square' requires the following strategy:

1. The agent filters the set of possible objects in the scene to retain only the squares.

2. He further filters the resulting set to retain only the green ones.

3. He orders the remaining green squares based on size and then picks out the smallest one.

4. Then he orders the objects in the scene based on their horizontal position (HPOS) and retains only those whose position is to the left of the smallest green square.

5. From the remaining set he filters out the triangles, and from this set those with a red colour.

6. This final set should contain only two members and they constitute the referents of the original phrase.

Our research has already led to mechanisms whereby agents can autonomously generate such semantic strategies using processes that compose primitive strategies into complex ones. The strategies compete for use in language games. New strategies form when needed by the environment or the agent's interactions and those that do not work or are irrelevant get pruned. The mechanisms for generating and selecting such semantic strategies are not unique to language. The invention and use of tools or the planning of a series of actions and the retrieval and use of ready-made plans requires exactly the same sorts of capabilities.

The spontaneous generation of repertoires of complex semantic strategies already explains some characteristics that are reflected in full-fledged languages: There is hierarchical structure, because one strategy may call upon another strategy to achieve a subgoal, and a strategy may potentially call upon itself thus introducing recursivity. There is also a functional specialisation of categories. They are now sometimes used for filtering the members of a set, sometimes for ordering them, sometimes for modifying another category before it is used for filtering, and so on. Hierarchical structuring, recursivity and functional specialisation therefore do not have to originate in language. The fact that we see them in language structure is a reflection of the generic hierarchical and functional nature of semantic strategies.[19]

Second, my hypothesis is that the need for communicating more and more complex semantic strategies and the conceptual structures they use, has pushed language users to start using more and more complex form characteristics, starting with word order but also intonation, stress patterns, function words, morphological variations of words, etc. Here another aspect comes into play: the ability to recognise forms and structures, which we also need to recognise structured objects in scenes for example, and the ability to assemble a structure satisfying a set of constraints. The collective dynamics which are responsible for the propagation and the spontaneous self-organisation of coherence in lexicons should also apply here. Grammars can be seen as ecologies, where form-meaning pairs compete in the population. New syntactic and semantic categories, new constructions and new uses of grammatical conventions are continuously created, and existing ones may destabilise and become in disuse.[20]

Each language user employs his own ideolect which is as well as possible co-ordinated with that of other language users but there is never complete similarity and never absolute stability. This explains perhaps why linguists have such a hard time to pin down "the" language of a community. As soon as someone speaks, language changes.

According to this theory, natural language structure is not the consequence of an autonomous innate language device which evolved by a genetic mutation or series of mutations. Instead cognitive mechanisms and structures already in place have been marshalled to get a language system off the ground, even though once language became essential for the rapid incorporation of new individuals and the general organisation of activities in human populations, it must have started to recruit vast amounts of brain capacity and stimulated other cognitive faculties, such as categorisation, episodic memory or problem solving, to become in turn much more complex and versatile.[21]

---

[19] The fact that languages change is, of course, well-known in linguistics even though it is less a focal research topic than used to be in the 19th century. See McMahon (1994) for a brief introduction into the subject. Language change has many of the characteristics of biological change but it takes place in cultural as opposed to biological time. See Labov (2000).

[20] The semantic strategies are similar to the cognitive processes that have been studied extensively in cognitive grammar (Langacker 1987). Formal versions of some of these processes have been formulated as part of Montague grammar (Montague 1974). In computational linguistics research, various attempts have been made to formalise conceptualisation and meaning application strategies (Gazdar & Mellish 1989).

[21] There has been an ongoing nature versus nurture debate with respect to the origins and acquisition of language. The different issues in this debate are already well illustrated in Piattelli-Palmarini (1980).

Before the problem of syntax can be tackled seriously, we must have a solid foundation showing how agents are capable of autonomously acquiring individual words or combinations of words without syntax. This is the subject of the remainder of the present volume.

2.6 Conclusions

The Talking Heads experiment examines with what kinds of mechanisms physically embodied autonomous agents might be capable of bootstrapping an ontology, a lexicon, and a syntax. The Talking Heads are situated embodied agents. This allows them to build up and co-ordinate language and meaning in tight interaction with a shared physical environment as perceived through their cameras. The Talking Heads are social agents, members of a language community. The collective dynamics of the community is a crucial ingredient to understanding how successful communications of a similar complexity as human natural language communications might have originated and how the underlying system can be maintained from one generation to the next.

This chapter has described the main hardware and software components of the agents and briefly sketched their internal architecture. The operation and effect of this architecture have been illustrated with some example games. The remaining chapters explore the various aspects of the agent's capacities in much more detail. First I will break the global task down into different subtasks, as suggested by the semiotic square. We will start by looking how agents may establish the relation between a real world object and a segmented image (Chapter 3). Then we study how they relate a segmented image to its conceptualisation (Chapter 4). Third, we study how a conceptualisation can be related to an utterance (Chapter 5). In Chapters 6 and 7 we couple these various components and study the lexical and ontological dynamic processes that result.

3 Perception

Our minds deceive us. Intuitively we feel we see very clearly and unambiguously the objects in our environment and are able to categorise objects or actions unequivocally in terms of perceptually grounded distinctions. For example, when I look out of the office window at the inner courtyard garden, I can clearly see the plants, trees and birds, as well as the walls, windows, and doors of the surrounding buildings. I can categorise their colours, sizes, and shapes and determine whether the leaves of the trees are moving with the wind. Because of this categorisation I can describe to another person what I see.

A categorisation and conceptualisation of reality is fundamentally based on sensors which output signals that directly reflect, in an analog and partially unreliable way, physical properties of the environment. For visual perception, human beings have photosensors in the eye which correlate with the amount of light, i.e. the amount of photons, falling on the sensor. The more photons, the stronger the sensor signal. But, a photosensor, or a matrix of such sensors as in the human retina, does not tell anything more than what the light intensity is at a tiny spot of the image captured by the eye. There is no obvious straightforward procedure that groups the spots into coherent patches. When you implement and try out different segmentation procedures on real world images, you quickly find that each procedure generates a multitude of possibilities instead of a clear segmentation. Even if coherent segments are detected, there is the problem of what features of the scene are going to be used for further conceptualisation. A very large, open-ended set of possible feature detectors can be imagined. The quality and reliability of their output depends on the scene being processed, and is in any case strongly context-dependent.

So we find that the world does not present itself neatly segmented, processed, and categorised. There is an enormous gap between the symbolic world of objects and categories and the subsymbolic world of analog sensing. The brain somehow performs a vast amount of processing to fill this gap, without us being in the least aware of it. This processing takes place in parallel. Many different segmentation procedures and feature detectors operate concurrently on streams of consecutive images, generating hypotheses that become stronger if they are confirmed by additional evidence, or weaker if they do not fit into a larger picture. We are only aware of the final result and therefore have no intuition of what is really going on, except in rare and pathological circumstances. Rather than viewing perception as a straight-forward step-by-step transformation of the raw sensory data into a segmented picture, it is better to think of the whole process as a boiling soup with thousands of hypotheses taking shape, some of them floating like bubbles up to the surface. Constraints and expectations flow down from the top so that the maximum amount of available information is used to construct the coherent segmented picture of reality we consciously experience.

3 Perception

The objective of this chapter is to examine this process in sufficient detail to move forward with the main topic of our investigations, namely language and meaning. My aim is not to delve into the full complexity of the visual system, because this would lead us too far astray of the main topic, but to have a sufficiently rich source of features so that conceptualisation and language communication can be studied.

3.1 What sensors sense

Sensors and actuators are the interfaces between the physical world and the internal world. They are dedicated hard-wired components which grow in biological systems strongly influenced by genetics and environmental inputs.[1]

A sensor transduces external physical states into internal states. For example, a touch sensor, of which there are hundreds of thousands all over the human body, transduces mechanical energy into neural signals. Other sensors respond to the intensity of certain sectors of the wave spectrum. Ears respond to audible waves. Photoreceptors in the eye respond to visible light waves. The body also has a large number of biochemical sensors responsive to internal chemical states so that we can feel the hunger in our stomach for example. In addition to sensors, bodies carry actuators, which transduce internal states into mechanical energy and thus make it possible to perform actions in the world. Actuators receive continuous signal streams and modulate their activity based on these signals.

3.1.1 Artificial sensors and actuators

Analogs of biological sensors can be artificially recreated to give robots sensory capabilities. Something similar to a touch sensor can be created using a contact switch that passes current when closed. A microphone has a functionality similar to the ear. A digital camera can be used to recreate the functionality of an eye; it records the light intensity of millions of small rectangles of the image, known as pixels, just like the retina. The set of all pixels is usually called an image map. Digital colour cameras provide three information elements for every pixel: the amount of red, green and blue of each pixel (RGB). We can build sonar sensors responding to low frequency waves, just like the ones bats use for navigation, or infrared sensors which are useful for obstacle avoidance because the amount of infrared light emitted and captured back by the sensor correlates with distance to objects.

A sensor should never be seen as measuring accurately an abstract property of reality. For example, an infrared sensor does not measure the distance to an obstacle. The infrared reflection depends not only on distance but also on the reflection properties of the object and on the amount of background infrared in the environment, thus distance must be inferred and projected onto reality. Similarly, the colour receptors do not really

---

[1] Possible biological implementations of the various sensors and sensory processes discussed in this chapter can be found in Churchland & Sejnowski (1992). The nature and neurophysiological implementation of visual processes are discussed in detail in Zeki (1993).

measure colour. They respond to reflections within segments of the wavelength spectrum but this reflection is again determined by many factors: how much and what kind of light falls on the object, and how the object reflects the light depending which varies with the position of the object. So colour is again a more abstract notion that needs to be reconstructed and projected on the image based on complex processing.

The Talking Heads use vision as the main source of sensory information because most of the perceptually grounded concepts used in language derive from visual sensing. The only actuator (apart from the speech synthesiser which I will not discuss in detail) is a pan/tilt motor for turning the head up and down or left and right.

3.1.2 Natural sensing

It is technically possible to build all sorts of sensors and actuators that have little to do with human capabilities. But clearly, human-like categories and languages that are similar to human categories and languages will only emerge if the sensors and actuators are at least to some degree similar to those of humans. This is not always technologically possible and when it is, it often requires non-trivial transformations of artificial sensor data. The Talking Heads use digital cameras as their main sensory source. These cameras give output in RGB (red, green, blue intensities) because this is the standard in current computer technology. But human vision operates on four quite different channels: the two chromatic opponent channels which provide a value on the yellow-blue and red-green dimensions, an achromatic channel which holds the brightness or light intensity, and a saturation channel which reflects the degree of saturation or purity of a colour. These channels can be reconstructed from RGB by a complex transformation.[2]

3.1.3 Behaviours

Although language requires that the image is segmented and categorised, a lot can already be done with raw or lightly processed sensory data by dynamically coupling them to signals controlling the actuators. The neural abilities of many simple animals probably do not get much further than this and it already has turned out to be a good way to construct the basic behavioural layers of robots that have to operate autonomously in a real-world environment in real time.

For example, suppose you want a robot of the sort seen in Figure 1.3 to move towards a light source. As originally suggested by the cybernetician Braitenberg (1984), we can do this by mounting two simple light sensors to the left and right of the body and by implementing a direct dynamical coupling between the output of the light sensors and the motors. The coupling is such that when the sensed left light is stronger than the sensed right light, the motor attached to the left wheel is slightly decreased and the

---

[2] There is a vast literature on colour perception from different points of view (physics, psychology, neurophysiology, linguistics). A representative sample is contained in Byrne & Hilbert (1997). In some of the experiments described later, the RGB values are converted to the CIE XYZ colour coding and from that to the opponent channels. These algorithms have been implemented by Michael Pollitis. See: Kaiser & Boynton (1996).

3 Perception

right motor slightly increased, so that the robot veers to the left. When the right light is stronger, the right motor is increased and the left motor decreased, so that the robot veers to the right. When these two dynamical couplings are put in place together with a forward movement, a zig-zag behaviour emerges which brings the robot to the light source.

Basic behaviours can be put together to form more complex behaviours.[3] Figure 3.1 shows a recording of the internal states of the robot in Figure 1.3 as it is performing phototaxis towards a light source, using two simple light sensors, and touch-based obstacle avoidance behaviour. When the robot strikes the box housing the light, it moves back in a kind of reflex behaviour triggered by the touch sensors mounted at the front. The LeftLight and RightLight sensory channels and the LeftMotorSpeed and RightMotorSpeed are shown in Figure 3.1. When the robot strikes the obstacle housing the light, its left and right motor is pulled down to a negative value so that it moves backwards. Then the robot zig-zags to the light source until it hits the obstacle again.

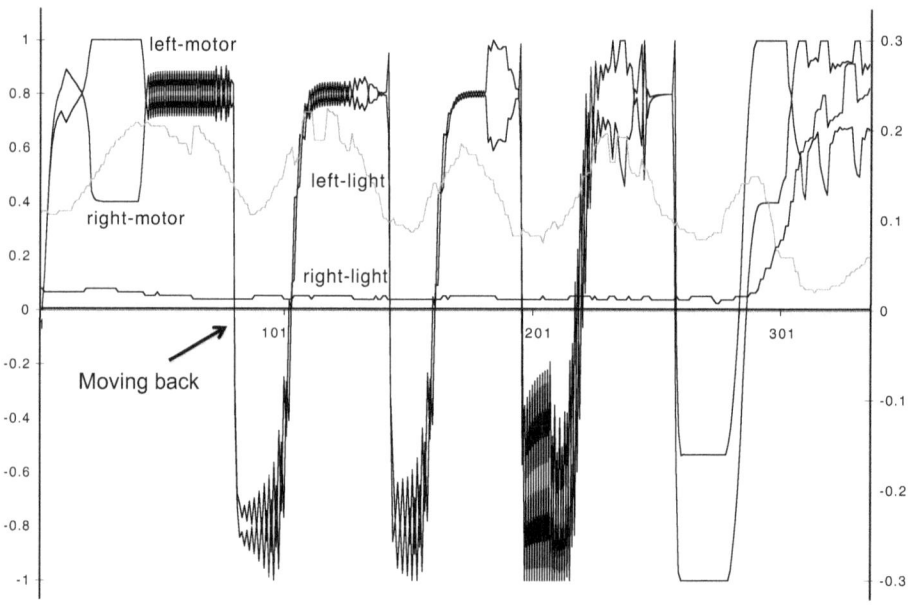

Figure 3.1: Internal states of a robot's sensory and actuator channels on the y-axis and time in periods of 1/40 seconds on the x-axis. The robot pushes against a box holding a light source.

These channel recordings illustrate clearly that sensor or actuator data is continuous in time and rapidly fluctuates in response to changes in the environment or the behaviour

---

[3] A representative sample of experiments in this direction is reported in: Steels & Brooks (1995). See also: Arkin (1998).

of the agents. Coupling sensory data to actuators is effective for quick reaction without the need for higher level processing. If an obstacle is rapidly approaching, it is important to get out of the way rather than trying to figure out what kind of obstacle it is. The observed behaviour is very complex, even though the underlying dynamical systems are relatively simple; the complexity is due to the complexity of the real world with which the robot is interacting.

Similar behaviour systems and networks have been experimented with for more complex tasks and it is actually the way that the Mars rover discussed in Chapter 1 works.[4] However, the gap between the continuous dynamics of sensori-motor intelligence and cognition remains unbridged. It is possible for *us* to see structure in the data but this structure is not perceived nor used for control by the robot itself. The robot does not segment nor categorise reality. It does not "know" that it is moving left or right and therefore cannot communicate this information to another robot. All processing remains at the analog continuous level. However because it remains at this subsymbolic level, it is doubtful whether we can ever hope to bootstrap cognitive intelligence simply by adding more of these dynamical systems.[5] The difference between behavioural intelligence and cognitive intelligence resides in an additional layer of processing which is no longer continuous and analog but discrete and symbolic. How this second symbolic layer could be formed but at the same time remain grounded in the analog sensori-motor layer is one of the main research topics addressed in this book.

3.2 Segmentation

The first step that bridges the gap between sensory layers and cognitive processing is segmentation. Segmentation means that a sensory data stream is divided into units either in space or in time. In the Talking Heads experiment, the environment is restricted to static images only, so that segmentation amounts to aggregating pixels into spatial patches.

A patch may have an irregular shape which makes it hard to apply some classifications without complex processing. Bounding boxes are much easier to compute and are already very useful. The bounding box of a segment is a rectangle around the contours of a segment (Figure 3.2).

It is generally not necessary for segmentation to always yield parts of the images that correspond to what we would call objects. This is an impossible demand. What counts as an object is to some extent task-dependent. Segmentation yields information that can

---

[4] At the risk of simplifying, we can say that the early work in cybernetics (such as that of Braitenberg (1984)) has focused on this subsymbolic layer and that *Artificial Intelligence*, as a research field emerging in the late 1950's, has focused on the symbolic layer. Some researchers involved in a bottom up approach to Artificial Intelligence strongly refocused on the subsymbolic layer. One of the most vocal advocates of this position is Brooks (1991). Obviously we need the two, but bridging the gap is a non-trivial problem, sometimes known as the grounding problem. See: Harnad (1990).

[5] Marr (1982) remains a classical reference outlining the features that can be extracted, the principled algorithms for doing it, and possible neurophysiological models. These are the main research topics that still dominate research in vision. See Ullman (1996) for an overview.

3 Perception

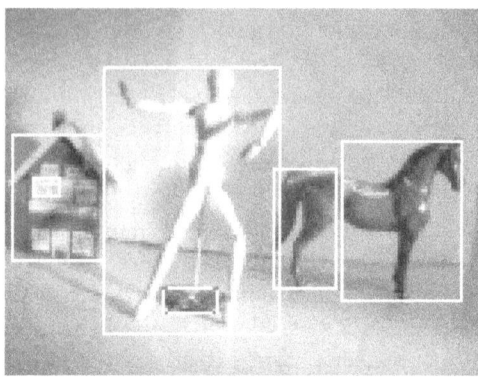

Figure 3.2: Example of a scene captured by the camera in Figure 1.6, containing a puppet, a wooden house, and a horse. Segmentation is based on aggregating grayscale patches, i.e. areas in the image that are lighter or darker than the general background. Bounding boxes have been drawn around the segments. Note that there can be bounding boxes within bounding boxes if an object forms part of a larger object.

be used for object identification but should not be equated with it. This is well illustrated in Figure 3.2. Segmentation has been done here by filtering out segments with lower or higher average grayscale values compared to the average in the scene. The segments that have been obtained are not necessarily those that we humans identify, because we use knowledge of the objects involved. This shows clearly that higher level constraints play a role even at the very first basic visual processing layers.

3.2.1 Feature extraction

Many methods for segmentation have been reported in the computer vision literature and all of them are useful even though they give slightly different results. Most methods assume that additional low level processing is first performed on the image map to detect small-scale structures, such as:

- Edges, which are possible boundaries between two surfaces. Edges can be aggregated in line segments.

- Junctions, which are regions where lines come together.

- Patches, which are regions where the colour or the grayscale values are relatively constant.

- Textures, which are small-scale regular surface markings, for example blobs.

- Optical flow, which are vectors indicating the direction and velocity of moving brightness patterns.

- Distance from the observer, computed by matching two image maps from binocular vision.

- Shadings, recovered from continuous variations in brightness.

The recovery of such features is in itself a non-trivial topic of research and a huge literature as well as many software libraries now exist.

The visual layer of the Talking Heads only extracts patches and edges which each leads to one way of segmenting the scene. Segmenting based on patches attempts to aggregate those parts of the image into patches (a process called *region growing*) that have more or less the same colour. More or less the same is of course a relative notion and larger or smaller segments will be found depending on the thresholds that are used for deciding whether a colour is similar or not. Segments that are too small are not considered further. Region growing starts by comparing for each pixel how similar it is to neighbouring pixels. Similar pixels are grouped as a patch. In the next step, each patch is examined to see whether it can be merged with a neighbouring patch, and so on recursively until patches cannot be combined further. Small patches or individual pixels that stand on their own are included as part of a larger patch so that we get sufficiently broad patches.

Segmentation based on edges starts by first detecting the edges themselves, which are colour discontinuities suggesting a boundary between two surfaces. The edges are then aggregated into lines, and these lines are connected to find the contours of an object. This method works well for the simple objects used in the Talking Heads experiment. Things are no longer so simple when contours are less clear, for example because they fuse with the background. Further complications arise when one object partly obstructs another object or when a set of lines can ambiguously be organised in different configurations (as in visual illusions like the Necker cube). This illustrates that one segmentation method must be balanced with others to offset unclear areas or local ambiguities.

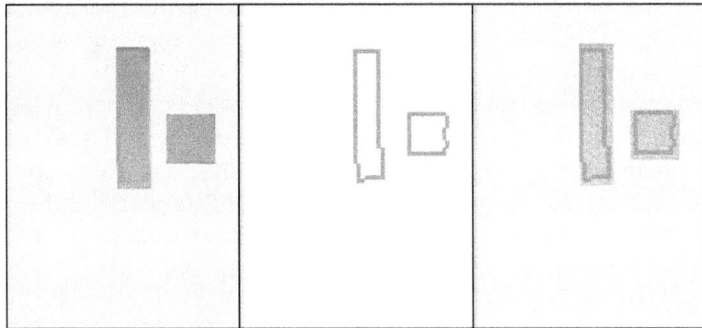

Figure 3.3: Left view shows an image as captured by a Talking Heads camera. Middle view shows the result of segmentation based on edge detection. Right view shows the integration of segmentation by color and by edge detection.

The results of applying these two segmentation methods can be seen in Figure 3.3. The top picture shows the image map itself as it is captured by a Talking Head camera. The middle image shows the result of segmenting based on edge detection. The contours of two objects have been found. Note that these contours are not straight lines as one might expect. They are obtained by connecting together line segments which are themselves based on connected edges. The bottom image shows the combination of edge detection and segmentation based on patches. Because the green objects stand out clearly against the white background they are easily recognised by the combination of these segmentation methods. Given the simplicity of the Talking Heads environment (geometric shapes on a white board), segmentation based on colour and on edge detection generally yields a segmentation that corresponds to the individual objects humans perceive in a scene.

3.2.2 Divergent perception

There is no guarantee that two Talking Heads looking towards the same area of the white board perceive exactly the same image. In fact, the contrary is true. Because the robots are physically grounded and situated in a particular context, standing roughly one meter apart from each other (as shown in Figure 1.1), they cannot see the same scene from exactly the same vantage point, and so images diverge. On the edges of the field of view, the differences might become so significant that different objects are seen and consequently different categories used.

Compare for example the recorded images for a speaker (top) and a hearer (bottom) as shown in Figure 3.4 (to the left). The same figure shows the segmentation performed by both agents in a separate window (to the right). The images are clearly different because they have been taken from slightly different camera positions and the hearer only approximately perceives in which direction the speaker is pointing. Agent **a1** (top of 3.4) has recovered the two circles, but not the rectangle which was deemed to small to be relevant. Agent **a2** (bottom of 3.4) has recovered the rectangle in the left top corner but only one circle. The yellow circle was not recognised by **a2** due to slightly different reflections perceived from **a2**'s angle of view, so that the yellow surface was no longer distinguishable from the white background.

Usually the situation is not so divergent, and even if there is divergent perception, the categorisation used by the speaker may still be compatible with the same topic for the hearer. Nevertheless, we must take into account that divergent perception of the scene might considerably confuse language communication and the feedback the speaker gives to the hearer. This is one example where it is useful to do grounded experiments because it shows clearly a major issue (namely perceptual and hence categorical divergence) which is usually swept under the carpet.

3.2.3 The sieve architecture

Segmentation exemplifies a dual kind of processing that we will encounter again and again as we focus on the different layers of the cognitive architecture (Figure 3.5). Various possible solutions are generated, expanded and combined in parallel. The possible

3.2 Segmentation

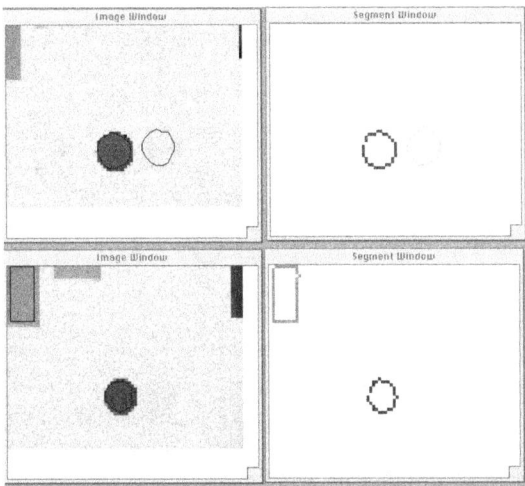

Figure 3.4: Top (left), image captured by the hearer. Bottom (left), image captured by the speaker. Because both have a different view on the scene, the images diverge and consequently the segmentation (bottom and top right) diverges as well, in particular the yellow circle is not perceived by the speaker. In contrast the speaker perceives a rectangle (bottom left corner) and has chosen this as the topic. The rectangle is not perceived by the hearer, so the game has no chance to be successful.

solutions enter into competition until globally coherent solutions emerge, which are ranked and handed to the next layer of processing. Often a solution does not emerge or multiple solutions are equally valid in which case constraints from expectations or from the further processing of partial solutions must flow down to influence earlier processing, which can be implemented as a *re-entry* of some solutions back into the previous layer. For example, hearing a word may stimulate the expectation that a certain category is relevant, which in turn may stimulate the computation of certain features and influence how the image is segmented. A speaker may have to choose between alternative segmentations and categorisations depending on whether the conceptualisation can be succinctly and accurately lexicalised and possible lexicalisations will only be acceptable when they can be integrated in a complete sentence.

The two way flow of constraints (from perception to high level cognitive processing and from high level cognitive processing to perception) suggests that the brain is best thought of as a massively parallel, densely connected processing system, in which multiple partial solution structures float up or down, gathering strength or weakening with new information entering the system. This contrasts with the view that information is processed in a serial step-by-step fashion through tightly compartmentalised modules.[6]

---

[6] See Fodor (1983). This book discusses a modular, sequential information processing architecture for cognition. A non-modular, parallel view is sketched in: Minsky (1986). A more realistic neurophysiological model similar to the one underlying the *sieve architecture* we have used is discussed by Edelman (1987).

3 Perception

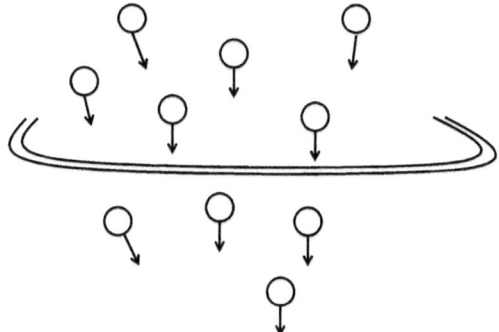

Figure 3.5: The different layers of cognitive processing act like a sieve. Inputs flow into the layer, where they are processed to generate hypotheses of which the best ones are transmitted to the next layer. Every layer can operate in both directions, so that constraints can flow from top to bottom and from bottom to top.

It is true that we have the illusion that there is some *homunculus*, a little man, which sees a single coherent picture of reality and finds quickly the right way to verbalise or interpret this picture, but closer examination of the actual informational requirements of each subprocess shows that this can never work. Constraints must flow in all directions, because the sensory data has not enough information to allow a unique segmentation, and categorisation and language is too full of ambiguities to allow a straightforward linear interpretation.

3.3 Sensory channels

Once segments have been found, further characteristics must be extracted. The values of these various characteristics will be communicated on sensory channels to later categorisation processes. A characteristic property of a segment, such as average gray-scale, is still in the analog continuous domain and should not be confused with a category (like dark or light) which is in the discrete symbolic domain. An open-ended set of possible sensory channels can be imagined, ranging from very general channels sensitive to often recurring properties relevant in common tasks and thus shared by most people, to very specific channels which only experts in specific domains possess.

3.3.1 Example channels

The segment characteristics which will be used later in various experiments are defined below. Their values are all derived by straightforward computations from the raw image maps captured by the cameras.

- AREA: The surface area of a segment is calculated by simply counting the number of pixels that are part of the segment.

- HPOS, VPOS: The x and y values of the central-position of a segment. The central position is calculated by taking the mid-point of the sides of the bounding box.

- HEIGHT: The height of the bounding box.

- WIDTH: The width of the bounding box.

- BB-AREA: The area of the bounding box, calculated by multiplying height by width.

- GRAY: The average gray-scale value of the pixels in a segment.

- R, G, B: The average R (redness), G (greenness), and B (blueness) values in a segment. To obtain more human-like colour channels, they are transformed in terms of YB (yellow-blue), RG (red-green), BW (black-white), SAT (saturation) and BRIGHTNESS channels.

- EDGE-COUNT: The number of edges in a segment, for example 3 in the case of a triangle.

- ANGLE-COUNT: The number of angles, determined on the basis of the junctions.

- RATIO: The ratio between the area of the segment and the area of its bounding box, which gives an idea how close a figure is to a rectangular shape.

Each of these segment characteristics or combinations of characteristics enables certain types of categorisations. For example, the GRAY channel makes it possible to distinguish between light and dark, HEIGHT between short and tall, HPOS between left and right, VPOS between top and bottom, AREA between big and small, etc. In the next chapter, we will study how such categorisations may form on the basis of their respective channels.

3.3.2 Conceptual spaces

The sensory channels used in the experiments have deliberately been kept to a minimum so that we can follow in detail the ontological and lexical dynamics, which is a non-trivial matter as I will demonstrate in Chapters 6 and 7. Obviously to get a richer lexicon, more channels need to be made available to the agents. These channels can often be grouped to form a CONCEPTUAL SPACE.[7] One of the best known examples is the colour space formed by the yellow-blue, red-green, black-white, saturation, and brightness channels.

---

[7] See Gärdenfors (2000). More cognitive oriented spaces, further removed from perception, are discussed in Fauconnier (1994).

Here are some other examples:

1. A set of sensory channels that are sensitive to characteristics of moving segments can easily be imagined. They include the speed of movement, the direction of movement (along the horizontal position (HPOS) and vertical position (VPOS) dimensions), or the change in area (getting bigger if the object approaches or smaller if it moves away). This is the foundation for categories about spatial change: moving left versus moving right, approaching versus retracting, speeding up versus slowing down.[8]

2. Various spatial relations between segments can be computed: inclusion and overlap between segments, distance between midpoints, hierarchical structure, etc. This leads to another batch of categories which are the basis for spatial distinctions like inside versus outside.

3. More properties of the shape of segments can be computed. I have already introduced the RATIO channel, which is the area of the segment divided by the area of the bounding box, giving an indication how rectangular a segment is. This can be generalised by using an ellipse around a shape so that we can calculate convexity. We can then also calculate elongation (by calculating the principal axes of the ellipse).

It is not at all necessary that the channels operate on visual input, they can also use actuator sensors or internal states like the level of the battery. It is moreover possible to consider channels for dynamic states, for example by transforming the sensor and actuator data into state-space representations and analysing them in terms of attractors.[9]

The ontological and lexical apparatus of the Talking Heads is generic with respect to the nature of the sensory channels that are used, they could just as easily be about other sensory domains like sound, tactile sensation or internal states of the robots.

3.3.3 Perceptual constancy

Real world sensory data is remarkably volatile due to the high variation and constant change of our physical environment, nevertheless human beings have the illusion of constancy. For example, the colour of an object is determined by the wavelength of the light reflected by its surface. For a long time, it was thought that colour was an intrinsic property of a surface, and that we therefore experience the colour of an object as constant, but psycho-experimental evidence has shown that this is not true. When we look at a surface in isolation which reflects light between 430 and 470 nanometres,

---

[8] Experiments using segmentation based on movement using the dedicated hardware shown in Figure 1.5 were carried out by Tony Belpaeme. More details can be found in: Belpaeme, Steels & van Looveren (1998) These channels have been used in language experiments where the agents were perceiving and communicating about moving images: Steels (1998) The segmentation used in this book based on output from the Sony EVI-D31 camera was implemented by Danny Van Tieghem. Angus McIntyre integrated the interfaces to this camera within the BABEL environment.

[9] Several examples of this type of approach are found in Port & van Gelder (1995).

we experience the colour blue. As a result, one might assume that blue can be equated with the experience of light in this particular wavelength region. However, if the same surface is perceived in a broader context and the light conditions are changed (so that objectively they now reflect light in a different spectral region), they still appear as blue! What should objectively appear green according to the measured wavelength values is still experienced as blue. This explains why we see colours as relatively constant even if the light conditions are changing (for example from broad daylight to evening light) which is obviously extremely useful for dealing with rich environments. But it implies that colour is *not* an intrinsic property that can be measured objectively with a light meter. It is actively mapped onto reality as a result of complex processing which takes the context into account.[10]

The same sort of context-sensitivity is important for the other sensory dimensions that the Talking Heads use, as well as for segmentation. An object will appear large or small depending on the other objects in the scene. It will appear light or dark depending on the average brightness. A scene may be segmented in one way or another depending on the objects it contains. Visual illusions arise when more than one context is consistent with an image and interpretations sometimes switch back and forth between different possibilities.

3.3.4 Transformations

Cognitive agents can stabilise the sensory data to achieve more perceptual constancy by transforming them so that the data become less context-sensitive. This implies that additional processing first recovers more information about the context. One of the best known examples of this concerns colour constancy. As mentioned earlier, wavelength reflection is strongly influenced by the background light in the environment. However, when the average surface reflectance is known, it is possible to transform the colour data to recover the colour that is experienced by humans as constant for a surface.[11]

3.3.5 Scaling

The second way in which the erratic nature of real world signals can be diminished is by scaling. Scaling means that the values actually recorded by sensors or feature extractors are calibrated with respect to a frame of reference.

A first frame of reference is based on the absolute minima and maxima of the values on a sensory channel. This can be used to do SENSOR-ORIENTED SCALING. For example, the image map captured by the camera contains 320 × 240 pixels, which means that the horizontal position (HPOS) has a value between 0 and 320 and the vertical position (VPOS) has a value between 0 and 240. Both values can be scaled to fall between 0.0 and 1.0 so that they become uniform with respect to other sensory channels. Given a value x and a

---

[10] See the discussion about colour in: Varela, Thomson & Rosch (1991)
[11] See the discussion in: Zeki (1993), particularly Chapter 23.

min and max value, then the scaled value is $x' = (x - min)/(max - min)$. Thus the sensed value of HPOS=200 becomes HPOS=0.62 after scaling.

In the experiments discussed later, sensor-scaling is always performed so that all sensory data is between 0.0 and 1.0, allowing values on different channels to be compared with each other. In addition, context-oriented scaling is performed. CONTEXT-ORIENTED SCALING uses the minima and maxima of the values that effectively appear in the context. For example, if the values for the HEIGHT of segments observed in the scene is between 500 and 700, then these can be the minimum and maximum of the HEIGHT scale, so that 500 maps onto 0.0 and 700 to 1.0. Context-oriented scaling acts like a lens magnifying the perceived values so that distinctions stand out more clearly. This scaling could be made more sophisticated by introducing an additional scaling factor so that differences are amplified but not necessarily blown up to their extremes.

Context-oriented scaling has two advantages. The context is now strongly taken into account, in a way similar to human perception: A segment looks dark when surrounded by light segments but light when surrounded by darker ones. The second advantage is that differences within the relevant subrange that actually occur in the scene are amplified, so that they stand out even if the range of possible values is much wider. Often both relative (context-oriented) and absolute (sensor-oriented) scaling are pertinent. Thus left can be the left-most of all the objects in the scene (context-oriented scaling) or left in absolute terms (sensor-oriented scaling). Some channels, such as the colour channels, should never be scaled for context, because the categorisation works best on the basis of the sensor-scaled values.

Context-oriented scaling is not necessarily based on the frame of reference imposed by the image map which is recorded by perceiving the scene from the viewpoint of the camera. Many contexts and hence other frames of reference are possible and are exploited in natural language conversations. Often a particular context is communicated through language. Scaling is then performed within the frame of reference suggested by that context, for example, if I will tell someone 'the chair is to your left', whereas it may perhaps be to the right of the hearer from my point of view.

A final form of scaling uses the typical values of the object being perceived. I will call this OBJECT-ORIENTED SCALING. For example, a small elephant is always very large next to a large mouse. We clearly have expectations about the typical size of an elephant at a certain distance and use it to scale perceptual data prior to size categorisation. Context-oriented and object-oriented scaling are examples how constraints must flow from non-visual cognitive processes to visual processing. These non-modular interactions are a strong indication that cognitive subsystems must be highly interconnected.

3.3.6 Saliency

The perceptual layer generates in parallel a wealth of sensory characteristics about each of the segments in an image and their relationships. But not all sensory characteristics are equally distinctive. For example, two segments in a scene may have almost the same area but one might be very thin and thus tall, and the other very wide and thus short. In our own human perception, those channels that reflect significant differences stand out and are preferred in referring to an object. Therefore, it is unlikely that area would be used in Figure 3.6 to distinguish object 1 from the others.

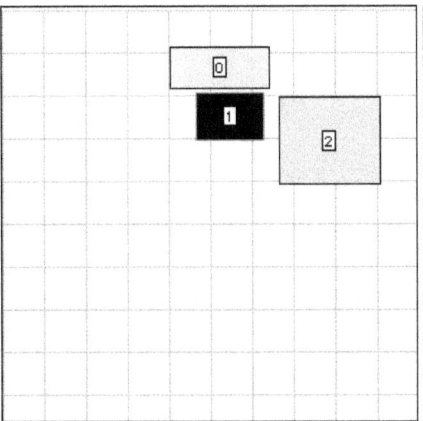

Figure 3.6: A scene with three objects. The sensory values on the grayscale channel are the most salient and will therefore be chosen preferentially for categorisation and verbalisation.

The saliency of a channel is the smallest distance (after sensor-scaling) between the perceived values of the topic and one of the corresponding perceived values of the other segments in the context. Thus the different perceived values (after sensor-scaling) for the segments in Figure 3.6 are shown in Table 3.1. The last line shows the saliency, assuming that the topic is segment 1. Clearly the GRAY-channel is the most salient one in this case, followed by the WIDTH-channel. Other sensory channels such as HPOS, VPOS or HEIGHT (which have almost the same values for object 0 and 1) are not salient at all.

Determining saliency has to be done before context scaling, because context-scaling stretches the values to their extremes and so saliency information is lost. Table 3.2 shows for the scene shown in Figure 3.6 the AREA channel with its raw data, the value after sensor-scaling (with minimum 1,000 and maximum 10,000), and the value after context-scaling.

Another example based on the segmented image is shown in Figure 3.7 (top images). Two circular segments have been identified, the others are ignored because they are too small. The different sensory values (after sensor-scaling) for the segments in the speaker's image are shown in Table 3.3.

The table shows clearly that HPOS is the most salient channel. The horizontal position also strikes us immediately as being the most salient when looking at Figure 3.7. For many of the other channels, the differences are almost insignificant. The use of saliency facilitates enormously communication and the acquisition of new categories. The case shown in Figure 3.7 (top images) is an excellent opportunity for the agents to learn about left versus right. If more channels are salient, it is no longer so easy for the hearer to

3 *Perception*

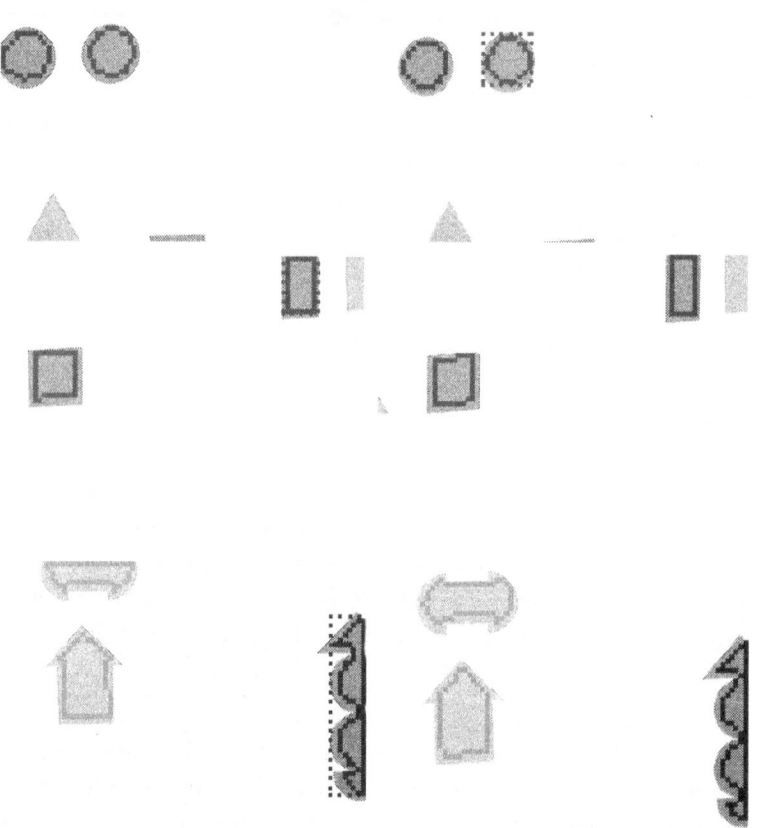

Figure 3.7: Three examples of segmented images. The topic is indicated by a dashed bounding box in the image of the speaker. Segments which are too small are ignored. The topics have all been conceptualised as being to the right and so the same word *gofubo* has been used to refer to them.

3.4 Methodology

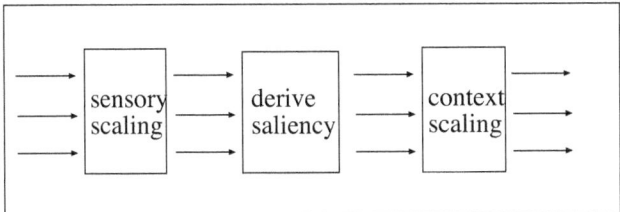

Figure 3.8: Processing converts data on a sensory channel into more usable data for later categorisation processes.

guess what meaning might have been used by the speaker and so incoherence would slip into the group's lexical system.

The various steps that the agents go through in preparing data on sensory channels are summarised in Figure 3.8. It is presented here as flowing in one direction, but in fact constraints coming from higher level cognitive processing may influence these steps. For example, if we say 'the largest square left of the triangle', we expect the hearer to scale the squares with respect to all the objects left of the triangle, not with respect to all the objects in the scene. The backward flow of constraints will be studied after I have covered the different layers separately.

3.4 Methodology

I hope the reader now has a much better idea of the enormous challenge that the Talking Heads face when trying to play a language game about a real world scene, particularly because they try to develop a lexicon and ontology as well. The images contain a multitude of ways to make distinctions and they differ slightly for both agents. It is enough fo a cloud to pass by causing the light conditions to change slightly, and different values are immediately seen on the colour channels possibly leading to different segmentations. So how can the agents ever get a repertoire of abstract categories and associated words when the real world shows such a perplexing variation? Very different scenes (for example the ones contained in Figure 3.7) can intuitively be distinguished with the same

Table 3.1: Perceived values for each segment in Figure 3.6.

obj	HPOS	VPOS	HEIGHT	WIDTH	GRAY	AREA
0	0.66	0.95	0.01	0.71	0.19	0.27
1	0.69	0.83	0.07	0.33	0.97	0.21
2	0.99	0.87	0.54	0.72	0.22	0.57
sal	0.03	0.05	0.07	0.39	0.75	0.06

Table 3.2: Data for the area channel for the scene in Figure 3.6.

Object	Raw data	Sensor-scaled	Context-scaled
0	24530	0.27	0.18
1	18924	0.21	0.0
2	50960	0.57	1.00

Table 3.3: Perceived values for each segment in Figure 3.7

channel	obj-0	obj-1	saliency
HPOS	0.27	0.16	0.11
VPOS	0.20	0.20	0.0
HEIGHT	0.15	0.15	0.0
WIDTH	0.10	0.11	0.01
AREA	0.10	0.10	0.0
R	0.23	0.25	0.02
G	0.32	0.34	0.02
B	0.63	0.65	0.02

categories (namely [LEFT] versus [RIGHT]). But how can such inductive leaps be made? Scaling and sensor transformation introduce some perceptual constancy, and saliency helps to restrict the attention to those channels that are potentially effective in communication, but there is clearly an enormous gap between sensory data and language.

In this book, I will not only report on the outcome of an experiment and what we learned about the nature of cognitive architectures, but I will also try to illustrate how we tackle such tremendously complicated problems. I will take a moment to explain this methodology because it runs like a red thread through the remaining chapters of this book and differs from the way other subdisciplines of cognitive science go about their investigations.

3.4.1 Putting up scaffolds

The standard means of attacking a difficult problem is to break it up in subproblems. In this case, the most obvious subdivision is along the different sides of the semiotic square I introduced in the previous chapter (Figure 3.9). This leads to three natural subproblems: perception, conceptualisation, and verbalisation. When breaking up a problem, we can initially assume that the other subproblems will be solved somehow and that they give perfect output to the others or provide the right feedback. We can then try to invent a mechanism that can do the job for the subtask we are investigating in these ideal circumstances, and test its strength and limitations. This is like putting up scaffolds to see whether partial solutions work, before putting it all together.

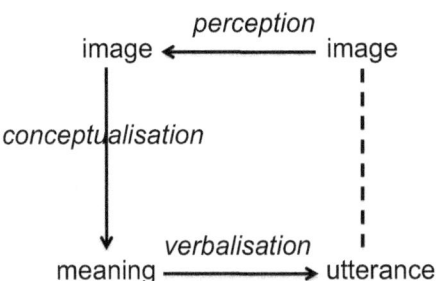

Figure 3.9: The general problem of production is broken up into three subproblems: perception, conceptualisation and verbalisation.

I will extensively make use of this methodology. This chapter has focused on perception, the next chapter focuses exclusively on conceptualisation, assuming that there is good segmentation and a decent set of sensory channels. Chapter 5 turns to the problem of lexicalisation, assuming that the agents have a shared repertoire of meanings and agree on what meaning to use in a particular game. Chapter 6 then puts the solutions for conceptualisation and lexicalisation together by coupling their inputs and outputs and establishing the appropriate feedback connections. Chapter 7 then couples this system to the perceptual processes discussed in this chapter, so that we get back to our original goal: understand how perceptually grounded language communication is possible.

The methodology of breaking a problem into its subproblems goes quite a distance, but is not without danger. The processes relating perception to language cannot be modular for reasons already mentioned. Each layer receives inputs which are not completely reliable and generates a set of possible suggestions rather than a single "correct" solution. Constraints have to flow from top to bottom because there is simply not enough reliable information to solve the problem with a straightforward sequential decision process. In addition, every layer is constantly adapting itself to the surrounding information context. New categories may develop, new words need to be learned, new sensory channels may even emerge. So, constructing a global system is going to be more than simply putting together its parts. There are complex behaviours that will only become visible when the appropriate non-modular couplings are put in place, and this is notoriously difficult to do and study.

3.4.2 Idealisation and realism

To make this problem more manageable I will adopt a second complementary method, widely used in engineering. We can keep the various aspects of the global process intact,

3 Perception

but simplify the challenge. We start with extremely idealised operational circumstances and then gradually add more and more realism, until the system is ready to face the real world. At every step we first establish whether the mechanisms still work, which means in the guessing game that communicative success moves up. If this does not happen, we must investigate what needs to be added or changed and perhaps reduce the complexity again to find a new solid ground. If a language system does get established, we can examine the limits of the process before increasing the challenge once more. During the original research, we extensively used this stepwise approach, often sliding down the mountain when too much complexity was introduced too quickly so that we were forced to take a few steps back and tackler simpler challenges until we got our feet on the ground again.

We can simplify or scale down in four dimensions. The first dimension is that of the agents. I will often start by investigating a group of only two agents, then scale up to larger and larger groups, and then tackle the problem of an open-ended population in which new members enter and others leave. Each of these steps introduces additional difficulties. For example, when there are only two agents, the risk of synonyms forming is low – as we will see later – because the agents only interact with each other and so they can rapidly see whether the other one has a word for the same meaning. But when the population is scaled up it is highly likely that different subgroups invent different words or develop new meanings. These variations take time to propagate until the group settles into a coherent state. When there is an open-ended set of agents, the new agents in the population must acquire a language which already exists, which implies that we must have demonstrated that language acquisition goes sufficiently fast to explain cultural transmission. When agents leave the community, they take some of the knowledge of the language conventions, and so we have to show that the whole community might destabilise.

Second there is the dimension of the real world and how it relates to perception and action. For this book, I will in any case only use worlds restricted to coloured shapes on a two-dimensional surface, thus drastically reducing the perceptual challenges, and constrain the perceptual task still further by supplying the agents only with a limited set of sensory channels. We also performed initially many simulations with artificial worlds (to be explained shortly) where we could carefully control various parameters, such as the number of objects in a scene, their complexity, or their variation.

But restricting the environment is not enough. Other aspects of perception can seriously disrupt language communication in a variety of ways and each of them can be neutralised. We have already seen that in normal circumstances, the agents do not share the same image of reality, which introduces a whole array of problems. They might consequently segment the scene differently, the pointing might not be accurate enough (even if they both were referring to the same object), the segments might have very different sensory characteristics (as already discussed for Figure 3.7). We have reduced these sources of difficulty by initially using only one camera, then scaling up to two cameras in the same room, and only then scaling up to many different cameras located all over the world.

Increasing or decreasing the importance of saliency also helps. When only the most salient sensory channel is used, agents have a higher chance to guess the right meaning (at least if their perception converges reasonably well), and so they can better guess the meaning of an unknown word or go less astray with words for which they have already a shared meaning. So by varying the saliency, we can control the degree of semantic ambiguity in the agents' communications. Divergent perception and confusing regularities in the environment are sources of polysemy in language, which the agents need to dampen if they want their communications to be efficient and reliable.

Another real world aspect that we can make more or less complex is related to the movements of the head and the pointing. A hearer must be able to look in the same direction as the speaker, so that there is a minimum shared context. The hearer must be able to point to the topic guessed, so that the speaker can see whether the communication succeeded. If it did not, the speaker must be able to point to the topic. These physical interactions are well within the state of the art in robotics, and there exist even various learning systems capable of bootstrapping this capacity from scratch.[12]

But these processes will never be completely reliable either. So we can increase or decrease the challenge to the agents by making the non-verbal communication and coordination more or less challenging. In the experiments reported in this book, speaker and hearer can communicate to each other the direction in which they are looking.[13] Because they still see a different image due to their physical position, the interaction is still partly unreliable but it is sufficiently stable to enable the agents to bootstrap a shared communication system, which then in turn can help to establish physical coordination.

Third, there is the cognitive apparatus of the agents implicated in language. Here we can start with a simple associative memory for the lexicon that can only handle single words associated with single meanings, and then scale up to conjunctions of meanings covered by single or multiple words, and then still further to open-ended complex meanings and syntax. Each step requires additional machinery in the agents, which will automatically lead to more complex linguistic forms, but it is our experience that there is great value in trying to understand the basic process of word meaning acquisition before attempting to install more cognitive complexity in the agents' architecture. Even for the acquisition and propagation of single word utterances there are still many open-ended problems.

A final dimension concerns the transmission and perception of the utterance. Here again we can scale up or down the challenge to the agents, from full-blown unconstrained speech in noisy environments down to perfect direct transmission of the language form by the speaker and perfect recognition by the hearer. Complexity along this dimension has been reduced to the minimum in the Talking Heads experiment. Agents transmit utterances directly although a speech sound is generated so that human listeners can hear which utterance is produced as part of a game.

---

[12] This is the problem of hand-eye coordination performed in living systems by the vestibulo-oculomotor systems. See: Anastacio & Robinson (1989).

[13] This real world interaction has been developed by Kaplan (1999).

3 Perception

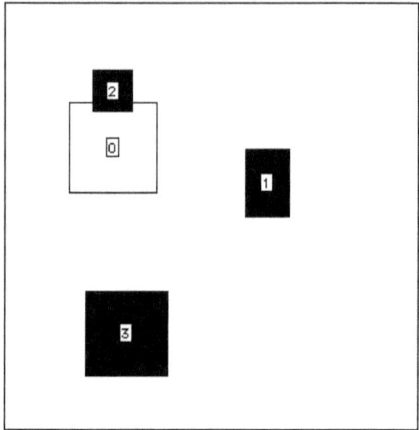

Figure 3.10: An example of the computer-generated scenes from the GEOM world. Each shape is labeled for further reference.

3.5 The GEOM world

One way to perform controlled experiments quickly and on a large scale consists of artificially generating the perceptual input to the agents. This has the additional advantage that we can simplify the situations the agents have to work in (for example have fewer types of shapes) and let them start initially with a shared perception. A simulation world that we have used extensively for many simulations reported later is the GEOM world.

The GEOM world generates geometric shapes similar to the physical figures we paste on the white board. Possible geometric shapes are circles, triangles, squares, rectangles, etc. We can control the complexity of the scenes that are generated through a few parameters, for example the number of minimum or maximum figures, or the possible repertoire of shapes. We ignore colour and use only different grayscale values. To construct a scene the computer simulation program chooses first a random number of figures. Then for each figure, a shape is chosen, and random values for the main characteristics (position, height, width, grayscale) are set.

An example of a computer-generated scene containing only rectangles is shown in Figure 3.10 (another one was shown earlier in Figure 3.6). Given such a scene, each agent calculates the bounding box and the segment-characteristics for every computer-generated figure. For the scene in Figure 4.3, which contains three squares and a rectangle, the values of the channels are summarised in Table 3.4. After sensory-scaling we get Table 3.5.

The output of the simulation is exactly the same as the one from real vision so that we can easily switch between simulation and physical experimentation.

Working with simulations has obvious advantages for speeding up development and systematic testing, but it does not replace experimentation with physical robots. It is true that building an experimental apparatus such as we built for the Talking Heads exper-

3.5 The GEOM world

Table 3.4: Sensory data for the scene shown in Figure 3.10.

	HPOS	VPOS	HEIGHT	WIDTH	GRAY	RATIO	AREA
0	116	166	293	293	0.777	1.0	85849
1	692	317	148	224	0.449	1.0	33152
2	192	64	137	137	0.408	1.0	18769
3	167	770	277	277	0.201	1.0	76729

Table 3.5: Sensory data after scaling for the scene shown in Figure 3.10.

	HPOS	VPOS	HEIGHT	WIDTH	GRAY	RATIO	AREA
0	0.09	0.13	0.64	0.64	0.78	1.0	0.95
1	0.55	0.25	0.16	0.41	0.45	1.0	0.37
2	0.15	0.05	0.12	0.12	0.41	1.0	0.21
3	0.13	0.62	0.59	0.59	0.20	1.0	0.85

iment is a very non-trivial engineering project, particularly because of the teleporting infrastructure that enables the agents to travel to multiple sites and thus experience different physical environments or the same environment from different points of view. One might therefore wonder why we have persisted to go to such great length in constructing a real-world physical infrastructure. Why are experiments with robotic agents necessary or desirable? Is it not enough to conduct simulation experiments given that they can be done so much more easily?

Computer simulations calculate the consequences of a theoretical model. For example, we can implement Newton's model of the solar system and simulate the movements of the planets around the sun by calculating for small time steps the position of each planet and hence the trajectories they follow. All the aspects of a calculation are under the scientist's control and it is therefore possible to use this method to examine whether a theory can be operationalised, whether it is coherent, and whether it is complete, i.e. whether it covers all aspects of the phenomena one tries to understand. Simulations can be inspected, re-executed or reprogrammed by anyone who cares to challenge them and other researchers can try to achieve the same performance with alternative approaches, so that different theories can be compared in an objective way.

Computer simulations can be set up for any theory which is formalisable, and hence for theories of cognition and language as well. We need to implement the cognitive architecture of the agent and then examine what happens when the agent engages in interactions, i.e. when data is supplied from real or simulated scenes. Computer simulations of cognitive mechanisms provide proof that they can be instantiated on physical systems, even though it may still be a mystery how the brain, itself a physical system, implements similar mechanisms. Computational simulation is of course not restricted to the theories I put forward in this book. Any theory claiming to explain the origins of language and meaning should be testable by computer simulation, so that it is clear what form the architecture takes and whether it does the job. All this is a big step compared to the early days of cognitive modelling when one was supposed to believe on faith whether a certain cognitive architecture could be instantiated by a physical system and whether it was indeed able to exhibit the functionality that was ascribed to it.

But computer simulations have two major shortcomings, which makes them only one of the tools in the toolkit of the cognitive scientist. First of all, computer simulations by themselves do not empirically validate a theory. When a computer screen shows pictures of planets moving around the sun, there is nothing that says that this is also the way the planets move. To validate the theory, large amounts of data need to be collected of the natural phenomena, and the simulation results have to be compared with the real world data to determine a sufficient fit. In this book, we are primarily concerned with formulating new plausible models for cognition and particularly for the origins of cognition, not yet with their empirical validation; this exciting work is left for the future.

However, there is a second shortcoming. Cognitive systems must deal with the real physical world in its infinite variety and complexity. If we perform only computer simulations, we not only model the cognitive mechanisms of the agents but also the environments which they are confronted with. We validate the model only with respect to stylised worlds. Of course we can make such worlds much more sophisticated, but there is never a guarantee that they are going to be representative of the real world that embodied cognitive agents have to deal with. The more realistic computer simulations become, that is the more aspects of reality they reliably take into account, the more the simulation starts to approach reality and the more a simulation may tell us whether the proposed mechanisms live up to realistic circumstances. But there will always be a huge difference between computer-simulated worlds and real worlds, as any roboticist knows all too well. And this is why we need to do experiments with physical robots and real-world environments.

Of course, it is useful and efficient to conduct simulations as part of the discovery process but true validation of a cognitive architecture can only come when the system is confronted with a real physical environment. It forces us to attack the final known or hidden assumptions in the theory's operational validation. It forces us to address the issue of sensing, using real world physical sensors. Therefore, an experiment like the Talking Heads experiment has a much greater force in convincing the sceptic. It is like testing the design for an airplane by building and flying one, as opposed to demonstrating the idea only in simulation.

3.6 Conclusions

This chapter focused on the perceptual layer which is responsible for interfacing the external physical world with the internal world of the agents. The interface is based on

3.6 Conclusions

sensors to transduce external states into internal states and actuators to transduce internal states into external states. Four sorts of operations take place on raw sensory data making them more amenable to categorisation, conceptualisation and consequently language communication: Features in the form of micro-structures are extracted, the image is segmented in coherent units using region growing or countour finding, segment characteristics such as average colour or size are derived, and characteristics are transformed or scaled to bring out salient features and aid to achieve categorial constancy.

The Talking Heads use standard techniques from computer vision research. Research in this field is indeed so advanced that a large number of algorithms for segmenting images and extracting information about image segments could be taken off the shelf and re-programmed to get a vision system that is adequate for the task setting of the Talking Heads experiment. This will, of course, no longer be the case if the environment is made more challenging and more open to novel situations. Very quickly we would then reach the limits of what can currently be done using standard techniques. Nevertheless for our purpose of exploring language and meaning, the Talking Heads vision system gives a sufficiently rich and reliable segmentation and characterisation of the scene so that an investigation of how real world scenes might be conceptualised and verbalised, has become possible.

4 The Discrimination Game

The previous chapter laid the perceptual groundwork for investigating conceptualisation and language communication. It proposed a set of mechanisms for segmenting a scene and extracting characteristics about each segment. The next task of the agent is to use these results from the perceptual layer to categorise and hence conceptualise the scene. For the time being, I will ignore the full complexity of natural language meaning and focus only on the most simple type of conceptualisation one can imagine, namely categories, which logicians refer to as unary predicates, as well as conjunctive combinations of categories. Words like *blue*, *light* or *square* name such categories. We not only need a way that the Talking Heads can use such categories to conceptualise a scene based on visual perception, but we also need mechanisms that can explain how such categories might develop or be acquired by each agent autonomously and without supervised training. This is clearly an enormous challenge and no known universally accepted solution exists to this problem.

Categorisation has fascinated philosophers and scientists since the onset of thought, not only because it is one of the most fundamental capabilities of the human mind, but also because the subject matter immediately raises some intriguing paradoxes and puzzles. First of all, we have already seen that there is an enormous gap between the symbolic world of objects and categories and the subsymbolic world of analog sensori-motor signal streams. A particular sensory signal is highly context-dependent and inherently noisy due to the partial unreliability of sensors and their limited accuracy. Sensory processing, transformation, and scaling go some way to achieve perceptual constancy but cognitive processes must clearly make up for the fleeting erratic nature of reality. Here we are immediately confronted with a first paradox. Univocal categorisation seems only possible when an interpretation of reality is within reach, for example when there are strong expectations, possibly coming from language utterances. But this interpretation depends itself on categorisation. How can this apparent causal circularity be broken?

Furthermore, if it is already so difficult to map categories on real world sensory data streams, how on earth can categories form and become stable? Young children appear to acquire perceptually grounded categories effortlessly and without systematic training. Psychologists have often observed the acquisition of distinctions with very few clear example cases and no overt feedback. On the other hand, categories appear to some extent culture-specific and different individuals make more refined distinctions depending on the sort of tasks they engage in. This is the case even in such a basic domain as colour categorisation. Painters or textile designers make distinctions ordinary humans do not see and have developed a very extensive repertoire of terms to talk about these distinctions. These observations highlight a second paradox: The effortless early acquisition of perceptual distinctions suggests that categories are innate. But the dependence on culture, individual variation and specialisation suggest that categories are learned. How can these two observations be reconciled?

Then there is a third paradox, first suggested by Jean-Jacques Rousseau. In order to communicate, the speaker and the hearer need to share the building blocks of the conceptualisations underlying their communication. If I say *the wine glass on the table*, I expect the hearer to be able to recognise what objects are tables, when something is on the table or not on the table, and when something is a wine glass versus another kind of glass. But if every individual learns categories independently and autonomously, how can they ever become shared? It is assumed that language helps in establishing a shared ontology within a language community but language itself depends on shared categories, so how can the whole system ever get off the ground; how can this chicken and egg situation be broken?

I will begin this chapter by outlining the empiricist and rationalist positions, which have dominated much of the philosophical discussion on categorisation and have indirectly influenced attempts to build artificial systems able to perform some form of categorisation. I will then propose an alternative SELECTIONIST approach and study a categorisation system based on it. It is shown that agents endowed with this system are able to develop an adequate repertoire of categories for distinguishing objects in their environment and that this repertoire remains adaptive when important changes occur in the environment. This goes some way to resolve the paradoxes of meaning, but the story remains incomplete. To explain how agents can share the same categories even if they develop their ontologies independently of each other, I will later argue for a co-evolution of language and meaning. I will show that when ontological development is coupled to lexical development, the two become co-ordinated with neither a central co-ordinator nor prior design.

4.1 The paradoxes of meaning

There are basically two philosophical doctrines that have tried to address the paradoxes of meaning. One doctrine is known as empiricism, the other one as rationalism. Many philosophical texts are available introducing these philosophical doctrines and their historical roots. The problem of the origins of language and meaning was for example already a highly debated topic among philosophers in the 18th century, see for example Rousseau (1781).

The debate between rationalism and empiricism is still very much alive today and now based on much more knowledge about what it means for something to be innate or what the limits are of induction. See Elman et al. (1996) for the most recent arguments and counterarguments. Compared to the full richness of human experience, I necessarily have had to adopt a very narrow view, focusing only on basic perceptually grounded categories. More complex categories related to human relationships, emotions, social organisation, or beliefs will not be considered and it would be very difficult to do so with the methodology used here. See Varela, Thomson & Rosch (1991) for a broader discussion.

4.1 The paradoxes of meaning

4.1.1 The empiricist's stance

The empiricist tradition has a long and reputable history. The first clear formulations emerged as a counterreaction to 17th century rationalism, with the work of Hume, Locke, and others. Empiricists were inspired by the early success of the natural sciences, which had insisted on observing reality as it is, through sensory experience and stepwise induction. The empiricist attitude has continued to dominate epistemology in the 19th and 20th century. It was formulated by Bertrand Russell in a doctrine called logical empiricism, and elaborated by generations of philosophers from Carnap to Quine into rich logical frameworks and precise inductive methods. Empiricist explanations about categorisation today very much dominate the neurosciences.

Empiricists argue that categories capture what is common or invariant between cases and that neural networks in the brain can detect this invariance. They also argue that these commonalities can be learned by progressively abstracting away from the details of specific cases, even if there is a poor stimulus. A child sees many examples of red objects and progressively grasps the abstract concept [RED] by retaining what is common to all of them. If categories are the result of a general inductive learning procedure, the areas of the brain responsible for categorisation do not have to be specialised or pre-programmed for recognising specific categories. Empiricists therefore believe that they can take the form of general purpose networks that learn any kind of category by making abstraction from the examples supplied by the environment. Categories are therefore not innate but learned.

In recent decades, various designs for neural network models have been proposed that reflect this empiricist stance.[1] The input nodes of these networks receive data from sensory channels of the sort discussed in the previous chapter. They are connected to higher level nodes which use the data to decide whether a category applies. The connections are weighted and a positive output signal is produced when the weighted sum of the inputs exceeds a certain threshold. Thus the networks exhibit some of the flexibility, tolerance to variation, and context-dependence seen in human categorisation. The weights and thresholds are learned by propagating back errors in categorisation. If a node makes a positive identification when it should not have done so, the weights of the incoming connections are lowered and the threshold is increased, so that it is less likely that the threshold will be exceeded again for the same situation the next time around. Conversely, if the network makes a negative identification where it should have made a positive one, the weights of the incoming connections are increased and the threshold lowered. It is known through mathematical proofs that such networks indeed stabilise on reliable categorisations, if the environment remains sufficiently constant.[2] These in-

---

[1] The first neural network models emerged in the fifties from the work of neurologists and computer scientists like Donald Hebb, McCullogh and Pitts, Rosenblatt, and others. There was a strong first wave of enthusiasm in the sixties, as illustrated for example in: Minsky & Papert (1969). A second wave developed in the mid-eighties when new more powerful network architectures were discovered that could handle intermediary representations and later on temporal structures (see the overview in Churchland & Sejnowski (1992).

[2] This type of neural networks and some of its main variants are discussed at length in the classical textbook by Rumelhart & McClelland (1986).

ductive neural networks therefore constitute their first serious proposal for bridging the gap between sensory signals and categories and for explaining the origins and acquisition of categories.

4.1.2 The rationalist's stance

A radically different approach to categorisation has been proposed by rationalists. The rationalist point of view had its first clear formulation in Plato's philosophy. A resurgence of rationalist ideas took place in the 17th and beginning of the 18th century, particularly through the work of Descartes and Leibniz. More recently, in the second half of the 20th century, a strong rationalist movement emerged again, mainly under the influence of Noam Chomsky. Today rationalist attitudes very much dominate linguistics and cognitive psychology.

Early rationalists, like Descartes, were dualists, which saw the mind and the body in totally different realms. In such a view, it becomes very difficult to scientifically investigate perceptually grounded categorisation, and an explanation how the brain works seems more remote than ever. However, most contemporary rationalists (like empiricists) now believe that categorisation is done by physical structures in the brain. Indeed, if certain parts of the brain are damaged, the capability to categorise disappears or is severely restricted and distorted (Deacon 1997).

Rationalists claim that categories exist *a priori* and therefore categorisation comes from within. They argue that humans have a repertoire of ideal universal forms, which they project onto reality. Reality itself is a weak, imperfect reflection of these forms, like the shadows of objects on the wall of a cave. Because of this poverty of stimuli, categories (particularly the perceptually grounded categories that are the focus of our attention in this book) are claimed to be unlearnable by induction and must therefore be innate.[3]

This innateness hypothesis suggests that the brain comes with CATEGORISATION ORGANS, small neuronal circuits capable of performing the mapping of some idealised universal form onto reality. Consequently the human genome must include a set of CONCEPT GENES which regulate how each of these categorisation organs should grow during development. Rationalists claim that it is absurd to think of categories as being learned from example cases supplied by the environment, just as it is absurd to say that the hand learns to grow five fingers.

4.1.3 Arguments for and against rationalism

There is something to say both for a rationalist and for an empiricist approach, indeed otherwise so many serious thinkers could not have believed fervently in one position

---

[3] Strong forms of innateness have been defended by Fodor (1983) and many philosophers and linguists associated with the generative grammar paradigm. See the discussion in Wierzbicka (1992), particularly the introductory chapter. In artificial intelligence research, particularly the logic-oriented tradition, there is often an implicit acceptance that basic categories are innate, but that derived categories, formulatable in terms of more primitive concepts, can be learned (see McCarthy 2008). There are also large-scale efforts going on to build an ontology as rich as human ontologies, see the discussions around Doug Lenat's CYC project in Steels & McDermott (1994).

4.1 The paradoxes of meaning

or the other. Rationalists point to the fact that children acquire concepts surprisingly quickly and apparently with very little stimuli and that anthropological observations have shown that there are strong universal tendencies for basic perceptually grounded categories, such as colour or space. However, more detailed observations show that the acquisition of categories in children goes in fact very slowly. For example, concepts like cause-effect and the correct use of the word *because*, the proper use of tenses, etc. all take years to develop. Adults keep acquiring new categories through out their lifetime, which makes it difficult to maintain that they are part of the human genome. For example, airline pilots and sailors categorise the direction and strength of winds and the shapes and colours of clouds, so as to predict turbulences, future weather, or advantageous trajectories. There are occasionally profound differences in how cultures conceptualise reality. These differences do not seem to be innate because everybody who has had sufficient exposure to the culture, preferably at an early age and therefore without too much preconception, can normally acquire them.[4]

Further objections against the innateness hypothesis have come from the camp of neurobiology. In lower animals, neural circuits have been identified which perform very specific categorisations of reality. For example, the frog is sensitive to objects of a particular size moving in front of it at a particular speed, specifically the kind of objects that constitute a potential source of food for the frog. The dedicated neuronal circuits performing this categorisation have been shown to be innate and shared by all frogs. But higher animals and humans exhibit an enormous plasticity, both in terms of the repertoire of categories they recognise and in terms of the actual brain structure.[5]

The difference between an animal reacting to a limited set of environmental stimuli with a rigid neural apparatus and a cognitively endowed human being is precisely the high degree of flexibility and adaptivity of the latter. It is therefore not surprising that clear-cut *categorisation organs* which have the same structure in all humans and are located at the same position in the brain have not been found. The microstructure of the brain does not consist of neatly separated organs and it therefore does not make sense to look for genes that regulate their maturation. Neurobiologists tell us that the brain appears more like an organically grown tissue rather than a delicately tuned machine laid out by genetic programs. In contrast to insect brains or brains of lower animals, the mammalian brain is capable of regenerating itself to some extent after damage, and brain tissue from one higher order animal can be implanted in another one, causing a resurgence of lost function, even if the source location of the transplant is different. For example, if tissue from the visual cortex is implanted in the auditory cortex, it will regenerate and function as part of the auditory cortex. Pathways to the visual cortex can be redirected to the auditory cortex, which will cause the auditory cortex to take on functions of visual processing.

---

[4] Rationalists often argue that there is no other way to explain the child's rapid acquisition of concepts but detailed psycholinguistic observations have shown that child language understanding (which is the clearest sign whether certain concepts have been acquired) is often deceptive because non-verbal strategies may lead to appropriate answers to adult questions and thus the appearance of understanding.
[5] Evidence for the remarkable plasticity of the human brain is reviewed in Edelman (1987) and Elman et al. (1996).

Even supposing that there is a strong genetic determination of micro-level brain structure, there is still the question how the hundreds of thousands of concepts employed by adult human beings might have become included in the human genome. Saying that a perceptally grounded category is innate does not explain anything. One has to show a plausible evolutionary history for the categories hypothesised to be innate and prove that the hypothesised concept genes can propagate sufficiently fast in the human population.[6]

4.1.4 Arguments for and against empiricism

Empiricists have had considerable success in coming up with inductive learning mechanisms. They have even been demonstrated on autonomous robots in direct interaction with the environment. At the same time, the learning mechanisms proposed so far turn out to be very fragile.[7] The human experimenter has to carefully set up the architecture of the network (the number of nodes, the number of layers of nodes, and how they are connected), tune the learning parameters, and supply just the right set of test cases. Performance may degrade when too many cases are seen. Even worse, when new cases are supplied that require a revision of categories already learned, a substantial portion of the earlier cases must be resubmitted to retrain the network. All this contradicts the robustness and open-ended extensibility of human categorisation. In addition, the learning mechanisms proposed have been slow to consistently acquire categories. A large number of cases are required and often cases must go through multiple iterations. Moreover any inductive method is a slave of the data. A category will only become reliably recognised when it is statistically significant.

So there are questions both for a rationalist and an empiricist approach. If categories are innate how can new categories, which are required when the environment or the task settings change, form so quickly? How can the genetic code store the vast repertoire of categories humans routinely employ, and how can we explain the diversity with which different cultures approach reality? On the other hand, if every child independently acquires categories by learning, we must question how can they do so, given the poor quality of the examples they see. How is it that learning is so rapid? How can different independent learners arrive at a repertoire of categories that is sufficiently shared to make language communication possible? How do we reconcile the apparent innate origins of perceptually grounded categories with their remarkable adaptedness to the changing needs and open-ended environments that the individual effectively encounters?

---

[6] See Worden (1995). This article argues, based on the genetic difference between humans and other primates, that there are limits to genetic transmission of cognitive content, like categories or grammars. For discussions on the speed of gene spreading compared to cultural evolution, see Cavalli-Sforza, Cavalli-Sforza & Thorne (1996).

[7] The weakness of traditional connectionist networks with respect to speed and resilience are discussed at length in Quartz & Sejnowski (1997).

4.2 Selectionism

The difficulties encountered with the empiricist *and* rationalist points of view make it worthwhile to explore alternative solutions. The one I propose and further explore in this book has been inspired by two key principles from biology. The first principle is that of selectionism. It requires a growth process in the agents that generates possible structures, even in the absence of examples, and a pruning process that removes those that are irrelevant. The growth and pruning process is assumed to be biologically given but not the categories that result from it. The second principle that I will adopt is interactionism, put forward by biologists to understand how genetic influences *and* environmental impact cooperate to shape an organism. Interactionism was first suggested by Piaget (originally a biologist) to explain the growth of mental capacity in the child. His numerous experiments show a gradual progressive construction of increasingly more complex ways of categorising and conceptualising reality. The child encounters situations that can be assimilated, and thus cause entrenchment of existing structures, as well as situations that cannot be handled and require the child to accommodate with new constructions or reorganisations.[8]

4.2.1 Principles of selectionism

Selectionism is a general means of explaining the origins of complexity. It requires: (1) a process that can generate a repertoire of possible solutions in a basically random fashion, (2) a process for preserving solutions so that there can be a gradual build up of more complex solutions, and (3) a selectionist force, which uses feedback from the environment and influences preservation so that adequate solutions are retained and others discarded.[9]

In the case of the Darwinian explanation for the evolution of species, a solution is an organism capable of surviving in a given environment. Types of organisms are preserved in the genetic material as it is copied from one generation to the next. Variations are produced due to errors in gene copying, mutations, gene insertion, etc. The feedback comes from the natural environment. Organisms that do not flourish are less successful in reproduction so that their genetic material and hence the organisms this material generates are less likely to be preserved. Selectionism contrasts with Lamarckian instructionism, which claims that the organism transmits its adaptations and what it has learned during its life time to its offspring.

---

[8] The work of Waddington is typical for the interactionist approach to development, see Waddington (1975). Such a view does not necessarily imply that there is a pre-determined course of development. Piaget emphasised a progressive, dynamical view on development Piaget (1985). His work arose prior to the detailed computational modeling that is now common place in cognitive science and there is still an enormous work left to demonstrate operationalisations of these insights. See for a more recent discussion of the issues: Thelen & Smith (1994).

[9] There are many excellent introductory accounts of selectionism. One of the best known is: Dawkins (1976). The recent application of selectionism to the automatic derivation of computer programs clearly demonstrates how general the principle is. See Goldberg (1989) and Koza, Goldberg & Fogel (1996). The principle has now even been applied to the development of computational hardware. See Sipper, Mange & Andres (1998).

From the viewpoint of instructionism, the neck of a giraffe is so long because at some point giraffes with shorter necks often stretched their necks. This was transmitted to the offspring which got born with slightly longer necks. They also stretched their necks further, and so on. In a selectionist framework, it is assumed that the natural variation in the population is exploited. Some giraffes have longer necks than others, and if this gives an advantage their genes proliferate. Within the population born with the new gene distribution there are still variations and once again those with a longer neck proliferate, and so on. Instructionist processes build further upon acquired characteristics. There is progressive learning from one generation to the next. Selectionism assumes natural variation and progressive dominance of fitter variants, with neither learning nor transmission of acquired characteristics. Selectionism can make sudden jumps and therefore has the potential to go much faster than the transmission of acquired characteristics.

In the case of the immune system, a solution is an antibody capable of combatting intruders foreign to the organism. Here again an instructionist approach can be envisioned and was believed for a long time to be the case. For this belief to be true would mean that the immune system somehow learns the appropriate response and then preserves that response. The selectionist viewpoint of the immune system argues instead that it generates autonomously a very large repertoire of possible antibody responses. When a foreign body invades, the response is already there, it is simply amplified (Varela et al. 1988).

4.2.2 Selectionist cognitive systems

The Talking Heads experiment explores the same line of thinking, both to the acquisition of categories, and later experiments (discussed in part II) to the acquisition of more complex meaning and even grammar. It implies that there is no learning taking place in the empiricist sense of induction from a series of examples, but that instead three processes are active:

1. a process whereby structures capable to categorise reality are generated in a basically random fashion,

2. a process to preserve these structures and build further upon them to enable a steady increase in complexity, and

3. a selectionist force which prunes away those structures that were irrelevant and retains the ones that are successful and needed.

As I will expand upon in more detail in this chapter, categorisation can be carried out by discrimination trees where the nodes in the tree filter objects depending on whether they fall within a sensory region or not. I will show that the discrimination trees grow in a more or less random fashion and those parts of the tree that are irrelevant get pruned. The selectionist feedback comes from the games in which the agent participates. Distinctions that are effective in discriminating the topic from the other objects in the context and have been successfully lexicalised, are maintained in the lexicon of the community, others are discarded.

When there is a high failure rate, the discrimination trees should expand, in the same way that the immune system gets stimulated (but does not strictly speaking learn) when the organism is invaded or genetic variation increases in periods of stress on a species. When there is a high success rate, some pruning might be possible. The growth and pruning dynamics creates an ecology of distinctions which is constantly adapting itself to the situations and tasks the agent encounters, without any innate *a priori* categories and without any inductive learning.

4.2.3 The tree metaphor

The growth of a tree or plant is a good metaphor to visualise this selectionist approach. The shape of a tree appears well adapted to its environment. Typically there are more branches and leaves where there is more sunlight. The height of the tree reflects the competition of neighbouring trees or the height of surrounding buildings. The overall shape reflects the shape of surrounding walls or other trees. It is obvious that a tree does not come with "shape genes" that determine exactly which shape the tree will have in a particular setting. Nor does it come with sophisticated sensors and a brain inductively learning about the environment so as to decide on which branch the next leaf should grow. Instead the tree grows in all directions following a steady, usually quite regular growth pattern. A tree standing alone in a landscape exhibits a beautiful balanced shape, expanding in all directions, but when the growth is constrained, the tree reflects these constraints. The branches and leaves that catch more sunlight receive more resources to flourish and develop further, whereas those pointing towards an area with no sunlight are stifled in their growth and may die altogether.

Given that the brain is a living tissue, it is possible to imagine a similar growth process in the brain.[10] Neural networks implementing discrimination trees could be expanding in all directions, just as other tissue forms. The overall growth dynamics is genetically determined but neutral with respect to the repertoire needed in a certain environment. The shape of the discrimination trees in a particular individual is due to the kinds of sensory data that have been produced in his interactions with the environment *and* their use and success in other cognitive processes such as language communication. The users of the discrimination trees and the environment act as selectionist forces molding the spontaneously forming repertoires.

Note that selectionism is *not* applied at the level of a species as in biological evolution but at the level of the cognitive structures in each individual as he or she develops and adapts during his or her life time. The parallel exploration and the competition of alternative ways to categorise reality take place in a single individual interacting with the environment and therefore are very rapid.

---

[10] Several neurobiologists have presented suggestions and evidence in this direction. See particularly Edelman (1987) and Changeux (1997).

4.2.4 Deriving new sensory channels

Obviously the sensory channels are a critical part of the categorisation process. When the sensory data is not available, it is simply not possible to develop discrimination trees along a particular sensory dimension. This raises the question as to where the sensory channels themselves may come from. The most basic raw data is directly supplied by the sensors themselves and is thus innately given. But processes calculating the values on the more complex channels must somehow form under the influence of the environment, and they are thus potentially partly influenced by language.

Here again both an inductive and a selectionist approach can be envisioned. In an inductive approach, a learning process, such as embodied by a connectionist network, is fed with a series of examples of situations exhibiting particular characteristics, and the network becomes sensitive to the characteristics of these situations. Several concrete examples of such a learning process have already been studied using the neural network techniques mentioned earlier.[11]

In a selectionist approach, a repertoire of primitive operations is given, presumably implemented by the basic biochemistry of the neural systems, and there are ways to combine these operations into more complex VISUAL PROGRAMS. Those programs yielding an outcome which is afterwards used successfully in categorisation are retained and the others discarded, thus establishing a co-evolution between a repertoire of sensory channels and a repertoire of categories. We have already done some successful experiments in this direction, see De Jong & Steels (1999), but this theme will not be pursued further here as a full discussion would be too much a digression from the main line of investigation. For the remainder of this book, the sensory channels will be pre-programmed, although it is still up to the selectionist categorisation process to discover which ones are useful in the environments presented to the agents and which ones are not.

4.2.5 Comparing approaches

A selectionist approach is different from both the rationalist *and* empiricist points of view. In contrast with rationalism, it is not assumed that categories are universal and *a priori* shared. Categories are not innate. In contrast with empiricism, it is not assumed that categories are derived by induction from a large set of cases. Categories are not learned. What is claimed to be innate is a general purpose growth and pruning dynamics which could be realised by the biochemistry of neural cells. The growth process may generate many categories which may turn out to be useless, but eventually it settles on a repertoire which is adequate for the environment in which the individual finds itself.

A selectionist approach to category formation has some characteristics that make it look like categories are innate. Categories may form in an individual without having ever seen one single example. They appear to pop up from nowhere, but this does not mean that genes determining this particular category have to be innate. They are the result of a random growth process which has simply generated these possibilities. Alternatively, a selectionist process has some characteristics that make it look like categories

---
[11] Examples are discussed in: Linsker (1990).

have been learned. The individual ends up with a repertoire which is adapted to the environments and tasks that are indeed encountered, and this ontology keeps evolving to remain adequate when the environment changes or new tasks are encountered. Because the selectionist approach has characteristics of innateness as well as learning, it is capable of helping resolve the paradoxes of the origins of categories discussed in the beginning of this chapter. It explains adaptivity without learning and fast development, even with a weak stimulus, but without innateness.

All of this sounds intriguing and brings in a refreshingly new point of view, but does it really work? Can we invent the required growth and pruning dynamics and identify the appropriate selectionist feedback loop? The remainder of this chapter focuses on this question.

4.3 Discrimination trees

First I will introduce structures that can perform categorisation. The next section shows how these structures may autonomously originate in an agent interacting with the environment.

4.3.1 Making distinctions

Empiricists start from the idea that categories capture what is common between objects. Thus [RED] is supposed to capture what is common or similar to all red objects. Hence in theories of (formal) semantics, the meaning of a predicate is equated with the set of all things that belong to the class it delineates. But we can also turn things around. We can view a category as a way to capture what is *different* between objects. For example, the distinction between [LEFT] and [RIGHT] is based on the horizontal position (HPOS) of an object with respect to the viewer. The distinction is imposed on the scene (as long as it is compatible) instead of recognised. This may seem a subtle difference, but it has profound consequences, particularly for acquiring categories.

Consider the category [LARGE]. What do all large objects have in common? At first sight very little. Almost any physical object can be called *large* in one context or another. It is going to be very difficult for a learning agent to determine some commonality, even if given thousands of examples of large objects. In the beginning, the agent might be confused by commonalities in colour or position or shape. Only with some luck, will the learning algorithm start to zoom in on size. This is what makes inductive learning so slow and why it is criticised, rightfully, by rationalists. In fact, searching for commonality hardly makes sense for many categories. [LARGE] is only meaningful in opposition to [SMALL], [LEFT] only makes sense in opposition to [RIGHT]. Often categorisation is relative to the context (a block which is large when surrounded by smaller blocks may be categorised as small when surrounded by larger blocks) and occasionally it is relative to the objects themselves (a large mouse is always categorised as much smaller than a small elephant).

4 The Discrimination Game

Few people would disagree that [LARGE] and [SMALL] are distinctions imposed on reality as opposed to intrinsic properties of classes of objects, but what about colour? Is it not an example where a category is absolute? We have already seen in the previous chapter that this is not the case. The colour reflection depends strongly on the surface reflection and thus on the light conditions and light sources in the environment. What should objectively appear blue when measuring the wavelength might actually appear green and vice-versa. Colour is *not* an intrinsic property but is actively mapped onto reality in a context-sensitive way.[12] This does not mean of course that categorisation does not make use of sensory data. On the contrary, without sensory data, categorisation would be entirely impossible.

Once categories are available, they can be used for much more than making distinctions. For example, if an agent has the distinction between [LARGE] and [SMALL], he can use it to group the objects in a scene into two subsets: those that are large and those that are small. So in this case, the categories are used to group objects based on a characteristic they have in common, namely being large and being small. My main argument here is that categories form driven by discrimination tasks, afterwards they can be used for many other semantic processes, including classification.

4.3.2 Categorisers

I will refer to the process capable of making a distinction as a CATEGORISER. It operates on the output of a sensory channel and decides whether a category or its opponent is valid. A categoriser keeps track of its success by maintaining an internal counter. Consider for example the category [LARGE] which operates on the output of the AREA-channel. This channel contains a scaled value between 0.0 and 1.0 for the area of a segment. A distinction can therefore be made simply by dividing the set of possible values in two halves: those whose area is between 0.0 and 0.5 and those whose area is between 0.5 and 1.0, giving us two categories, [SMALL] and [LARGE]. When the agent needs to categorise an object, he checks in which region an object's area falls. If it is between 0.0 and 0.5, the category is [SMALL], if it is greater than 0.5 the category is [LARGE].

It is clearly possible to refine each category c by introducing categorisers that further divide the region of possible values of c into smaller subregions. For example, the category [SMALL] which is applicable if the area is between 0.0 and 0.5, can be refined by introducing two more specific categorisers: one responding to a region between 0.0 and 0.25 for [VERY-SMALL] and another one for a region between 0.25 and 0.5 for [MEDIUM-SMALL]. The total set of distinctions using values of the same sensory channel can be organised in a discrimination tree (Figure 4.1).

As mentioned earlier, I will label categories by using the sensory channel from which a category operates, followed by the minimum and maximum values of the region carved out by the category. For example, [AREA 0.0–0.25] carves out the region [0.0,0.25] of the area channel. When it must be emphasised that a category belongs to a particular agent, for example a1, I will write [AREA 0.0–0.25]$_{a1}$.

---

[12] As mentioned earlier, see the discussion about colour in Varela, Thomson & Rosch (1991).

4.3 Discrimination trees

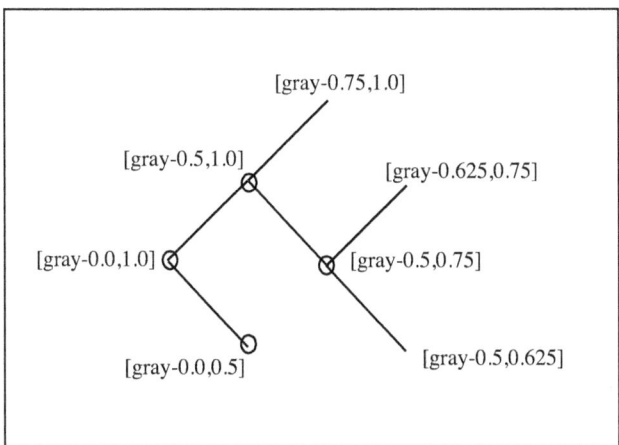

Figure 4.1: A discrimination tree contains a set of categorisers which categorise by checking whether a sensory value falls in the region of one category or not. The discrimination tree shown operates on values on the GRAY channel.

Conjunctive combinations of categories also have dedicated categorisers which are linked to the categorisers of their components (see Figure 4.2). A conjunctive combination often yields a more efficient way to pick out the topic compared to a single, possibly very fine-grained distinction. For example, it might be that [AREA 0.0–0.25] *and* [GRAY 0.5–1.0] together are distinctive but none of the two on their own is. Other logical combinations are equally of interest but I will restrict my attention to conjunctive combinations. Conjunctive combinations of categories will be written between curly brackets ({,}) as in {[AREA 0.0–0.25] [GRAY 0.5–1.0]}.

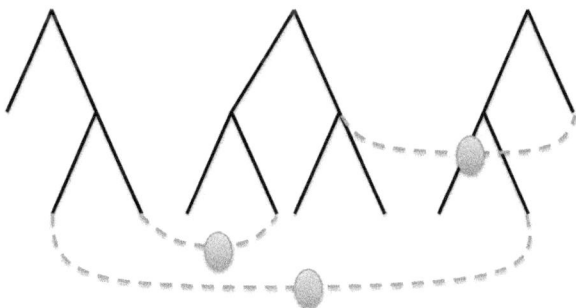

Figure 4.2: More complex categorisers (shown as circles) are formed from the combination of primitive categorisers.

87

4 *The Discrimination Game*

4.3.3 The Discrimination Game

Here is a game, which I call the Discrimination Game, which is useful to study categorisation in a systematic way.[13] The game is played by a single agent, randomly drawn from a population of agents, and is equivalent to the conceptualisation phase of the guessing game. The agent perceives the scene and chooses a topic from the possible objects segmented in the scene. He then uses his discrimination trees, as developed so far, to come up with a category or a conjunction of categories that is valid for the topic, but not for any other object in the context. The Discrimination Game succeeds if the agent has found distinctive categories, otherwise the game fails. When the game succeeds, the success counter of the categorisers involved go up.

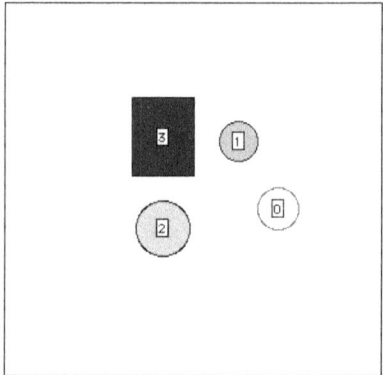

Figure 4.3: A computer generated scene from the GEOM world.

I will now develop some concrete examples, which imply that I make choices for the kinds of sensory channels and scenes that the agents use. I will first use scenes from the GEOM world as in Figure 4.3 and later real world scenes captured with a Talking Heads camera.

Consider the scene in Figure 4.3. Assuming that the agent already has a well-developed set of categories, he could use the category [GRAY-0.75,1.0] (very dark) to distinguish shape 3 from the others. On the other hand, if shape 2 is chosen as topic, the grayscale will not be enough because shape 2 has the same grayscale as shape 1. Maybe a combination of categories can be chosen, like [VPOS 0.0–05] (lower), and [HPOS 0.0–0.5] (left). Indeed shape 2 is lower in the scene, as opposed to shape 1 and shape 3, and it is more to the left compared to shape 0 and 2.

---

[13] The Discrimination Game model together with the discrimination trees and its growth dynamics was presented for the first time in Steels & Brooks (1995). Based on this paper a new implementation of single category discrimination was implemented by Angus McIntyre within the BABEL environment. Later on, Joris Van Looveren re-implemented the use of conjunctive combinations.

4.3 Discrimination trees

4.3.4 The Pachinko machine

Any visitor to Japan sooner or later comes across a Pachinko hall where eager players sit before a machine in which a metal ball, inserted at the top, falls through a series of gates until it falls in a winning or a losing bin. These games are a possible metaphor to visualise the categorisation process based on discrimination trees.

Imagine that for each object in the scene and for each sensory channel, there is a ball containing the value for that object on that channel. It is introduced in the top categoriser of the discrimination tree associated with that channel. For example, suppose that there are three objects in the scene: *O1*, *O2*, and *O3*, with gray-scale values 0.6, 0.4, and 0.9 respectively. We can therefore imagine three balls labeled with these datavalues which are input to the top categoriser of the GRAY discrimination tree (Figure 4.4). A categoriser divides the balls in two bins, those that fall in the range of one category and those that fall into the range of the other category. In this case, the left bin contains {*O2*} (category [GRAY 0.0–0.5]) and the right bin {*O1*, *O3*} (category [GRAY 0.5–1.0]).

A distinctive category is found when the ball of the topic is the only one left in one of the bins. If the topic is *O1*, then this is not yet the case, because it is together with *O3* in the bin of [GRAY 0.5–1.0]. However when the next categoriser is exercised, it splits the set {*O1*, *O3*} into two subsets: {*O1*} for [GRAY 0.5–0.75] and {*O3*} for [GRAY-0.75,1.0]. [GRAY 0.5–0.75] is a discriminating category because only *O1* is left in its bin.

Balls thus trickle down from the top to the bottom of a discrimination tree, like in the Pachinko game or a lottery machine. The trickling down process can stop as soon as a distinctive category is found because finer grained distinctions are not necessary.

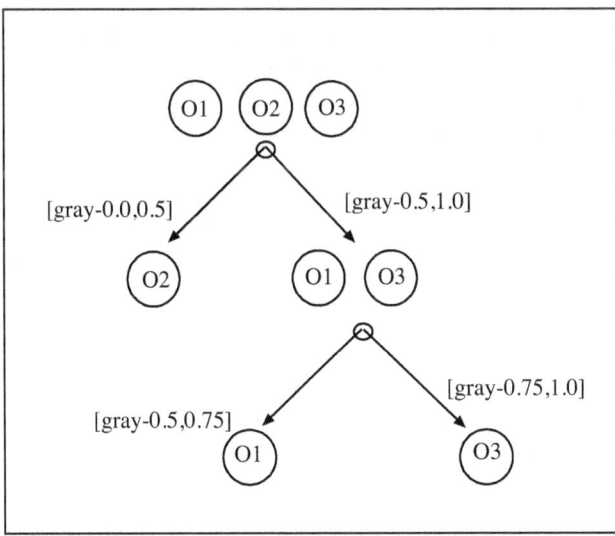

Figure 4.4: Balls containing the data value for the different objects *O1*, *O2*, *O3* in the scene. *O1* is the topic. *O1* has the value 0.6 on the GRAY-channel, *O2* has 0.4 and *O3* 0.9.

4.3.5 Competition between categories

A realistic agent has hundreds of sensory channels, and humans probably have tens of thousands of them, probably grouped with respect to the domains to which they apply.[14] There are discrimination trees for each of these channels or for combinations of them, and each can possibly yield a distinctive category. The categorisation process can therefore be envisioned like a huge Pachinko hall, in which balls are trickling down in parallel in hundreds or thousands of machines. It is highly likely that more than one solution is found when there are a lot of trees, particularly if combinations of categories are allowed as well. So, an additional competitive process must take place to rank categories even though multiple solutions are offered to subsequent verbalisation processes. We see therefore the same characteristics as for the perceptual layer, and thus the "sieve architecture" also applies for the conceptual layer (Figure 3.5).

There are many possible criteria for preferring one category over another, equally distinctive one. The first is based on simplicity. A single category is less complex than a combination of categories, and a more abstract category is preferred over a more specific one. The second criterion is based on success in earlier games. Each categoriser monitors how many times it was used and how many times it was successful, i.e. how many times it could distinguish the topic and participate in a successful language game. Another criterion, that I will bring in later once I have introduced the lexical layer, refers to success of the lexicalisations of the category. The agent will prefer categories where it is known that there is a well-accepted way to express it. When ranking categories, these criteria are combined and the best ones enter with the most force in the lexicalisation layer.

Notice the hidden positive feedback effect between success and use: A categoriser which has already achieved a higher score wins the competition, everything else being equal, causing its score to increase even more. This way a consistent behaviour emerges where the same category tends to be used in the same circumstances, similar to the way a walking path sometimes emerges for crossing a patch of grass between buildings. Initially many paths are possible, but once one path is used a bit more than others, it gets used more and more, as people reuse a path they perceive to be there. I will show later (chapter 6) that this entrenchment of a particular solution by a positive feedback loop can be exploited through the structural coupling between the ontology (the set of categories) and the lexicon (the set of form-meaning pairs verbalising categories), so that they become co-ordinated without a central co-ordinator.[15]

---

[14] This is strongly suggested by psychological data on the presence of conceptual spaces in human categorisation. See Gärdenfors (2000).

[15] I adopt here other general principles of complex systems. The notion of structural coupling has been introduced by Maturana & Varela (1998) and is now widely used to explain various forms of biological co-ordination.

4.3.6 Variations on discrimination

There are obviously many variations on categorisation that could be imagined. For example, a categoriser could make use of focal points instead of regions. A focal point is a single significant data value of a sensory channel. The categoriser then has to compute the distance between the value for a segment and the focal point of each possible category. The category whose focal point is closest to the sensory value of a segment applies. This implements a prototype-like approach to categorisation which has been argued to be more realistic with respect to human categorisation.[16] For example, humans typically label light at 482 nanometres as the most typical blue, so that a given object reflecting light at or near this point is categorised as [BLUE]. Categories based on focal points are interesting and have clear advantages but I will stick nevertheless in the first instance to binary discrimination trees operating on single sensory channels to simplify the explanations and to analyse better what is going on.

Still another way to categorise reality is by imposing an order on the segments based on their values for a particular sensory channel. For example, we can order the segments based on the HPOS channel (i.e. from left to right) and then introduce relational categories like *left of one segment in the series*, or *the left-most object*. Similarly we can order the segments based on the HEIGHT channel (i.e. in terms of their size) and then have categories that select the smallest (i.e. the first segment in this ordering), or those greater than some other one.

Of course, I am well aware that this categorisation process captures only the most basic way of generating meaning. Human beings make extended use of metaphor, analogy, metonymy, and other processes that adapt conceptual structures from one domain to another one, see Johnson (1987). But before we can study such processes we must understand how basic perceptually grounded categories can originate.

4.3.7 The Discrimination Game in action

Let us now look at some example games for an agent a1 taken from simulations using computer generated scenes from the GEOM world and showing the internal structures generated as well as the reports from the commentator. At first I will not take saliency nor context-scaling into account. The first game (Game 8) fails. It takes place near the very beginning when a1 has practically no repertoire of distinctions yet. The scene and the discrimination trees available so far are shown in Figure 4.5. The object labeled 0 is the topic. Only two channels have top level categorisers: HEIGHT and WIDTH. The data on these channels for the scene in Figure 4.5 are shown in Table 4.1.

HEIGHT and WIDTH have been scaled with respect to the minimum and maximum height and width of a figure (sensor-scaling) but no context-scaling has been performed.

The game is reported by the commentator as follows:

---

[16] See Varela, Thomson & Rosch (1991) and Taylor (1995).

4 The Discrimination Game

Table 4.1: Sensory data for the scene in Figure 4.5.

Object	HEIGHT	WIDTH
0 (square)	0.413	0.317
1 (circle)	0.410	0.410
2 (square)	0.163	0.163

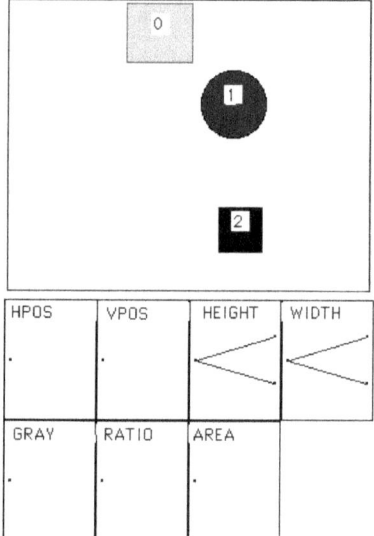

Figure 4.5: Top: The scene used in Game 8. Shape 0 is the topic. Bottom: The discrimination trees available for this game.

```
Game 8
  a1 segments the context in 3 objects:
    square-0, circle-1, square-2
  a1 chooses square-0 as the topic
  The discrimination game fails
```

The game fails because for the two sensory channels for which there are discrimination trees, the values of the segments are all within the lower range and so no distinctive category or category set could be found. This failure stimulates the discrimination network to expand, but any node, including a top node of some of the other sensory channels can be chosen for further expansion.

The next example shows a game (Game 22) based on the scene in Figure 4.6. The topic is the triangle, shape 0. The discrimination trees for HEIGHT and WIDTH have already

4.3 Discrimination trees

Table 4.2: Sensory data for the scene shown in Figure 4.6.

Object	HPOS	WIDTH	HEIGHT
0 (triangle)	0.167	0.437	0.573
1 (rectangle)	0.789	0.563	0.287

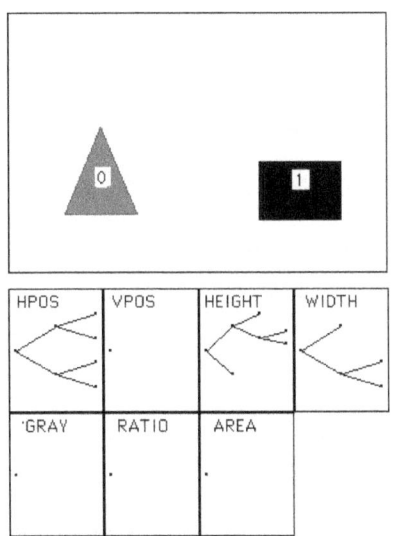

Figure 4.6: Top: The scene used in Game 22. Bottom: The discrimination trees available to the agent.

more than one level and a discrimination tree for HPOS has developed. The relevant sensor-scaled data for these three sensory channels is shown in Table 4.2.

The scene is very simple so there are several possible solutions: The triangle is more to the left, it is less wide and taller. Each of these possibilities is discovered and their score (purely based on past performance) is looked up. The game is reported by the commentator as follows:

```
Game 22
  a1 segments the scene in 2 objects:
    triangle-0, rectangle-1
  a1 chooses triangle-0 as the topic
  a1 categorises the topic as [HPOS 0.0-0.5] (score 0.57),
    [HEIGHT 0.5-1.0] (score 0.09), or
    [WIDTH 0.0-0.5] (score 0.0)
  The discrimination game succeeds
```

4 The Discrimination Game

4.3.8 The importance of scaling and saliency

Game 22 shows at once why context-scaling and saliency is important. When we inspect the scene in Figure 4.6, we do not quite see so clearly that the triangle is less wide than the square, so why is [WIDTH 0.0–0.5] nevertheless considered? Examination of the data shows that the WIDTH values, 0.437 for the triangle and 0.563 for the square, are very close to each other, but just by luck fall within the two regions carved out by the WIDTH discrimination tree. On the other hand, the values on the HPOS channel are much further apart and so they are preferred.

As we have seen in the previous chapter, saliency is the smallest of the absolute values of the distance between the topic and any other object. It gives us an indication why a certain sensory channel should be preferred over another. For the scene in Game 22, the saliency for each channel with respect to the triangle is as in Table 4.3:

Table 4.3: Sensory data for the scene in Game 22.

HPOS	WIDTH	HEIGHT
0.622	0.125	0.286

From this table we see immediately that HPOS is the most salient channel and should be preferred by far, followed by HEIGHT and then WIDTH. Thus we can expect the agent to choose HPOS based on saliency. When the saliency threshold is set to a reasonably high value, the other channels would not even be considered, they would not pass the sieve of the perceptual layer.

The sensory channel data for the same scene now scaled for context is shown in Table 4.4. Such context-scaling pulls the data further apart and makes categorisation therefore much easier and much more stable, but the information on saliency is lost and so it is no longer clear which channel is to be preferred for reasons of saliency.

Table 4.4: Sensory data for the scene shown in Figure 4.6.

Object	HPOS	WIDTH	HEIGHT
0 (triangle)	0.0	0.0	1.0
1 (rectangle)	1.0	1.0	0.0

So the best thing to do (and this is what the Talking Heads effectively do) is to first perform sensor-scaling, then compute saliency to determine which channel should be preferred, then perform context-scaling, to get clearly distinguished sensory values, and then do categorisation. Note that context-scaling has the same effect as using prototype-based categorisation because the actual values are pulled towards extremes, and thus

4.3 Discrimination trees

perceived as prototypes. Context-scaling is not always desirable. For example, in the case of colour categorisation the actual channel data should be maintained because here categorisation takes place on the basis of actual values.

4.3.9 Combinations of categories

The next game (Game 24) is based on the scene in Figure 4.7. The topic is triangle-0. The discrimination trees are the same as for Game 22. The game (based on sensor-scaled values) succeeds with a conjunctive combination of two categories:

```
Game 24
  a1 segments the scene in 4 objects:
    triangle-0, triangle-1, square-2, rectangle-3
  a1 chooses triangle-0 as topic
  a1 categorises the topic as
    {[HEIGHT 0.0-0.5] [WIDTH 0.5-1.0]}
  The discrimination game succeeds
```

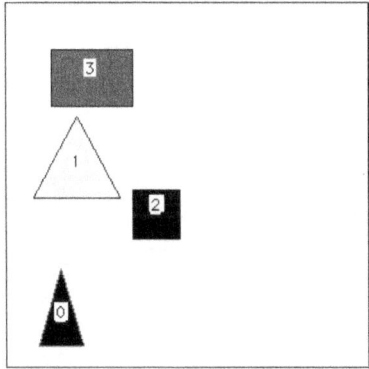

Figure 4.7: The scene used in Game 24.

The relevant data after sensor-scaling for the two sensory channels involved is shown in Table 4.5.

[HEIGHT 0.0–0.5] is valid for triangle-0 and square-2 but filters out the other segments. [WIDTH 0.5–1.0] is valid for triangle-0 and triangle-1 and filters out the others. The conjunctive combination of these two categories only retains triangle-0 and is therefore the one that is chosen.

4.3.10 A real world scene

The next example is taken from a series of discrimination games played by physically instantiated agents using real world images. The series is discussed more extensively in

4 The Discrimination Game

Table 4.5: Sensory data for the scene in Figure 4.7.

Object	HEIGHT	WIDTH
0 (triangle)	0.170	0.513
1 (triangle)	0.653	0.570
2 (square)	0.213	0.213
3 (rectangle)	0.613	0.310

Chapter 7. The agent a2 has captured the image shown in Figure 3.7 (top left) and done the necessary segmentation and gathering of sensory characteristics. The resulting sensory values (after sensor-scaling) for the segments are shown in Table 4.6. Object-0 has been selected as the topic.

Table 4.6: Sensory data from a real world scene with segmentation shown in Figure 3.7.

channel	obj-0	obj-1	Saliency
HPOS	0.27	0.16	0.11
VPOS	0.20	0.20	0.0
HEIGHT	0.15	0.15	0.0
WIDTH	0.10	0.11	0.01
AREA	0.10	0.10	0.0
R	0.23	0.25	0.02
G	0.32	0.34	0.02
B	0.63	0.65	0.02

Clearly HPOS is the most salient channel and should be preferred by the agent. When performing context scaling, the two values for HPOS are drawn apart with 1.0 for object-0 and 0.0 for object-1 so that the category [HPOS 0.5–1.0] (to the right) easily distinguishes the topic (object-0) from object-1. The game is reported as follows:

```
Game 3
   a2 is the speaker. a1 is the hearer.
   a2 segments the context into 2 objects:
        object-0 object-1
   a2 chooses object-0 as the topic
   a2 categorises the topic as [HPOS 0.5-1.0]
```

This example illustrates well why the categorisation of the Talking Heads is so robust and why agents often share the same conceptualisation even if the details of their raw perception is quite different. The saliency factor helps to focus the agents on those aspects of the scene that stand out. There is an enormous reduction of variation, first by scaling then by the categorisation process itself.

4.4 An ecology of distinctions

The previous section introduced mechanisms that enable agents to find a distinctive category or conjunctive combination of categories given a set of segments and data on a series of sensory channels for each segment. I will now focus on the issue how discrimination networks and hence repertoires of possible categories may develop.

4.4.1 Growth dynamics

The process of growing categorisers is relatively straightforward. In the very beginning, the agent constructs top level categorisers for each channel which have contained at least once in the recent past relevant and distinctive data. If a channel has the same data for every possible segment it is obviously not going to be possible to find a distinctive category no matter how hard the agent tries.

A new subcategoriser is constructed by taking a categoriser node in the tree and dividing its range into two new subranges and thus two new subcategorisers. For example, if there is a categoriser [HPOS 0.0–0.5], which triggers when the object is in the left most half of a scene, i.e. with HPOS within [0.0,0.5], then two subcategories are created by dividing [0.0,0.5] into two halves, one for the range [0.0,0.25] ([HPOS 0.0–0.25] or totally left) and one for the range [0.25,0.5] ([HPOS 0.25–0.5] or mid-left). A new categoriser is added to the tree for each of these halves.

A categoriser based on a combination of categories is constructed by combining existing categories into a new one. Of course, if done without limits, this could create potentially a combinatorial explosion of possibilities. In the current implementation, the construction of combinations is restricted by combining only those categories that have been partially successful in a given scene, just as only categories that have ever been relevant are expanded.

There are two key parameters to the growth process: (1) which category should be expanded and (2) when should growth take place. In the Talking Heads experiment, agents expand a category which was effectively applied in the recent past, even though it may have failed in the game. This way the network is more likely to develop branches that are potentially relevant, although there is still no guarantee that the expansion gives the distinctions required for the case at hand, because it is not based on an in-depth analysis of the case.

Growth rate is proportional to failure. The more failures occur, the higher the likelihood of more nodes growing. This has the net effect of many new nodes growing in the beginning because there are many failures, but that the repertoire of categories stabilises once discriminatory success is steady. When the environment starts to change

4 The Discrimination Game

again, causing new failures, more active growth is automatically triggered, which may lead to a renewed expansion of the repertoire.

4.4.2 Pruning dynamics

Growth needs to be balanced by pruning. Pruning simply means that a categoriser and thus its pending branches is cut away. There are again two issues: (1) which nodes should be pruned and (2) when pruning should take place. Obviously the score of a category should play a role in deciding whether it should be pruned. categorisers that have not been used very much or have a low success rate are prime candidates for removal, unless any of their subcategorisers has a high score. The monitoring of use and success already played a role in determining which category should be preferred, so this information is available to decide on pruning as well.

Whereas the growth rate is proportional to failure, the pruning rate is made proportional to success, so that in the case of a high failure rate the new categorisers are given time to improve their score or to grow refinements that may be successful. A new categoriser obviously should be given a grace period to encounter enough cases to prove its worth, otherwise it could be cut out too quickly. Categorisers therefore not only monitor their use and success but also their age.

4.4.3 Average discriminatory success and repertoire size

The Discrimination Game is a dynamical system.[17] A repertoire of categories emerges in an agent gradually as an attractor of the growth and pruning dynamics coupled to the environment. If growth is strictly proportional to failure and there is no pruning, a point attractor is reached as soon as the repertoire is adequate, i.e. as soon as the agent consistently has success for all the possible cases it encountered. However, as soon as the environment or the sensory capabilities of the agent change, in other words when new types of figures appear or when new sensory channels become available to the agent, we expect that the repertoire of categories starts expanding again. This could be seen as an illustration of the assimilation-accommodation dynamics envisioned by Piaget.

Let me introduce a few measures to test whether all this is really happening with the mechanisms introduced so far. The first (crucial) measure monitors how well the agent is doing by tracking the average success in the most recent n Discrimination Games. Figure 4.8 shows the outcome of this measure, for agent **a1**, playing 500 Discrimination Games in a simulation with scenes from the GEOM world. Success is averaged per 25 games. We see clearly that **a1** has become successful in discriminating randomly chosen topics from a consecutive series of scenes. Success rapidly climbs and reaches 100%, even though the scenes are randomly generated combinations from a repertoire of figures along continuously varying dimensions making for literally billions of possibilities. The Discrimination Game is successful because it does not try to detect invariants or

---

[17] The theory of complex dynamical systems, which is well developed in the natural sciences, provides the theoretical foundation for studying the Discrimination Game. For a general introduction, see Peitgen, Jurgens & Saupe (1992).

4.4 An ecology of distinctions

commonalities between consecutive cases but focuses on finding what is distinctive between the topic and the other objects. This enables the agent to make such a gigantic abstraction leap and to make it at an amazingly rapid speed.

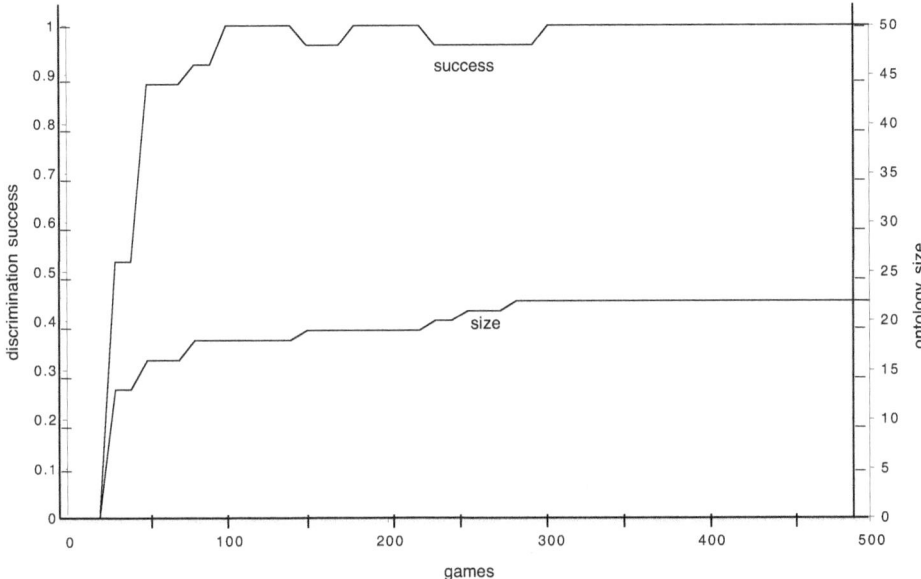

Figure 4.8: The graph displays the average success per 25 Discrimination Games for a series of 500 games played by a single agent. Success climbs to 100%. The graph also displays the size of the agent's repertoire of categories. Each scene contains between 3 and 6 objects.

We can see whether a stable attractor has been reached by tracking the size of the repertoire, which is simply the number of categorisers in the agent's discrimination trees. The result of this measure is also displayed in Figure 4.8. Once success is steady, the size of the repertoire remains constant, which means that no new elementary distinctions arise nor do any distinctions disappear. This is because there has been no pruning yet and growth is strictly proportional to failure.

Figure 4.9 shows some snapshots of the evolution in the discrimination trees of a1 as the simulation continues and as additional situations arise. There are expansions, contractions, and shifts in the constitution of the discrimination trees but gradually there are fewer and fewer changes, compare for example (c) and (d), as a stable core emerges.

These simulations show that the category formation process based on a growth and pruning dynamics is capable of creating a repertoire of discrimination trees adequate for distinguishing the topic from other objects in the scene. The simulations worked with computer-generated, stylised environments so that it is possible to probe the behaviour of the mechanisms and vary the complexity of the environment. Note that the mechanisms are neutral with respect to the type of channels supplied. The discrimination trees

4 The Discrimination Game

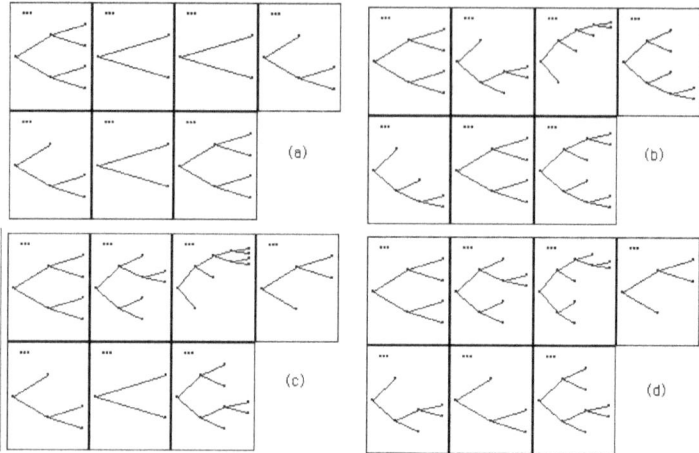

Figure 4.9: Some snapshots of an evolving repertoire in a single agent using growth and pruning. Trees are shown after 500 games (a), 1000 games (b), 1500 games (c) and 2000 games (d).

and growth and pruning dynamics can operate over auditory or bodily sensory channels, or other kinds of visual information that is produced by low level perception.

4.4.4 Adaptivity in categorisation

An agent operating in a real world environment is always going to be confronted with situations that he has not seen before. The growth and pruning dynamics of the Discrimination Game is capable of dealing with this because new distinctions grow when the failure rate is increasing. Here are the results of a computer simulation based on scenes generated by the GEOM world that test whether this is indeed the case.

The simulation starts with a new virgin agent playing a series of Discrimination Games involving scenes which only contain rectangles of the same graylevel. The agent has only channels for HEIGHT (0), WIDTH (1), RATIO (between the actual area of the shape and the area of the bounding box), (2), GRAY (3) and AREA (4). We expect to see that the discrimination trees on the RATIO (channel 2) and GRAY channels (channel 3) do not develop because the values on those channels are the same for all objects ever seen. This is clearly confirmed in Figure 4.10: The ratio between actual area and bounding box area is always 1.0 in the case of rectangles and they always have the same grayscale value. We see clearly that the RATIO (channel 2) and GRAY (channel 3) do not develop and that the others develop to very fine levels of detail to still successfully discriminate. So discrimination trees only develop as needed in a particular environment, which is important for applying the selectionist principle to the generation of sensory channels. The categorisation process gives feedback to the sensory processing on the adequacy of particular sensory channels.

4.4 An ecology of distinctions

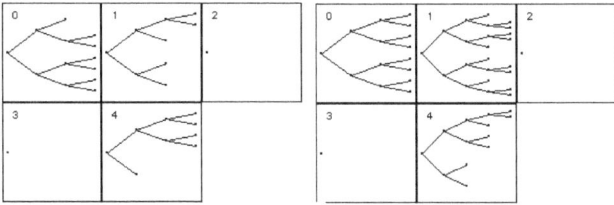

Figure 4.10: Two snapshots from a series of 500 discrimination games developing categories to distinguish rectangles of the same average graylevel. Channel 2 (the ratio channel) and channel 3 (the grayscale channel) do not develop.

Let us now make the environment richer by letting the GEOM world also produce scenes with circles and triangles, as well as rectangles. If the discrimination process is adaptive, the RATIO and GRAY channels should start to expand because these channels now contain significant data. This is indeed the case as shown in Figure 4.11.

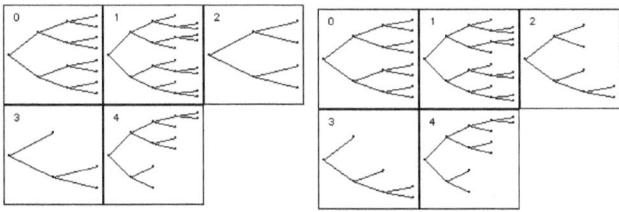

Figure 4.11: Two snapshots from an additional series of 500 Discrimination Games after the environment has become more complex. RATIO (channel 2) and GRAY (channel 3) have started to develop.

The simulation demonstrates that the proposed discrimination process is adaptive to changes in the environment, because growth picks up as soon as the environment poses new challenges, just like the immune system starts generating a larger repertoire (and expanding already existing antibodies that partially matched) when challenged by the invastion of foreign bodies. The adaptation can be tracked with the success and repertoire size measures introduced earlier. When these measures are collected for the example shown in Figure 4.12, phase one shows clearly that when only rectangles are present, a stable repertoire gradually develops and that the success rate reaches 100 % after about 500 games. In phase two, when other types of shapes have been introduced, the discrimination trees begin to expand again, now exploiting the RATIO and GRAY channels to cope with the new types of objects. Existing categories will of course still be adequate for many cases. After 500 more games, a new equilibrium is reached. Steady discrimination success is seen with an enlarged repertoire.

4 The Discrimination Game

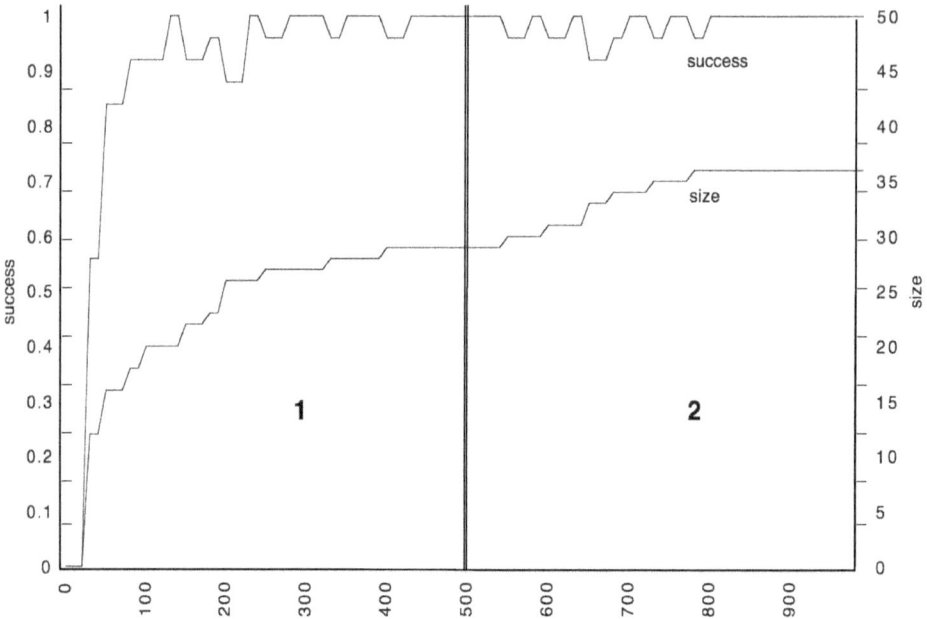

Figure 4.12: Evolution of success and ontology size in a series of 1000 Discrimination Games played by a single agent. In phase 1, only rectangles of the same graylevel are generated by the GEOM world. In phase 2, additional types of shapes are generated by the environment.

4.4.5 Real world scenes

Very similar developments can be seen when we do experiments with embodied agents, capturing real world scenes through their cameras. Figure 4.13 shows two snapshots of developing discrimination trees for two agents. The game discussed earlier, based on Figure 3.7 top, has been played with these trees. HPOS is the most salient channel and a distinction can be made easily. Note that the HEIGHT and WIDTH channels have not developed yet because no clear cases emerged in the environment where those channels provided salient data.

4.5 Conclusions

This chapter addressed the problem of how agents may categorise their environment using information on sensory channels about each segment in the scene. I argued in favour of a selectionist approach, which generates possible solutions in a relatively random growth process and tests them in the cases presented by the environment. This approach contrasts with instructionism, where the agent is assumed to make gradual

4.5 Conclusions

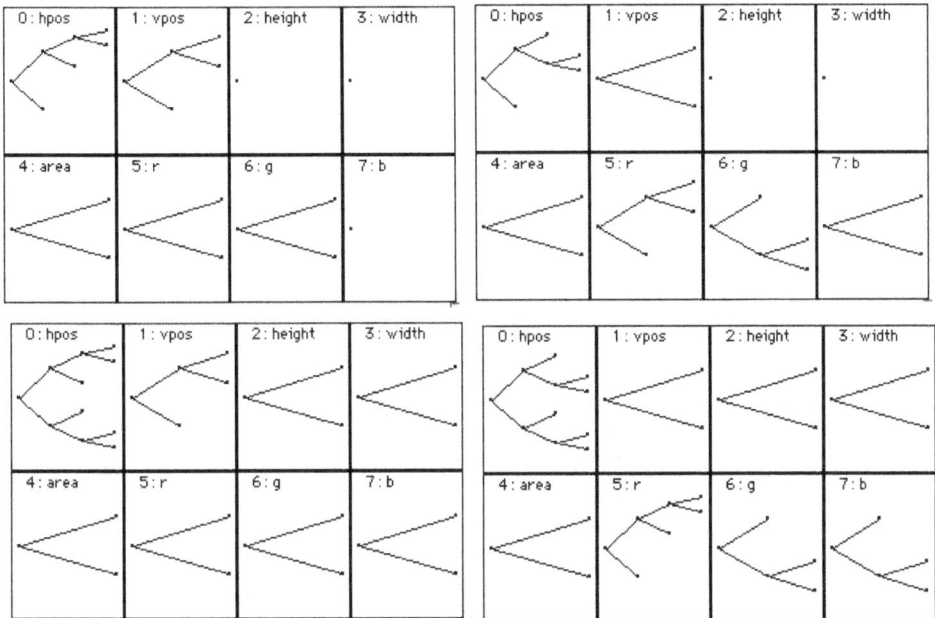

Figure 4.13: The discrimination trees developed by two physically embodied agents **a1** (left) and **a2** (right). The top of the figure shows the trees after playing 100 games and bottom after 200 games.

abstraction from a series of examples using induction, and with a rationalist approach, where perceptually grounded categories are assumed to be innate and hence derived through genetic evolution.

The main conclusion of this chapter is that a selectionist approach to the origins of categories is theoretically and practically feasible. I have defined a growth and pruning dynamics which leads to an adequate repertoire for discriminating one object from the others in the same context and I showed that the repertoire is continuously adapted when the environment changes.

We will have plenty of opportunity in later chapters to further test the mechanisms for categorisation presented here. I will also introduce additional feedback couplings from the lexical layer to these categorisation processes. Nevertheless we are now sufficiently advanced to be able to turn to the next subtask the agents face when engaging in a language game: establishing a relation between categories or combinations of categories and an utterance.

5 The Naming Game

The semiotic square captures the four entities in a linguistic interaction: the REFERENT, which is the object in the physical world that the speaker wants to communicate, the SEGMENTED IMAGE, which is the internal perception of the referent, the MEANING, which is a category or combination of categories that picks out the referent in the present context, and the UTTERANCE, which is the word form or set of word forms transmitted by the speaker. In the previous chapters we looked at two sides of the semiotic square. The relation between the real world and the perceived image was studied in chapter 3 and the relation between the perceived image and a conceptualisation that could act as the meaning for a language communication was studied in chapter 4. We now turn to the next side of the semiotic square: the relation between meaning and utterance.

We need to find an architecture by which an agent can establish the relation between form and meaning, in other words verbalise a meaning to produce an utterance and parse an utterance to retrieve its meaning. This mechanism needs to be flexible enough to deal with the unavoidable synonymy and ambiguity that will arise. Second, we need to find a mechanism by which an agent can acquire and help construct the lexicon of the group. A shared lexicon should emerge through the distributed activities of the agents without any prior design or global co-ordination. Third, the lexicon formation process should scale up to handle a growing and ever changing set of meanings and continue to work even with large populations whose constitution changes in time. It should be possible for new agents to enter the population and acquire the existing language and for agents to leave without destabilising the whole system. These are formidable challenges, particularly because we want to find the simplest possible solution, something a one year old child could do without fully developed intelligence.

Immediately we observe a major difficulty. In realistic language games, where agents cannot inspect each others' brain states nor transmit meanings directly, there is no feedback about the meaning of a word, only about the referent. For example, when a speaker says *wabo* and the hearer has correctly pointed to the referent that the speaker intended, neither the speaker nor the hearer can know whether they were using the same meaning. They can only know that they arrived at the same referent. When a game fails, the speaker can only point to the topic and the hearer then tries to figure out what possible meaning could have been applicable. The speaker cannot communicate directly the "right" meaning, and very often more than one meaning is possible to distinguish a topic from other objects in the context, so that the hearer will not necessarily guess the meaning used by the speaker. I will call this the gavagai-problem, because Quine used this word to illustrate exactly this difficulty.[1] Quine evoked the problem of an anthropologist

---
[1] See Quine (1960: 29–30).

trying to figure out what a native speaking an unknown language might mean when he utters *gavagai* while pointing to a white rabbit scurrying by.

In this chapter, I will bypass the gavagai-problem by assuming that agents get direct feedback about the meaning of a word. This is done by assuming that all agents share the same perception, that they already have a repertoire of shared meanings, that for every agent a particular meaning always picks out a single referent, and that a given referent is conceptualised with the same meaning by every agent. This scaffold allows us to focus on the problem of how form-meaning associations might form and propagate in a population without worrying how agents get feedback about the meanings of forms. However, it does means that we cannot do experiments with embodied physical agents but will have to accept the limitation of working only with computer simulations. The next chapter will take the scaffold away, as any serious theory for word meaning acquisition should. I will then show that given an appropriate coupling between lexicalisation and categorisation, a communication system can still get off the ground based on the mechanisms described in this chapter.

5.1 Inventing a lexicon

I will now introduce another game, the Naming Game, to allow us to focus on the origin of the lexicon. The Naming Game defines a situation requiring a group of distributed autonomous agents to develop and use a shared lexicon relating forms and meanings, assuming they have a shared repertoire of meanings and get direct feedback about what meaning corresponds to a certain form. The Naming Game can be thought of as the lexical side of the Guessing Game.[2] The game can be implemented with different mechanisms compared to the ones I will use, so it defines a task setting in which different solutions can be compared. See also Hutchins & Hazlehurst (1995). A different task setting for studying language acquisition (but not how a language may emerge from scratch) is illustrated in Regier (1996). In this case, the agents are shown examples and counter-examples together with words they should use in each case.

It can be objected that the Naming Game (and the Guessing Game) already assumes that the agents want to communicate. This is true, but the game can be embedded in a larger setting where communication is vital for survival. An example of such a setting is discussed in Werner & Dyer (1991).

Another issue concerns the evolution of the game itself. This topic is discussed in: Hurford (1989). This paper is also the earliest paper posing the problem of the origins of a lexicon through computational simulations. See also Oliphant (1996). Hauser (1996) contains a further discussion of these topics from the viewpoint of biological continuity.

The Naming Game is played by two agents, a speaker and a hearer, which are picked randomly from a population. The speaker selects a meaning from the shared repertoire of meanings, looks up a possible word for this meaning in his lexicon, and transmits the word to the hearer. The hearer interprets the word by looking it up in his lexicon,

---

[2] The Naming Game and associated computer simulations were presented for the first time in Steels (1996).

5.1 Inventing a lexicon

and transmits the meaning he thus obtained. If this meaning is the one that the speaker originally had in mind the game succeeds, otherwise the game fails. When the game fails, the speaker communicates the meaning directly so that the hearer can acquire a new form-meaning pair for later conversations. When a speaker does not have a word yet for a meaning he wants to communicate, he may create a new one.

5.1.1 Representing lexical associations

What cognitive architecture do agents need to engage in naming games? Clearly they need some sort of ASSOCIATIVE MEMORY to store their individual lexicons. Let us assume that agents can construct and recognise arbitrary consonant-vowel combinations, like *coba* or *wabidu*, for forming words, and that they have a repertoire of possible meanings in the form of categories, for example [LEFT], [DARK], [LARGE], etc. The contents of the associative memory of a single agent can be displayed in a table as follows:

Table 5.1: Associative memory of a single agent

meaning	form
[DARK]	coba
[LARGE]	wabidu
...	...

As an agent is acquiring his lexicon, there are going to be stages when he is not yet sure about the meaning of a certain form. So it must be possible for the agent to store different meanings for the same form and different forms for the same meaning. This can easily be done by extending the memory capacity to cross-associate multiple items. Agents can then handle ambiguity (one word can have different meanings) and synonymy (one meaning can be associated with many different words).

A speaker can only transmit a single choice for expressing the meaning. When there are alternative words for the same meaning in his lexicon, he must decide which one to use and this decision should be such that it maximises success in the game. To estimate this success, each agent should monitor for each form-meaning association how successful it has been, which could be implemented by associating with every form-meaning pair a SCORE. The score of a form-meaning pair is specific to an agent and based only on his own local interactions with other agents, in line with the principle that no single agent has a complete overview of the lexicon nor controls the others. An example of a lexicon with multiple associations and a score for every association is illustrated in Table 5.2.

From this table we see that the agent prefers to use the word *pama* for [DARK] and *limiri* for [LARGE].

Table 5.2: Example lexicon with multiple associations

	coba	zapo	bila	pama	wabidu	limiri
[DARK]	0.3	0.2	0.1	0.8	-	-
[LARGE]	-	-	-	0.5	0.3	0.6

5.1.2 Updating the score

One of the crucial aspects of the Naming Game model is how scores are updated based on the outcome of a game. Intuitively the score should be related to use and success. The more a word is used and the more success it has, the higher the score should be. Moreover there should be a time dimension, as recent use and success should obviously contribute more to the current score. The following is a scheme that captures these characteristics.

Every time an agent successfully uses a form-meaning pair for speaking, he increments the score with a specific increment δ. δ is relatively high, typically equal to 0.1. The scores of competing associations, i.e. associations that used another form for the same meaning are decremented with δ. The score remains however bounded between 0.0 and 1.0. This way the "best" form-meaning pair stands out more clearly next time around.[3]

When an agent plays the role of hearer, he also increments the association that was successful with δ, and decrements competing associations, i.e. associations that related another meaning to the same form. When a game fails, the associations used by the speaker and the hearer that contained the transmitted word form are both decremented.

The operations of speaker and hearer are summarised in Figure 5.1 assuming that speaker and hearer use both the score table above (in reality they of course always have different score tables). The speaker collects all possible forms for a given meaning [DARK], chooses the one with the highest score (*pama*), and transmits that form. The hearer collects all possible meanings for the transmitted form ([DARK], [LARGE]) and again chooses the one with the highest score. If the hearer's meaning is equal to that of the speaker's, the game succeeds. The score of two used associations increases and the others decrease, implementing lateral inhibition. If the game fails, only the two used associations go down.[4]

It is possible to impose an even stronger lateral inhibition, by assuming that in the case of success, the speaker decreases the score of all the associations that imply the word used in the game but with another meaning, and the hearer decreases the score of

---

[3] A systematic investigation of alternatives for the updating function is contained in Oliphant (1997). The dynamics of the mechanisms used in the Talking Heads experiments are being investigated in the Ph.D thesis of Frederic Kaplan.

[4] More or less neural realism can be introduced to model this associative memory. In our experiments we have a perfectly working memory that can store an association as soon as it has seen it once. This makes theoretical investigation easier and makes it possible to better follow the simulations and experiments. An example of a neural network solution to lexical memory is discussed in Cangelosi & Parisi (1996).

5.1 Inventing a lexicon

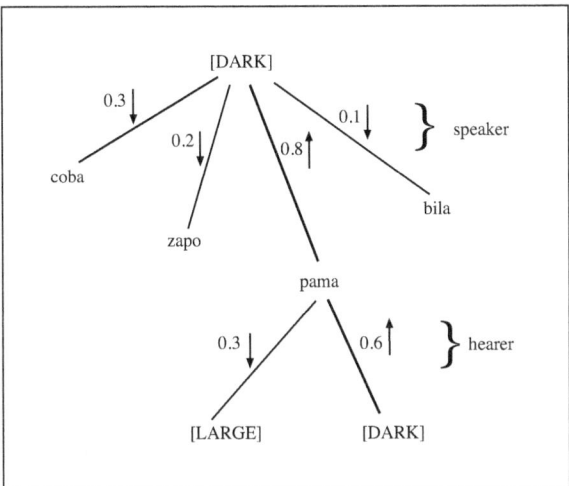

Figure 5.1: Score adjustments after a successful game. Scores of used associations go up and their competitors go down.

all the associations that imply the same meaning but with another word. This obviously requires additional processing from the side of the agents.

5.1.3 Constructing and acquiring words

When virgin agents start playing naming games, their associative memories are completely empty. Each agent needs two additional activities to get a lexicon emerging:

- When an agent does not have a word for a meaning he wants to communicate, he is allowed to create a new word (by random combination of vowels and consonants) and add that to his lexicon. Agents are assumed to have a shared repertoire of syllables which they can all produce and recognise. This happens with a certain probability, the WORD CREATION RATE w_c. This rate reflects how "free" the agent feels to extend the lexicon.

- When an agent hears a word he has never heard before, he may add this new word to his repertoire. Again this happens with a certain probability, the WORD ABSORPTION RATE w_a. This rate reflects the critical attitude with which an agent accepts the linguistic authority of other agents.

These rates are not critical but must of course be positive. Experiments continue to work when agents always make a new word ($w_c = 1$) and always absorb the word of the other ($w_a = 1$).

109

5 The Naming Game

5.1.4 The Naming Game in action

To become more familiar with the Naming Game, I will now go through a few examples of its application, assuming a group of five agents: $\mathcal{A} = \{$a1,a2, a3, a4, a5$\}$ and five possible shared meanings: $\mathcal{M} = \{[\text{DARK}], [\text{LARGE}], [\text{LIGHT}], [\text{SMALL}], [\text{RED}]\}$.

Here is a trace of a first game as reported by the commentator, when the agents do not have any lexicon at all.

```
Game 0
   a5 is the speaker. a3 is the hearer.
   a5 categorises the topic as [LIGHT]
   a5 does not have a word for [LIGHT]
```

This trace lists the number of the game, the speaker, the hearer and the categorisation of the topic. The speaker did not have a word and did not create one (because the word creation probability is $w_c = 0.1$): the game has failed. In the beginning most games fail if the word creation rate has been set to a low rate.

In the next game shown below, the speaker is **a4**, the hearer **a5** and the topic [SMALL]. Now the speaker is successful in creating a word, namely *di*. The hearer receives the word, does not know it, but stores it in association with [SMALL]. The game still fails.

```
Game 29
   a4 is the speaker. a5 is the hearer.
   a4 categorises the topic as [SMALL]
   a4 creates a new word: di
   a5 does not know di
   a4 points to the topic
   a5 categorises the topic as [SMALL]
   a5 stores di as [SMALL]
```

In game 32, something similar happens. This time **a5** creates a new word *pida* for [LARGE]. **a3** does not know the word but stores it.

```
Game 32
   a5 is the speaker. a3 is the hearer.
   a5 categorises the topic as [LARGE]
   a5 creates a new word: pida
   a5 says: pida
   a3 does not know pida
   a5 points to the topic
   a3 categorises the topic as [LARGE]
   a3 stores pida as [LARGE]
```

A first success occurs in game 43, when **a5** uses again *pida* for [LARGE]. **a3** hears *pida*, has associated it in his lexicon with [LARGE], and so the game succeeds.

5.1 Inventing a lexicon

```
Game 43
    a5 is the speaker. a3 is the hearer.
    a5 categorises the topic as [LARGE]
    a5 says: pida
    a3 interprets pida as [LARGE]
    a3 points to the topic
    a5 signals OK
```

It is quite tedious to go through such games by hand. For large populations of agents or meanings, even the most diligent researcher soon loses patience. Fortunately it is not so difficult to implement the Naming Game model on a computer. This makes large-scale simulations, even with hundreds of agents and meanings feasible, and ensures that they have been done correctly. All traces and graphs of games reported in this book have been produced by computer simulations or physical experiments with the Talking Heads.

5.1.5 Characterising the lexicon

The individual lexicon of one agent, **a5**, after 100 games is shown in 5.3.

Table 5.3: Associative memory of a single agent after 100 games.

Meaning	Word	Score
[LARGE]	pida	0.20
	fobu	0.1
[LIGHT]	gi	0.0
[SMALL]	di	0.10

Both the words *di* and *pida* are present but with weak scores. There are two synonyms for [LARGE]: *pida* and *fobu*, but *pida* is preferred. There is a word *gi* who is available for [LIGHT] but does not have a positive score, because successive trials failed to yield a successful game.

A table such as the one above only represents the lexicon of a single agent. It is highly unlikely that two agents share the same lexicon because each agent will have had different encounters and hence different language experiences. A picture of the lexicon of the group from the viewpoint of an outside observer can be obtained by inspecting the internal states of each agent to construct the GROUP LEXICON. It groups the dominating meaning-form associations for all possible meanings and the frequency of each association. It gives a picture of "the" lexicon in the group. The group lexicon for the complete population of five agents after 50 language games is shown in Table 5.4.

This reflects a situation where 40 % of the agents prefers to name [LARGE] with *pida*. 60 % of the agents use *gi* for [LIGHT], and 40 % *di* for [SMALL]. The other meanings ([DARK] and [RED]) do not have names yet.

5 The Naming Game

Table 5.4: Population lexicon after 50 games

Meaning	Word	Frequency
[LARGE]	pida	0.40
[LIGHT]	gi	0.60
[SMALL]	di	0.40

Note that the group lexicon is not known by the agents and is not stored anywhere in the total system. The only information which is locally stored in each agent is his own lexicon, which might be quite different from that of the group lexicon. For example, the lexicon of **a5** shown earlier is different from the group lexicon. **a5**'s score for *gi* is 0.0 even though the word is already preferred by 60 % of the agents according to the group lexicon. The group lexicon is a macroscopic structure that we as observers construct from inspecting the internal states of the agents.

Let us now continue the simulation. Here are two additional games showing how *ga* propagates from **a4** to **a2** in game 101 and from **a2** to **a1** in game 104.

```
Game 104
    a4 is the speaker. a2 is the hearer.
    a4 categorises the topic as [RED]
    a4 says: ga
    a2 does not know ga
    a4 points to the topic
    a2 categorises the topic as [RED]
    a2 stores ga as [RED]

Game 104
    a2 is the speaker. a1 is the hearer.
    a2 categorises the topic as [RED]
    a1 says: ga
    a1 does not know ga
    a2 points to the topic
    a1 categorises the topic as [RED]
    a1 stores ga as [RED]
```

After a total of 250 games, the consensus is complete. The group lexicon is shown in Table 5.5.

Once the agents have reached this stage, the lexicon does not change anymore, because all agents now prefer the same word for each possible meaning and would never choose another one nor encounter another one.

The lexicons of individual agents contain quite a few form-meaning pairs that did not make it in the shared lexicon that gradually emerged. It is entirely feasible to envision

Table 5.5: Consensus in group lexicon, reached after 250 games.

meaning	form	frequency	meaning	form	frequency
[DARK]	go	1.00	[LARGE]	pida	1.00
[LIGHT]	gi	1.00	[SMALL]	di	1.00
[RED]	ga	1.00	-	-	-

a pruning mechanism that would eliminate from memory those form-meaning pairs whose success has been non-existent (for example because an agent created it as speaker but it was never picked up by anybody else), or whose score has become zero (because another word became dominant). The impact of such a forgetting function has not been explored yet in our experiments.

5.1.6 Monitoring

I use various measures both for actual lexicon use and for the coherence and evolution of the lexicons of the individuals to see better what is happening. The first and easiest measure is the AVERAGE GAME SUCCESS, also called the COMMUNICATIVE SUCCESS, of a population of agents $\mathcal{A}$ in a set of n language games. When this measure is graphed continuously for consecutive sets of games, the progress in the population towards successful communication can be followed easily. This is shown in Figure 5.2 which plots data from the games discussed in the previous paragraphs. We see at once that average success climbs from a starting point of zero to a maximum of 1.0. This can only be because a shared lexicon emerged in the population.

When the population (both of meanings and agents) is larger, one would expect that it takes longer to reach total average success. This is indeed the case (Figure 5.3).

We see for example that for 20 agents and 20 meanings success climbs to total success after about 10,000 games. This is still surprisingly low particularly as success is are already above 95 % after about 5000 games. Games can be played in parallel by different agents because the system is entirely distributed. If we divide the number of agents by the number of games, we see that about 250 games are needed by the agents to get 95 % success, which means that every meaning needs to appear about 10 times for each agent. Interestingly enough, the larger the population of agents, the more the success curve approximates an S-shape, which has been observed empirically in the spreading of new linguistic conventions. The same curve shape is familiar to biologists studying models of competitive growth, suggesting a strong relationships between ecological dynamics and language spreading.[5]

---

[5] The S-shaped curve is discussed in McMahon (1994) p. 52. For examples of biological models with similar properties, see May (1976).

5 The Naming Game

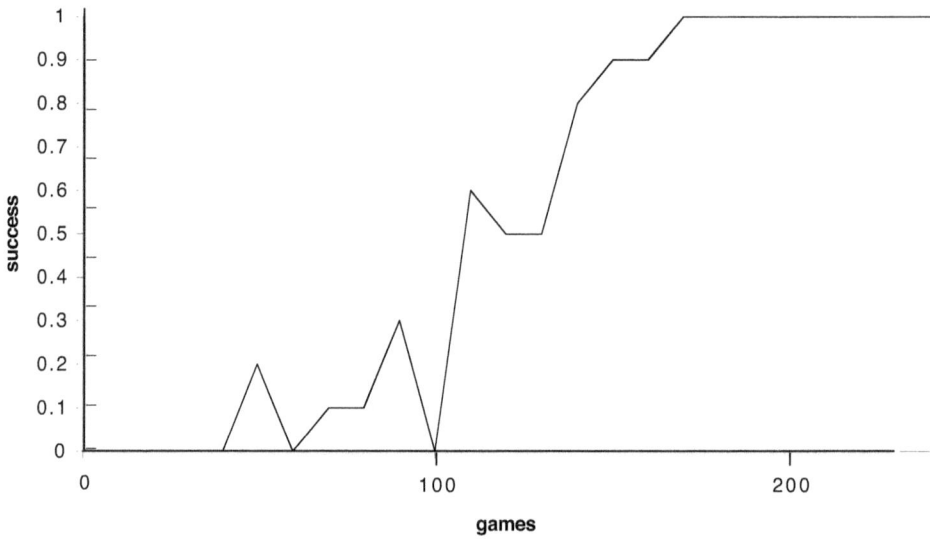

Figure 5.2: The graph displays on the y-axis the average success every 10 games in a population of five agents lexicalising five different meanings. The x-axis shows the number of games. Average success rapidly climbs until it reaches total success after about 180 games.

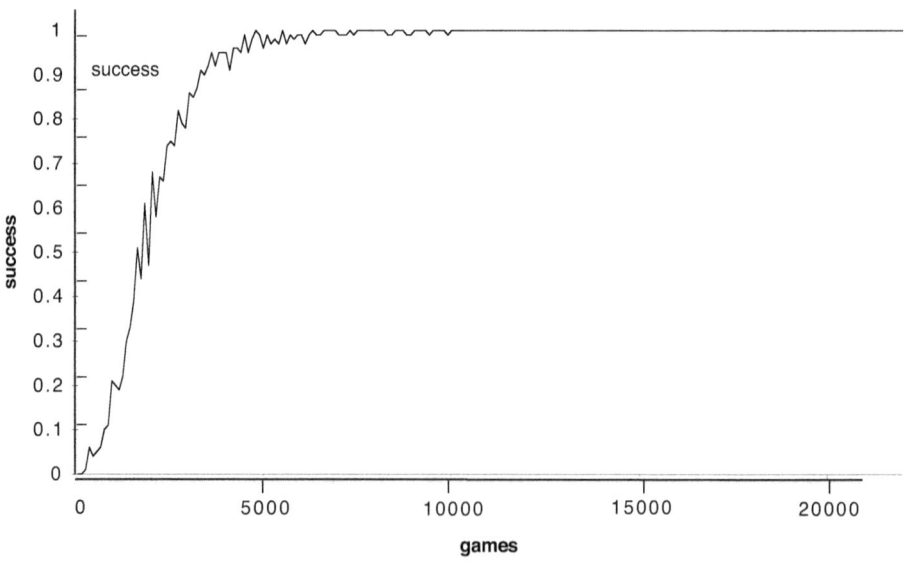

Figure 5.3: The graph displays the evolution of communicative success for larger and larger populations. The number of games on the x-axis is divided by the number of agents.

5.1.7 Measuring lexical coherence

To monitor to what extent the agents share the same lexicon, I propose a second measure, the LEXICAL COHERENCE. The lexical coherence is defined as the average of the frequencies of all the form-meaning pairs in the group lexicon. If all agents prefer the same form-meaning pair for all meanings, lexical coherence is 1.0. If they agree on none, it is 0.0.

Consider the following group lexicon after 3000 games for the previous simulation (with 20 agents), shown in Table 5.6.

Table 5.6: Group lexicon after 3000 games.

meaning	form	frequency	meaning	form	frequency
[DARK]	dato	1.00	[LARGE]	biti	0.80
[LIGHT]	pitu	0.60	[SMALL]	dopu	1.00
[RED]	gabi	1.00	[GREEN]	gu	0.85
[SQUARE]	koti	0.50	[RECTANGLE]	totu	0.65
[LEFT]	toga	0.90	[BLUE]	ku	0.80
[YELLOW]	gubo	0.55	[CHARMING]	ge	1.00
[TRIANGLE]	bu	0.85	[SQUARE]	ba	0.60
[FAST]	beke	1.00	[SLOW]	tu	0.95
[CIRCLE]	ke	0.75	[RIGHT]	gaba	0.95
[UP]	butu	1.00	[DOWN]	ki	0.95

The lexical coherence is at this point equal to 0.835.

Lexical coherence can be graphed alongside average success (see Figure 5.4). As expected, lexical coherence increases and we can see that as coherence increases the success rate increases.

Does total success imply that all agents use the same lexicon? Not really. To have success, the hearer must associate the form used by the speaker with the same meaning. But it is not required that the hearer himself prefers to use the same form for the same meaning, synonyms may occur. A speaker of British English typically uses the word *pavement*, whereas an American prefers *sidewalk*, even though he understands *pavement*. Thus there can be several forms active in the same population, even though the outcome of a game is always successful. We will see later that synonyms do get damped, as is the case in human natural lexicons.

Initially lexical coherence is higher than success, because a game fails if the hearer is acquiring the form-meaning association used by the speaker. So two agents could have stored the same association, and thus coherence would have increased, without already having enjoyed the benefit in a successful communication. However, once success is total, agents no longer make changes based on negative feedback from failure, simply because there is no failure, even the less common forms are understood correctly by

5 The Naming Game

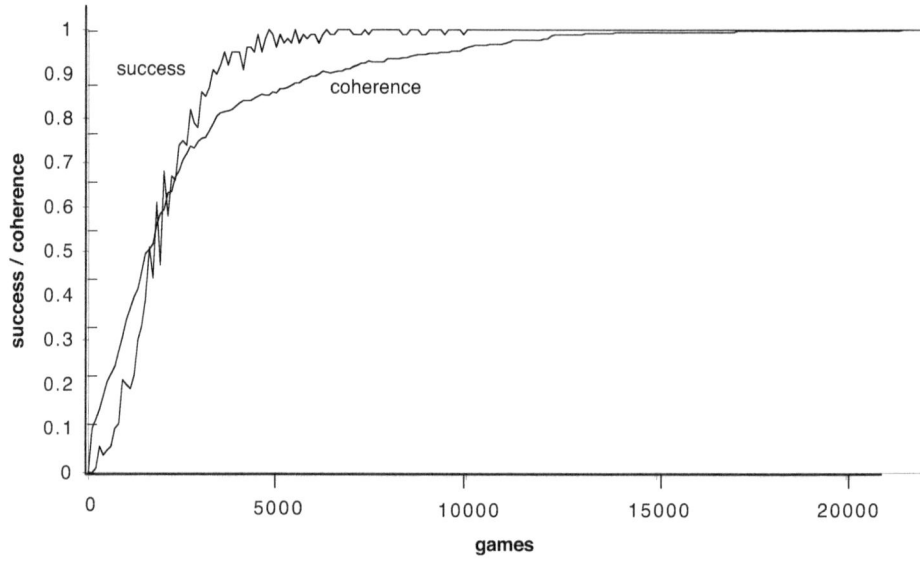

Figure 5.4: This figure shows the evolution of both average success and lexical coherence for a group of 20 agents and 20 meanings. Total lexical coherence climbs more slowly once the population has reached a high average success.

everybody. Further progress towards more coherence is therefore only due to the fact that the more common forms occur more often so that their scores keep going up as they are used more.

5.2 Scaling up

The associative memory and the score updating introduced in the previous section appears to allow a group of distributed agents to establish a shared repertoire of form-meaning pairs. Of course, I still need to show that this mechanism remains adequate when it is incorporated in a complete game, in which case there is no direct feedback about meaning. But before doing so, let us see whether the mechanisms are adequate from the viewpoint of scaling: Can they handle variation in the set of meanings to be expressed? Do they cope with a changing population?

5.2.1 Coping with new meanings

In natural languages, new meanings arise every day while other meanings become irrelevant. For example, none of the terms used for talking about the Internet (e-mail, surfing, home page, etc.) would have made sense to anyone a few decades ago. On the other

5.2 Scaling up

hand, most of us now have lost many categories and concepts for classifying plants, simply because they are no longer such a prominent part of our urbanised environments. It follows that a mechanism claiming to explain the origins and acquisition of a lexicon in a population of agents should cope with a fluctuating set of meanings as well. This property is moreover crucial in the Talking Heads experiment because new meanings will continuously arise as the agents encounter new situations in the environment.

Because the Naming Game included ways to handle new meanings from the start, nothing should have to be changed to handle an increased set of meanings. Let us see whether the Naming Game indeed copes through the next simulation (see Figure 5.5), using arbitrary labeled meanings ([M1], [M2], etc.). In a first phase, the system is closed and a shared lexicon emerges for the initial set of 20 meanings, as expected. The group's lexicon is now as in Table 5.7.

Table 5.7: Group lexicon after first phase.

meaning	form	frequency	meaning	form	frequency
[M1]	gebo	1.00	[M2]	goge	1.00
[M3]	koto	0.70	[M4]	da	1.00
[M5]	peko	1.00	[M6]	ki	1.00
[M7]	gipe	1.00	[M8]	kedo	1.00
[M9]	do	1.00	[M10]	gige	1.00
[M11]	pi	1.00	[M12]	bu	1.00
[M13]	pa	1.00	[M14]	kipa	1.00
[M15]	depi	0.95	[M16]	pudi	1.00
[M17]	tegi	1.00	[M18]	ba	0.90
[M19]	ko	1.00	[M20]	guda	1.00

In phase 2, a relatively small meaning flux is introduced (one new meaning every 1000 games). As can be seen from Figure 5.5, the population copes with the change. New words are created and propagate in the population. The following group lexicon shows that for newcomers like [M22] or [M25] a total consensus has emerged. Words for the latest new meanings, [M28] and [M29], still have low frequencies.

Next (phase 3 in Figure 5.5) a much higher meaning flux is imposed (one new meaning every 100 games). Lexical coherence decreases and average success plummets. There is not enough time to propagate the new conventions in the group. Note that lexical coherence drops slower than success when the lexicon disintegrates. Coherence is based on the average for all meanings, thus only the new ones are therefore affecting overall coherence. Success drops more rapidly because of the high rate of failure of new meanings.

The system restores itself when the flux of meaning is brought back to 1/1000 games (phase 4). Interestingly enough, coherence now increases slower than success. The in-

5 The Naming Game

Table 5.8: Group lexicon after second phase.

meaning	form	frequency	meaning	form	frequency
[M1]	gebo	1.00	[M2]	goge	1.00
[M3]	koto	1.00	[M4]	da	1.00
[M5]	peko	1.00	[M6]	ki	1.00
[M7]	gipe	1.00	[M8]	kedo	1.00
[M9]	do	1.00	[M10]	gige	1.00
[M11]	pi	1.00	[M12]	bu	1.00
[M13]	pa	1.00	[M14]	kipa	1.00
[M15]	depi	1.00	[M16]	pudi	1.00
[M17]	tegi	1.00	[M18]	ba	1.00
[M19]	ko	1.00	[M20]	guda	1.00
[M22]	to	1.00	[M23]	de	0.85
[M24]	tabo	0.95	[M25]	piku	1.00
[M26]	ku	1.00	[M27]	pugu	1.00
[M28]	tete	0.35	[M29]	todu	0.35

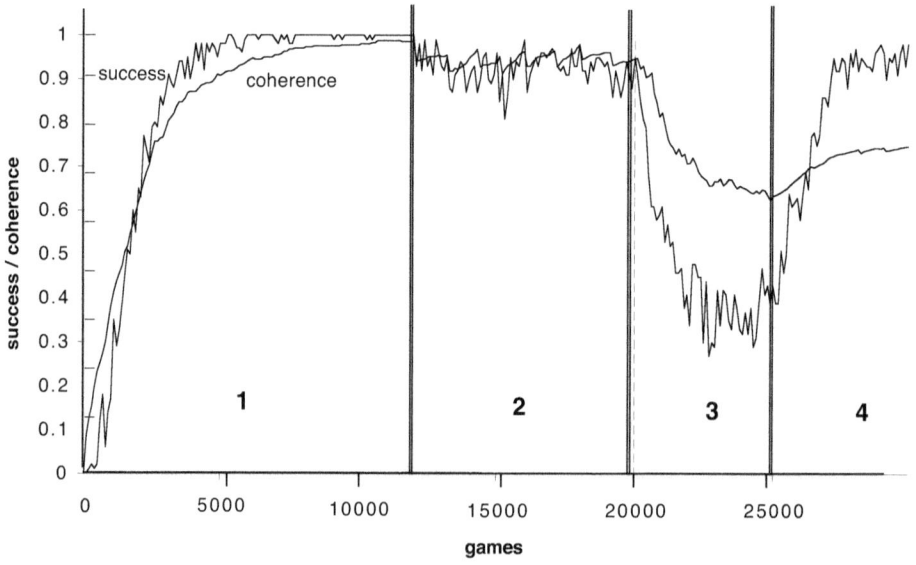

Figure 5.5: Both average success (every 100 games) and lexical coherence is shown in cases of an inflow of meanings for a population of 20 agents starting with 20 meanings (phase 1). The inflow is 1/1000 in phase 2, 1/100 in phase 3 and 1/1000 in phase 4.

stability caused by a rapid influx of new meanings has lead to many new forms for the same meanings. These synonyms now spread in the population and lead to a rapid increase in communicative success. Coherence climbs up more slowly because competing synonyms are only gradually weeded out, based on their frequency of use.

We can conclude that the agent architecture manages to handle an influx of meaning, as long as the flux stays within certain bounds.

5.2.2 Lexicon acquisition by virgin agents

The next question we need to investigate is whether the mechanisms explain how a lexicon, once it has formed, can be preserved from one generation to the next. This clearly happens in human populations. Although lexicons show profound change, large parts get preserved even over very large periods of time. Some linguists even claim that the roots of certain words still in use today go back to the very beginnings of language which is hypothesised to have been around 50,000 years ago, see Ruhlen (1994). A genetic solution, where the lexicon is stored in the genetic code and thus transmitted from parent to child, seems clearly out of the question. Nevertheless, a lot of the early work on computational modeling of language origins relied on a genetic approach for transmitting the lexicon, possibly with some additional adaptation. See for example: MacLennan & Burghardt (1993: 603–631). This approach sheds light on the issue how signaling systems may evolve in animals but is not applicable to the transmission of human lexicons. The lexicon of human languages is too diverse and changes too quickly to allow genetic transmission. So lexicons must somehow be transmitted in a cultural process.

It turns out that the agent architecture I introduced in the previous sections does not need to be changed at all to obtain a cultural transmission of a lexicon, illustrating the explanatory power of the model despite its simplicity. New virgin agents entering the group may occasionally create a new word, if they do not have one themselves, but if a particular set of words with particular meanings is already strongly entrenched in the population, these new words have a very low probability to survive. Instead, the virgin agents will adopt the words that they abundantly hear in their environment, and the score of these words goes up quickly.

Here is a computer simulation testing whether this is indeed the case (see Figure 5.6). We begin with a population of 20 agents and let them develop a shared lexicon for 20 meanings (phase 1). Then I *add* new virgin agents at regular time intervals, at a rate of 1 every 1000 games (phase 2). A new agent has no knowledge of the existing lexicon and therefore must acquire the lexicon present in the rest of the group. Figure 5.6 (phase 2) shows that the population indeed copes. A new member initially causes some failures in communication, but he quickly picks up the lexicon of the community and success moves back up. The lexicon does not change, it is stable against minor perturbations.

However, when the birth rate is increased to 1/100 games (phase 3) the population is less able to cope. Success stays relatively high (70 %), but there are too many new agents coming in too fast. The lexicon cannot spread sufficiently quickly to the new agents and therefore starts to disintegrate. In a final stage (phase 4), the birth rate is set again to 1

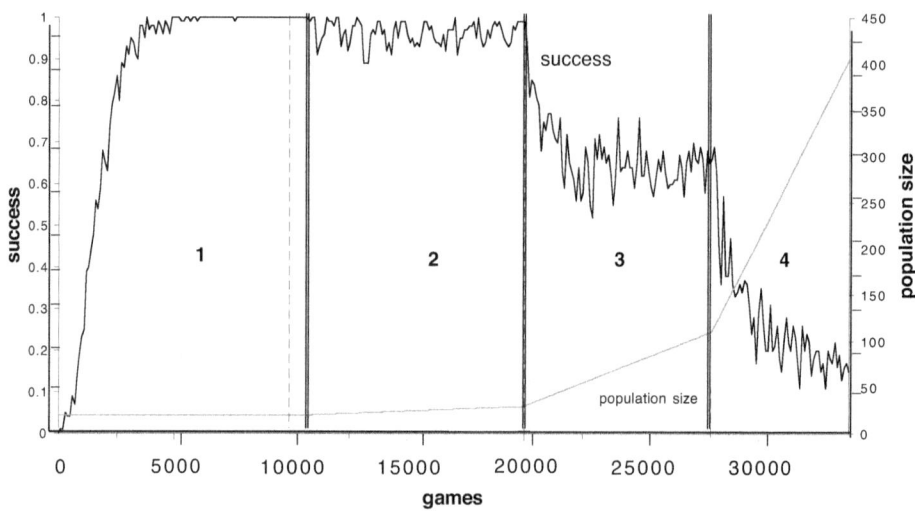

Figure 5.6: Evolution of communicative success with different birth-rates, starting from a population of 20 agents (phase 1). Next the birth rate is increased from 1 new agent every 1000 games (phase 2) to 1 new agent every 100 games (phase 3), and then to 1 every 50 games (phase 4).

new agent every 50 games. The population is no longer able to cope with the influx of new members and disintegrates. If inflow is brought back to a lower rate, the population would again establish a shared lexicon. However, the lexicon is now a different one from the one that was established before. The dynamical process has moved from one stable lexical state to another one.

We have seen earlier that the Naming Game scales up with respect to the size of possible meanings. Now we see that it scales up with respect to the size of the population. As long as the rate of influx is not too high, the population can keep expanding. The only constraining factor is that new agents must have sufficient opportunities to acquire the lexicon present in the group.

5.2.3 Preservation in changing populations

In human populations, there is not only an influx of new members but also an outflux. When somebody leaves the community knowledge about the lexicon should disappear as well. Nevertheless, a lexicon clearly gets preserved from one generation to the next, which implies that the know-how is distributed robustly over the agents.

The next computer simulation tests whether this is also true in the Naming Game model. The simulation starts with a population of 20 agents who are left to develop a shared lexicon for 20 meanings (phase 1). Then an in- *and* out-flux is introduced (phase

2 in Figure 5.7) with one new virgin agent coming in and another agent leaving the population every 1000 games. The new agent has to acquire the lexicon present in the group. Average success therefore dips but is quickly regained. In fact, the population can be completely renewed without affecting the lexicon at all. After 16000 games nine agents (50 %) have been replaced, but the lexicon has not changed. So, the Naming Game model not only explains the formation of a lexicon but also its transmission: This transmission is entirely cultural. New agents enter the population with no prior knowledge.

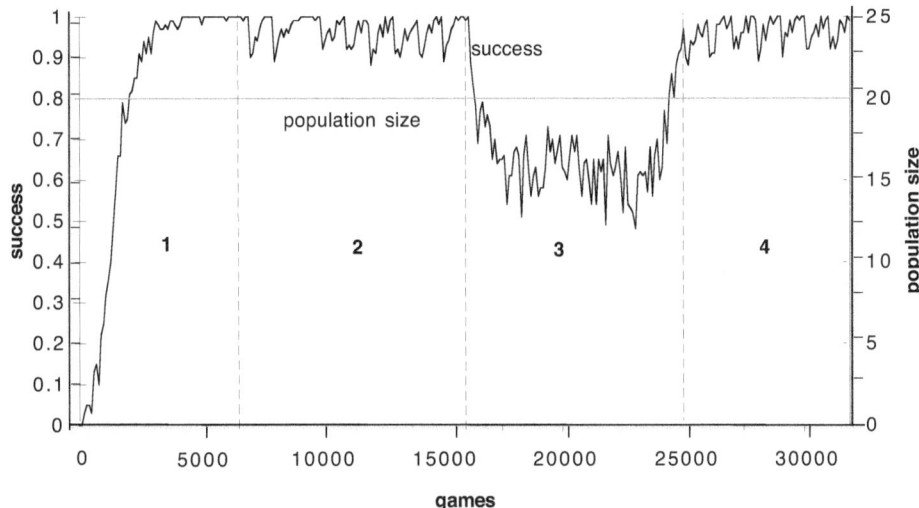

Figure 5.7: Success and population size is shown for a series of 35,000 language games. The population starts with 20 agents and 20 meanings (phase 1). Then an influx and outflux is introduced at the rate of 1/1000 games (phase 2). The lexicon maintains itself. In phase 3 agents enter and leave at the rate of 1/100 games. Success lowers. In phase 4 the rate of change is brought back to 1/1000 games and success is regained.

Can we increase the flux in the population indefinitely? This is examined in phase 3 of Figure 5.7. In this phase a higher flux has been introduced. One agent is added and removed every 100 games. Success goes down, although it is still maintained at a high level. The lexicon is still not changing. However, previous examples have already shown us that if we continue to increase the rate, the lexicon would disintegrate. Too many new agents would be flowing in, who do not have a lexicon yet. On the other hand, if we bring the rate of change back down to 1/1000 games (phase 4 in figure 5.7), success regenerates.

These simulation illustrates how we can study lexicon transmission using a language game approach. We have to set up an in- and outflow of the agents and study the impact on their communicative success and their lexicon. In principle, we should not have to change the architecture of the individual agents, and indeed I have not done so. Language acquisition is such an integral part of language use that a realistic agent architecture must intimately integrate both capacities from the start. Of course, at this stage we have only tested this with the agents getting direct feedback about meaning, we still must that whether it will continue to work with the physically instantiated Talking Heads.

5.3 Self-organisation

These various simulations show that the Naming Game embodies robust mechanisms for the emergence of a lexicon and we will use it as a core component for the Talking Heads experiment. In retrospect, the following mechanisms are crucial for the success of the model:

1. Agents must be able to represent multiple associations (one form can be associated with many meanings and one meaning with many forms). Multiple associations naturally arise in a population of distributed agents because an agent may create a new form not knowing that one already exists in the population, or guess a different meaning for a form than the one intended by the speaker. I will discuss such examples in more detail later.

2. An agent must be able to record a score for each association. The score is necessary for the agent to decide which meaning or which form should be preferred in a particular interaction. When random choices are made lexicons do not converge.

3. Agents must be able to create new words when no words are available yet. When there is a fixed set of words, the problem is much harder and the distributed search process may get stuck into local minima. Lexical systems must be able to cope with a steady influx of new meanings so restricting the set of words from the beginning would be odd.

4. Agents must perform lateral inhibition, which means that they must decrement the score of competitors to the form-meaning pair which won a competition. This is necessary to achieve convergence.

5. Agents must get feedback in the case of failure. At the moment the feedback is direct, but I will soon embed the naming game into a more complex guessing game in which feedback comes from the externally observed outcome of the language game as opposed to the direct transmission of the intended meaning.

When any of these characteristics of the agent architecture or the game are eliminated, the system does not work. Communicative success does not climb, convergence will not go beyond a small percentage, the size of the lexicon explodes, and so on. The fact that these architectural properties are crucial and non-trivial to discover strongly suggests that similar mechanisms must be in place in the emergence of human lexicons.

It is also important to stress what is not in the model. The mechanisms used by the agents are deliberately kept as simple as possible. Complexity should arise only from the enactment of simple construction rules. Agents do not go through complex reasoning about words, they simply store the new associations they encounter and rely on the updating processes to weed out wrong hypotheses.

5.3.1 Winner-take-all processes

The most remarkable and at first mysterious property of the Naming Game model is that the agents somehow reach a consensus without any central supervisor. They do *not* do this by having a general overview or by changing their internal parameters so as to become more conservative as the lexicon solidifies. It is solely due to the subtle interaction between language use, which gradually becomes uniform, and each agent's adaptation to the language heard in the environment. If a certain word comes to be preferred by a group of agents for a certain meaning, its frequency of use goes up so that others encounter this word more often and hence their scores for that word continue to increase as well. The more agents use a word, the higher its chance of success and the more it will be used. This effect is still enforced by lateral inhibition. The scores of competing associations decrease, making it less likely that they will win in the future. This positive feedback therefore introduces an AUTOCATALYTIC (self-enforcing) effect until the population locks into an equilibrium state.[6]

To follow better how a consensus gradually emerges, I will visualise the competition between different words for the same meaning in a MEANING-FORM (MF) COMPETITION DIAGRAM, such as the one in Figure 5.8, which monitors the frequencies of the different forms in use for one meaning. The diagram shows clearly the struggle between different forms until one form (*pe*) emerges as the winner. When we later study grounded lexicon formation processes, we will see that the competition becomes much more complex and the whole system is in constant evolution. A form-meaning pair which is dominating may become weaker because its meaning fails to pick up the right referent in a new context. This in turn may trigger the creation of new words or the resurgence of existing words.

5.3.2 Collective behaviour and self-organisation

Biology is full of examples where structures spontaneously self-organise from the uncoordinated activity of distributed elements through a winner-take-all process. Each time the same basic components as in the Naming Game model are seen: Random behaviour creates various possibilities and the reinforcement of some of these variations through positive feedback creates an autocatalytic effect. Perhaps the clearest examples can be found in the collective behaviour of social insects, such as the formation of nests by termites, although beautiful explanations have also been reported for the formation of

---

[6] Such positive feedback loops and the stability criteria associated with them have been widely studied in non-linear dynamical systems and applied to chemical and biological processes. See Babloyantz (1986).

5 The Naming Game

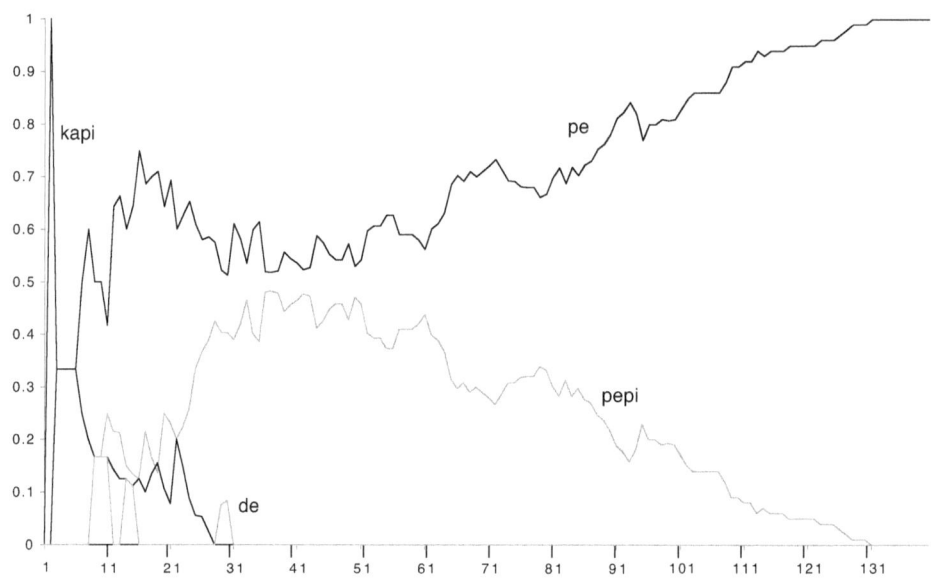

Figure 5.8: Simulation with a population of 20 agents. The meaning-form competition diagram shows the frequency of all competing forms for a single meaning. We see a winner-take-all situation with one word (*pe*) dominating.

patterns on sea shells, the growth of cell tissue, the aggregation of individual cellular slime mold amoebae into a slug, the flocking and collective movement of birds or mammals, etc., Meinhardt (1982). A classical example for collective behaviour, first developed by Jean-Louis Deneubourg, is the formation of paths in an ant society through mass recruitment, Pasteels & Deneuborg (1987).

When ants carry food or other materials, they organise themselves in a chain which is typically the shortest path between the source and the nest. These chains can sometimes be surprisingly long (20 meters is quite common for European ants) and are maintained as long as the food supply lasts. The whole process has many intriguing properties. First of all, there is no central planning agency that regulates which food sources are to be explored. The coherence and co-ordination between hundreds or sometimes thousands of ants is established in a completely distributed fashion. There is no dependence on individual ants. Ants can be removed from a path or new ones can be introduced randomly without too much interference for the stability of the path as a whole. The paths are robust. If objects are put in the way or if the path is destroyed, the ants manage to reestablish it in a relatively short time span. The paths are adaptive. If the food supply terminates, the path disintegrates and a new path will appear linking the ants to an alternative food source.

We see here many of the properties found in natural languages and integrated in the

Naming Game model: absence of central planning, no critical dependence on a single element, resilience to influx or outflux of elements, and adaptation to changing circumstances. Even more interestingly, the ants manage to establish these dynamic paths by a process which is similar to the language formation process used in the Naming Game, namely a positive feedback loop having an autocatalytic effect. An individual ant appears to move around in a random fashion while searching for a source of food. When a food source is discovered, the ant returns to the nest using a global landmark like the sun. The food-carrying ant also deposits a chemical substance known as a pheromone as he travels back to the nest. This pheromone influences the otherwise random movement of the other ants, in that ants are attracted by the pheromone. Thus more ants are drawn to the path and hence led to the food source. As these ants in turn go back to the nest they also deposit pheromone. This gives the self-enforcing, autocatalytic effect: The more ants are on the path, the more pheromone is deposited, and therefore the stronger the attraction to the other ants. Very soon all the ants which were sufficiently close to the path form a chain. There is no central planning agency needed and the whole system does not depend on an individual ant. The order is emergent.

These simple mechanisms also explain other features of the process. When the food source is depleted, the ants going back no longer deposit pheromone. And because the pheromone is a chemical that evaporates, it will soon have disappeared and consequently the ants will return to a random movement. When a path is interrupted because obstacles are put in the way or because the pheromone is temporarily removed by an experimenter, the ants resort back to a random movement. This introduces a random search process which will eventually lead to the discovery of a connection and the reestablishment of the path. When two ants find two food sources one closer than the other, the society will go for the closest source. Not because they exchange sophisticated signals but because the trail leading to the closest source will be amplified faster. Adaptivity is explained in terms of errors in following the path. Although ants are attracted to the pheromone, the attraction is only partial and very often (how often depends on the species) they will go astray. This sloppiness is however a source of new discoveries. When a lost ant hits upon a new food source the path formed by the whole society may gradually shift particularly if it is more abundant.

5.3.3 Increasing-returns economics

Self-organisation is not unique to biological phenomena, on the contrary, similar situations have been intensively studied in economics, where the complex adaptive systems paradigm has recently also led to many interesting new insights, as discussed in Arthur (1996). For certain types of products, particularly in information technology where the cost of manufacturing and distribution is neglectible compared to the cost of design, a winner-take-all situation can be observed. One product, for example a particular operating system or a particular microprocessor, comes to dominate the market.

Brian Arthur and others have analysed these economic situations and identified a positive feedback loop as being the ultimate cause. The more customers choose a product, the more others are attracted to it, particularly because other suppliers develop useful derivative products. Prices can be decreased keeping newcomers out of the market and customers get locked in, unable to move to other suppliers because they have invested too much and became dependent. For the companies who manage to manoeuver their products in such a situation there is a bonanza of increasing returns. This contrasts with the decreasing returns familiar from traditional equilibrium economics, where there is a damping of profits due to proliferating production and distribution cost as a product's market share increases.

5.3.4 Lessons from nature

The analogies between self-organisation in language and other fields is important for three reasons. First of all, if self-organisation is ubiquitous in nature and has successfully explained so many phenomena, its incorporation into a model of language becomes independently motivated, and therefore the explanatory force of the model increases. What is new and different is that the principle is applied to a non-material self-organising entity, but nevertheless the same sort of dynamics can be seen.

Second, the large arsenal of mathematical tools and analysis techniques developed in the sciences of complexity over the past decades can be carried over to the study of language. For example, the mathematical models of economists like Arthur or biologists like Deneubourg help us develop mathematical explanations why language reaches coherence if autocatalysis is present.

Third it suggests many aspects of the mechanisms which might be relevant for language. For example, the errors ants make in following a trail allow them to discover occasionally better food sources. Could such stochasticity also play a role in the adaptive capabilities of language? The chaotic regime seen in many natural systems is known to be a source of new order (Kaneko 1996). Could language innovation also be explained that way? In other words, is it possible that language may occasionally exhibit a chaotic dynamics out of which new order emerges?

5.4 Lexical dynamics

This discussion begins to illustrate a major theme of the present book, namely that language as a macroscopic phenomenon can be viewed as a complex adaptive system with the same characteristics as other complex adaptive systems.

It is well known that the dynamics of language change are related to the dynamics of the underlying population. Basically we can see two phenomena. On the one hand, human populations are not fixed for ever. New children without any knowledge of the language are born and other members die, taking knowledge about the language away with them. Populations renew at a certain rate which is known to have a significant impact on language. If the population changes quickly a language evolves more quickly and subsystems may even destabilise. For example, linguists have argued that English lost its case system due to the Black Plague which decimated the population so that there was not enough opportunity for children to acquire the existing conventions.

Second, human populations mix. Throughout the history of mankind there have been migrations or intense contact between geographically diverse groups. This again impacts then the languages of the groups. When a given population splits into groups that have no longer contact, their languages start to deviate. Conversely when there is an intense and prolonged contact between languages, structures from one language get adopted by the other and vice-versa. The degree of adoption depends on which group is dominant. Sometimes groups adopt another lexicon while retaining their own syntax, and sometimes they take over the syntax while retaining their own lexicon.[7]

These phenomena are fascinating and interesting from the viewpoint of language evolution, and may even explain some of the characteristics of human languages. Linguistic systems must be such that they can be transmitted from one generation to the next, otherwise they will not survive. In the Talking Heads experiment, new agents may enter into the group at any time and agents are geographically distributed. The local interactions with humans at a particular site, which is a kind of language contact between human and artificial populations, may impact the evolving lexicons and ontologies.

5.4.1 Spatially distributed naming games

Language game models provide us with new fantastic tools to study language transmission and language contact: We can introduce a particular dynamics in the population in a controlled way and then study the impact on the dynamics of the language itself. I now focus on such a model to investigate the impact of the migratory dynamics of a population on the dynamics of language. We can introduce a two-dimensional grid and assign every agent randomly a position on this grid. The position assignment can be modulated so that the agents form clusters (Figure 5.9). Such a population structure can be thought of as a geographical distribution in space but might as well represent a social, genetic or economical structure. We could even envision models integrating several of these alternate dimensions. The physical Talking Heads network connecting installations in different geographical locations allows to do these experiments for real.

In earlier simulations agents were randomly picked out of the population. Now we can base the probability with which two agents interact on their respective distance and on an interaction factor, which determines the weight of the distance. If the interaction factor increases, the role of distance becomes more important and interactions tend to reflect the spatial clustering more. Based on this parameter we can study the evolution of language when communications between clusters of agents increase.

Initially we let each subgroup evolve towards a shared communication. Success is never total because there are occasional interactions with members of other communities, however inner-cluster communication reaches total success. However inspection of the agent lexicons reveals that agents will develop a stable language within their cluster,

---

[7] A representative example of empirical investigations into language dynamics is contained in Nichols (1992). See also Romaine (1988).

5 The Naming Game

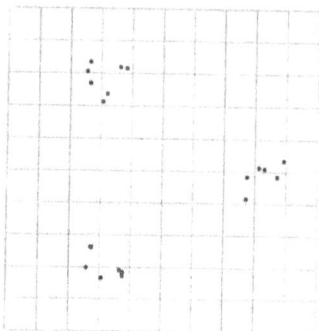

Figure 5.9: The figure shows the spatial distribution of a set of 20 agents. There is clustering around three centers.

but also a second language, an INTERLINGUA, which is weaker but shared among the different clusters. This interlingua will become stronger as more agents interact between clusters. Thus we observe language diversity due to the spatial distribution but at the same time the rise of an interlingua.

The following vocabularies illustrate this point clearly. The first vocabulary is taken from an agent from the leftmost cluster in Figure 5.9. All the words associated with a particular meaning are shown together with their score.

```
{}[M0]: kube[0.88] gutida[0.00] moko[0.00]
{}[M1]: nugini[0.97] gi[0.83] majiba[0.00]
{}[M2]: go[0.98] ta[0.00]
{}[M3]: moma[0.98] ti[0.00] nudo[0.00] kene[0.00]
{}[M4]: nebu[0.98] me[0.83]
{}[M5]: tine[0.98]

{}[M6]: bo[0.94] babige[0.82]
{}[M7]: mepabo[0.97] jabeto[0.71] di[0.00]
{}[M8]: kude[0.90] nado[0.00]
{}[M9]: pe[0.94] da[0.00]
{}[M10]: na[0.94] nuguge[0.90] pa[0.80] ne[0.00]

{}[M11]: mu[0.98] gite[0.00] paku[0.00]
{}[M12]: gema[0.96] do[0.33] gapu[0.00]
{}[M13]: ja[0.67] jo[0.00]
{}[M14]: dodine[0.88] pibo[0.83] gije[0.00] pupeto[0.00]
{}[M15]: jiti[0.94] gato[0.64]

{}[M16]: bimogu[0.98] ba[0.00]
{}[M17]: bapi[0.96] ki[0.81] damuti[1,0,0.00]
```

```
{}[M18]:  kutume [0.94]  bu [0.00]  ni[0.00]
{}[M19]:  mugu[0.95]  NINU[0.50]  pi[0.43]  ji[0.00]  tu[0.00]
```

This is the vocabulary for an agent taken from the rightmost cluster in Figure 5.9:

```
{}[M0]:   gutida[0.79]  kube[0.00]
{}[M1]:   gi[0.89]  matu[0.85]  pumoni[0.00]
{}[M2]:   go[0.95]  ta[0.20]
{}[M3]:   kene[0.89]  moma[0.82]  nudo[0.00]  koko[0.00]
{}[M4]:   nebu[0.97]  me[0.00]  bukugo[0.00]
{}[M5]:   tine[0.90]

{}[M6]:   babige[0.93]  bo[0.00]
{}[M7]:   mepabo[0.90]  junipe[0.75]  di[0.00]
{}[M8]:   nado[0.96]  kude[0.80]  puto[0.00]
{}[M9]:   da[0.86]  nine[0.71]
{}[M10]:  pa[0.87]

{}[M11]:  gite[0.88]
{}[M12]:  gema[0.90]  gapu[0.87]
{}[M13]:  jo[0.96]  ji[0.89]  ja[0.00]
{}[M14]:  dodine[0.96]  pupeto[0.56]  pibo[0.00]  gije[0.00]
{}[M15]:  jiti[0.97]  gato[0.46]

{}[M16]:  bimogu[0.97]  ba[0.83]  pipebe[0.00]
{}[M17]:  ki[0.97]  bapi[0.00]  ke[,0.00]
{}[M18]:  ni[0.94]  kutume[0.80]  moko[0.80]  mekami[0.00]
{}[M19]:  ninu[0.81]  mugu[0.00]  pi[0.00]
```

Some words (for example *tine* for [M5] or *go* for [M2]) are shared. But generally there are at least two words. One word is used preferentially inside the cluster, the other is known but preferentially used by members of another cluster. Thus the word *mugu* for [M19] is preferred for the first object in the first cluster and known but not preferentially used by the agent in the second cluster. Conversely, *ninu* is preferred for the same meaning by the agent in the second cluster, although he also knows *mugu*. *mepabo* for [M7] belongs to the interlingua. Both agents know and use it but they have a strong alternative *jabeto* for the first and *junipe* for the second agent.

5.4.2 Language contact

When the interaction factor increases, we see further differentiation because there is less communication between clusters. When it is decreased, we see more coherence because there is more intercluster communication. Thus we can effectively tune divergence or convergence in the simulations based on the probability of interaction between communities (clusters) of agents. The effect of increased language contact and hence convergence is demonstrated in Figure 5.10. The simulation starts from the situation described

5 The Naming Game

earlier with three clusters of agents that have each evolved a lexicon. The interaction between clusters is initially very weak. At some point (after 4000 games) the intercluster communication is increased drastically. At first there is a drop in communicative success but then total communicative success is again reached.

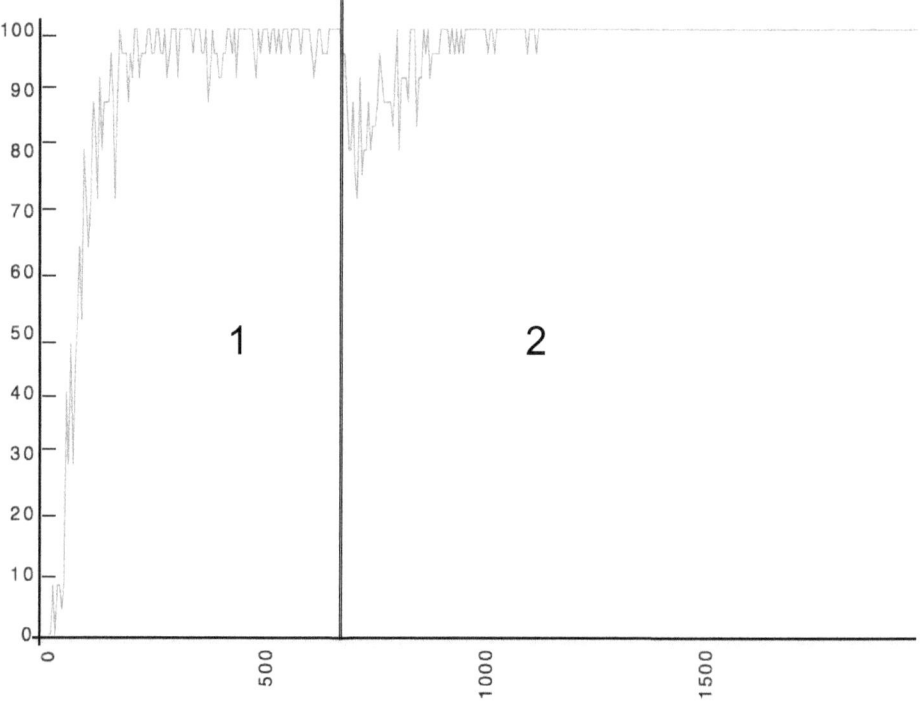

Figure 5.10: Evolution of average communicative success per 25 games in a group of agents with first weak (phase 1) and then strong interactions (phase 2).

However, this general evolution hides the more interesting developments. Figure 5.11 shows the evolution of coherence for each cluster (a, b, c) separately and also for the total set of agents. As long as the agents have relatively little contact, total coherence is low although the lexical coherence within each cluster is high. Total coherence starts to increase with increased contact. Coherence in each cluster diminishes somewhat because the agents in the cluster are in the process of accommodating to the global lexicon. This means that the languages of the different groups are in the process of merging due to the increased language contact.

Simulations show that, just as in human languages, increased contact causes at first a rapid increase in bilingualism, then a gradual mixing of the languages, and, if the contact continues, an evolution towards complete coherence. The more rapid the contact is increased, the faster the three phases can be observed.

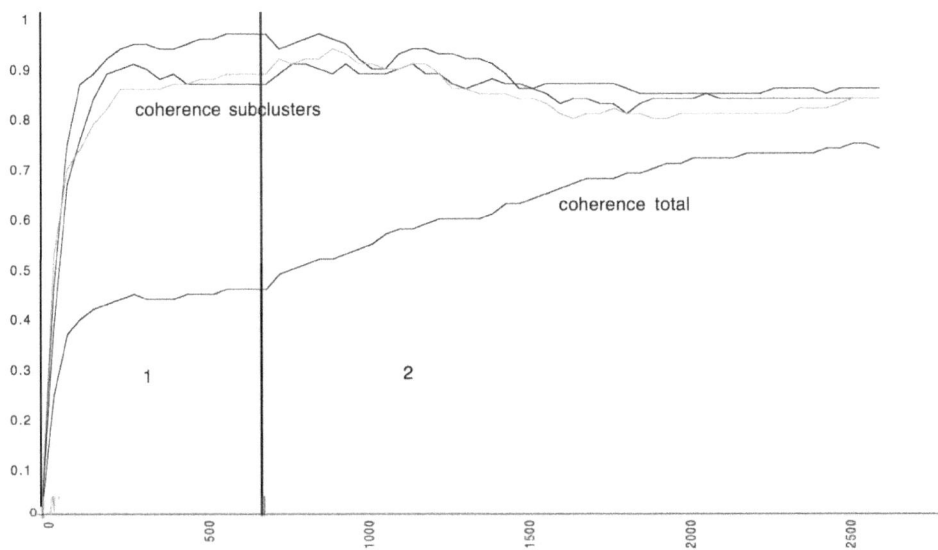

Figure 5.11: Evolution of coherence in the total population and in the individual clusters is shown on the same scale as the previous figure. When contact is increased (phase 2), global coherence begins to rise steadily.

5.5 Conclusions

A population of agents following a simple set of behaviour rules and using an associative memory can give rise to a shared repertoire of form-meaning associations, giving the agents a total average success in communication. Once a shared repertoire comes into existence, it locks into an equilibrium state and gets transmitted from one generation to the next in a cultural process, as long as the rate of population change is not too high. The population can also cope with an in- and outflux of meanings, in the sense that the lexicon constracts or expands in relation to the demands from an evolving set of possible meanings.

The mechanisms I have proposed here for the Naming Game are remarkable in many ways. It clearly shows that a shared set of conventions can arise without an omniscient central co-ordinator and without any prior knowledge of the lexicon built into the agents. The Naming Game also demonstrates a new way to model and thus investigate linguistic phenomena. Existing formal models of language, such as generative grammars, only model static competence of a single idealised speaker in a homogeneous language community. Using the framework of language games played by populations of agents, we can model the emergence and evolution of language in an inhomogeneous community and study language use as well as change through language contact.

5 The Naming Game

The Naming Game is a minimal model of communication between agents and far removed from the full complexity of human natural language. Moreover we made a number of simplifying assumptions, thus putting up scaffolds to construct this initial model. The most important assumption was that the meaning of a word can be unambiguously known by the speaker and hearer independently of language. This assumption is of course not valid for human beings, and neither is it valid for the Talking Heads.

6 The Guessing Game

The problem how a physically embodied situated agent might refer to objects using language is extraordinarily difficult. If we then further want to find out how a group of such agents might autonomously bootstrap a language system, the task seems almost unsurmountable. That is why I proposed earlier on to start by dividing this task into its three main subtasks along the lines of the semiotic square (Figure 6.1). The previous chapters each focused on one of these tasks. Chapter 5 has introduced perceptual mechanisms to process the raw image, segment the scene, derive characteristics about each segment, and give feedback by pointing to the referent. Chapter 4 studied categorisation mechanisms needed for conceptualising a scene and thus for generating the possible meanings of a verbal communication. Chapter 5 looked at how agents can lexicalise meanings and build up a sufficiently shared lexicon to engage in verbal interactions.

Given that we now have reasonable solutions for these basic processes, at least for its most simple instantiations, we can now start to put the pieces together and thus study the complete guessing game. I will proceed in two steps. First I will but the lexical layer and the conceptualisation layer together in this chapter, and then I will ground the whole system by coupling the conceptualisation layer to the perceptual layer in Chapter 7.

Another technique I proposed earlier on for handling the enormous challenges addressed in this book, is to scale up gradually. I will follow this strategy as well. In this chapter, I will assume that the referent and the perceived image are the same. This implies that we are really dealing with semiotic triangles as opposed to semiotic squares (Figure 6.1). I will start simulations with only 2 agents and then scale up to a larger number. This increases the degree of synonymy in the lexicon. I will furthermore start by letting the agents consider only the most salient channel, so that they much more easily guess the same category for the same scene. Then I will scale this up so that the agents now consider more sensory channels and hence more categories. This increases the degree of ambiguity in the lexicon. Both synonymy and ambiguity are sources of incoherence and we will have to make sure that agents still manage to be successful despite of these.

This chapter shows that agents still manage to bootstrap a shared lexicon due to carefully established feedback couplings between the different processing layers introduced in the previous chapters. The language game gives feedback to the lexical layer so that words become preferred that are understood by others. The lexical layer gives feedback to the conceptual layer so that categories become preferred that have been successfully lexicalised. Each layer is a selectionist system that generates possible ways to solve a subproblem, of which some are kept and others discarded based on feedback of their use. I will examine in this chapter whether these couplings indeed cause a coordination of

6 The Guessing Game

the different internal layers in a single agent and whether they lead to shared ontologies and lexicons.

6.1 Defining the Guessing Game

The guessing game was already introduced in Chapter 2. Here is a first example game, game 500. **a2** plays the role of speaker and **a1** the role of hearer. The game is about the scene in Figure 6.2. The topic is the rectangle labeled 1. The grayscale channel is the most salient channel. The different sensory values (after sensor-scaling) for the segments in Figure 6.2 are shown in Table 6.1. The last line shows the saliency of the topic segment 1. Clearly the grayscale channel is the most salient.

Table 6.1: Sensory data for the scene shown in Figure 6.2.

obj	HPOS	VPOS	HEIGHT	WIDTH	GRAY	AREA
0	0.66	0.95	0.01	0.71	0.19	0.27
1	0.69	0.83	0.07	0.33	0.97	0.21
2	0.99	0.87	0.54	0.72	0.22	0.57
saliency	0.03	0.05	0.07	0.39	0.75	0.06

All rectangles are relatively close to each other and have more or less the same height and width. But the grayscale is clearly the more salient because rectangle-1 is much darker than the others. I assume that there are only two agents in the population and that they always use only the most salient to conceptualise the scene. The speaker and hearer have to traverse only two sides of the semiotic square (Figure 6.1) because we assume that perceived image and object being referred to are identical for both agents.

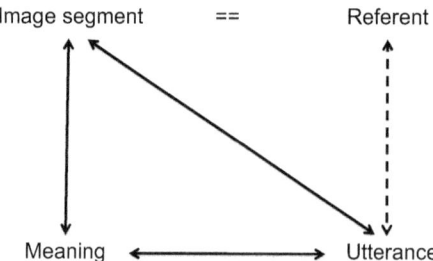

Figure 6.1: The semiotic square becomes a triangle when the perceived image and the referent in the real world are assumed to be identical.

6.1 Defining the Guessing Game

6.1.1 Example of a coupled game

The speaker first plays a Discrimination Game traversing the semantic side of the square going from the referent *rectangle-1* to a possible meaning [GRAY 0.5–1.0]. He then plays a Naming Game traversing the lexical side of of the square to find the word *pokuneso* for this chosen meaning. The hearer traverses the lexical side of the triangle in the other direction to interpret the word *pokuneso* as [GRAY 0.5–1.0], and then identifies the referent by filtering the objects in the context with this meaning. Only rectangle-1 remains, so the game succeeds. The whole game is reported by the commentator as follows:

```
Game 500
    a2 is the speaker. a1 is the hearer.
    a2 segments the context into 3 objects:
        rectangle-0 rectangle-1 rectangle-2
    a2 chooses rectangle-1 as the topic
    a2 categorises the topic as [GRAY 0.5-1.0]
    a2 says: pokuneso
    a1 interprets pokuneso as [GRAY 0.5-1.0]
    a1 points to rectangle-1
    a2 signals OK
```

The game is perfectly successful because both agents associate the word *okuneso* with [GRAY 0.5–1.0] (dark) and they perceive the scene in the same way.

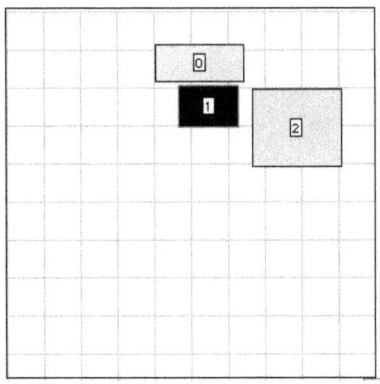

Figure 6.2: Example scene used in game 500.

Before examining the architecture behind these games in more detail, we can already see from Figure 6.4 that **a1** and **a2** clearly manage to build autonomously a communication system and its underlying ontology from scratch by playing the guessing game. The communicative success moves up to reach almost 100 % after a mere 500 games. Given that the environment keeps generating novel situations, there is always a chance that a scene occurs which requires new categories. So there is always a chance of failure, but it will further trigger expansion of the discrimination trees and of the lexicon.

6 *The Guessing Game*

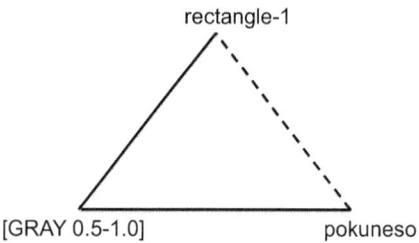

Figure 6.3: Semiotic triangle underlying game 500.

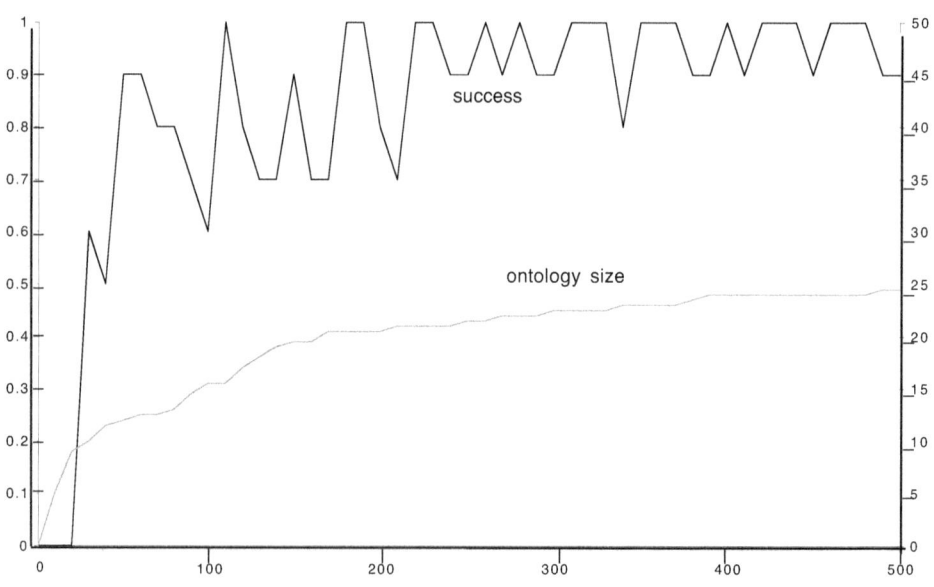

Figure 6.4: Success (left y-axis) and average ontology size (right y-axis) for two agents playing 500 guessing games.

6.1 Defining the Guessing Game

Figure 6.4 also shows the average number of categories in each agent. There is a steep rise in the early phases, when no categories exist, but then the creation of new categories levels off as discrimination mostly succeeds. When the environment becomes more complex, possibly exercising additional sensory channels, the discrimination trees would start to expand again, as we have seen in the previous chapter and then the lexicon would start to expand as well. Obviously the lexicon can only start to develop when there is an adequate ontology which explains some of the delay before the communicativesuccess curve starts to climb.

Table 6.2 displays the complete lexicon of the two agents after 100 games, together with the score for each assocation for **a1** and **a2**. Only associations where the score is above 0.0 for at least one agent are shown. A dash (-) indicates that the agent has not stored this association yet.

Table 6.2: Complete lexicon of **a1** and **a2** after 100 games

Meaning	Word	Translation	a1	a2
[HPOS 0.0–0.5]	vapola	left	-	0.1
[HPOS 0.5–1.0]	gonapa	right	0.1	-
[HEIGHT 0.0–0.5]	suwaxugo	short	0.6	0.8
[HEIGHT 0.5–1.0]	kusone	tall	0.4	0.5
[WIDTH 0.0–0.5]	bepupepa	narrow	0.1	0.1
[WIDTH 0.0–0.25]	kutaki	very narrow	-	0.1
[WIDTH 0.5–1.0]	zikorika	wide	0.0	0.3
[GRAY 0.0–0.5]	fesasado	light	0.5	0.7
[GRAY 0.5–1.0]	pokuneso	dark	0.8	0.9
[AREA 0.5–1.0]	mafanoda	large	0.1	0.1

We see that, at this point, the agents have lexicalised only the most general distinctions, such as 'dark' (*pokuneso*) versus 'light' (*fesasado*) or 'short' (*suwaxugo*) versus 'tall' (*kusone*). Words for the grayscale and height dimensions have the strongest scores, although this is purely accidental. When we would start another simulation from scratch, we would end up with different words and perhaps other distinctions would be more successful.

Table 6.3 is the complete lexicon after 500 games and Table 6.4 after 1000 games.

We see that words for basic distinctions have further established themselves. Words for 'short' (*suwaxugo*) and 'tall' (*kusone*), or 'light' (*fesasado*) and 'dark' (*pokuneso*) now have scores of 1.0. Words for more refined categories, like 'very short' (*tawube*) or 'very narrow' (*kutaki*), are beginning to establish themselves.

Two steps in the evolution of the discrimination trees underlying this lexicon are shown in Figure 6.5. There is a progressive refinement of all trees as time goes on, because all sensory channels have the same chance of being most salient. But the trees are

Table 6.3: Lexicon of **a1** and **a2** after 500 games

Meaning	Word	Translation	a1	a2
[HPOS 0.0–0.5]	vapola	left	0.7	1.0
[HPOS 0.5–1.0]	gonapa	right	0.6	0.5
[VPOS 0.0–0.5]	rixuzime	up	0.2	0.7
[VPOS 0.5–1.0]	gofugage	down	0.6	1.0
[HEIGHT 0.0–0.5]	suwaxugo	short	1.0	1.0
[HEIGHT 0.0–0.25]	tawube	very short	0.4	0.5
[HEIGHT 0.25–0.5]	narofi	medium short	0.1	0.4
[HEIGHT 0.5–1.0]	kusone	tall	1.0	1.0
[HEIGHT 0.5–0.75]	wuruzo	medium tall	0.3	0.6
[HEIGHT 0.75–1.0]	bowaluro	very tall	0.6	0.2

Table 6.4: Lexicon of **a1** and **a2** after 1000 games

Meaning	Word	Translation	a1	a2
[WIDTH 0.0–0.5]	bepupepa	narrow	1.0	1.0
[WIDTH 0.0–0.25]	kutaki	very narrow	0.1	0.5
[WIDTH 0.25–0.5]	wukogo	medium narrow	0.2	-
[WIDTH 0.5–1.0]	zikorika	wide	1.0	1.0
[WIDTH 0.5–0.75]	mitula	medium wide	0.1	-
[WIDTH 0.75–1.0]	wupixo	very wide	-	0.2
[GRAY 0.0–0.5]	fesasado	light	1.0	1.0
[GRAY 0.0–0.25]	sanize	very light	-	0.1
[GRAY 0.5–1.0]	pokuneso	dark	0.9	1.0
[GRAY 0.5–0.75]	wavosoru	medium dark	0.2	0.5
[GRAY 0.75–1.0]	kuragoni	very dark	0.3	0.2
[AREA 0.0–0.5]	babifewa	small	-	0.1
[AREA 0.25–0.5]	togule	medium small	0.1	0.1
[AREA 0.5–1.0]	mafanoda	large	0.2	0.5

6.1 Defining the Guessing Game

not the same for the two agents at every stage of development because even though they prefer to expand the salient channel, the agents have encountered different environmental situations in which different channels were salient. For example, after 100 games, a1 has less refinements for the WIDTH channel than a2. After 500 games, all trees have at least one level of refinement. Not all categories have been lexicalised. For example, the WIDTH channel is three levels deep in both agents but no words exist yet for the deepest level.

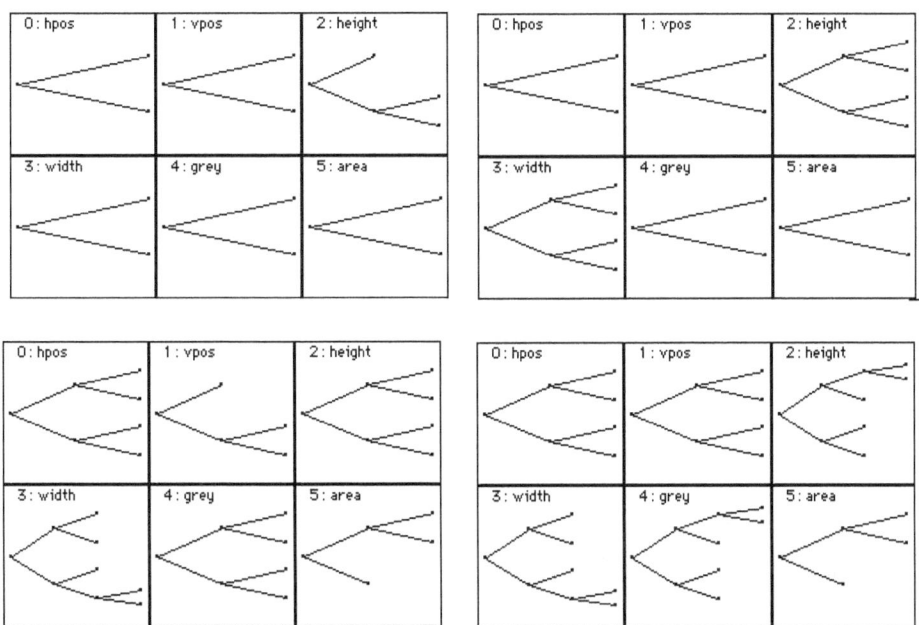

Figure 6.5: Evolution of the discrimination trees of **a1** (left) and **a2** (right). Snapshots have been taken after 100 games (top) and 500 games (bottom).

Note that this simulation is very different from the ones shown in the previous chapter. The agents now get only feedback through overt selection of the referent. The hearer points to the identified referent and the speaker decides on the outcome of the game based on this non-verbal information, but speaker and hearer do not know whether they have used the same meaning or not. Very often there are alternative ways to conceptualise reality, so even if agents would have completely shared ontologies, there is still the possibility of guessing the wrong meaning. I have called this the gavagai-problem, inspired by the philosopher Quine, who tells the story of the anthropologist puzzled by the word *gavagai* uttered by a native in an undecoded language. Does *gavagai* mean rabit, animal scurrying by, the direction in which I will go now, or white furry object? The child who is acquiring a lexicon has exactly the same problem. It explains why overex-

6 The Guessing Game

tensions or underextensions are seen in a child's first words. For example, the word for orange is applied to any small circular round object, including a ball, or a doorknob.

6.1.2 Input-output coupling

Obviously the first thing I had to do to get these results, is make the inputs of one layer the outputs of the other (Figure 6.6). When the speaker has conceptualised the scene, the possible solutions enter the lexical layer for lexicon lookup. The resulting words get into a competition and the one with the highest score wins. In a more complete system with a syntactic layer, different lexicalisations would be considered by the syntactic layer to find the one that fits with the rest of the grammatical structure.

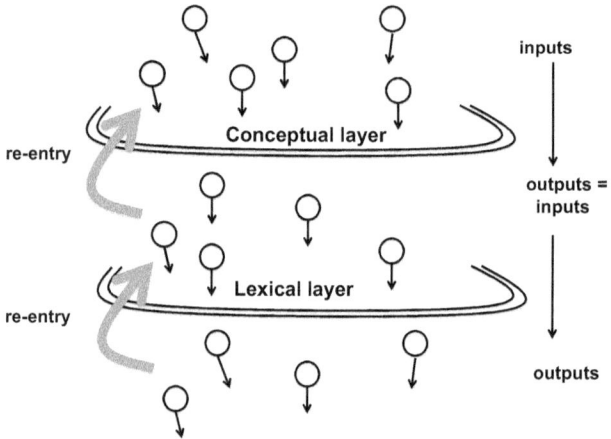

Figure 6.6: Flow of solutions through coupled layers from perception to conceptualisation and lexicalisation with re-entry links between them.

The importance of having re-entry links now becomes clear. The choice which conceptualisation is finally chosen as the best one will depend on the lexical layer because the speaker should prefer those categories whose lexicalisation is best established, if he wants to maximise success in the game. Due to the constant evolution of the lexicon and the presence of synonyms, the conceptual layer cannot know once and for all what the most appropriate conceptualisation from the viewpoint of language will be. And it needs to know the outcome of the lexical layer to later update the scores of participating categorisers.

The hearer uses the same layers but now with solutions flowing in the other direction. He gets a set of words which generate possible conceptualisations through lexicon lookup and these then are applied to the scene to find the referent (Figure 6.7). Because layers have this dual mode of operations, it is perfectly possible that the hearer has already guessed words and thus strong expectations based on the scene and his own conceptualisation of it, although this has not been implemented in the Talking Heads yet.

6.1 Defining the Guessing Game

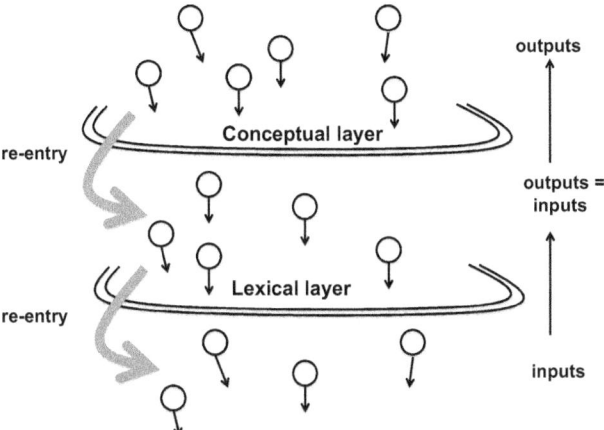

Figure 6.7: Layers operate in two directions. The flow of solutions in the hearer is shown from words to categories and perceptions and in the other direction through re-entry.

Also for the hearer, the re-entrant flow is important. A hearer can only know which meaning was intended for a particular word after trying out the meaning on the scene. He therefore uses the context to determine the meaning of the utterance. For example, a particular word may mean both [LARGE] and [DARK], particularly during the phase of early language acquisition. However if only one of these categories picks out a single referent, it is chosen as the meaning, and the hearer will act upon this choice by pointing to the object it singles out from the scene.

This architecture takes care of synonymy and ambiguity and makes sure that the most plausible form/meaning/referent chain stands out. A similar architecture may explain how humans effortlessly pick out the appropriate meanings from the many possible meanings a word typically has and not even be aware of the alternatives. If our language sytems could not cope this way with ambiguity and ambiguity we would have had to use a lexicon where every word can have only a single meaning. Language has had to recruit whatever capacity was already available.

6.1.3 Updating the scores

The next thing I had to do is reconsider the score updating mechanisms, even though they are basically the same as used earlier (Figure 6.8). For a given referent, there are multiple meanings possible (in case more than one channel is considered to be sufficiently salient), and for each meaning there are multiple words. The best one of this whole lot is chosen by the speaker and used for the utterance transmitted to the hearer. We have seen that it is important for the hearer to use lateral inhibition based on the outcome of a game. But although the speaker is considering *all* the possible conceptualisations, lateral inhibition should only take place between the lexicalisations of the meaning that was finally chosen.

6 The Guessing Game

So when the game was successful, the speaker increases the association that was used with δ and decreases all the other associations *with the same meaning*. delta is still set to a reasonable low value, namely *delta* = 0.1. The hearer does the same as explained earlier in the Naming Game. The score of all the alternative meanings for the word (or words) that are used by the speaker are decreased. When the game fails, both the speaker and the hearer decrease the association that they used with δ. No change takes place to the scores of any of the other associations.

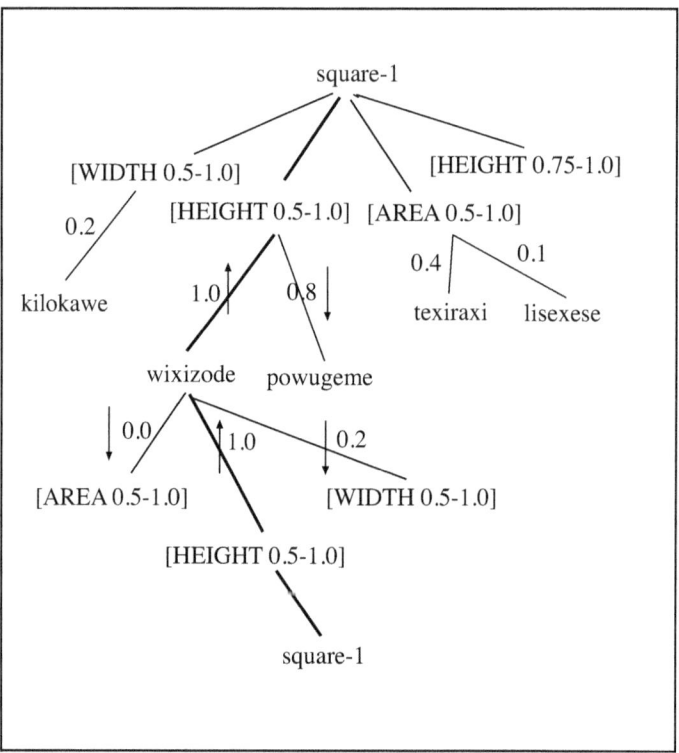

Figure 6.8: Score adjustments after a successful game. Used associations go up and competing associations go down. The game producing these relationships is discussed later as game 10008.

The scores of the categories and category combinations in the discrimination trees should also be updated. When a category or category combination is used as part of the communication in the game (as meaning for the speaker or the hearer), its use counter goes up. When the game is successful, its success counter goes up. To know the score of a particular category or category-set, the agent simply divides success by use. Because the score of the categories thus depends on their success in the language game, a strong co-ordination gradually arises between conceptualisation and lexicalisations. After a while, categorisations will be preferred that are amenable to yield successful language games and of course the language only lexicalises categories that are nodes in discrimination trees. We thus get a progressive coordination of both the repertoire of categories and the lexicon, as I will discuss in more detail later.

The other criteria discussed earlier (simplicity of the categories and level of depth in the tree) are still used for ranking the possible conceptualisations coming out of the lexicon, particularly when none of the meanings has been lexicalised yet or whether there are multiple possibilities. The human brain is clearly capable to integrate many more criteria in lexical choice. For example, when talking to a child we might use more common words than we would use when talking to another adult.

6.1.4 Repair processes

Of course the other repair processes discussed earlier are still going on as well. Agents expand their discrimination trees when they fail to categorise and they invent new words or adopt words from the other if necessary. The task is more complicated compared to the simple Naming Game because the hearer now gets no direct feedback of the meaning only of the referent. In case of failure, the hearer must try to find himself a distinctive category or category set discriminating the referent from the other objects in the context.

Here is an example game illustrating this type of repair process. The data for game 77 (after sensor-scaling) is shown in Table 6.5.

Table 6.5: Sensory data for game 77 after sensor-scaling.

Obj	Hpos	Vpos	Height	Width	Gray	Area
0	0.51	0.98	0.90	0.47	0.79	0.60
1	0.75	0.68	0.26	0.09	0.14	0.20
2	0.76	0.54	0.56	0.26	0.94	0.36

The speaker is again a2. HEIGHT is the most salient channel. a2 has a word for [HEIGHT 0.75–1.0] (very tall), namely *bowaluro*, and uses it. The hearer a1 does not know the word, conceptualises the scene, and arrives at the same category, so the hearer stores the new word with the same meaning as the speaker.

```
Game 77
    a2 is the speaker. a1 is the hearer.
    a2 segments the context into 3 objects:
        rectangle-0 rectangle-1 rectangle-2
    a2 chooses rectangle-1 as the topic
    a2 categorises the topic as [HEIGHT 0.75-1.0]
    a2 says: 'bowaluro'
    a1 does not know 'bowaluro'
    a1 says: 'bowaluro?'
```

6 The Guessing Game

```
a2 points to rectangle-1
a1 categorises the topic as [HEIGHT 0.75-1.0]
a1 stores 'bowaluro' as [HEIGHT 0.75-1.0]
```

The reason why **a1** has guessed the right meaning of *bowaluro* is because both agents use only the most salient channel and they both share the same perception of reality. We will soon see that if these constraints are not valid, agents are not always so lucky and hence multiple meanings start to circulate for the same word.

A similar repair action takes place when the hearer cannot guess a unique referent, as illustrated in game 96 drawn from the same simulation series. The scene contains three rectangles and the topic is the most narrow rectangle. The segments in the scene of game 279 have the characteristics (after sensor-scaling) shown in Table 6.6.

Table 6.6: Sensory data for game 279

Obj	Hpos	Vpos	Height	Width	Gray	Area
0	0.51	0.71	0.64	0.61	0.80	0.56
1	0.51	0.91	0.53	0.41	0.42	0.41

The hearer guessed the meaning used by the speaker right away, because both share the same perception and both use the most salient channel as basis for categorisation.

```
Game 96
  a1 is the speaker. a2 is the hearer.
  a1 segments the context into 3 objects:
      rectangle-0 rectangle-1 rectangle-2
  a1 chooses rectangle-1 as the topic
  a1 categorises the topic as [WIDTH 0.0-0.25]
  a1 creates a new word: 'kutaki'
  a1 says: 'kutaki'
  a2 does not find a unique referent
  a2 says: 'kutaki?'
  a1 points to rectangle-1
  a2 categorises the topic as [WIDTH 0.0-0.25]
  a2 stores 'kutaki' as [WIDTH 0.0-0.25]
```

6.2 Synonymy

When we scale up the population, synonyms (several words for the same meaning) will start to appear. Indeed, when there are only two agents, the hearer picks up a word as soon as the speaker has created it. With a larger group, it is much more likely that agents

6.2 Synonymy

create words not knowing that words already exist in the population, and it takes time for a new word to propagate.

Synonyms are not a positive feature of a language. They make it less efficient for the speaker to find the most appropriate word to express a meaning, they require more memory to store the lexicon, and confuse a new virgin agent coming into the group. In natural languages, synonyms get damped and we have seen in the previous chapter that the positive feedback loop between use and success (implemented by lateral inhibition in the agent's score updating process) has the same effect. Let us now see whether this is still the case if the hearer does not get any feedback about the meaning used.

The following simulation uses a group of ten agents. Each agent still only uses the most salient channel so that the agents can guess the meaning easily in case a word is not known. The evolution of communicative success for a series of 4000 games, which means about 800 games per agent, is shown in Figure 6.9. An effective lexicon and ontology is emerging because we see communicative success rise.

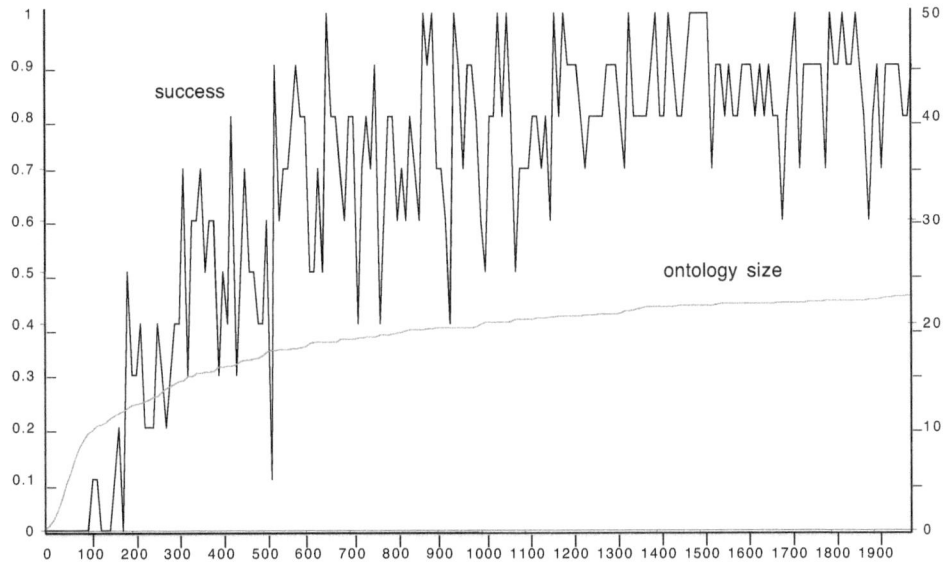

Figure 6.9: Communicative success (left y-axis) and average ontology size (right y-axis) is shown for a series of 4000 language games played by 10 agents.

Part of the lexicons of five of the ten agents after 2000 games (only those words which have positive scores) are shown in the Table 6.7. We see that synonymy does indeed occur. For example, two words are in the running for [HPOS 0.5–1.0]: *rutaxese* and *xomupovi*, and three for [VPOS 0.5–1.0]: *wavone*, *zaxawe*, and *dazofo*. Some words are already well established, for example *numefuli* for [GRAY 0.5–1.0] (dark).

145

6 The Guessing Game

Table 6.7: Lexicon of five agents after 2000 games.

Meaning	Word	a1	a2	a3	a4	a5
[HPOS 0.5–1.0]	rutaxese		0.1			
	xomupovi	0.1		0.2		0.1
[VPOS 0.5–1.0]	wavone			0.3		
	zaxawe				0.1	
	dazofo	0.1			0.2	
[WIDTH 0.0–0.5]	buxevo					
	vubupo	1.0	0.6	1.0	0.1	1.0
[WIDTH 0.5–1.0]	pawixona			0.1		
	rikepule	1.0	0.8	1.0	1.0	1.0
[WIDTH 0.5–0.75]	gowinoge			0.1		
	wesurodi				0.2	
[WIDTH 0.75–1.0]	besabi			0.2		
	lituvi	0.1				
[GRAY 0.5–0.75]	goxomixe		0.1			
	korufo				0.2	
[GRAY 0.0–0.5]	numefuli	1.0	0.7	1.0	1.0	1.0
[GRAY 0.0–0.25]	rekemaxi	0.2				
[GRAY 0.5–1.0]	faluleru	0.6	0.6	1.0	1.0	1.0
	nupanu					0.2

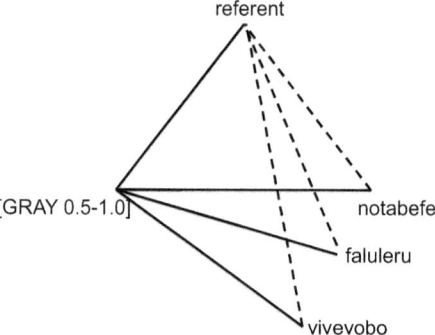

Figure 6.10: In the case of synonymy, there are multiple words for the same meaning and hence the same referent.

6.2 Synonymy

The positive feedback loop between use and success has already dampened some synonyms. For some cases, like [GRAY 0.5–1.0] the competition has died out with one word *faluleru* being the winner. For others, like [HPOS 0.5–1.0], the competition is still going on, although we can guess that *xomupovi* is probably going to be the winner.

It is instructive to follow the history of the words in use for a particular meaning. For example, let us look at the words for [GRAY 0.5–1.0] (dark) in the very early phases of lexicon development. Three different words are quickly created, and *faluleru* is the first one that has some success.

```
Game 76
  Speaker a4 creates 'notabefe' for [GRAY 0.5-1.0]
  Hearer a5 adopts 'notabefe' for [GRAY 0.5-1.0]
Game 79
  Speaker a2 creates 'vivevobo' for [GRAY 0.5-1.0]
  Hearer a7 does not adopt 'vivebo'
      (failed to discriminate)
Game 88
  Speaker a7 creates 'faluleru' for [GRAY 0.5-1.0]
  Hearer a4 adopts 'faluleru' for [GRAY 0.5-1.0]
Game 100
  Speaker a7 uses 'faluleru' for [GRAY 0.5-1.0]
  Hearer a4 correctly interprets 'faluleru'
```

The semiotic triangles existing at this point in the population are summarised in Figure 6.10. Agent **a4** is now already in a dilemma because he has created *notabefe* and picked up *faluleru* from a7.

With a lower word creation rate (w_c), fewer new words would be created. The initial bootstrapping of the lexicon would then take a bit longer but the process of weeding out synonymy would be shorter. With a lower word adoption rate (w_a), agents are less inclined to adopt a word and that again diminishes the chance that new words spread, if words already exist for the same meaning. But even with high word creation and word adoption rates, the whole system stabilises automatically. The stronger a lexicon is already in place, the fewer new synonyms arise because new words created by virgin agents entering the population have hardly any chance to propagate.

Note that the word creation rate can never be completely zero because then the agents would no longer be able to handle new meanings. The word adoption rate can never be equal to zero either because then new words cannot spread in the population and there would be a high chance that the lexicon does not become coherent with subgroups getting stuck with different words for the same meaning.

Because there are synonyms, agents must now choose which word to use. The one with the highest score should clearly be preferred because based on the evidence the agent has gathered so far, this gives the highest chance of success in the game. **a4** is faced with this kind of choice in the next game in the series involving the meaning [GRAY 0.5–1.0]. **a4** chooses *faluleru* because this word has the highest score. It is immediately picked up by **a1**:

6 The Guessing Game

```
Game 101
  a4 is the speaker. a1 is the hearer.
  a4 segments the context into 2 objects:
      rectangle-0 rectangle-1
  a4 chooses rectangle-1 as the topic
  a4 categorises the topic as [GRAY 0.5-1.0]
  a4 has two words for [GRAY 0.5-1.0]:
      'faluleru' (0.20)
      'notabefe' (0.00)
  a4 says: 'faluleru'
  a1 does not know 'faluleru'
  a1 says: 'faluleru?'
  a4 points to rectangle-1
  a1 categorises the topic as [GRAY 0.5-1.0]
  a1 stores 'faluleru' as [GRAY 0.5-1.0]
```

After this game, three agents "know" the word *faluleru* for [GRAY 0.5–1.0]: **a4**, **a1**, and **a7**. When we continue to inspect the simulation we see that *notabefe* takes a bit of a revenge. The next games with the meaning [GRAY 0.5–1.0] all involve the word *notabefe*:

```
Game 111
  Speaker a5 uses 'notabefe' for [GRAY 0.5-1.0]
  Hearer a4 correctly interprets 'notabefe'
Game 113
  Speaker a4 uses 'notabefe' for [GRAY 0.5-1.0]
  Hearer a9 adopts 'notabefe' for [GRAY 0.5-1.0]
Game 127
  Speaker a9 uses 'notabefe' for [GRAY 0.5-1.0]
  Hearer a6 adopts 'notabefe' for [GRAY 0.5-1.0]
```

But then there is another occurrence of *faluleru*:

```
Game 135
  Speaker a1 uses 'faluleru' for [GRAY 0.5-1.0]
  Hearer a2 adopts 'faluleru' for [GRAY 0.5-1.0]
```

And now **a6**, which has not been involved yet in any interaction concerning the meaning [GRAY 0.5–1.0], further confuses the situation by creating a new word, *sopine*, which a5, playing the role of hearer, adopts.

```
Game 140
  Speaker a6 creates 'sopine' for [GRAY 0.5-1.0]
  Hearer a5 adopts 'sopine' for [GRAY 0.5-1.0]
```

This kind of evolution continues with a struggle between *notabefe* and *faluleru*. The agents know both words so the games do not fail. But *faluleru*, just by chance, starts to occur a bit more often which causes its score to go up a bit more. This results in *faluleru* being used even more, and, due to lateral inhibition, *notabefe* used less. Gradually *faluleru* dominates for the whole population. After 2000 games, the competitors to *faluleru* have all disappeared from the group lexicon.

6.3 Ambiguity

We now continue in small steps to scale up the challenge to the agents by progressively adding more realism to the simulation. So far I assumed that agents use only the most salient channel for categorising the topic and that their perception of the world is identical. Consequently a hearer can guess with 100 % success the meaning of an unknown word and it is therefore no wonder that the agents arrive at a shared communication system, even though neither the lexicon nor the repertoire of categories has been supplied in advance by a designer nor their development centrally coordinated. The main problem for them so far is the rise of synonyms which need to be damped to increase the probability of successful and efficient communication.

I now relax the saliency assumption. When there is a lower saliency threshold, more than one sensory channel is considered by the conceptual layer, possibly leading to several alternative conceptualisations of the scene. The question is then whether the agents are still able to reach a shared communication system despite the unavoidable word ambiguities that this generates.

We begin again by looking at simulations with two agents so that we can clearly see the impact of multiple conceptualisations. The architecture of the agents has not changed, I only lowered the saliency threshold. The scenes have become a bit more complex as well. They now not only contain rectangles but also squares, circles, and triangles. This has a limited impact because the same sensory channels are used as before and none of them is really sensitive to shape properties.

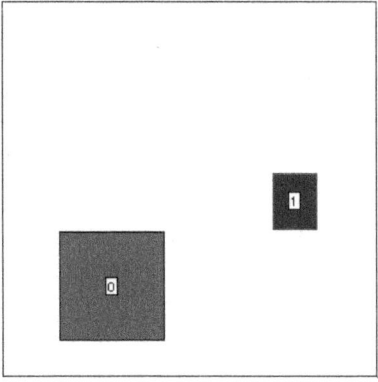

Figure 6.11: Scene used in game 3.

6 The Guessing Game

6.3.1 How words may still get the same meaning

When inspecting the simulation results, we see first of all that we may still accidentally get the same situation as before, i.e. one where the hearer selects the same channel as the speaker for conceptualising the scene, even though several channels are salient. This happens in the following game which involves a scene with a rectangle and a square (Figure 6.11).

The data for game 3, after sensor-scaling, are shown in Table 6.8.

Table 6.8: Sensory data for game 3 after scaling.

Obj	Hpos	Vpos	Height	Width	Gray	Area
0	0.37	0.44	0.92	0.92	0.69	0.10
1	0.98	0.55	0.25	0.11	0.78	0.88

Values for VPOS and GRAY are very close so they are not considered as sufficiently salient.

```
Game 3
   a1 is the speaker. a2 is the hearer.
   a1 segments the context into 2 objects:
       square-0 rectangle-1
   a1 chooses rectangle-1 as the topic
   a1 considers as salient AREA WIDTH HEIGHT HPOS
   a1 categorises the topic as [HEIGHT 0.0-0.5]
   a2 creates a new word: \smplenquote{mibati}
   a1 says: 'mibati'
   a2 does not know 'mibati'
   a2 says: 'mibati?'
   a1 points to rectangle-1
   a1 considers as salient AREA WIDTH HEIGHT HPOS
   a1 categorises the topic as [HEIGHT 0.0-0.5]
   a1 stores 'mibati' as [HEIGHT 0.0-0.5]
```

[HEIGHT 0.0–0.5] has been chosen by the speaker because HEIGHT was one of the salient channels (even though clearly not the only salient one) and because a successful distinction already existed in the ontology. The same distinction was chosen by chance by the hearer, but he could just as well have chosen a distinction based on the AREA, WIDTH or HPOS.

In the next game of the simulation series, *mibati* is used again, now by a2 as speaker. It is based on a scene with a triangle and a rectangle. The data for game 4 are shown in Table 6.9 (after scaling).

6.3 Ambiguity

Table 6.9: Lexicon of a1 and a2 after 500 games.

obj	HPOS	VPOS	HEIGHT	WIDTH	GRAY	AREA
0	0.47	0.23	0.90	0.83	0.49	0.34
1	0.21	0.22	0.67	0.79	0.86	0.63

The rectangle is chosen as topic. Two alternative categories can be used by a2 (and are listed by the commentator) but the one preferred is the one with the strongest lexicalisation, which is *mibati*.

```
Game 4
  a2 is the speaker. a1 is the hearer.
  a2 segments the context into 2 objects:
      triangle-0 rectangle-1
  a2 chooses rectangle-1 as the topic
  a2 considers as salient AREA GRAY HEIGHT HPOS
  a2 categorises the topic as [HEIGHT 0.0-0.5]
{}[GRAY 0.5-1.0]
  a2 has the word
      mibati for [HEIGHT 0.0-0.5] (1.0)
  a2 says: 'mibati'
  a1 interprets 'mibati' as [HEIGHT 0.0-0.5]
  a1 points to rectangle-1
  a2 signals OK
```

This example illustrates two points. First of all the language interpretation process influences which conceptualisation of the scene is preferred. For the speaker, both [HEIGHT 0.0–0.5] (short) and [GRAY 0.5–1.0] (dark) are possible ways to distinguish the topic from the other objects in the context. But [HEIGHT 0.0–0.5] is chosen because its lexicalisation has a higher score. Second, we begin to see why agents will manage to coordinate their ontologies, even though they do not have any direct feedback about each other's internal structures. The score of [HEIGHT 0.0–0.5] goes up after this game and if the agent has to choose a category later purely based on the score of the categories themselves, [HEIGHT 0.0–0.5] will be the one being preferred. Unless [GRAY 0.5–1.0] manages to become successfully lexicalised itself, it even risks to get pruned away.

6.3.2 How words get different meanings

Here is an example where ambiguity slips in the lexicon. The game involves two objects: a rectangle and a square (Figure 6.12). The data for game 9, after sensor-scaling, are shown in Table 6.10.

The discrimination trees of the two agents at this point are shown in Figure 6.13. The speaker uses a distinction based on the VPOS channel namely [VPOS 0.5–1.0] (top), cre-

6 The Guessing Game

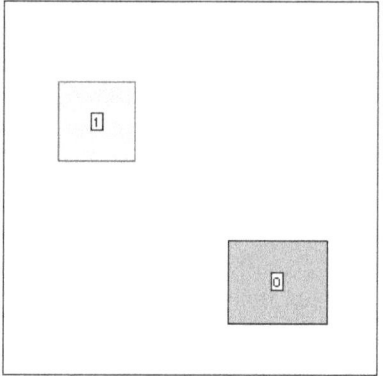

Figure 6.12: Scene used in game 9. Square-1 is the topic. Several conceptualisations are possible so the agents get divergent meanings.

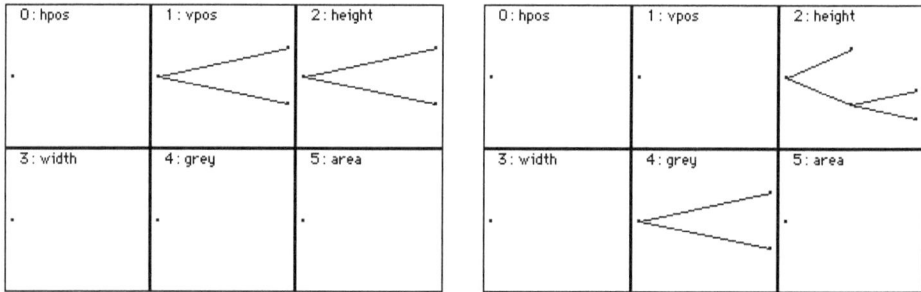

Figure 6.13: Discrimination trees of speaker a1 (left) and hearer a2 (right) available in game 9

Table 6.10: Data for game 9 after sensor-scaling.

obj	HPOS	VPOS	HEIGHT	WIDTH	GRAY	AREA
0	0.92	0.38	0.59	0.83	0.36	0.61
1	0.32	0.88	0.54	0.54	0.12	0.42

ates a word for it *puxazi*, and transmits this to the hearer. The hearer does not know the word, conceptualises the scene based on this non-verbal hint from the speaker, and identifies the category [GRAY 0.0–0.5] (light) as distinctive. So this meaning is stored and it is different from the one used by speaker. The current constellation of meanings is summarised in Figure 6.14.

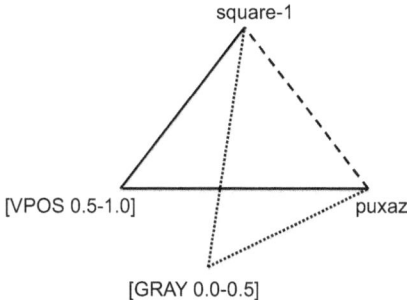

Figure 6.14: Semiotic triangles underlying game 9. For the same referent and the same word, there are two different meanings. Dashed lines indicate the relations used by the speaker a2. Straight lines indicate those used by the hearer a1.

```
Game 9
  a1 is the speaker. a2 is the hearer.
  a1 segments the context into 2 objects:
      rectangle-0 square-1
  a1 chooses square-1 as the topic
  a1 considers as salient GRAY WIDTH VPOS HPOS
  a1 categorises the topic as [VPOS 0.5-1.0]
  a2 creates a new word: 'puxazi'
  a1 says: 'puxazi'
  a2 does not know 'puxazi'
  a2 says: 'puxazi?'
  a1 points to square-1
  a2 considers as salient GRAY WIDTH VPOS HPOS
  a2 categorises the topic as [GRAY 0.0-0.5]
  a2 stores 'puxazi' as [GRAY 0.0-0.5]
```

A subsequent game (game 11) illustrates that despite semantic incoherence, a game can still succeed. The agents do not know that each of them means something else by *puxazi* and if the meanings are compatible, they have no reason to change their internal lexicon:

6 The Guessing Game

```
Game 11
  a2 is the speaker. a1 is the hearer.
  a2 segments the context into 3 objects:
      circle-0 rectangle-1
  a2 chooses rectangle-1 as the topic
  a2 considers as salient AREA GRAY WIDTH HPOS
  a2 categorises the topic as [GRAY 0.0-0.5]
  a2 says: 'puxazi'
  a1 interprets 'puxazi' as [VPOS 0.5-1.0]
  a1 points to rectangle-1
  a2 signals OK
```

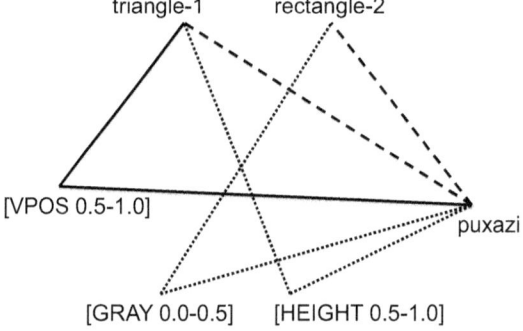

Figure 6.15: Semiotic triangles used in game 14. Dashed lines are the relations used by the hearer a2. Straight lines those of the speaker a1. After this game, a1 adopts yet another meaning for *puxazi*, namely [HEIGHT 0.5–1.0].

Here is next a game (game 14) where a2 comes to adopt the other meaning of *puxazi*, because the first meaning does not work in the present context. The game involves three objects: two rectangles and a triangle (Figure 6.16). The data for game 14, before context scaling, are shown in Table 6.11.

Table 6.11: Sensory data for game 14 after scaling.

obj	HPOS	VPOS	HEIGHT	WIDTH	GRAY	AREA
0	0.60	0.49	0.12	0.09	0.78	0.06
1	0.95	0.71	0.51	0.60	0.07	0.15
2	0.29	0.31	0.29	0.65	0.03	0.33

6.3 Ambiguity

a1 conceptualises the scene using [vpos 0.5–1.0], which he has lexicalised as *puxazi*. For a2, *puxazi* means [gray 0.0–0.5] (light), but this meaning identifies both rectangle-2 and triangle-1 (Figure 6.15). The game therefore fails and the speaker points to the topic. The hearer conceptualises the scene based on this non-verbal hint from the speaker using the HEIGHT dimension and adopts this as the second meaning of *puxaxi*.

```
Game 14
   a1 is the speaker. a2 is the hearer.
   a1 segments the context into 3 objects:
       rectangle-0 triangle-1 rectangle-2
   a1 chooses triangle-1 as the topic
   a1 considers as salient HEIGHT VPOS HPOS
   a1 categorises the topic as
{}[VPOS 0.5-1.0] [HEIGHT 0.5-1.0]
   a1 says: 'puxazi'
   a2 interprets 'puxazi' as [GRAY 0.0-0.5]
   a2 identifies rectangle-2 triangle-1
   a2 says: 'puxazi?'
   a1 points to triangle-1
   a2 considers as salient HEIGHT VPOS HPOS
   a2 categorises the topic as [HEIGHT 0.5-1.0]
   a2 stores 'puxazi' as [HEIGHT 0.5-1.0]
```

Note that the hearer could in principle also have categorised the scene using vpos and hpos, because they are equally salient. So there was absolutely no guarantee that *puxazi* would have been associated with [height 0.5–1.0] by a2. Moreover a2 stores an association between *puxazi* and [height 0.5–1.0], even though there is already another word for [height 0.5–1.0] in his lexicon. The fact that several meanings are possible to distinguish the topic in a given context has not only the consequence that ambiguity arises but also that synonyms may enter into the lexicon, even with only two agents!

6.3.3 Competition between word meanings

Once a word has more than one meaning (ambiguity), and once several words exist for the same meaning (synonymy), a struggle between word-meaning pairs sharing the same word or the same meaning develops. The lateral inhibition carried out by the speaker in case of a successful game pushes down alternative lexicalisations for the same meaning, thus damping synonyms, and the lateral inhibition carried out by the hearer pushes down alternative meanings for the same word, thus damping ambiguity.

Game 25 illustrates this effect of lateral inhibition. The situation before the game is as depicted in Figure 6.17. Two words (with different meanings) are competing in a2 to identify the referent: *puxazi* (meaning [gray 0.0–0.5], i.e. light) and *torigusu* (meaning [vpos 0.0–0.5], i.e. lower). *puxazi* has a higher score and wins the competition. Because the game was successful, the score of *puxazi* goes up. The score of *torigusu* does not

6 The Guessing Game

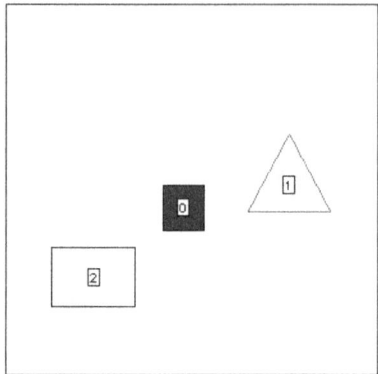

Figure 6.16: Scene used in game 14. Synonymy arises because the hearer conceptualises the scene differently from the speaker.

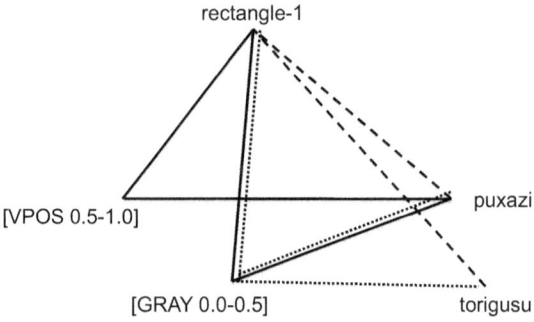

Figure 6.17: Semiotic triangles used in game 25. The score of the relation between [GRAY 0.0–0.5] and *puxazi* is increased in both agents. The relation between *puxazi* and [GRAY 0.0–0.5] gets damped.

change because it concerns another meaning. Two meanings for *puxazi* are competing in a1: [GRAY 0.0–0.5] (light) and [VPOS 0.0–0.5] (down). [VPOS 0.0–0.5] gets damped and the score of [GRAY 0.0–0.5] goes up, thus helping to further disambiguate *puxazi*.

```
Game 25
    a2 is the speaker. a1 is the hearer.
    a2 segments the context into 2 objects:
        rectangle-0 rectangle-1
    a2 chooses rectangle-1 as the topic
    a2 considers as salient GRAY VPOS
    a2 categorises the topic as [VPOS 0.0-0.5]
{}[GRAY 0.0-0.5] [GRAY 0.0-0.25]
    a2 has the words
```

156

```
            puxazi   for [GRAY 0.0-0.5] (0.20)
            torigusu for [VPOS 0.0-0.5] (0.0)
     a2 says: 'puxazi'
     a1 interprets 'puxazi' as
{}[GRAY 0.0-0.5] (0.20)
{}[VPOS 0.0-0.5] (0.0)
     a1 points to rectangle-1
     a2 signals OK
```

After this game, the association between [GRAY 0.0–0.5] and *puxazi* will have a score of 0.3 in both agents. The association between *puxazi* and [VPOS 0.0–0.5] in the hearer is decreased, but because it was already 0.0, it cannot decrease further.

Note that the speaker not only conceptualises the scene using the most generic distinctions ([GRAY 0.0–0.5], [VPOS 0.0–0.5]) but also with more specific ones ([GRAY 0.0–0.25]). Indeed it may happen that there is no word for a more generic distinction, but there is one for a more specific one, in which case it should be used. So, all discriminative distinctions, whatever their level of detail, are transmitted from the categorisation layer to the lexical layer and it is up to the lexical layer to choose. Of course, everything else being equal, other criteria are still important. If there is a more abstract category (meaning one higher in the discrimination tree) it is preferred over a more specific one if they have equal lexical scores.

6.3.4 Lexical and ontological development

Despite additional complication of mutually compatible meanings for unknown words, the two agents nevertheless manage to build up a shared communication system, as can be seen from Figure 6.18. Each time the ontology is extended, communicative success dips because a new word needs to be acquired, but the agents clearly manage to become successful in the guessing game.

Success does not mean that the lexicons are completely identical. As we have seen in game 11, it is possible to have communicative success with different meanings for the same word as long as the different meanings pick out the same referent. Of course in the domain of the GEOM world, it is a pure coincidence that two categories pick out the same referent and therefore alternative meanings for the same word will get damped. However, if there are more regularities, ambiguity persists much longer. In fact, ambiguity may persist in natural languages if the different meanings of a word are so closely related that it is sufficiently often unclear which meaning is intended.

Here are some snapshots of the developing lexicon. After 30 games, the lexicon of the established words (i.e. associations with a score greater than 0.0 for at least one agent) is as in Table 6.12.

Note that there are two meanings for *puxazi*: [GRAY 0.0–0.5] (light) and [HEIGHT 0.5–1.0] (tall).

The lexicon after 200 games is shown in Table 6.13.

The second meaning of *puxazi* has now disappeared from the lexicon. So we basically see the same situation as before when only one most salient channel was considered by

6 The Guessing Game

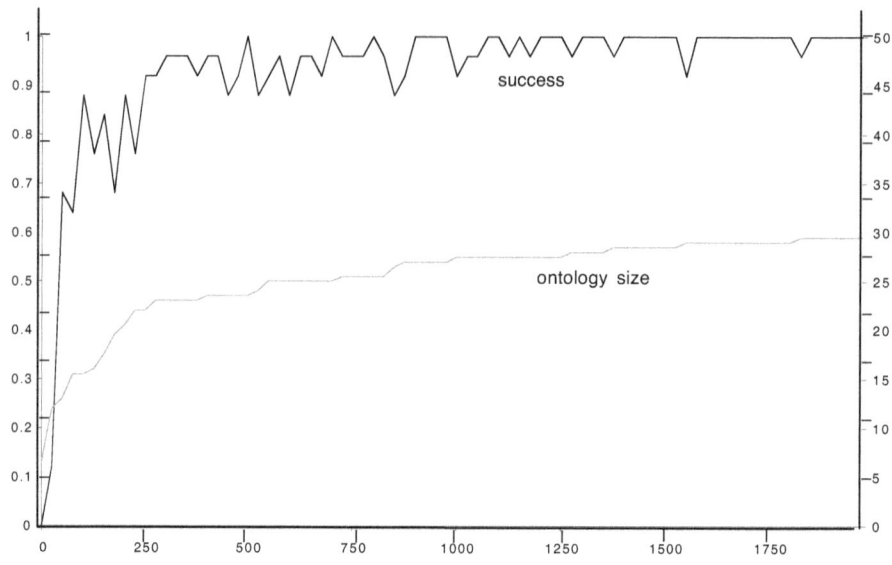

Figure 6.18: Communicative success (left y-axis) and average ontology size (right y-axis) for a series of 2000 language games played by two agents.

the agents. Words for more general distinctions happen to be lexicalised first because they are more often useful in the game, but when needed words for more specific meanings start to develop.

Table 6.12: Group lexicon after 30 games.

Meaning	Word	Translation	a1	a2
[VPOS 0.0–0.5]	torigusu	left	0.4	0.3
[HEIGHT 0.0–0.5]	mibati	short	0.6	0.6
[HEIGHT 0.5–1.0]	puxazi	tall	0.2	0.0
[GRAY 0.0–0.5]	puxazi	light	0.6	0.7
[GRAY 0.25–0.5]	turawa	medium light	0.1	0.0
[GRAY 0.5–1.0]	xubevilo	dark	0.0	0.1

Table 6.13: Group lexicon after 200 games.

Meaning	Word	Translation	a1	a2
[HPOS 0.0–0.5]	lefividi	left	0.2	0.2
[HPOS 0.5–1.0]	vuvovo	right	0.2	0.4
[VPOS 0.0–0.5]	torigusu	left	0.8	0.2
[VPOS 0.5–1.0]	rugomoto	right	1.0	1.0
[HEIGHT 0.0–0.5]	mibati	short	1.0	0.9
[GRAY 0.0–0.5]	puxazi	light	0.3	0.6
[GRAY 0.25–0.5]	turawa	medium light	0.4	0.4
[GRAY 0.5–1.0]	xubevilo	dark	0.4	0.5
[GRAY 0.5–0.75]	visuxa	very dark	0.3	0.3

6.4 Scaling up

Conforted by having reached a new plateau in the challenges confronting the agents, I now go one more step further. First we scale up the population to see whether despite the ambiguity now persistently present, a larger group of agents still manages to develop a shared communication system.

6.4.1 Increasing the population size

We already know from the previous section that a larger population automatically increases the risk for synonymy. Figure 6.19 shows the evolution of communicative success and average ontology size in a population of ten agents. We see again a steady progression towards an effective communication system. Recall that these games are played with randomly generated scenes from the GEOM world.

It is instructive to examine in detail the lexicon that has emerged after this series, where every agent has on average played about 2000 games. The table shown in Table 6.14 shows word-meaning pairs whose frequency is larger than 0.8.

We see that for all the sensory channels, solid words exist for the top level categories. There is however one exception: there are no words in this group for AREA nor for [HEIGHT 0.5–1.0]. We do find these words, and words for more refined notions as well, in the batch of word-meaning pairs whose scores are between 0.5 and 0.8, shown in Table 6.15.

Although most of these words are on their way towards total coherence, because the competition has already been damped completely, this is less the case for AREA/HEIGHT words. Closer inspection reveals that there are two words competing for expressing AREA and HEIGHT: *texiraxi* and *wixizode* (Figure 6.20). Both words have both meanings but there is a strong divergence of opinion in the population. Some prefer the AREA

6 The Guessing Game

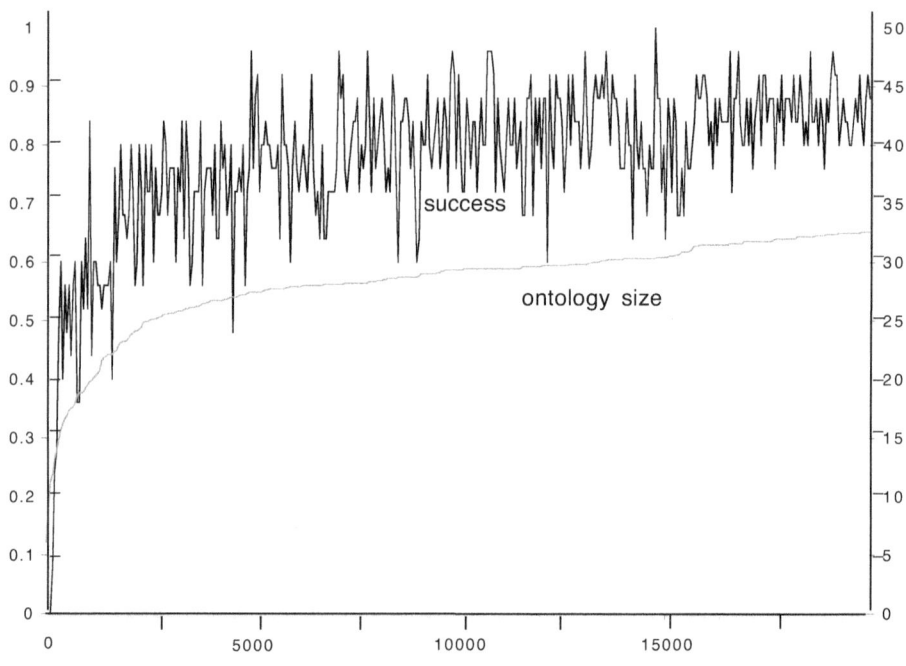

Figure 6.19: Communicative success (left y-axis) and average ontology size (right y-axis) for a series of 20,000 language games played by ten agents.

Table 6.14: Group lexicon after 2000 games.

Word	Meaning	Translation	Frequency
larubo	[HPOS 0.0–0.5]	left	1.00
tituroxu	[HPOS 0.5–1.0]	right	1.00
fumetese	[VPOS 0.0–0.5]	top	1.00
tokadapa	[VPOS 0.5–1.0]	bottom	1.00
povomovi	[WIDTH 0.0–0.5]	thin	1.00
kilokawe	[WIDTH 0.5–1.0]	wide	1.00
legoka	[HEIGHT 0.0–0.5]	short	0.94
vuwusugu	[GREY 0.0–0.5]	light	1.00
kewenoku	[GREY 0.5–1.0]	dark	1.00

6.4 Scaling up

Table 6.15: Table of word meaning pairs and their average scores.

Word	Meaning	Translation	Frequency
nifavipa	(HPOS 0.0–0.25)	very left	0.55
nodanova	(VPOS 0.0–0.25)	very top	0.58
texiraxi	(HEIGHT 0.5–1.0)	tall	0.69
poxalu	(HEIGHT 0.0–0.25)	very short	0.70
fovibilo	(HEIGHT 0.25–0.5)	medium short	0.61
wixizode	(AREA 0.5–1.0)	large	0.78
tebuwona	(GREY 0.75–1.0)	very dark	0.76
mogevo	(GREY 0.25–0.5)	medium light	0.60
toduwe	(GREY 0.0–0.25)	very light	0.65

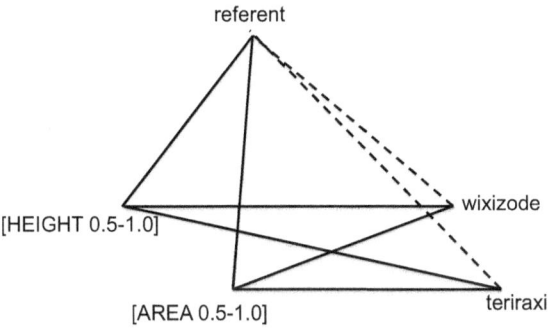

Figure 6.20: Two different words have the same two meanings and have difficulty disambiguating because they are often both equally distinctive in a given situation.

meaning, others prefer the HEIGHT meaning. This can be seen from the scores of the different meanings.

For the word *texiraxi*, the scores of the different agents for the AREA and HEIGHT categories is as in Table 6.16.

A game where the two meanings are compatible is shown below:

```
Game 10008
   a2 is the speaker. a4 is the hearer.
   a2 segments the context into 2 objects:
       circle-0 square-1
   a2 chooses square-1 as the topic
   a2 considers as salient AREA WIDTH HEIGHT
   a2 categorises the topic as
{}[HEIGHT 0.5-1.0] [HEIGHT 0.75-1.0]
```

161

6 The Guessing Game

Table 6.16: Scores for area and height categories.

Agent	Scores texiraxi		Scores wixizode	
	HEIGHT	AREA	HEIGHT	AREA
a1	0.00	0.9	0.6	0.4
a2	0.0	1.0	1.0	0.0
a3	0.90	0.2	0.0	1.0
a4	1.00	0.0	0.0	1.0
a5	1.00	0.0	0.2	0.6
a6	1.00	0.0	0.0	1.0
a7	1.00	0.0	1.00	1.0
a8	1.00	0.0	1.00	1.0
a9	1.00	0.0	1.00	1.0
a10	0.0	1.0	0.0	0.8

```
{}[WIDTH 0.5-1.0] [WIDTH 0.75-1.0]
{}[AREA 0.5-1.0] [AREA 0.75-1.0]
{}[HEIGHT 0.5-1.0] [HEIGHT 0.75-1.0]
  a2 has the words
      wixizode for [HEIGHT 0.5-1.0] (1.0)
      kilokawe for [WIDTH 0.5-1.0] (1.0)
      texiraxi for [AREA 0.5-1.0] (1.0)
      powugeme for [HEIGHT 0.5-1.0] (0.8)
      wetami for [HEIGHT 0.75-1.0] (0.5)
      wofetizo for [WIDTH 0.5-1.0] (0.4)
      kufule for [HEIGHT 0.75-1.0] (0.1)
      lisexese for [HEIGHT 0.75-1.0] (0.1)
  a2 says: 'wixizode'
  a7 interprets 'wixizode' as
{}[AREA 0.5-1.0] (1.0)
{}[WIDTH 0.0-0.5] (0.0)
{}[HEIGHT 0.5-1.0] (0.0)
  a7 identifies square-1
  a2 signals OK
```

Note the abundance of choices for the speaker. He finally picks *wixizode*. The hearer interprets this using AREA and the game succeeds. A partial overview of the different choices and subsequent updating is given in Figure 6.8. The speaker decreases the score of *powugeme* which is also competing for expressing [HEIGHT 0.5–1.0]. The hearer on the other hand damps the alternative meanings of *wixizode*, which includes the meaning [HEIGHT 0.5–1.0] used by the speaker.

6.4 Scaling up

This example shows that there will be a divergence of opinion among the agents if the environment does not provide enough disambiguating cases. It is still possible of course that the semantic incoherence will disappear from the lexicon, but it is understandable that agents have difficulty in this domain to disentangle the meanings of words for tall and large. French has one word *grand* encapsulating both of these categories.

Here are the words in the lexicon with still lower frequencies in the population (between 0.2 and 0.5). We see more clearly several synonyms in heavy competition, for example *kodawika* and *togixa* for [GRAY 0.5.0.75], or *vavuvosi* and *radude* for [WIDTH 0.75–1.0]. See Table 6.17.

Table 6.17: Lexicon with lower frequencies.

Word	Meaning	Frequency
lovifo	[HPOS 0.5–0.75]	0.21
petenuga	[HPOS 0.5–0.75]	0.25
gafizuru	[WIDTH 0.25–0.5]	0.24
vavuvosi	[WIDTH 0.5–0.75]	0.27
radude	[WIDTH 0.5–0.75]	0.30
wofetizo	[WIDTH 0.75–1.0]	0.42
wetami	[HEIGHT 0.75–1.0]	0.40
donadewe	[HEIGHT 0.5–0.75]	0.41
turede	[AREA 0.0–0.25]	0.26
likiwewe	[AREA 0.0–0.5]	0.27
savifo	[AREA 0.25–0.5]	0.21
rapoguwe	[AREA 0.5–0.75]	0.22
texiraxi	[AREA 0.5–1.0]	0.31
kodawika	[GREY 0.5–0.75]	0.23
togixa	[GREY 0.5–0.75]	0.45

So all the mechanisms proposed earlier do what they are supposed to do, even when we scale up the population. The Discrimination Game generates the repertoire of distinctions necessary in this domain, the Naming Game generates the shared repertoire of form-meaning pairs. The coupling between the two based on feedback from the environment causes a convergence even if the agents do not have any direct knowledge about which meanings are used by the others.

6.4.2 Lexicon acquisition by new agents

We finally scale up on the same dimension but now towards an open population. The following simulation examines what happens when a new agent enters into the population. The agent has no prior ontology nor any knowledge of the existing lexicon in the

6 The Guessing Game

group and no additional components or processes are added, compared to the agents in the simulation so far. Introducing a new agent tests in how far the cognitive architecture put in place enables a new agent to acquire a lexicon that already exists.

The first words learned (after about a dozen games by the agent) are shown in Table 6.18.

Table 6.18: First words after about a dozen games.

Word	Meaning	Score
larubo	[HPOS 0.0–0.5]	0.30
sakezomo	[HPOS 0.0–0.5]	0.00
tituroxu	[HPOS 0.5–1.0]	0.50
tokadapa	[VPOS 0.5–1.0]	0.20
legoka	[HEIGHT 0.0–0.5]	0.30
kuvodogi	[WIDTH 0.0–0.5]	0.00
gafizuru	[WIDTH 0.25–0.5]	0.10
nopofi	[WIDTH 0.5–1.0]	0.00

As expected, the new agent sometimes creates new words (this is the case for *sakezomo* and *nopofi*). But these words are very short-lived. The new agent has already picked up *larubo* which is the word in use expressing the meaning of *sakezomo*. *larubo* has already a higher score so *sakezomo* will definitely disappear.

The most widespread words in the lexicon such as *tituroxu* or *legoka* are the ones that are most likely to be picked up because the chance that they will be heard is higher. This suggests that the entry of new agents in the population does not destabilise the lexicon but on the contrary it makes it more coherent [1]

For example, the new agent has solidly associated the word *texiraxi* with [HEIGHT 0.5–1.0] and *wixizode* with [AREA 0.5–1.0] as the majority of the population. Thus resolving the incoherence shown in Figure 6.20.

Notice also that the new agent first acquires words for the more abstract categories. This is the case because (1) the discrimination trees are still developing and so more specific categories are not yet available, and (2) even if more specific categories are available, agents do not try to be more specific than needed in the game.

Table 6.19 is the set of words of the new agent with scores above 0.4 after 500 total games (which means more or less 100 games in which the new agent was involved).

The agent clearly picks up the lexicon circulating in the population and generally associates the same meanings to the words (compare with the lexicons given earlier for the total population). Occasionally there are still incoherences. For example, *fumetese*

---

[1] The importance of a flux in the agent population for streamlining a language has been stressed by Simon Kirby, who has applied this principle in a remarkable simulation concerning the origins of hierarchical structure, Kirby (1999).

Table 6.19: Score of new agent after 500 games.

Word	Meaning	Score
texiraxi	[HEIGHT 0.5–1.0]	0.80
lepowaxu	[HEIGHT 0.25–0.5]	0.50
kewenoku	[GREY 0.5–1.0]	0.80
wixizode	[AREA 0.5–1.0]	1.00
vuwusugu	[GREY 0.0–0.5]	0.50
tokadapa	[VPOS 0.5–1.0]	1.00
tituroxu	[HPOS 0.5–1.0]	1.00
legoka	[HEIGHT 0.0–0.5]	1.00
larubo	[HPOS 0.0–0.5]	1.00
fumetese	[WIDTH 0.0–0.5]	0.40

has been associated with [WIDTH 0.0–0.5] whereas the rest of the population uses this word for a distinction on the VPOS-channel. The meaning of this word will later shift as the agent encounters disambiguating cases. We can conclude that the guessing game shows not only how a population may emerge a lexicon from scratch but also how new agents entering the group may acquire the existing lexicon.

6.5 Conclusions

This chapter has coupled the Discrimination Game and the Naming Game, so that agents now can play language games without getting explicit feedback about meanings. As in the case of humans, feedback only comes through the non-verbal outcome of a game. This may generate semantic confusion because usually more than one conceptualisation is possible to distinguish a topic from the other objects in the context. However we have seen that despite this complication agents still manage to build up an ontology and a lexicon which is effective for communicating in their environment.

Although this chapter took away the assumption of direct meaning feedback, it still made a number of simplifying assumptions with respect to real world physical agents, in particular it assumed that the perception of the scene was identical for the speaker and the hearer. The next chapter takes away this assumption and thus sets the final step to test whether a perceptually grounded lexicon may emerge in a population of EMBODIED distributed autonomous agents.

7 Grounding

Ludwig Wittgenstein went through two major periods in his thinking. During the first period he worked within the framework of logical empiricism, initiated by Bertrand Russell and others at the end of the 19th century. The logicist approach defines a language by listing the elementary building blocks (the words), the combination rules (the syntax), and a mapping from words and syntactic structures to semantic interpretations (the semantics). It assumes that there is a universal, logical structure to the world which can be captured once and for all in a non-ambiguous logical language and that the permissible inferences can be catalogued exhaustively. This project has its roots in the 17th century dream of Leibniz and Descartes to streamline rational thinking so that it becomes as clear and non-controversial as numerical calculation. Wittgenstein enthusiastically participated in this project, which is still vigorously being pursued today by logicians and linguists alike, even though many of them do not necessarily subscribe to the universalist thesis motivating the early developments of logic.[1]

But some drastic events happened in Wittgenstein's life which caused a radical shift in his philosophical orientation. One of them was that he became headmaster of a small school in the Austrian mountains, without losing his interest for philosophising about language and meaning. By working with children and by seeing concretely how they engaged with language, Wittgenstein realised that the logicist approach did not address some basic questions one can ask about language, particularly how the semantics of a language might arise, or how people ever develop a shared communication system. Wittgenstein saw clearly that a language imposes a certain view on the world, which gives each language its own strength as well as its limitations. The logicist framework might be ideal as a tool for constructing a *post factum* formal description of the semantics of an (ideal) language, just as a structuralist grammar identifies the frozen state of its syntax, but not for modeling how language achieves its communicative purpose, comes about, or evolves.

Wittgenstein proposed to study the use of language in terms of games. This notion captures that the most basic form of language involves a social interaction between individuals within a specific setting, which acts as a context restricting the possible meanings. The interaction is played out along a conventionalised set of rules, as is chess or any other game. The notion of a game captures that a language interaction has a purpose, for example, to identify an object in a context, to gather information, to transmit emotion, to try and invoke an action by another person, etc. Words get their meaning as part of a language game. Language is a tool fully integrated in the rest of human social activity.[2]

It should be abundantly clear by now that the mechanisms explored in this book are

---

[1] Wittgenstein's main work from this period is Wittgenstein (1922). A prototypical example of the logicist research program is found in Carnap (1928).
[2] See in particular Wittgenstein (1953).

strongly indebted to a Wittgensteinian point of view. Of course, we studied only one relatively simple language game, but we have explored it at great depth so that there is now a framework for studying language games with the same rigor as the framework of classical logic or structural syntax.[3]

We are also exploring many issues that were not raised by Wittgenstein, the most important one being the origins of words and meanings and how they may spread in a population. In this chapter, I set the ultimate step on this path, which is to ground the cognitive architectures of the agents in the world through their perceptual and behavioral apparatus. I will show concrete examples from a series of language games played by autonomous robotic agents perceiving real world scenes and we will see that very similar phenomena as the ones observed in the previous chapter emerge.

The second goal of this chapter is to study the semiotic dynamics that thus unfolds in the population. Already in the beginning of this book, I introduced the notion of a semiotic square, which captures the relation between a referent, a perceived image, a meaning, and a form. The collection of semiotic squares that can be observed in an agent's behavior or in the behavior of a group of agents forms a semiotic landscape. This landscape undergoes continuous change as new words are created, word-meaning relations shift, and meanings are applied to new referents. This chapter introduces additional tools to study this dynamics, focusing in particular on how synonymy and ambiguity get introduced or damped and how language influences the conceptualisation of reality.

7.1 A first grounding experiment

We have arrived at a point where experiments with physically embodied autonomous agents become conceivable. To do so, we first have to ground the language game, which means that we have to couple the conceptual layer to the sensory-motor layers of the agent.

7.1.1 Integrating perception and action

The coupling between the perceptual layer and the conceptual layer is from an architectural viewpoint very similar to the coupling of the conceptual layer and the lexical layer which we studied in the previous chapter. For the formulation of an utterance, the outputs of the perceptual layer are inputs to the conceptual layer which in turn provides inputs to the lexical layer (Figure 7.1). Just as the other layers, the perceptual layer generates a set of possibilities: a set of possible segmentations and a set of sensory characteristics about each segment. These possibilities are ranked based on various criteria such as saliency and made available to the conceptual layer which further expands on the best solutions. The conceptual layer in turn generates a set of possible solutions with different rankings which are then processed by the lexical layer. Re-entry is nec-

---

[3] There have been several attempts to develop a more formal investigation of language games, see one of the earliest efforts in Hintikka (1998).

essary because the final perception of the scene depends on the ontological and lexical repertoires of the agent and cannot be decided on the basis of sensory processing alone.

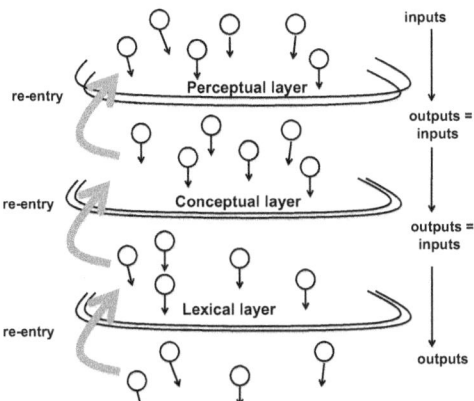

Figure 7.1: Flow of solutions through the different cognitive layers when an utterance is being produced. Re-entry is necessary because the decision at each layer depends on decisions at subsequent layers.

For the interpretation of an utterance, the main flow of information goes in the other direction. The lexical layer sends a variety of hypotheses to the conceptual layer and the conceptual layer makes use of data from the perceptual layer to see which conceptualisation yields a referent. Several solutions are considered by the conceptual layer because words are typically ambiguous and so the perceptual layer must produce the appropriate segmentations and sensory characteristics to test each solution. Even if a sensory channel was not considered to be very salient by the hearer, it may have been used by the speaker in his conceptualisation of the scene and hence the hearer's perceptual processes must actively try to seek in the image the information required to see whether it is applicable to the specific context. The interpretation of an utterance thus strongly takes the real world context into account. The utterance literally influences the way the hearer sees the world. The two-way flow (from perception to conceptualisation and language and from language and conceptualisation to perception) resolves one of the paradoxes of meaning discussed in Chapter 4. The clear picture of reality that we consciously experience results from a dynamical process in which local constraints keep propagating until a globally coherent solution emerges.[4]

Grounding language games in the real world not only requires a link between conceptualisation and real world perception. Of equal importance is the physical actions undertaken by the agents to point to the object they believe to be the topic. The accuracy of pointing heavily influences overall communicative success. Indeed, a game may

---

[4] Dynamical systems which enter into an attractor based on a similar relaxation process have been widely studied, particularly in physics. One of the prototypical examples is a spin glass whose magnetic states keep switching until a globally coherent state is reached.

7 Grounding

fail not because the speaker and the hearer did not agree on the meaning nor because they did not refer to the same object, but because the speaker misperceived which object the hearer has pointed to. These differences in perception leading to difficulties in communication do happen and may cause communicative failures despite a shared lexicon.

7.1.2 Concept acquisition

I now show a series of example games taken from an experiment in which two situated embodied agents, a1 and a2, play grounded language games based on coloured figures pasted on the white board in front of them. The following channels are available to the agents in the experiments in this section: HPOS (the horizontal position of the midpoint of the segment's bounding box), VPOS (the vertical position of the midpoint of the segment's bounding box), HEIGHT (the height of the bounding box), WIDTH (the width of the bounding box), AREA (the area of the segment, calculated by counting the number of pixels that belong to it), R (the average redness of the pixels in the segment), G (the average greenness of the pixels in the segment), B (the average blueness of the pixels in the segment). These "colour" channels are not to be confused with the human opponent colour channels so the distinctions that form of them are not directly perceivable by human observers.

Because there are only two agents, the risk of synonymy is almost non-existent. The saliency threshold is sufficiently low so that more than one sensory channel might be salient and hence ambiguity is unavoidable.

A first word is acquired by the agents in game 3 based on the segmented images shown in Figure 7.2 (top). The different sensory values (after sensor-scaling) for the segments in game 3 are shown in Table 7.1.

Table 7.1: First words after about a dozen games.

channel	obj-0	obj-1
HPOS	0.27	0.16
VPOS	0.20	0.20
HEIGHT	0.15	0.15
WIDTH	0.10	0.11
AREA	0.10	0.10
R	0.23	0.25
G	0.32	0.34
B	0.63	0.65

7.1 A first grounding experiment

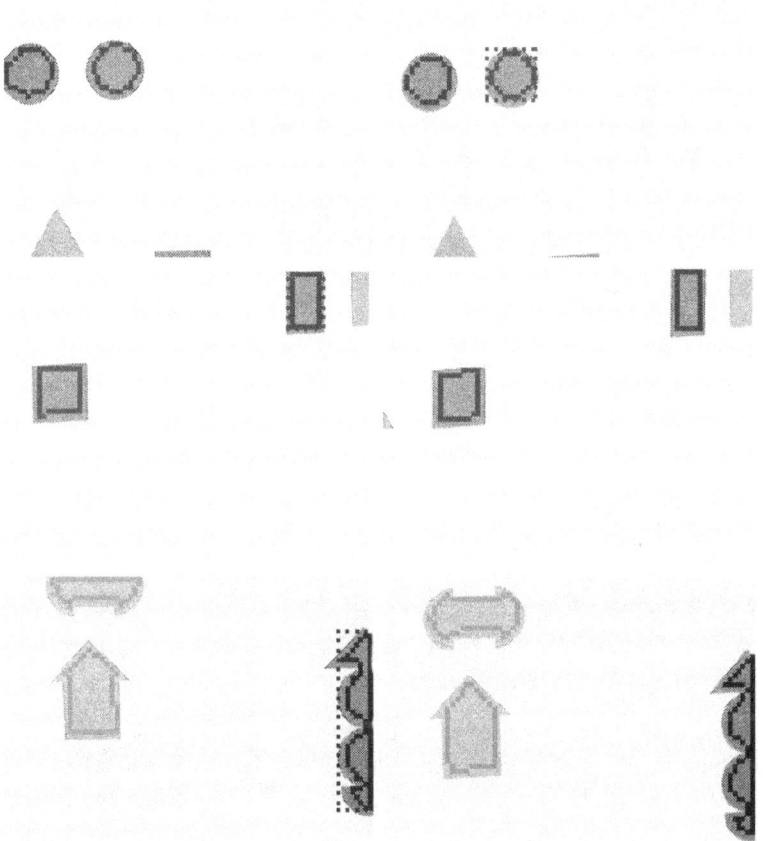

Figure 7.2: Three examples of segmented images. The topic is indicated by a dashed bounding box in the image of the speaker. Segments which are too small are ignored. The topics have all been conceptualised as being 'to the right' and so the same word *gofubo* has been used to refer to them.

7 *Grounding*

HPOS is the most salient channel. After sensor-scaling, the two values for HPOS are still be drawn further apart with 1.0 for object-0 and 0.0 for object-1 so that the category [HPOS 0.5–1.0] easily distinguishes the topic (object-0) from object-1.

The left image is that of the hearer **a1**, the right one that of the speaker, **a2**. **a2** had already invented the word *gofubo* for [HPOS 0.5–1.0] (to the right) in an earlier game, but the word was not acquired in that game by **a1** because he still missed the appropriate distinction. Meanwhile the HPOS category is available to **a1** due to an expansion of his discrimination networks and so he can store the word:

```
Game 3
  a2 is the speaker. a1 is the hearer.
  a2 segments the context into 2 objects:
      object-0 object-1
  a2 chooses object-0 as the topic
  a2 categorises the topic as [HPOS 0.5-1.0]
  a2 says: gofubo
  a1 does not know gofubo
  a1 says: gofubo?
  a2 points to object-0
  a1 categorises the topic as [HPOS 0.5-1.0]
  a1 stores gofubo as [HPOS 0.5-1.0]
```

This game proceeds essentially like in the computer simulations studied before. The major difference is that now real images have been used, the objects considered are the outcome of segmentation processes, the sensory characteristics have been derived from the image itself, and the pointing has been done by physically moving the cameras.

7.1.3 Generalisation without learning

Immediately the agents apply this word to very different scenes, such as the ones in Figure 7.2 (middle and bottom). The middle picture shows on the left the segmented scene from the speaker in game 5, and on the right the one from the hearer. In game 5, the figures are blue rectangles. They are much further apart than the two circles in game 3. Nevertheless, after scaling, they are categorised and conceptualised similarly and therefore the same word could be used effectively. The concept of [HPOS 0.5–1.0] and hence the word *gofubo* is general *from the very start*. The agents do not need to see many examples because they do not use inductive generalisation. Instead, the HPOS category is constructed in a top-down fashion as soon as the HPOS channel has been salient and is immediately available for use in the discrimination game and hence in verbalising the scene. This explains why the word-meaning acquisition process observed in the experiments goes so amazingly fast.

The bottom of Figure 7.2 shows yet another scene where the word *gofubo* was used with success. The topic is the rightmost shape in the scene and so [HPOS 0.5–1.0] is once more distinctive. To an outside observer it may look like the agents have performed a

7.1 A first grounding experiment

gigantic inductive leap, but this is not the case at all. The agents do not try to abstract the commonalities from different examples but construct distinctions in a top down fashion and try to apply them to the perceived image.

After a mere 50 games, the lexicon shown in Table 7.2 has emerged. Only associations with scores greater than 0.0 are shown.

Table 7.2: First words after about a dozen games.

Word	Meaning	Translation	a1	a2
wawosido	[HPOS 0.0–0.5]	left	0.4	0.4
meluri	[HPOS 0.25–0.5]	medium left	0.1	0.0
gofubo	[HPOS 0.5–1.0]	right	1.0	1.0
wiwigapo	[VPOS 0.0–0.5]	left	0.1	0.0
fozumoba	[AREA 0.5–1.0]	large	0.0	0.1
wefoto	[R 0.0–0.5]	low redness	0.2	0.2
togene	[R 0.5–1.0]	high redness	0.5	1.0
fumudanu	[G 0.0–0.5]	low greenness	0.2	0.2
puxedu	[G 0.5–1.0]	high greenness	0.4	0.4

There is already a word (*gofubo*) which has a score of 1.0! After 100 games, the lexicon has become more solid and now looks as in Table 7.3.

Table 7.3: Population lexicon after 100 games.

Word	Meaning	Translation	a1	a2
wawosido	[HPOS 0.0–0.5]	left	0.7	0.5
meluri	[HPOS 0.25–0.5]	medium left	0.4	0.4
gofubo	[HPOS 0.5–1.0]	right	1.0	1.0
vokomutu	[HPOS 0.5–0.75]	medium right	0.2	0.2
buwonipo	[HPOS 0.75–0.875]	strongly right	0.1	0.0
wiwigapo	[VPOS 0.0–0.5]	down	0.6	0.6
fozumoba	[AREA 0.5–1.0]	large	0.2	0.4
wefoto	[R 0.0–0.5]	low redness	0.2	0.3
togene	[R 0.5–1.0]	high redness	1.0	1.0
fumudanu	[G 0.0–0.5]	low greenness	0.7	0.7
puxedu	[G 0.5–1.0]	high greenness	0.7	0.9

7 Grounding

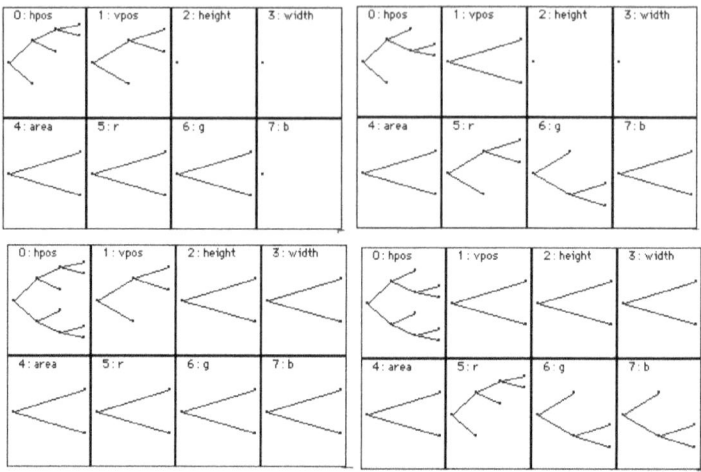

Figure 7.3: The discrimination trees of two embodied agents a1 (left) and a2 (right) after playing 100 games (top) and after 200 games (bottom).

7.1.4 The influence of the environment

One thing is striking about this lexicon. It contains words for fine-grained distinctions along the horizontal position axis, but none for width or height. Indeed if we look at the discrimination trees as they exist at this point (figure 7.3 top) we see that there are no discrimination trees for the HEIGHT and WIDTH channels. This is entirely due to the environment. There have simply been no situations on the white board yet where these distinctions are salient enough.

As human experimenters, we can stimulate conceptual development by configuring scenes where these channels are needed, for example, a scene which contains two objects with the same size, colour, and position but of significantly different width. The conceptual layer in each agent should then start to develop again and the lexical layer should follow with the construction of new words.

A game where this happens is game 126 with the segmented images shown in Figure 7.4 (top). Width is now the most salient channel. The segments and sensory data for game 126 (after sensor-scaling) are shown in Table 7.4.

Clearly width is the most salient channel for the speaker. It is therefore chosen and because the agents have already grown distinctions on this channel, discrimination succeeds and a new word can be constructed and stored.

```
Game 126
    a2 is the speaker. a1 is the hearer.
    a2 segments the context into 2 objects:
        object-0 object-1
    a2 chooses object-0 as the topic
```

7.1 A first grounding experiment

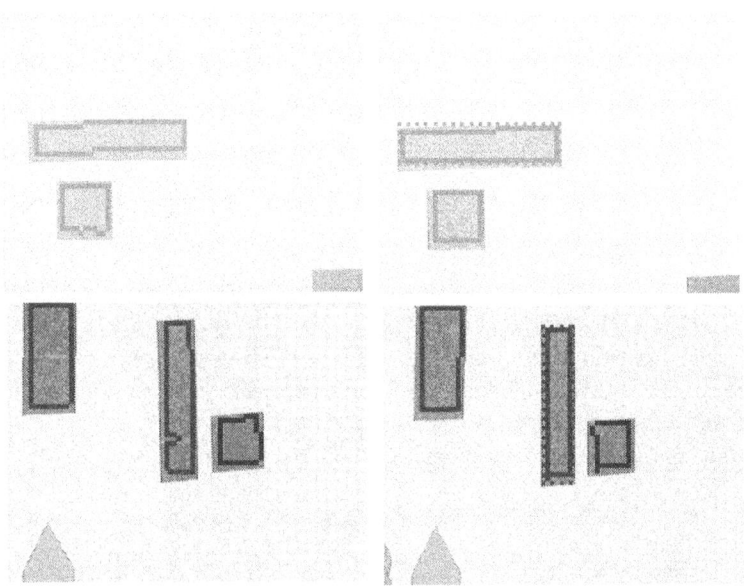

Figure 7.4: Top and bottom: Examples of new segmented scenes that stimulate conceptual development and hence expansions of the lexicon. The most salient characteristic in the top scene is WIDTH and in the bottom scene HEIGHT.

Table 7.4: Sensory data for game 126.

channel	obj-0	obj-1
HPOS	0.08	0.09
VPOS	0.21	0.10
HEIGHT	0.10	0.15
WIDTH	0.42	0.11
AREA	0.34	0.16
R	0.33	0.31
G	0.68	0.65
B	0.52	0.50

7 Grounding

```
a2 categorises the topic as [WIDTH 0.5-1.0]
a2 creates a new word: vaviwumu
a2 says: vaviwumu
a1 does not know vaviwumu
a1 says: vaviwumu?
a2 points to object-0
a1 categorises the topic as [WIDTH 0.5-1.0]
a1 stores vaviwumu as [WIDTH 0.5-1.0]
```

Figure 7.4 (bottom) contains another example of segmented images which have stimulated conceptual growth and hence an expansion of the lexicon. In this case, categorisations on the HEIGHT channel are relevant and a word developed for tall.

Figure 7.5 shows another series of image segments, where categorisations based on the AREA channel were effective and Figure 7.6 shows additional image segments exercising VPOS, HPOS and colour distinctions.

After 200 games, the lexicon of the population looks as in Table 7.5.

Table 7.5: Population lexicon after 200 games.

Word	Meaning	Translation	a1	a2
wawosido	[HPOS 0.0–0.5]	left	0.9	0.4
gixepo	[HPOS 0.0–0.25]	very left	0.4	0.4
wonuxa	[HPOS 0.0–0.25]	very left	0.10	0.0
meluri	[HPOS 0.25–0.5]	medium left	0.4	0.4
gofubo	[HPOS 0.5–1.0]	right	1.0	1.0
vokomutu	[HPOS 0.5–0.75]	medium right	0.4	0.4
buwonipo	[HPOS 0.75–0.875]	strongly right	0.1	0.0
wiwigapo	[VPOS 0.0–0.5]	down	0.5	0.4
putuwenu	[VPOS 0.5–1.0]	up	0.5	0.5
vaviwumu	[WIDTH 0.5–1.0]	wide	0.5	0.5
pesidumu	[AREA 0.0–0.5]	small	0.2	0.2
fozumoba	[AREA 0.5–1.0]	large	1.0	1.0
wefoto	[R 0.0–0.5]	low redness	0.2	0.1
togene	[R 0.5–1.0]	high redness	0.9	1.0
fumudanu	[G 0.0–0.5]	low greenness	0.7	0.9
puxedu	[G 0.5–1.0]	high greenness	0.9	0.9

Note that new words have come into the lexicon for 'up' (*putuwenu*), 'down' (*wiwigapo*), and 'wide' (*vaviwumu*). The discrimination trees of the WIDTH and HEIGHT channel have started to expand (Figure 7.3 bottom).

7.1 A first grounding experiment

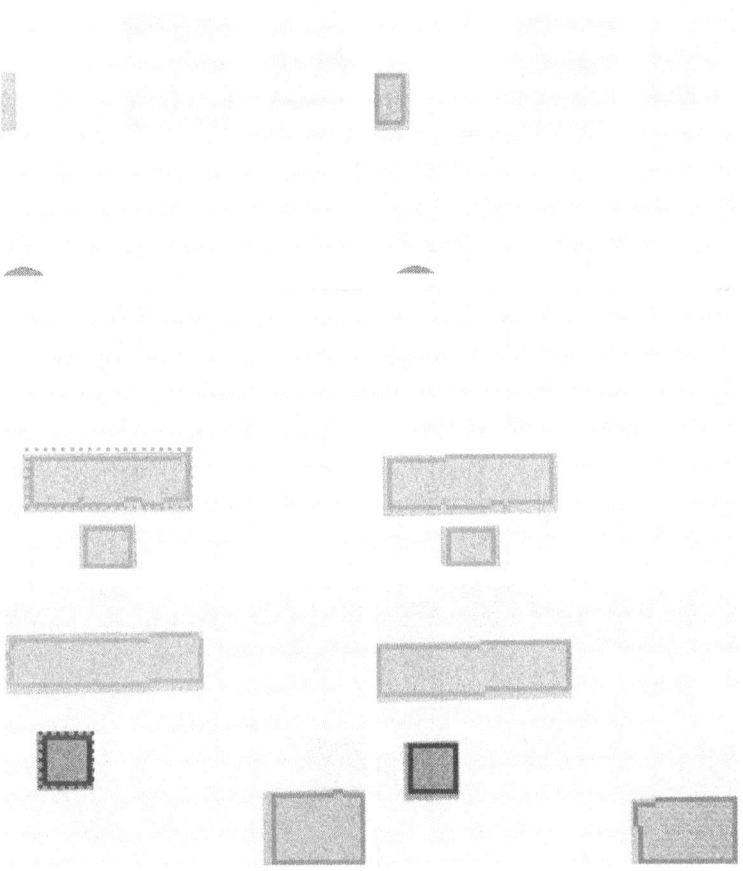

Figure 7.5: Segmented images where distinctions on the AREA channel have been used. The topic (with dashed bounding box) in the two top cases has been categorised as large. In the bottom case, a word meaning 'small' was used.

7 *Grounding*

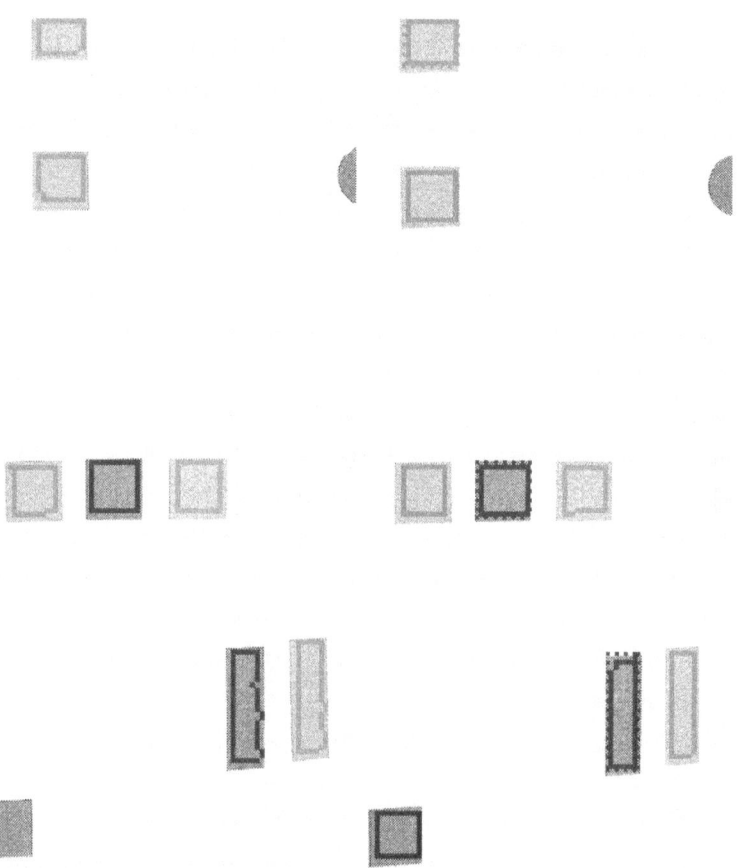

Figure 7.6: The image segments from the top game require distinctions on the vpos channel and caused the creation of a word for 'upper'. The image segments in the middle led to the use of refined distinctions on the HPOS channel, so as to identify the middle square. The topic in the image segments at the bottom was done with a conjunction of categories: blue and tall.

7.1.5 Coping with perceptual anomalies

Grounding language games in physical environments makes it obviously harder for the agents in a number of respects. First of all because perception and segmentation may differ, the salient characteristics of objects may not be the same and as a result the hearer may guess another meaning for an unknown word, compared to the one used by the speaker. This happens for example in the following game (game 128) which is based on the segmented images shown in Figure 7.7 (top). The speaker's perception is shown to the left and the hearer's to the right.

```
Game 128
   a1 is the speaker. a2 is the hearer.
   a1 segments the context into 3 objects:
       object-0 object-1 object-2
   a1 chooses object-0 as the topic
   a1 categorises the topic as
       [HPOS 0.0-0.25] [HPOS 0.0-0.125]
   a1 creates a new word: 'bagaxe' for [HPOS 0.0-0.25]
   a1 says: bagaxe
   a2 does not know bagaxe
   a2 says: bagaxe?
   a1 points to object-0
   a2 categorises the topic as [AREA 0.5-1.0]
   a2 stores bagaxe as [AREA 0.5-1.0]
```

Although the difference may not appear significant to the human eye, the topic (the left most rectangle) is in the raw perception of the speaker less wide as the same rectangle perceived by the hearer. The segments and sensory data of the speaker in game 128 (after sensor-scaling) are shown in the Table 7.6.

Table 7.6: Sensory data for game 128.

channel	obj-0	obj-1	obj-2
HPOS	0.03	0.15	0.33
VPOS	0.29	0.29	0.01
HEIGHT	0.37	0.39	0.07
WIDTH	0.10	0.08	0.27
AREA	0.29	0.22	0.16
R	0.95	0.97	0.97
G	0.33	0.40	0.93
B	0.35	0.44	0.26

7 Grounding

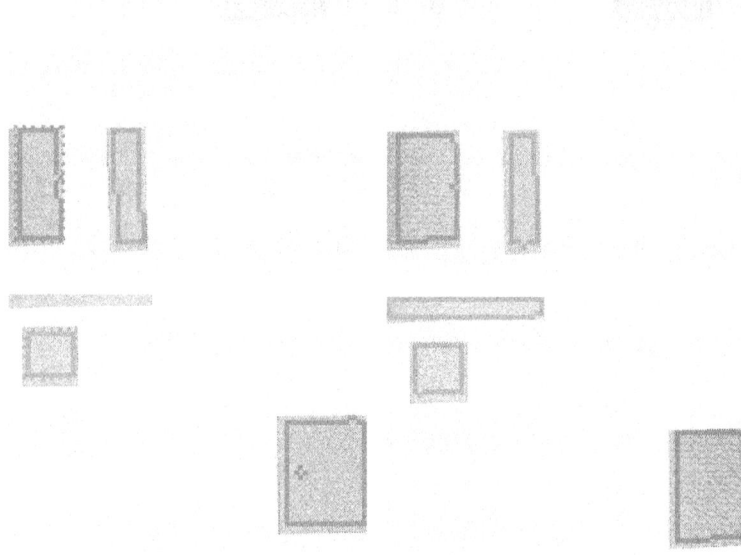

Figure 7.7: Examples of scenes causing confusion due to perceptual anomalies. In the top scene, the segmentation of the speaker (left) makes the topic's most salient characteristic the horizontal position, whereas for the hearer (right) the most salient characteristic of the same segment is its area. In the bottom scene, speaker and hearer have segmented the scene into two, respectively three segments. This causes the game to fail even though both agents had the same meaning for the word used by the speaker.

Context-scaling further amplifies this difference which shows that it is not always beneficial to do so. a1 uses the horizontal axis, creating a new word *bagaxe* meaning 'very left' [HPOS 0.0–0.25] whereas a2, for whom the area is the most salient characteristic, associates this word with [AREA 0.5–1.0] (large). This example shows that grounding introduces additional risks for the introduction of semantic incoherence in a group's lexicon.

Due to perceptual anomalies, a game may fail even though both agents already have the same meaning for the same word. This happens when this meaning yields different objects (or no objects at all) for the speaker and the hearer. As a consequence, the hearer adopts another meaning for the word which starts to compete with the one he already had. This happened in the following game (game 127) based on the segmented images shown in Figure 7.7 (bottom). The speaker (left image) has identified only two objects, but the hearer three. The speaker (left image) uses green as distinguishing characteristic which is indeed appropriate. but because the hearer's third object (the top rectangle) is also green, this distinction fails for him. Even though the hearer had already a well estab-

7.1 A first grounding experiment

lished meaning for *puxedu*, he associates a new meaning based on the WIDTH-channel with this word because this channel is now the most salient.

```
Game 127
  a1 is the speaker. a2 is the hearer.
  a1 segments the context into 2 objects:
       s-object-0 s-object-1
  a1 chooses object-0 as the topic
  a1 considers as salient G R AREA HPOS
  a1 categorises the topic as
       [HPOS 0.0-0.5] [HPOS 0.0-0.125]
       [AREA 0.0-0.5] [R 0.0-0.5] [G 0.5-1.0]
  a1 has the words
       puxedu for [G 0.5-1.0] (1.0)
       wawosido for [HPOS 0.0-0.5] (0.7)
       pesidimu for [AREA 0.0-0.5] (0.2)
       wefoto for [R 0.0-0.5] (0.2)
       buwonipo for [G 0.5-1.0] (0.0)
  a1 says: puxedu
  a2 segments the context into 3 objects:
       h-object-0 h-object-1 h-object-2
  a2 interprets puxedu as
       [G 0.5-1.0] (0.20)
  a2 identifies h-object-0 h-object-1
  a2 says: puxedu?
  a1 points to s-object-0
  a2 categorises the topic as [WIDTH 0.5-1.0]
  a2 stores puxedu as [WIDTH 0.5-1.0]
```

After 500 games, the lexicon is as in Table 7.7.

The global evolution of success and ontology is shown in the graph in Figure 7.8. The graph is not fundamentally different from the ones we have seen in the computer simulations in the previous chapter, except that more failures occur after a lexicon is established due to the contingencies of real world images and the unavoidable stochasticity associated with physical interactions.

So despite the difficulties caused by perceptual anomalies and errors in non-verbal real-world interaction, the mechanisms used by the agents appear sufficiently robust that a shared communication system manages to get off the ground. We have been able to take away all the scaffolds put up in earlier chapters and the complete language system now stands on its own feet. Of course we now need to further scale up the challenge to the agents, particularly along three dimensions: complexity of the environments, complexity of the sensori-motor apparatus (particularly the number of sensory channels available to the agents), and size of the agent population. Only the latter type of scale-up is studied in the remainder of this chapter.

7 Grounding

Table 7.7: Population lexicon after 500 games.

Word	Meaning	Translation	a1	a2
wawosido	[HPOS 0.0–0.5]	left	0.9	0.4
gixepo	[HPOS 0.0–0.25]	very left	0.4	0.4
wonuxa	[HPOS 0.0–0.25]	very left	0.10	0.0
meluri	[HPOS 0.25–0.5]	medium left	0.4	0.4
gofubo	[HPOS 0.5–1.0]	right	1.0	1.0
vokomutu	[HPOS 0.5–0.75]	medium right	0.4	0.4
buwonipo	[HPOS 0.75–0.875]	strongly right	0.1	0.0
wiwigapo	[VPOS 0.0–0.5]	down	0.5	0.4
putuwenu	[VPOS 0.5–1.0]	up	0.5	0.5
vaviwumu	[WIDTH 0.5–1.0]	wide	0.5	0.5
pesidumu	[AREA 0.0–0.5]	small	0.2	0.2
fozumoba	[AREA 0.5–1.0]	large	1.0	1.0
wefoto	[R 0.0–0.5]	low redness	0.2	0.1
togene	[R 0.5–1.0]	high redness	0.9	1.0
fumudanu	[G 0.0–0.5]	low greenness	0.7	0.9
puxedu	[G 0.5–1.0]	high greenness	0.9	0.9

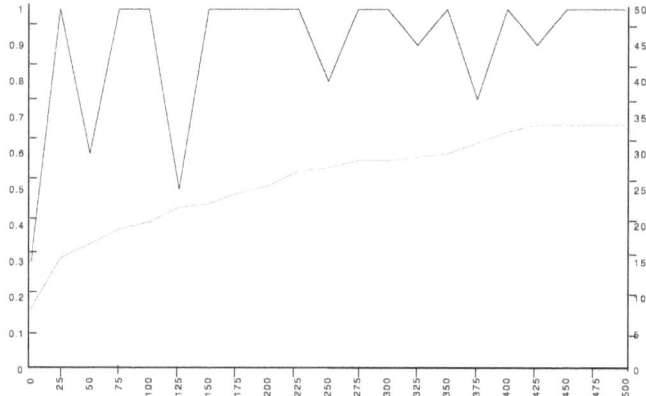

Figure 7.8: Success (left y-axis) and average ontology size (right y-axis) for two agents playing 500 guessing games about real world scenes perceived through their cameras. Occasionally new situations have been introduced to stimulate conceptual development.

7.2 Semiotic dynamics

Semiotic dynamics refers to the changing relationships between words, meanings, perceptions, and real world scenes observed while a group of autonomous distributed agents play language games about scenes from an open evolving environment. The possible utterances and possible meanings are not fixed but continuously changing as the agents autonomously evolve their communication systems and adapt to changing environments. Tracking and understanding these changes is a non-trivial task. It is comparable to the investigation of other non-linear complex dynamical systems and therefore similar tools are useful.[5] The study of semiotic dynamics is an entirely new subject for linguistics, and I will give here only some examples to illustrate the approach.

7.2.1 Tracking language evolution

The first thing we need is a systematic way to collect data. In studying the lexical and ontological development of the agents, I have so far played god, inspecting the internal states of the agents. With larger agent populations that are travelling over the Internet and engage in interactions in different physical sites, it becomes impossible to perform these computations, because ontologies and lexicons are distributed over many agent servers throughout the world and different language games are going on in parallel. We are forced in these circumstances to adopt the viewpoint of a linguist, who can only observe the overt linguistic behavior in the community, not the internal states of each individual. So we have built tools that track the language games as they take place in parallel on a world-wide scale. The tools are available to anyone who logs on through the Internet and wants to see for him or herself how the language system is evolving.[6]

Of course, an external observer's point of view is only partial. As we have seen in the previous chapters, many words and categories are latently known by the agents, without their being used in overt behavior, just as we carry genes in our bodies that are not being expressed. Nevertheless, observations of the actual behavior of the agents is in a sense a more natural way to characterise ontologies and lexicons and reflects well the semiotic dynamics in the population. For the remainder of this chapter, all data are taken from observing experiments with the Talking Heads as they play grounded language games.

7.2.2 Semiotic landscapes

A semiotic landscape contains all the semiotic relationships that effectively occurred at least once in the games played by a particular population of agents during a certain period of time. The semiotic landscape is a graph. The nodes in the graph are formed by situations (referents in a specific context), meanings, and forms (words), and there are links if the items associated with two nodes indeed co-occur (Figure 7.9). In a more

---

[5] See Badii & Politi (1997). Examples of ways to model evolutionary systems are shown in Kauffman (1993) and Maynard Smith (1989).
[6] The website http://talking-heads.csl.sony.fr/ contains the latest statistics on this world-wide evolution. The observational tools were mainly built by Joris Van Looveren and Frederic Kaplan.

7 Grounding

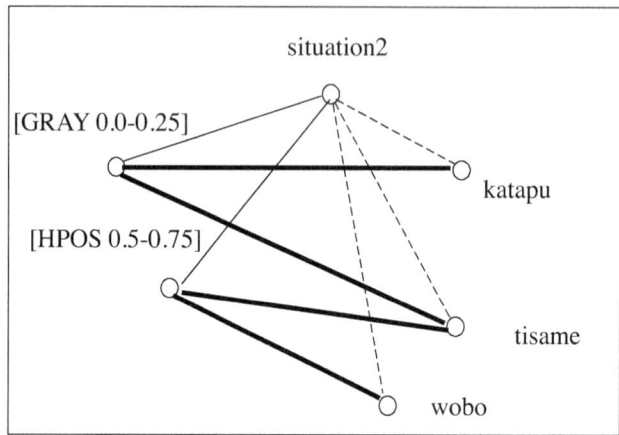

Figure 7.9: Typical segment of a semiotic landscape capturing the co-occurrence relations between referents, meanings and word forms. The FM/MF relations are in thick lines, the RM/MR relations in regular lines, and the RF/FR relations in dashed lines.

complete picture, the landscape makes a distinction between external referents and segmented images but I will not do so in the present chapter. The relations in the landscape are labeled as in Table 7.8.

The partial landscape in Figure 7.9 (taken from an actual experiment) contains an example where the agents use two possible meanings for conceptualising *situation2*, namely [GRAY 0.0–0.25] (very light) and [HPOS 0.5–0.75] (medium right). The words *katapu* and *tisame* lexicalise [GRAY 0.0–0.25] and *wobo* and *tisame* [HPOS 0.5–0.75]. Each meaning has therefore two synonyms and *tisame* is ambiguous; it can mean both [GRAY 0.0–0.25] and [HPOS 0.5–0.75]. Three words are used to communicate the situation: 'katapu', 'tisame', and 'wobo'. Such a structure is typical for grounded lexicon evolution and complexity rapidly increases when the same meanings are used to communicate about other situations (which is obviously very common and indeed desirable).

Table 7.8:

Label	Relation
RM	referent to meaning
MR	meaning to referent
FM	form to meaning
MF	meaning to form
RF	referent to form
FR	form to referent

7.2.3 Competition diagrams

The degree of coherence of a language system can be studied by collecting data on the frequency of the members of each relation in the semiotic landscape for given periods of time (for example periods of 100 games). The result is represented in competition diagrams, such as the RF-diagram in figure 7.10 taken from actual experiments. It plots the evolution of the frequency of the referent-form relations for a given referent. In other words, all games during a certain period are collected where this particular situation (i.e. a specific referent in the same context) occurred and then the frequencies of all words used to refer to this referent in the same series of games are computed. Similar diagrams can be constructed for the other semiotic relationships. The FR-diagram plots all the referents for a given form, the MF-diagram all the forms for a given meaning, the FM-diagram all the meanings for a given form, the MR-diagram all the referents for a given meaning and the RM-diagram all the meanings for a given referent.

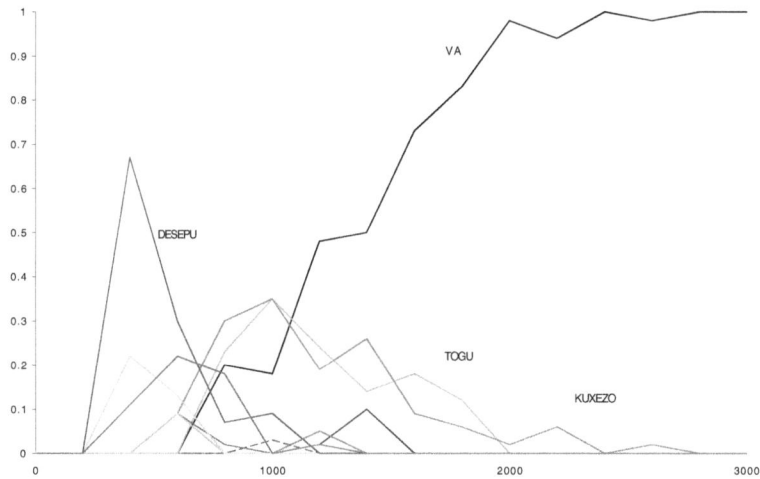

Figure 7.10: This RF-diagram shows the frequency of all forms used for the same referent in 3000 language games, played by a group of 20 embodied situated agents.

The RF-diagram in Figure 7.10 shows the frequency with which certain words were used to communicate a particular situation. We see that in the beginning the word 'desepu' has been dominant, then there is a period of turbulence in which different words compete, but after a while a new word *va* wins the competition and becomes the dominant way to communicate about this situation. Figure 7.11 shows another competition diagram plotting the evolution of the FM-relation, for the word form *va*, in other words the frequencies of all the meanings that co-occurred with the word *va*. We see an early peak when *va* was used in 70 % of the games with the meaning [B 0.3125–0.375], i.e. a particular shade of blue. Then there is a struggle during which additional distinctions (on the RED and VPOS-channels) are competing for the dominant meaning of *va*. [R 0.0–0.125] finally becomes dominant.

185

7 Grounding

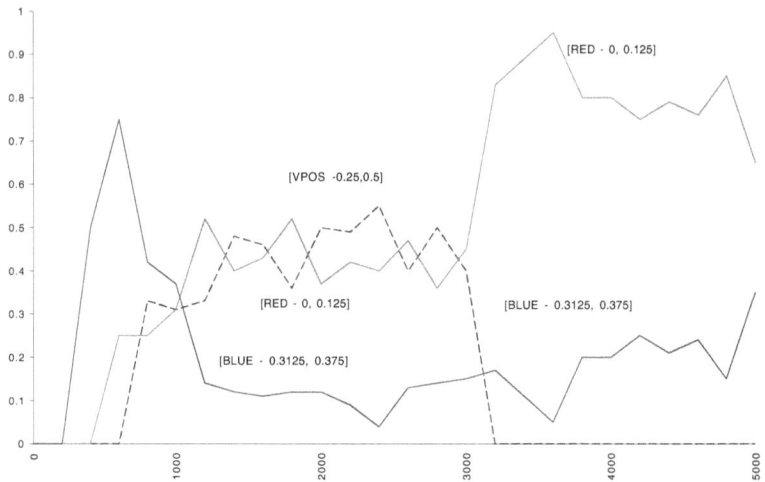

Figure 7.11: This FM-diagram shows the frequencies of each form-meaning pair with the form equal to *va* in a series of 5000 games. A disambiguating situation occurs in game 3000 causing the loss of one meaning of *va*.

These competition diagrams are an important tool to try and make sense of the ontological and lexical evolution taking place in evolving groups of agents as they are playing their language games. Typically we pick a dominating word, for example the word *va* in Figure 7.10, and try to understand why it has become dominant. The FM-diagram for *va* (Figure 7.11) explains part of the story. Three stable meanings for *va* have emerged at around 1000 games: [R 0.0–0.125], [B 0.3125–0.375], and [VPOS 0.25–0.5]. They are all equally adequate for distinguishing the object *va* designates, and there are no situations yet that would have forced the disambiguation of *va*. In game 3000, the environment (which is continuously changing in this experiment) produces a scene in which a category which was distinctive for the object designated by *va* is no longer distinctive. The lexicon adapts immediately. Around game 3000 the VPOS-based meaning disappears, and the distinction based on RED shoots up and becomes dominant.

7.2.4 RMF coherence

The average frequency of the dominating relations along a particular semiotic dimension is an indication how coherent the community's language system is along that dimension. For example, suppose we want to know the coherence along the meaning-form dimension, in other words whether there are many synonyms in the lexicon or not. For a given series of games, we calculate for each meaning that was indeed used in the series, the frequency of the most common form for that meaning. Then we take the average of these frequencies and this represents the MF-coherence. If all meanings had only one form, the MF-coherence is equal to 1.0. If two forms where used for the same meaning with equal frequency, MF-coherence is 0.5. When plotting the MF-coherence we can therefore follow the tendency towards an increase or decrease of synonyms.

Examining the coherence along the other dimensions is equally instructive. Studying the coherence along the FM dimension informs us about the degree of ambiguity in the lexicon, because it is based on the average frequency of the preferred meaning for each word. When all word forms have only one meaning, the FM-coherence is 1.0. The more the forms in a language have different meanings with non-zero frequencies, the lower the FM-coherence becomes.

The coherence along the RM dimension informs us about how many possible conceptualisations of the same situation are used by the population. If RM-coherence is high, this means that the population has uniform conceptualisations. For every referent, all agents typically use the same meaning. Usually there are initially many possible ways to conceptualise a scene, but there is a tendency for agents to view the world in a similar way under the influence of language because the scores of the discrimination trees are affected by success of a distinction in language games. I will discuss this in more detail in the final section of this chapter.

The inverse relation (MR, between meanings and referents) tracks the frequency with which certain situations are covered by specific meanings. It informs us about the generality of the categories available to the agents, assuming that all agents statistically encounter the same sort of environments. If a particular meaning can pick out many possible referents in many contexts, this meaning must be abstract and the agents must have managed to develop a lexicon that is not tied up completely to specific situations.

7.3 The ideal language

Complex adaptive systems show a tendency to optimise their internal functioning despite the absence of a global overall control center. For example, each species in a single ecology tends to become better in exploiting its niche and the global system moves towards a balanced equilibrium where different species play different roles in a complex ecological web.[7] This book explores the idea that language is a complex adaptive system like a natural ecology, which is shaped and reshaped by the local interactions of autonomous agents without a central controlling agency regulating what linguistic conventions should be adopted. We have seen that in computer simulations and experiments with robotic agents a shared communication system emerges, but in how far is this system optimal?[8]

7.3.1 Total coherence

A first desirable property of a language system is perhaps that it is totally coherent along all semiotic dimensions. In terms of semiotic landscapes, this means that the graph consists of unconnected triangles. Each object in a specific context has a unique meaning,

---

[7] See examples in Margulis (1991).
[8] See for the discussion on whether languages ever can be said to optimise: Kirby (1999).

7 Grounding

each meaning has a unique form and picks out a unique referent, and each form has a unique meaning and hence a unique referent as well. The coherence along all possible dimensions is then always 1.0. Given such a system, the agents would not need to consider different hypotheses while speaking or listening, there would never be any confusion, and a new agent learning the language would never be confronted with different uses of the same word.

Such an ideal language has been a dream of many philosophers, including Descartes and Leibniz, but the investigations reported here show clearly that it is not attainable.[9] A language must be open to the expression of new meanings because the communicative objectives and the environments which are the subject of communication keep changing. Hence synonymy (incoherence along the MF dimension) is unavoidable because words are created by some agents not knowing that words already exist in the population for the same meaning. In addition, one agent may "wrongly" infer that a certain word has a particular meaning due to perceptual anomalies, even though the same word had already another meaning in the lexicon. Word-meaning pairs that thus arise may start to propagate in the population and actually supersede the "original" word-meaning pairs.

Ambiguity (incoherence along the FM dimension) is unavoidable as well for similar reasons. The same situation can often be conceptualised in more than one way and so an agent guessing the meaning of an unknown word or trying to make sense of a word in a particular context may easily derive another meaning than the one used by the speaker. Perceptual anomalies further aggravate the risk that a certain form becomes associated with another meaning by the hearer, as we have seen in some grounded example games earlier on.

Different conceptualisations of the world (incoherence along the RM and MR dimensions) are even harder to avoid because every agent develops its own ontologies independently and without any direct feedback from the other agents. The ideal language system is not only impossible to attain for autonomous agents engaged in grounded language games, it would be very inefficient to store and use as well because new words and meanings would be required for every new situation ever encountered. The larger the lexicon, the harder the task of a language learner to acquire it. So there is a trade off between coherence and expressibility. This is why natural languages constantly try to recruit existing words to keep down the repertoire of forms that have to be stored and hence learned.

7.3.2 Communicative success despite incoherence

A grounded language system cannot be fully coherent. This implies that communication among autonomous embodied agents can only work if their internal architectures are capable to handle incoherence. Of course, incoherence may not necessarily impinge on communicative success. Alternative conceptualisations may be compatible with the same situations. Agents may not even realise that their language systems are different because even though their words have different meanings these meanings may always pick out the same topic. Thus the RMF-landscape in Figure 7.9 leads to total success for communicating situation2. Even if a speaker uses 'tisame' to mean [GRAY-0.0,0.25] and

---

[9] The history of this search for such an ideal language is discussed by Eco (1997).

the hearer understands 'tisame' to mean [HPOS-0.5,0.75], they still have communicative success. The goal of the language game is to find the referent. It does not matter whether the meanings are the same. The agents cannot even know which meaning the other one uses because they have no access to each other's internal states.

The architecture of the agents in the Talking Heads experiment has been carefully designed so that incoherence can be handled. The context is at every level strongly taken into account. When producing an utterance, the meaning of a word is partly determined by whether that meaning makes sense in the specific context of the language game. This makes it possible to handle ambiguity. To handle synonymy, agents store several words in their lexicons so that they can understand more words than the ones they prefer themselves. Agents maintain different ways to conceptualise reality so that they can apply conceptualisations used by others even though they would not prefer these themselves.

The agents behave in their own selfish interest to maximise success in the game. They increase the score of the word-meaning pairs that yielded success and decrease those that resulted in failure so that next time around they are more likely to use that word-meaning pair. But a side effect of this behavior is that synonymy and ambiguity get damped. Success depends on use in the rest of the population. The more agents use a word, the more it will have success, the higher the scores will be, and the more it will be used. The global effect is that the language becomes more coherent without a central coordinator.

7.4 Damping synonymy and ambiguity

To conclude this chapter, I now discuss in more detail an example of this kind of semiotic dynamics as gleaned from an actual experiment with twenty Talking Heads, taking turns to materialise themselves in two robotic bodies at a single physical site. The agents have only R, G, B, and gray-scale channels. This case study illustrates how the tools introduced in the previous section help us to make sense of the very complex lexical evolution spontaneously arising in the system. We have set up the experiment in such a way that the agents first see a limited set of objects. Then we have progressively added new situations to the environment (by pasting new figures on the white board or reconfiguring existing figures) and studied the impact on the lexicons and ontologies of the agents.[10]

Figure 7.12 plots the global result of the experiment for 35,000 games. It shows the progressive increase in environmental complexity (after every 5000 games) and the average communicative and discriminative success in the game. During the final 15,000 games, no new objects were introduced.

We see clearly that the agents manage to bootstrap a successful lexicon from scratch in the first 1000 games. Success then drops every time the environment increases in complexity but regains as the agents invent new words or create new meanings. Progressively it is less and less difficult to handle increased environmental complexity be-

---

[10] These experiments work were done in strong collaboration with Frederic Kaplan, see for example Steels & Kaplan (1999).

7 Grounding

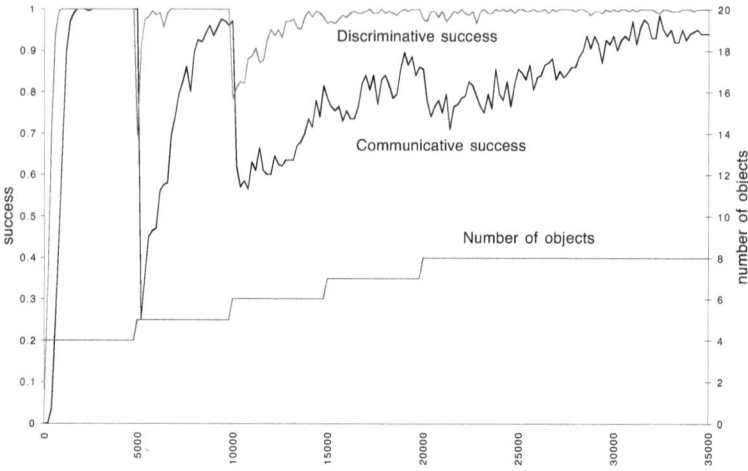

Figure 7.12: The graph shows the communicative and discriminatory success for a series of 35000 language games played by a group of 20 Talking Heads. The environment has progressively been made more complex.

cause distinctions are already available to cope with the novel situations, words are less ambiguous, and the lexicon is covering more and more meanings.

7.4.1 The story of *fepi*

Only looking at macroscopic measures like communicative success hides away the interesting rich lexical dynamics that unfolds in the population. Let me examine just one word, *fepi*. By looking at the FR-diagram, we see that this word is used consistently for identifying two objects (*O3* and *O5*) in a certain set of contexts (Figure 7.13).

We can see the meanings of *fepi*, by inspecting its FM-diagram (Figure 7.14). The dominant meaning of *fepi* is a particular shade of green [G 0.25–0.5]. There are some other competing meanings (including [GRAY 0.25–0.3125]) but most of them are hardly ever used. We observe clearly the tendency for ambiguity to get damped.

What about synonymy? Let us look at the MF-diagram of [G 0.25–0.5], so that we can see whether there are any other words in use for expressing the same meaning (Figure 7.15). *fepi* has indeed emerged as dominant for this meaning, but this has not been without an intense struggle. The tendency for synonymy to get damped is clearly present. Even though the lexicon occasionally destabilises, the lateral inhibition and the positive feedback loop between use and success causes self-organised MF-coherence. There is however something curious going on. In the early phases *xu* was dominant. Why did it destabilise and how has *fepi* has managed to become the dominant expression for [G 0.25–0.5]?

190

7.4 Damping synonymy and ambiguity

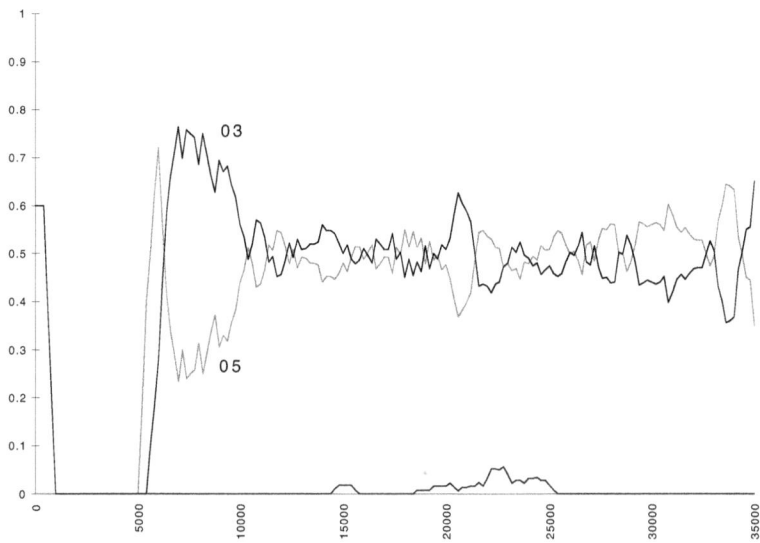

Figure 7.13: FR-diagram showing the frequencies of the objects referred to by the word *fepi*. *fepi* is consistently used for *O3* as well as *O5*.

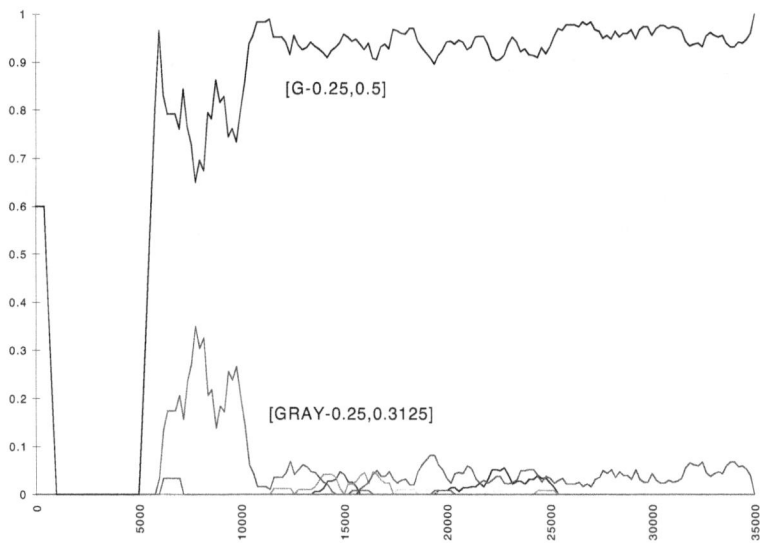

Figure 7.14: FM-diagram showing the different meanings of *fepi*. One meaning [G 0.25–0.5] dominates.

7 Grounding

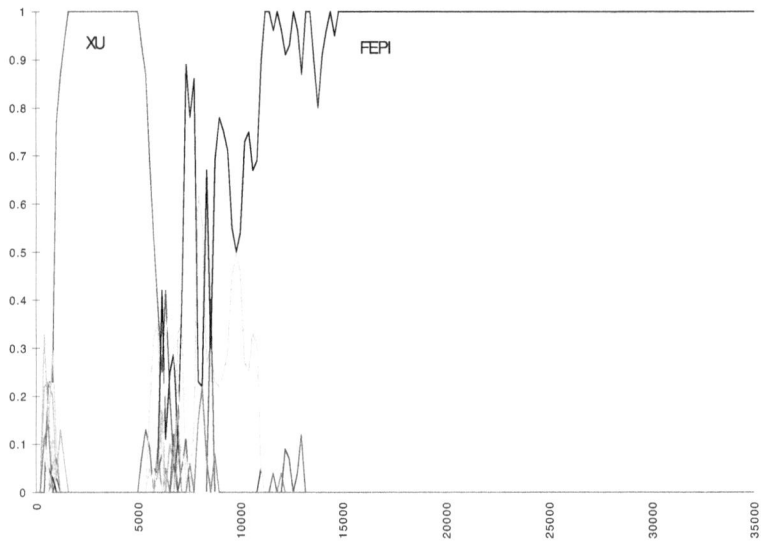

Figure 7.15: MF-diagram showing the different words circulating in the population for expressing the category [G 0.25–0.5]. First *xu* dominates and then *fepi* wins the competition after an intense struggle.

7.4.2 The story of *xu*

When inspecting in more detail the game traces, we see that *fepi* is created in game 328 by agent-3, playing the role of speaker, in order to refer to object *O3* using the meaning [G 0.25–0.5]. Agent-19, the hearer in the same game, acquires the same meaning for [G 0.25–0.5]. In one sense, we could say that agent-19 has learned this meaning of *fepi* from agent-3 but that is not entirely accurate. Agent-19 has constructed a possible meaning for *fepi* and this happened to be the same as the one used by agent-3, but this is partly accidental. Agents only indirectly learn the language from others. They construct a language which is compatible with the language used by others. Coherence among the individual language systems occurs through the positive feedback between language use and communicative success.

fepi entered into the lexicon to refer to *O3*, but we see from the RF diagram for *O3* (Figure 7.16) that *xu* was already well established for *O3* and initially *fepi* had no success at all. So the puzzle is still there, how did *fepi* manage to overtake *xu*?

Let us look at the different meanings of *xu* on a magnified scale by inspecting the FM-diagram of *xu* (Figure 7.17). Only the first 10,000 games are shown because after that *xu* is no longer used. In the first 5000 games, *xu* has the same dominant meaning as *fepi*, namely [G 0.25–0.5]. There are some other meanings associated with *xu*, which are all effective to conceptualise *O3*.

7.4 *Damping synonymy and ambiguity*

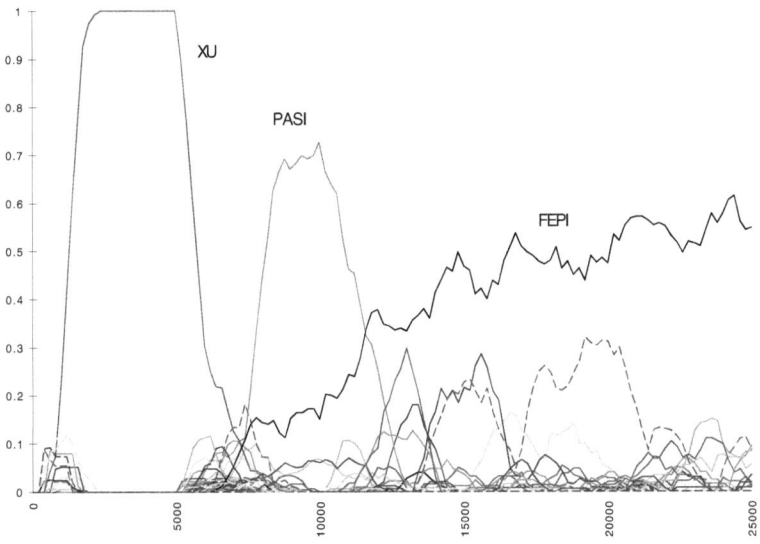

Figure 7.16: RF-diagram showing the different words being used for identifying *O3*. Initially *xu* dominates

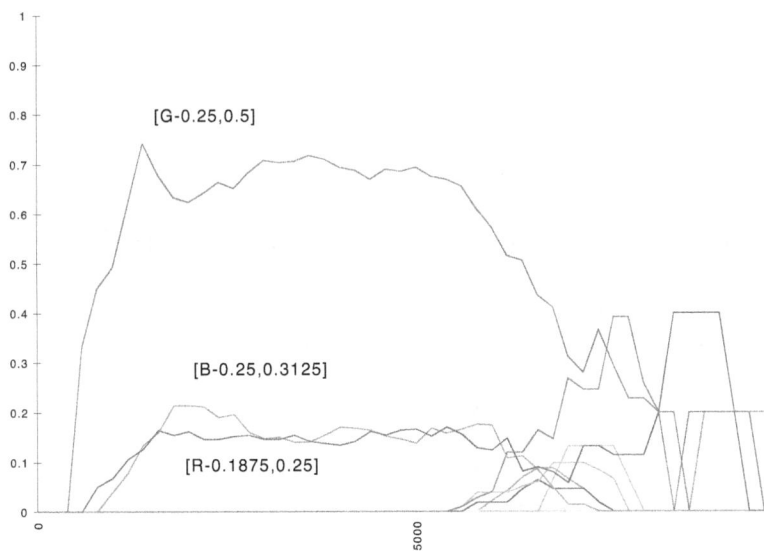

Figure 7.17: FM-diagram showing the different meanings of *xu*. After game 5000, the meaning of *xu* becomes unclear and the word falls in disrespute.

7.4.3 The entry of O3

The mystery is unveiled by looking at what happened when *O3*, a new object, entered the environment around game 5000. The word *xu* now not only picks out *O3* in certain contexts but *O5* as well. Hence games where both objects are occurring fail and consequently the association between *xu* and [G 0.25–0.5] is weakening. Closer examination reveals that *O5*'s green value is a bit lower (in the range [0.25,0375]) than that of *O3* (which is in the range [0.375,0.5]), so that a more refined distinction on the G-channel is necessary if both objects occur in the same context.

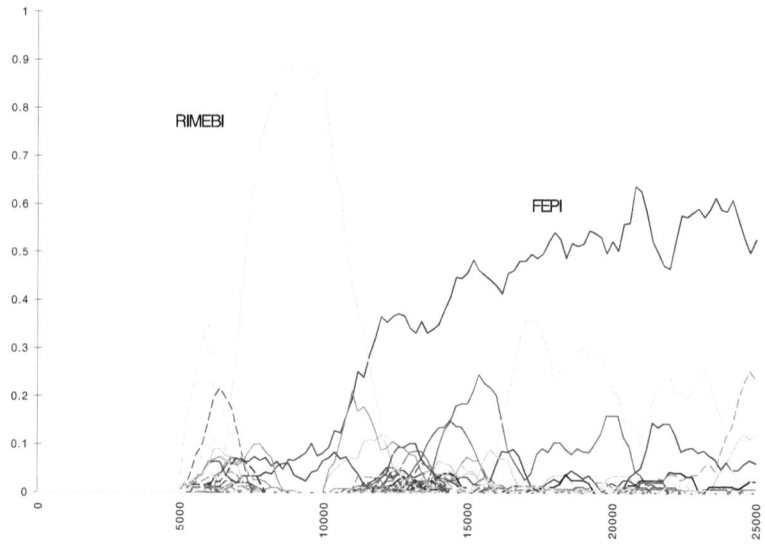

Figure 7.18: RF-diagram showing the different words used for *O5*. Initially a word *rimebi* dominates. It destabilises and *fepi* takes over.

As seen from the RF-diagram in Figure 7.16, *xu* is no longer used for *O3*. Instead the word 'pasi' comes to dominate. 'pasi' has indeed the more specific meaning [G 0.375–0.5] which is only applicable to *O3*, not to *O5*. At the same time we see from the RF-diagram for *O5* (Figure 7.18) that the word 'rimebi' initially dominates for designating *O5*. 'rimebi' has the more specific meaning [G 0.25–0.375] which is not applicable to *O3*. The more general word *xu* is still useful in some contexts where the refined distinction is not necessary (for example where either *O3* or *O5* is present but not both). So we would expect that *xu* continues to exist. However this is not the case. *xu* loses out completely and its role is taken over by *fepi*.

Understanding why this is the case tells us a great detail about the kind of hidden semiotic dynamics that takes place. *xu* loses its strength because (1) it fails in games where its meaning is not distinctive enough so that its score goes down, and (2) because there are other meanings competing with *xu* which do not have strong alternatives and are therefore less prone to failure. This is notably the case for *fepi*. *fepi* carries the more general meaning of green and does not have competitors. It therefore overtakes *xu*.

This example shows many things. Clearly lexical dynamics can be very complicated, despite the fact that the underlying mechanisms are relatively simple. Complexity comes partly from the complexity of the environment that continues to challenge the agents with novel , and partly from the internal complexity the semiotic dynamics spontaneously generates. There are strong tendencies in the agents' lexical systems towards FM and MF coherence, in other words towards shared lexicons. These tendencies are not due to a central controlling authority which has a global view of the lexicon and dictates to the agents what they should do but because incoherent form-meaning pairs do not resist when the environment changes. As we have seen, the word *fepi* could overtake *xu*, because *xu* had alternative meanings that caused failures in novel situations and *fepi* did not. *fepi* had a higher coherence and therefore survived, even though *xu* was used more often but with an ambiguous meaning.

7.5 Rousseau's paradox

The self-organised coherence of lexicons is an important outcome of the experiments, but what about the other semiotic dimension, the relation between situations and their conceptualisation? In how far do the agents use the same conceptualisations of reality in the same situations (RM-coherence) and in how far do they pick out the same topics given the same meaning (MR coherence). Many different ways to conceptualise reality may exist side by side and if each one can be expressed, it would lead to successful communication. So there is less a clear pressure to make the RM-coherence increase. The advantage of high RM-coherence is that the agents are more uniform in their behavior, so that fewer hypotheses need to be considered and the acquisition of the lexicon by virgin agents is easier.

7.5.1 Universality versus relativism

This raises a fundamental question, which has been heavily debated throughout the history of philosophy, namely in how far have different languages different ontologies and in how far does the use of a language influence ontological coherence in a population. From one point of view, words are seen as labeling existing (innate or learned) categories, and so the problem of learning a lexicon consists in learning the association between unknown labels and known internal categories.[11] On the other hand, ethnologists and linguists studying non-European languages almost invariably arrive at the conclusion

---

[11] "The speed and precision of vocabulary acquisition leaves no real alternative to the conclusion that the child somehow has the concepts prior to experience with language, and is basically learning labels for concepts that are already part of his or her conceptual apparatus." p.21. in Chomsky (1987).

7 Grounding

that there are profound differences between languages, not simply in which words they use but also in which way they conceptualise reality. This implies that there is a kind of co-evolution between language and meaning.[12]

Here is a seemingly trivial example of the interaction between language and meaning. In French, the second singular person pronoun ('you') has two forms: 'tu' and 'vous'. Textbooks say that the first is colloquial and the second form is polite. A speaker is therefore required to categorise the social relation between himself and the hearer, which he is not forced to do in English. But polite/colloquial is too simplistic to capture the underlying usages. The categorisation of the speech situation is quite subtle, possibly incorporating age differences, professional status, class differences, pragmatic context, speaking style, etc. Someone learning to speak French must not only learn that 'you' has two forms but also what the subtle distinctions are between the situations where you use one or the other. If you think learning this distinction is difficult, just consider Japanese, where there are dozens of words for 'I', some of them listed in Table 7.9.

Table 7.9: Words for 'I' in Japanese

A	Chin	As-shi	Fu-sho
A-i	Da-i-ko	A-ta-i	Ge-kan
A-ta-ki	Ge-se-tsu	A-ko	Da-ra
A-ta-ku-shi	Ge-sho	A-re	Fu-bin
A-te	Gi-ra	A-shi	Fu-ko-ku
A-ta-shi	Go-jin	Bo-ku	Gu

Here is another example which is more related to the perceptually grounded distinctions we are studying here. To categorise space, a viewer typically imposes a frame of reference on the scene before him and categorises regions and positions in terms of this frame of reference. For example, standing in front of a chair we could say in English *the table is to the right of the chair*, where *to the right of* designates an area to the right within the frame of reference relative to axes emanating from the observer. This seems the most natural and simplest way to categorise space and it is used by the Talking Heads when they expand the HPOS channel. However, there are quite a few languages which impose an absolute frame of reference, see Levinson & Wilkins (2006). For example, the Tenejapans from Chiapas, Mexico speak a Mayan language known as Tzeltal. They live in a mountaneous region that is generally sloping north-northwest. They use this regional characteristic to introduce an absolute frame of reference with three distinctions: uphill, downhill, and across. Standing in front of the chair, they would literally say something like 'standing at its uphill chair the table', in other words, 'the table is uphill from the chair'. The spatial categories left, right, front, back, etc. simply do not exist in Tzeltal. Something that is *to the left* from the viewpoint of English could be 'downhill', 'uphill', or 'across' depending on its absolute position. If we want to translate *to the left of* in

---

[12] The best known representative of this position is Whorf (1956). See for a wider discussion Lee (1996).

Tzeltal, we first have to conceptualise the global reference frame that is valid in the situation being described, and only then we can choose whether 'uphill', 'downhill', or 'across' are appropriate translations. It could be argued that these differences are purely due to differences in lexicalisation. But this is not so. An absolute frame of reference has not only an impact on language but also deep implications for other cognitive tasks. Psychologists have invented non-verbal tasks where speakers of Tzeltal make other spatial inferences than Europeans. Ignoring such profound cultural differences is therefore a sure recipe for disastrous misunderstandings.

The degree of sharing (or non-sharing) of an ontology in a group raises the paradox, first expressed by Jean-Jacques Rousseau. Language requires a sufficiently shared categorisation of reality, otherwise no communication is possible. But, if every language employs its own categorisation (even if there are large overlaps), how is a particular individual entering a language community supposed to know the categorisation implicit in his or her language? It is clear that language helps foster shared meaning because meaning is transmitted through language, for example when a speaker explains the meaning of a word to a hearer. On the other hand, successful language interaction already requires at least some shared meaning, how could the system otherwise bootstrap itself? So we have a chicken and egg situation, a causal circularity that somehow must be broken.

7.5.2 Ontological coherence

The Talking Heads experiment shows a way to resolve this paradox. Different agents develop their own ontology in a selectionist fashion, using the growth and pruning dynamics discussed in Chapter 4. Because there is some randomness in the growth process and because different agents see different cases in which other channels may be salient, it is highly unlikely that they all end up with exactly the same set of categories, even though agents operating in the same environment with a similar sensori-motor apparatus will develop similar distinctions.

On the other hand, the coupling between the conceptual and lexical layer discussed in the previous chapter causes a strong interaction between the two. Those distinctions whose lexicalisations are the most successful are preferred, and the scores of categorisers is influenced by the outcome of the games in which they were used. This structural coupling causes a progressive coordination of the ontology and the lexicon of the agents, even though ontologies will never be completely identical.

Figure 7.19 shows the result of some experiments focusing on ontological coherence (i.e. RM-coherence). The agents reach a close to 100 % discriminatory success, and coherence climbs to 75 %. Multiple solutions are possible, and so there is no reason why the agents would have completely convergent ontologies.

A more fine-grained way to visualise the emerging coherence between the agents' ontologies is through a COHERENCE WEB (see Figure 7.20). There is an axis for each agent as well as a line emanating from the center of the web. Let *a1* and *a2* be two agents, then *a1*'s line intersects with *a2*'s axis at the level of coherence between *a1* and *a2*. For example, if *a1* and *a2* have a 50 % ontological coherence, then *a1*'s line intersects *a2*'s

7 Grounding

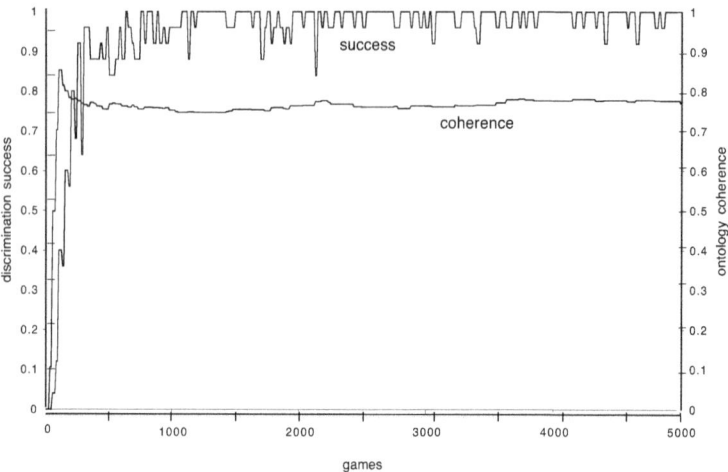

Figure 7.19: This figure shows the discrimination success as well as the ontological (RM) coherence for a series of 5000 discrimination games in a group of 10 agents.

axis at point 0.5. The intersection between an agent's line and its own axis represents the average coherence of this agent with respect to all the other agents. When there is little coherence, the lines cluster around the center of the cobweb. As coherence increases, the lines approach more and more the edges of the diagram. If all lines end up exactly on the edges, there is complete coherence. Similar coherence webs can be constructed for the other semiotic relations studied earlier.

The evolution in the coherence webs in Figure 7.20 shows clearly that the agents are coordinating their ontologies, despite direct feedback about the meaning of a game. Feedback only comes from the pointing through the external world. More experiments need to be done to with more channels so that the set of possible alternative conceptualisations is sufficiently significant to investigate the co-evolution of language and meaning more precisely. Nevertheless, the experiments show that ontologies can be coordinated without needing to be innate.

7.6 Conclusions

The experiments reported in this chapter have demonstrated that the various mechanisms introduced in earlier chapters not only work in computer simulations but also in experiments with embodied situated agents. The grounding of language games in physical reality introduces perceptual and behavioral anomalies which may cause failures and additional ambiguities in the lexical systems of the agents. However the mechanisms introduced before, particularly the forces damping synonymy and ambiguity, still prove to be adequate to lead the population towards a coherent successful language system.

The lexical and ontological evolution observed even in small populations of agents quickly becomes too complicated to investigate by hand. I therefore introduce a number of tools, such as the semiotic landscape, the coherence diagrams, and the coherence web. We clearly need more of these tools and we need to study additional properties of emergent lexicons, such as the semantic relations between the words and how they may evolve.

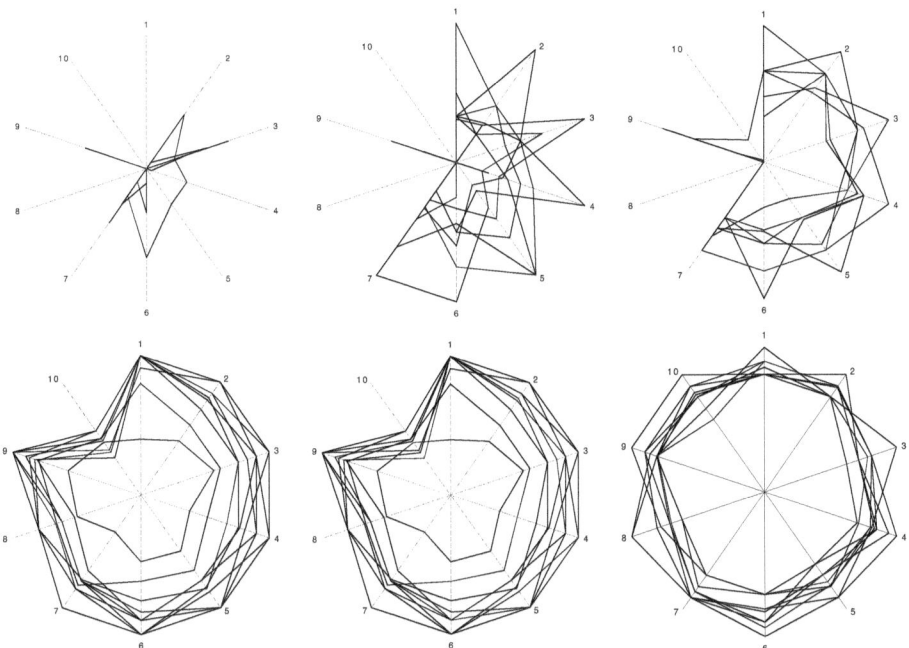

Figure 7.20: Coherence diagrams visualising the coherence of ontologies in a group of 10 agents for a series of 1000 discrimination games. Lines emanate from the center when there is close to 0 % coherence. They approach the edges in the case of 100 % ontological coherence.

Part II

Installations and experiments

8 The first series (1999)

The ideas and results that have been discussed in Part I of the present volume were based on results obtained in idealised conditions. Computer simulations are able to test the validity of the basic algorithms, but simulations are still theoretical in nature. It is well known that technologies can only become a reality after experiments have been carried out in open-ended real world conditions. Nobody would want to fly an airplane that has only been tested in computer simulations.

We did the same for the Talking Heads experiments and this was a huge step. Many more people had to get get involved: for making the code more robust, setting up the teleportation infrastructure, and installing and maintaining the physical installations in different countries. The mechanisms about language evolution discussed in Part I of this book did not significantly change. On the contrary, they received solid experimental confirmation. At the same time, we learned a huge amount about the dependencies between these mechanisms and the environments in which agents use them. We also learned a great deal about running software agents in an open infrastructure distributed over the entire globe. Furthermore we learned a lot about the interaction between humans and agents ranging from enthusiastic participation and enjoyment to nasty attacks by English hackers, set on destroying the experiment.

This chapter provides more detail on the first main experiment that took place in the summer of 1999 as part of the Laboratorium exhibition in Antwerp. The next chapter documents follow up experiments that took place within the context of the N01SE exhibition in Cambridge and London and at several other locations.

8.1 The Laboratorium exhibition

The Laboratorium exhibition was a major artistic event in Europe during the summer of 1999 organised by Bruno Verbergt of an organisation called *Antwerpen Open*. It was one of the first exhibitions that put so much emphasis on art as a research activity and on profound interactions between art and science. Participants included both scientists and science historians such as Peter Galison, Bruno Latour, Israel Rosenfield and Isabelle Stengers, as well as architects such as Rem Koolhaas and artists with an affinity for research such as Peter Fischli and David Weiss, Gabriel Orozco, Carsten Höller, Panamarenko, Lawrence Weiner and others. The exhibition was visited by 8000 people.

The introduction to the catalog edited by curators Hans Ulrich Obrist and Barbara Vanderlinden[1] stated the objectives as follows:

---

[1] The catalog of the Laboratorium exhibition was published as Obrist & Vanderlinden (1999).

8 The first series (1999)

> Laboratorium is an interdisciplinary project in which the scientific laboratory and the artist's studio are explored on the basis of their various concepts within the different disciplines. How can we attempt to bridge the gap between the specialized vocabulary of science, art and the general interest of the audience, between the expertise of skilled practitioners and the concerns and preconcepts of the interested audience?
>
> Laboratorium will search the limits and possibilities of the places where knowledge and culture are made. Throughout the summer we will establish within the city of Antwerpen networks, fluctuating between highly specialized work by scientists, artists, dancers, and writers. "Working places" where the participants communicate their findings on the "work in progress". Also the scientific laboratories in Antwerpen will be involved in the initiative.
>
> Laboratorium started as a discussion that involves questions such as: What is the meaning of laboratories? What is the meaning of experiments? When do experiments become public and when does the result of an experiment reach public consensus? Is rendering public what happens inside the laboratory of the scientist and the studio of the artist a contradiction in terms? These and other questions are being offered in this interdisciplinary project that starts with the "workplace" where the artists and the scientists experiment and work freely.

The event was part of the activities, celebrating the famous Antwerp painter Anthony van Dyck born 400 years earlier. In preparation of the exhibition a series of discussions were held between Carsten Höller, Bruno Latour, Hans-Ulrich Obrist, Luc Steels and Barbara Vanderlinden. These discussions helped to shape the general concept of the exhibition and the selection of the artists and scientists who would participate. Excerpts appeared in the exhibition catalog and other publication fora, Obrist (2003).

The exhibition took place in two locations: the photography museum in Antwerp, which was the main location, and an annex occupying several floors in a high rise office building close to the central station (the so called President's Building). The Photography Museum Exhibition featured work by several well known artists, architects and scientists. The annex featured the Talking Heads experiment as well as work by artists Joseph Grigely and Matt Mullican and science philosopher Isabelle Stengers, who had set up a reconstruction of Galileo's famous experiments. There were also a number of public presentations under the heading "The Theatre of Proof", organised by Bruno Latour. The catalog was designed by Bruce Mau and his team.

In addition to the installation at the exhibition in Antwerp itself, there were two additional external sites for the Talking Heads experiment operating within the same time frame: The Paris site at the Sony Computer Science Laboratory in Paris and the Brussels site at the Free University (Vrije Universiteit) of Brussels.

Months of preparation and testing took place before we attempted to go "live" and public. Once this happened, work continued frantically to shake out bugs, get the semiotic dynamics right and then maintain the general communication infrastructure and the ongoing interactions with participants. The fascinating email correspondence (see section 8.3) shows that most of the difficulties initially came from running the agent

8.2 The installation

Figure 8.1: Hans-Ulrich Obrist and Luc Steels during the opening of the Laboratorium Exhibition in Antwerp, summer 1999.

teleportation infrastructure. The reader has to keep in mind that this was late nineties, when large-scale uploading and downloading, cloud computing, agent architectures, etc. were totally in their infancy.

The real heros of the first Talking Heads series were Angus McIntyre, who was the chief architect of the agent teleportation infrastructure, Fréderic Kaplan, who kept an eye on the Paris site in particular, Joris Van Looveren, who looked after the Brussels and Antwerp sites, and Mario Campanella, an aeronautical engineer from Brazil who had shown up at the last minute to help keep track of the Antwerp installation. I focused on the overall dynamics of the experiment, which initially was certainly not going the way it should, and on handling the contact with the exhibition organisers and the press. Silvere Tajan, Alexis Agahi and Holger Kenn helped to create the telecommunication infrastructure.

8.2 The installation

The installation in Antwerp was announced as a "Laboratory for Cognitive Robotics and Teleportation" (Steels 1999). It featured various rooms as shown in the layout in Figure 8.2. The rooms had different functions:

1. The CENTRAL ROOM which was visible on entering the space contained the experiment itself, i.e. the two cameras mounted on tripods, the computers driving them, the screen with geometric figures, and a projection of what went on. The activities of the agents were audible through a narration.

8 The first series (1999)

2. A READING ROOM contained background philosophical and scientific papers and excerpts from books about language, meaning and their origins.

3. A USER INTERFACE ROOM contained a workstation where visitors to the exhibition could create their own agents, direct them to play games on certain sites, and teach new words to their agents.

A typical example of the kind of images that the cameras picked up are shown in Figure 8.4. To play a game, the agent had to find a sufficiently delineated group of objects and each object had to exceed a minimal size. Initially quite complex configurations were put on the white board but this made it very difficult for agents to find a coherent group and to develop good concepts for referring to the topic. The right image in Figure 8.4 provides clear examples of up, down, left and right, different colors, and also opportunities to use multiple words (such as *red bottom*).

A typical example of an interaction is shown in Figure 8.5. The speaker (called "rubber", an agent created and named by a user) has selected the blue object at the bottom left of the screen. We see the discrimination trees of the agent at that point and the data for each of the objects recognised. The coordinates of the respective objects (scaled within the coordinate system of the captured image) are (0.0,1.0) for the blue object, (1.0, 0.96)

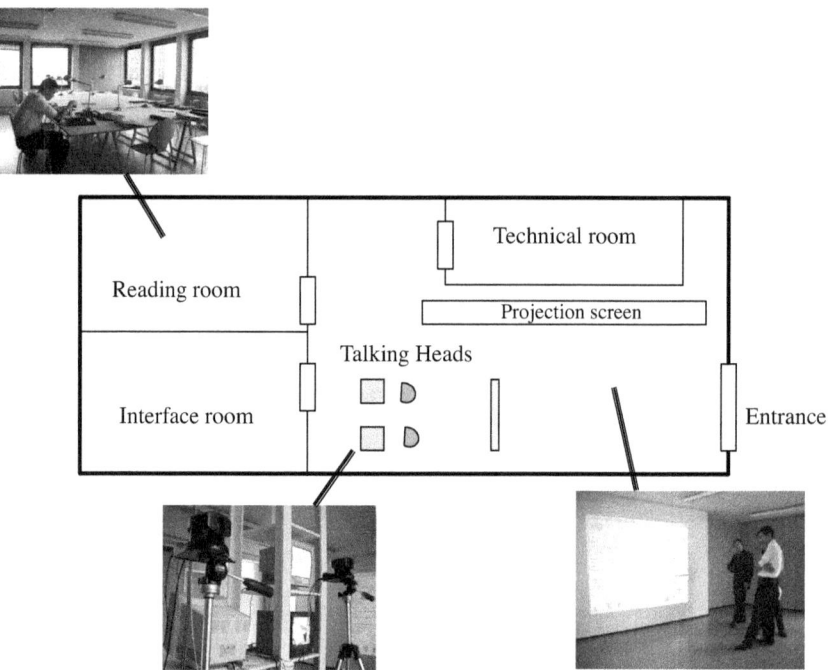

Figure 8.2: Layout of the "Laboratory for Cognitive Robotics and Teleportation" at the Laboratorium exhibition in Antwerp.

206

8.2 The installation

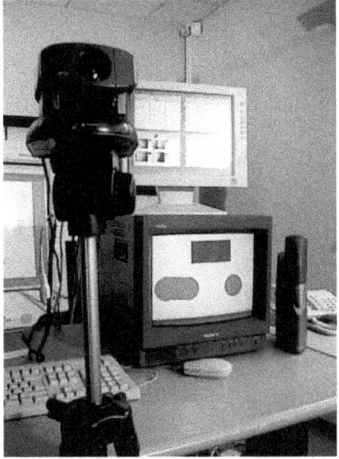

Figure 8.3: A single Talking Head at the Paris site. In the background we see (bottom) the display with an image that the agent picked up, (on top of that) a screen displaying the processed image and the discrimination trees, and to the right the loudspeaker broadcasting the speech output of the agent.

Figure 8.4: Examples of images picked up by the cameras. The chosen topic was signalled by drawing a bounding box around it. During experimentation, it was found that configurations such as in the right image led to more stable performance.

207

for the red one, and (0.42, 0.0) for the green one. The values are displayed as HP (horizontal position), VP (vertical position), H (height), W (width), A (area), R (red), G (green), Y (yellow), B (blue), L (lightness). The blue object is chosen as the topic and the value on the blue channel has the most discriminative power, although there are other possibilities. There are three competing words for naming blue: *Xagadude*, *Nibidesu*, and *Tetipi*. None of them have a score higher than 0 and so a random choice of *Xagadude* is made.

The hearer (called "me") perceives an image which is slightly different from the one seen by the speaker. Also the discrimination trees built up so far by this agent are different from the ones used by the speaker. The hearer does not know the word, so the game fails. After the speaker has then pointed to the topic, the hearer conceptualises and guesses that the meaning of this word is 'blue' because that is also for him the most discriminating feature of the topic (which has coordinates 0.0, 1.0) compared to the other objects in the context.

The experiment had also a presence on the web, designed by Angus McIntyre. Anyone could log in on the Talking Heads website, create an agent with a given name, and launch it on a tour of the various physical sites. There was also a forum on which users could discuss the experiment as it was progressing, a hall of fame for the agents that were the best communicators, and an overview of the lexicon that had formed so far. The website allowed inspection of what was happening at each site (Figure 8.6): Users could check which agents were waiting there to play a game, and what the current game was about. It also displayed statistics about the communicative success and agent activity at each site. The site is no longer operational due to changes to the underlying software but some remnants can be visited here: https://ai.vub.ac.be/talking-heads/

An example of how the web interface displayed a single game is shown in Figure 8.7. There are two agents: Antonusius is the speaker and Zelebot is the hearer. The green object has been chosen as topic and correctly recognised by the hearer using the word *kazozo*. The meaning of the word was not visible through the interface because we wanted users to learn themselves the language of the agents.

8.3 Start up of the experiment

Once the physical installation at the Antwerp site was completed, work focused on getting the experiment itself up and running. It is interesting and instructive to look at some snippets of the email correspondence during the first weeks. The despair when trying to cope with the unavoidable problems but also the excitement as a language began to emerge shines through. The English humor of Angus McIntyre was a welcome antidote to all the stress. The correspondence reprinted here is a small selection but also necessary fragmentary because a lot of communication took place face-to-face or through the telephone, as email was not always possible.

8.3 Start up of the experiment

Rubber hole
speaker

"xagadude"

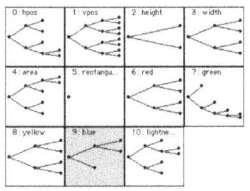

(0.00, 1.00): HP=0.37 VP=0.71 H=0.48 W=0.21
  A=0.45 R=0.17 G=0.00 Y=0.00 B=0.39 L=0.28
(1.00, 0.96): HP=0.70 VP=0.69 H=0.38 W=0.22
  A=0.45 R=0.98 G=0.00 Y=0.52 B=0.00 L=0.36
(0.42, 0.00): HP=0.51 VP=0.31 H=0.21 W=0.51
  A=0.70 R=0.00 G=0.99 Y=0.73 B=0.00 L=0.46
Categorization: ((B 0.25-0.5))
Words: ((XAGADUDE ((B 0.25-0.5)) 0.00)
  (NIBIDESU ((B 0.25-0.5)) 0.00)
  (TETIPI (B 0.25-0.5)) 0.00))
Choose: ((B 0.25-0.5)) -- (XAGADUDE)

me
hearer

"xagadude?"

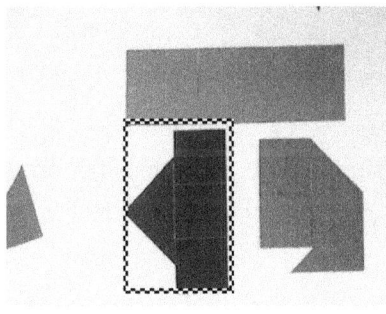

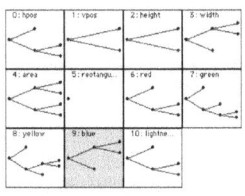

(1.00,0.96): HP=0.70 VP=0.69 H=0.38 W=0.22
  A=0.45 R=1.00 G=0.00 Y=0.50 B=0.00 L=0.32
(0.00,1.00): HP=0.45 VP=0.67 H=0.50 W=0.22
  A=0.48 R=0.17 G=0.00 Y=0.00 B=0.39 L=0.23
(0.42,0.00): HP=0.59 VP=0.25 H=0.23 W=0.54
  A=0.77 R=0.00 G=0.77 Y=0.82 B=0.00 L=0.40
Unknown word.
New association: (XAGADUDE) + ((B 0.25-0.5))

Game 1140 Thu-24-02-2000 5:20 PM

Figure 8.5: Top: Source image, conceptualisation, and word choice of the speaker. Bottom: Source image, parsing and interpretation of the hearer.

8 *The first series (1999)*

Figure 8.6: The Talking Heads website main interface. Users could create and manage their own agents and inspect what was happening at each site. Here 12 agents located at the Brussels site are listed.

8.3 Start up of the experiment

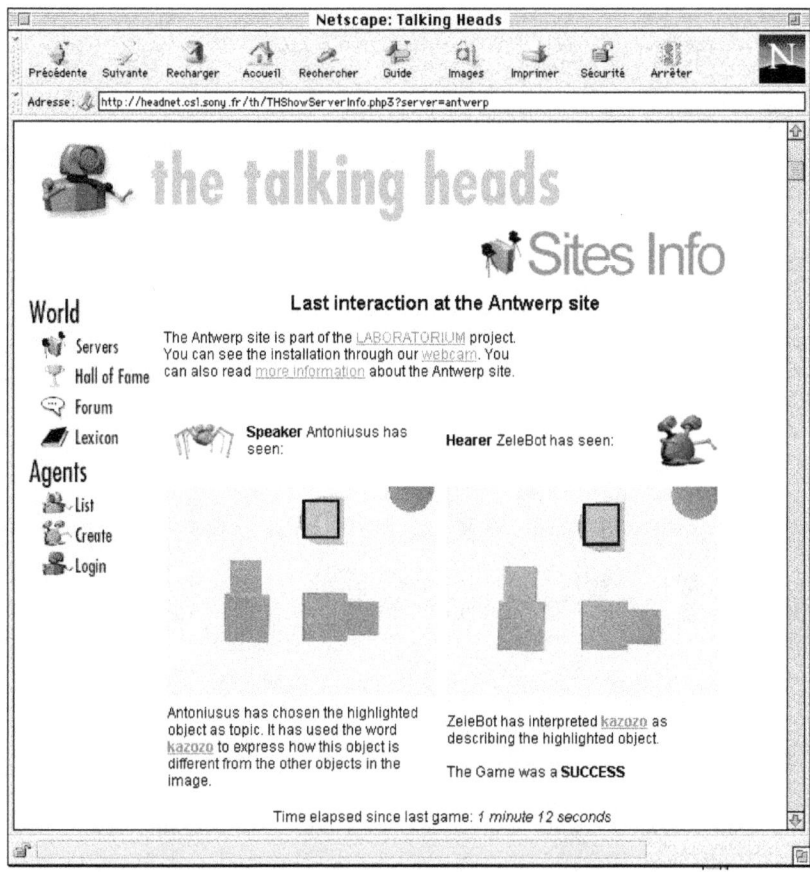

Figure 8.7: Example of an interaction that took part in Antwerp. This game was a success. The agents recognised the same set of objects and the meaning of *kazozo* was effective in finding the same topic.

8 The first series (1999)

We pick up the email correspondence on June 23, 1999 when the first experiments are taking place to try and make language games at the three sites possible and allow the scheduling and activation of agents.

23 June 1999

```
-============_-1278188520==_d============
From: Angus McIntyre <angus@csl.sony.fr>
Subject: Re: Brussels is back
At 9:04 pm +0200 23.06.99, Joris Van Looveren wrote: >Brussels
is officially back on line. I forgot to make sure that there
>were no agents here before I launched it, so don't be surprised
if it
>turns out that some agents have suddenly been cloned :)
I don't think agents can be cloned; 'headnet' will probably just
say "Oh, back so soon?" and overwrite existing definitions.
This may lead to inconsistencies if two copies of an agent are
out and about at the same time ...
Brussels is active, which is good. Paris appears to have gone
to sleep, either because the lights are out, or because it's
past its pre-defined bedtime. Still, the Babel software still
seems to be running with nothing more than the usual email
process errors.
>- The machine is still fast enough to do other work. The only
> thing that is a bit annoying is that it stalls when images
> are being grabbed (read: sent over the bus).
There's a lot of data moving over a slow line, and evidently the
MacOS is giving it priority to prevent dropped frames when doing
video capture.
>- Since there is no sound, it is blazingly fast compared to
> the Antwerp installation (2-3 games per minute or so)
Speech and camera motion are the big slow downs. This means
that we're not under a lot of pressure to optimize the agent
code, as the agents can do all their discriminations faster than
we'll ever be able to drive the cameras (until we try using the
little EVI-G21's, which only have to move a little CCD unit
rather than a whole camera assembly, and apparently track very
quickly indeed).
I've announced the site to a handful of links pages (Peter
Norvig's AI links collection, Chris Bogart's Constructed
Languages page, the NASA real robots page - links to all these
sites are under 'background' on our site). I haven't yet done a
massive submit of the site to the big search engines or
```

announcement sites; I suggest that we let traffic build slowly
so we can find out what we can handle. A

24 June 1999

The (faster) machines that were planned are now available, so that a switch has to be made while the experiment is already running.

```
-============_-1278188520==_d============
```
From: Angus McIntyre <angus@csl.sony.fr>
Subject: 'headnet' now running on new PII 400 server.
Silvere and Alexis have installed Linux and the headnet software
on the new 400Mhz Pentium II server, and I've done the DNS
switch (and updated /etc/hosts, and csl.zone, and sony.rev, and
sony.zone, and killed half a dozen in.named processes, and
killed squid, and restarted squid, and killed squid, and
restarted squid, and killed squid, and deleted squid's cache,
and restarted squid, and flushed my Netscape cache, and flushed
everyone else's Netscape cache, and flushed the Netscape cache
of eight dozen people in Australia who I've never met, and
individually inspected and edited every packet on the Internet
to make sure that 'headnet.csl.sony.fr' now points to the new
box).
The result of this is that 'headnet.csl.sony.fr' should now get
you the P400 server, and 'headnet-dev.csl.sony.fr' should get
you the old 200Mhz Vectra, which can be recognised because it
has the words 'test site' in the banner that appears at the top
of the page.
With luck, the change should be transparent and you shouldn't
need to do anything. You should however check to make sure that
your agents are going to the right server, however, and that
when your browser looks for 'headnet', that it gets the correct
machine. If your Babel server accesses 'headnet' via a cacheing
proxy server, you may also need to ask your sysop to clear the
server's cache and restart it.
Enjoy A

-============_-1278188520==_d============
To: Joris Van Looveren <joris@arti.vub.ac.be>
From: Angus McIntyre <angus@csl.sony.fr>
Subject: Re: Brussels 2pm
At 2:00 pm +0200 24.06.99, Joris Van Looveren wrote: >We're planing to go to Antwerp in 1 hour. There is no telephone there, >so we will communicate by email ... We're thinking of clearing the
>database around 4 pm. ... do you want to do it from Paris ?
You do it. At 3:55pm, I'll kick all the agents off 'paris' and pause it. When I see headnet has been cleared, I'll restart 'paris' and make some new agents.
I'll upload the changed TH website with the direct links to 'headnet' at the same time.
A

-============_-1278188520==_d============
From: Angus McIntyre <angus@csl.sony.fr>
Subject: Things to do in Antwerp when you're head(net) ...
There seems to be some problem with the changeover of the machines. What's happened is that the new address for 'headnet' (193.105.194.10, which is to say the PII 400, rather than 193.105.194.8, which is the Vectra formerly known as 'headnet' but now represented by an unpronounceable symbol that means 'headnet-dev') has not yet propagated through the DNS as far as Belgium.
So Antwerp (yeah! welcome to the net!) is sending its agents to 'headnet-dev', rather than 'headnet'. There's no great problem here as far as testing your installation goes, except that 'paris' is pointing at the new 'headnet' and 'brussels' is apparently dead, so you won't be seeing any foreign agents.
In theory, if you reboot, the DNS results cached on the Macintosh should go away, forcing a re-lookup which ought to get the correct values. If that doesn't work, you could try taking the MacTCP DNR file which lives in the System Folder *out* of the System Folder and then rebooting. And if that doesn't work, we just have to be patient and wait for the changes to propagate. You could also consider entering the address of 'headnet' as dotted IP (193.105.194.10) in the network configuration dialog.
A

8.3 Start up of the experiment

From: Angus McIntyre <angus@csl.sony.fr>
Subject: Re: Database cleared
At 5:47 pm +0200 24.06.99, Joris Van Looveren wrote: >The databases have just been cleared. You can create new agents now.
>Brussels might be down for some more time, so check if it's up before you
>send any agents there.
OK. I notice there are bugs in the server code which cause it to generate scads of errors when the database is empty, but those should clear.
I've restarted 'paris', and I'm now going to make some agents to send there. Antwerp is showing up on 'headnet', and the error messages strewn all over the site should go away when we get some data into the database.
When it begins to look a little more solid, I'll upload the changed pages on 'talking-heads', and then we'll really be live.
A

From: Angus McIntyre <angus@csl.sony.fr>
Subject: Re: Webcam
At 6:28 pm +0200 24.06.99, Joris Van Looveren wrote: >The Antwerp webcam is on-line:
I've added a link from the Antwerp page on the main site, and I've also added a link in the descriptive text about the Antwerp server which appears on the 'server overview' page.
I actually saw one of you - Fred? - through the Antwerp webcam a moment ago.
> Also, the Antwerp and Brussels site are up 'permanently',
> so can send agents to them.
I've created a bunch of agents and sent them round the sites. The server seems to be acquiring consistency.
I'm off home now. If you need me to come back and kick the server, call me on: +33-1-42-78-xx-xx Bye, A

25 June 1999

The different sites and the teleportation infrastructure are now running but there are still basic problems stemming from hardware and software glitches.

```
-=============_-1278188520==_d=============
Date: Fri, 25 Jun 1999 05:13:55 EST
From: "frederic kaplan" <fred@captage.com>
Subject: First night
```
The talking-heads in Antwerp have passed the night OK... 34 agents 18 users... It goes fast
It seems that Paris and Brussels are not playing anymore ?
Fred.

```
From: Angus McIntyre <angus@csl.sony.fr>
Subject: Re: Antwerp & Brussels live!
```
At 10:52 am +0200 25.06.99, Joris Van Looveren wrote: >I got e-mails from Antwerp and Brussels that they resumed normally this
>morning. So they both survived their first night on the job! Paris seems to be still ticking along. One thing I notice is that it's quite easy for agents to 'pool' on one particular server at the expense of others. The more agents you have on any one server, the longer it takes for each agent to get through its assigned 50 games or whatever. So servers with many agents tend to stay occupied, and others which are waiting to receive agents can often stand empty waiting for the agents to play out their games on the crowded servers.
It's probably a good idea to have a few agents (either the ones owned by 'adm' or your own agents) set up to make round trips, playing five games here, five games there, and so on. Long routes of small numbers of games rather than short routes involving many games is probably the way to load balance and prevent servers drying up.
> ... the database is still accessible through a simple URL,
>without any protection (password). I think since headnet has gone
>public, it would be a good idea to change this ...
The same idea had occurred to me. I'll look into that (trans: I'll try to find the piece of paper on which I wrote down the root password to 'headnet' and, if I find it, I'll set up an .htaccess file to keep strangers out).

8.3 Start up of the experiment

I've told a few friends of mine about it, and the response so far has been generally positive, although Sylvia – Luc's proofreader – apparently has some reservations about the usability of the site.
Hmm. News update.
A friend of mine, who shall be nameless, sent down an agent with route: 'brussels paris antwerp' As I predicted a few days ago, this will (and did) cause a LISP-level error.
I patched the route by hand and then made the mistake of trying to use MCL's rather flaky 'Restart frame' option to go on. At first this seemed to have worked, but about one game later things went bad and the whole machine locked. One of the three agents then on the server managed to get out just seconds ahead of the meltdown, but two more were caught on the server and are now in limbo. I've edited the database for one of them to try to resurrect it, and if that works, I'll try to revive the other as well.
I'll also write a quick bit of code to do route-checking to try to make sure that this doesn't happen again.
A

-=============_-1278188520==_d=============
From: Angus McIntyre <angus@raingod.com>
Subject: The Lazarus Syndrome
When a Babel server falls over and agents get lost, it's possible to restore them to life by going onto Headnet's 'admin' page and editing the agent's entry in the 'THAgent' table. Basically, if you reset the 'isonserver' field to 1 (it will be 0 when the agent's away), the agent should spontaneously reappear on headnet and then move off to wherever it was meant to go. There will be inconsistencies in the database – 'headnet' will remember all the words that the agent used before the crash, but the agent's own memory is reset to what it was when it left 'headnet' – but with luck they shouldn't be too serious.
By the way, there's a bug in the 'headnet' software with respect to routes; there's a finite limit on the field length for the 'route' field. If you make a route that's too long, it gets truncated, so you can have an agent whose route goes:
... paris 10 bruss The agent will complete its games on 'paris' and then go into stasis waiting for a server called 'bruss' to pick it up. A patch for this would probably be nice to have at some point. A

8 The first series (1999)

```
-============_-1278188520==_d============
```
From: Holger Kenn <kenn@arti9.vub.ac.be>
Subject: Alpha box in Antwerpen gone...
Hi !
The alpha box in Antwerpen is gone.
Please somebody reboot it ASAP, or we won't have a connection to
Antwerpen anymore...
Holger p.s.: To reboot: Disconnect Printer. Switch alpha box
off. Switch on again. Wait about 5 Minutes. Reconnect printer.
Holger

28 June 1999

After the basic hardware appeared to be operational, attention turned to the actual behavior of the emergent language system. Initial results are not very encouraging.

```
-============_-1278188520==_d============
```
From: Luc Steels <steels@arti.vub.ac.be>
Subject: paris site
I just examined the Paris site a bit. The error rate is
distressing. This is due to many things.
1. The calibration is way off. Even if they get it right,
calibration mixes up completely the game. It is obligatory to
calibrate much better tomorrow morning (can you do this
frederic?)
2. The light conditions were very bad and have been improved a
bit so that patches of white light are no longer seen as objects.
3. The visual situations about which the agents are playing
games are way too complex. Even humans would not be able to play
the game. I simplified enormously. We need to make similar
clear situations AT ALL sites so that the agents can really
learn the very basic concepts first. Also salience might have
to be set lower to have multi-categories and consequently
multi-words (although there is a fundamental bug in the
multi-word thing it seems). Now the agents are making much too
deep discrimination trees because of the confusing nature of the
situation and the errors in pointing. If the top agent only has
20 in the setup because it is pure chance. The fact that success
drops means that self-organisation is NOT taking place.
4. We might have to change the word creation rate to be less
than 1.0. In the present circumstances I believe that every

8.3 Start up of the experiment

agent will make for every node in the tree at very great depth his own word.
I suggest that tomorrow we go through games with the agents step by step and fix the environment and the lights, etc. so that the game is at least feasible; at the moment it is not. The same exercise will have to be done in Brussels and Antwerp. There is a question how we can get rid of all the garbage that is being created right now.
luc

Date: Tue, 29 Jun 1999 13:07:48 +0200
From: Joris Van Looveren <joris@arti.vub.ac.be>
Subject: Re: paris site
Luc Steels wrote: > 2. The light conditions were very bad and have been
> improved a bit so that patches of white light are
> no longer seen as objects. The problem is reflections on the whiteboard. In brussels the lights are covered so that there is no direct light falling onto the whiteboard. Consequently, it happens rarely if ever that parts of the background are seen as objects.
Also, turn on the 'back light' option of the cameras. This improves the image quite a bit, especially at lower light intensities. I'll try to find out if it can be turned on and off from software, so that the setting can be saved along with the other configuration data.
Joris.

-=============_-1278188520==_d=============
From: Luc Steels <steels@arti.vub.ac.be>
Subject: Major error in feedback
Based on the dismissal performance in Paris, we discovered a major error in the feedback. I suggest that all sites at this point PAUSE until we fix this and then we update versions on different sites. This bug may explain why the lexicon has disintegrated.
more news soon.
luc

29 June 1999

```
-============_-1278188520==_d============
```
Date: Tue, 29 Jun 1999 11:38:23 +0200
From: Joris Van Looveren <joris@arti.vub.ac.be>
Subject: Antwerp OK
Antwerp has not been down, contrary to what the server page showed. The problem whas that the network was not accessible any more because the network interface of the alpha machine was down. This meant that the proxy was not available. According to Mario, the games have continued, so probably in a couple of hours when all interactions and agents have been uploaded, the database will be up to date again.
At this moment, Brussels and Paris have been paused until further notice. Interactions continue to be uploaded until the network interface has caught up.
Joris (in Brussels) & Mario (in Antwerp).

```
-============_-1278188520==_d============
```
Date: Tue, 29 Jun 1999 16:35:46 +0100
From: Frederic Kaplan <kaplan@csl.sony.fr>
Subject: Patches
Bugs fixed
1. Feedback mechanisms and find-segmented-pointed by the hearer (this was not working at all...) corrected in: segment-tools.lsp and th-world.lsp
2. scaling. If a value is higher than the maximum, it gives max as opposed to 1.0!!! corrected in: geom.lsp
3. Masking. Eliminating zero channels should be done on the source not on value (= value after scaling, so it is often zero). corrected in: prototype.lsp (in the functions folder)
After theses patches, sites can be running again.
Fred and Luc.

```
-============_-1278188520==_d============
```
Date: Tue, 29 Jun 1999 23:25:45 +0200 (MET DST)
Subject: There is hope for robokind
After fixes to the Paris site by Frederic and me, I relaunched
some agents. Things are now beginning to work as they should.
We can see the agents quickly build up a successful lexicon.
It is a pity that at the moment one can no longer give more than
20 games (although I can see the goal of getting to a global
coherent lexicon that way). I try to circumvent by immediately
sending them 3 times to Paris but I am not sure this works.
Brussels and Antwerp should wait until all the fixes have been
made before re-entering the network. Frederic and I will send a
mail tomorrow morning. Once the system works, it is quite
exciting to see your agents move forward quickly!
Luc

30 June 1999

```
============_-1278188520==_d============
```
Date: Wed, 30 Jun 1999 11:16:41 +0200 (MET DST)
From: Luc Steels <steels@arti.vub.ac.be>
Subject: progress
The mails to talking-heads go in a log file and I suggest that
everybody not only sends technical issues but remarks.
The Paris site is really taking off now. A lexicon is beginning
to be in place, mostly focusing on positional information (left,
right, up, down). Because the lexicon is getting established,
it is now easier for new agents to acquire the existing lexicon
and be successful. The agents have less bushy discrimination
trees and fewer but effective words. This was demonstrated by
frederic's agent (Kant) which quickly came to the top as speaker
after only a few games!
The word "green" apparently means red. So I am teaching my
agents the word rouge instead of green. It is not yet clear to
me whether you can influence the lexicon once it is already
firmly established.
Later this afternoon we might enrich the agents' experiences by
changing the environment a bit.
Luc

8 The first series (1999)

```
-=============_-1278188520==_d============
Date: Wed, 30 Jun 1999 17:16:19 +0200
From: Joris Van Looveren <joris@arti.vub.ac.be>
Subject: Re: paris site
Luc Steels wrote: > 4. We might have to change the word
creation rate to be less than
> 1.0. In the present circumstances I believe that every agent
will
> make for every node in the tree at very great depth his own
word.
Don't do this yet. It will cause the system to crash sooner or
later, as I experienced in Antwerp and Brussels today. The
reason is the method utterance-word-string is not defined on
null-utterances. I'm trying to find out what result this method
should return.
I've been in Antwerp today to get it running again and to apply
the patches. It had run well for quite some time when I left,
but something caused it to crash again half an hour later. I'll
try to fix it tomorrow with Mario, if he has the time to go
there.
Joris.
```

By mid July, the basic infrastructure, the teleportation mechanisms and the semiotic dynamics were running smoothly and so the experiment could operate without constant care.

8.4 Results of the experiment

The first Talking Heads experiment ran for 4 months during the summer of 1999 and showed the validity of the mechanisms that were used for the agent architecture and of the interaction patterns and group dynamics of the agents. A shared lexicon and an underlying conceptual repertoire emerged, enabling successful communication by the agents about the scenes before them. In total, 400,000 grounded games were played. The population of agents rose to just under 2000, increasing steadily over the period of the experiment. Despite the many perturbations due to grounding, intermittent technical failures, a continuous influx of new agents entering the population, and unpredictable human interaction, the lexicon was maintained throughout this period.

The rate of communicative success for the first 200,000 games is shown in Figure 8.8. We see that the success rate is generally between 70 and 80 %. There are occasionally crashes (e.g. around 90,000) caused by problems at a particular site (such as bad light conditions).

8.4 Results of the experiment

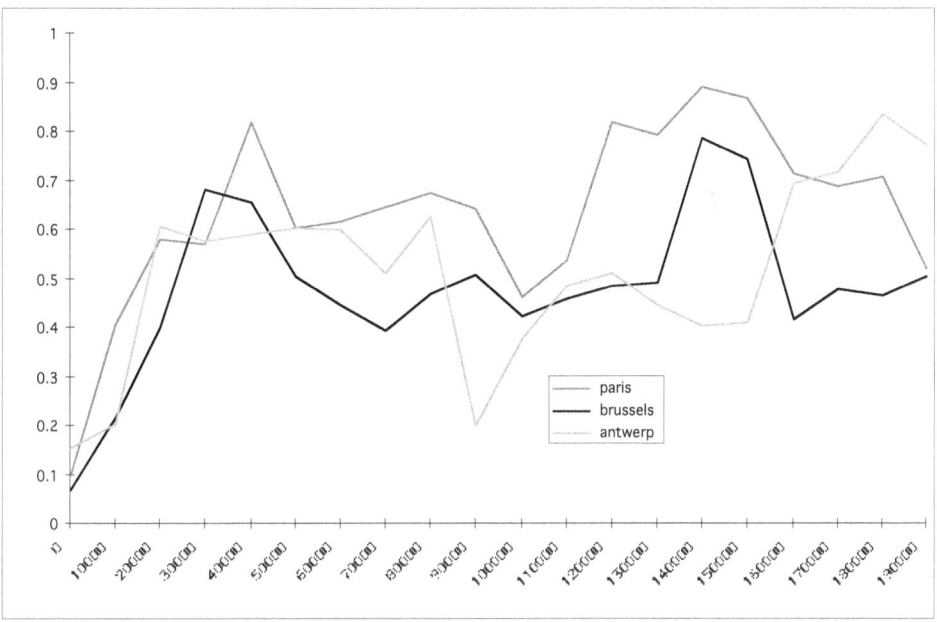

Figure 8.8: The y-axis shows the average communicative success of agents at each of the three different sites for a total of 190.000 games shown on the y-axis.

A total of 8000 words and 500 concepts were created by the agents, with a core vocabulary consisting of 100 basic words expressing concepts like up, down, left, right, green, red, large, small, etc. Of these, 8 words represent a large majority of words used (about 80 %). 4 of these words refer to the position of objects: GOREWA (top), DOWN (bottom), WOGGLESPLAT (left), and SESUBIPU (right). 4 other words refer to colors: ROUGE (red), KAZOZO (green), WEGIRIRA (blue), and EMPTY (light). The distribution of these words after 130,000 games is shown in Figure 8.9.

Figure 8.10 shows the semiotic dynamics related to an expression of the meaning for the concept 'left', i.e. a horizontal position between 0.0 and 0.25 (after scaling). The word "wogglesplat" becomes dominant although there is a very strong competition in the beginning. We see that users try to give other words to the same meaning, such as "gauche" or "links" (both words expressing left in French and German or Dutch respectively). We also see that other words such as "red" or "yellow" get associated with this meaning, because the hearer may guess the wrong meaning in learning the word for left.

Figure 8.11 shows another example of the semiotic dynamics in the experiment, this time looking at all the meanings for a particular word, namely *droite* (meaning 'to the right' in French). This word clearly has been introduced by a human user and the dominating meaning progressively becomes a region (between 0.75 and 1.0) on the horizontal position, as could be expected. On the way we see some confusion, Specifically there must be objects that appear both on the right and up (vertical position between 0.5 and 1.0).

223

8 *The first series (1999)*

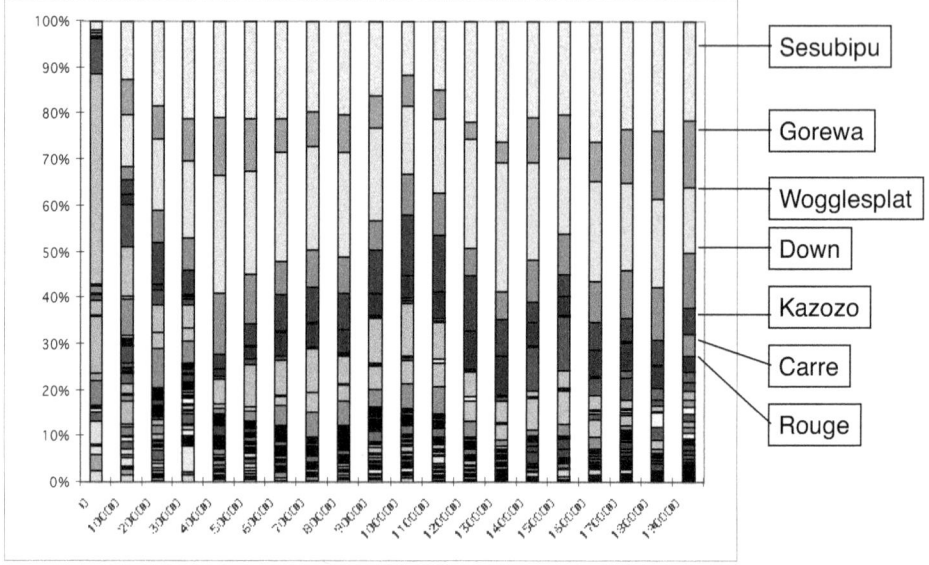

Figure 8.9: Distribution of word use. There are only a few words that are dominant. Many words are short-lived, either because the circumstances in which they fit are rare or because they do not get settled in the population. Moreover sometimes users create agents which they do not keep rescheduling for new games.

Figure 8.12 shows different meanings competing for the same word *bozopite*. Dominant ones are a large area (AREA scaled between 0.5 and 1.0) or extended width (WIDTH scaled between 0.5 and 1.0). These two concepts apparently could both be applied in many situations, but at some point new situations appeared that caused a symmetry breaking and AREA became dominant.

It was also possible that different meanings which were highly compatible were maintained in the population. An example is shown in the form-meaning diagram in Figure 8.13, which plots the average frequency of meanings for the word *down*. The meanings are all concepts on the vertical position channel VPOS, but they carve out smaller and smaller regions.

8.5 Conclusions

The Talking Heads experiment was without doubt a success from many angles. The mechanisms for concept formation, lexicon formation and alignment (as discussed in Part I of this book) all worked out the way it was expected, even in very difficult 'real world' conditions. The complex hardware could be maintained at the different physical sites and the general web infrastructure and agents teleportation mechanisms held up

8.5 Conclusions

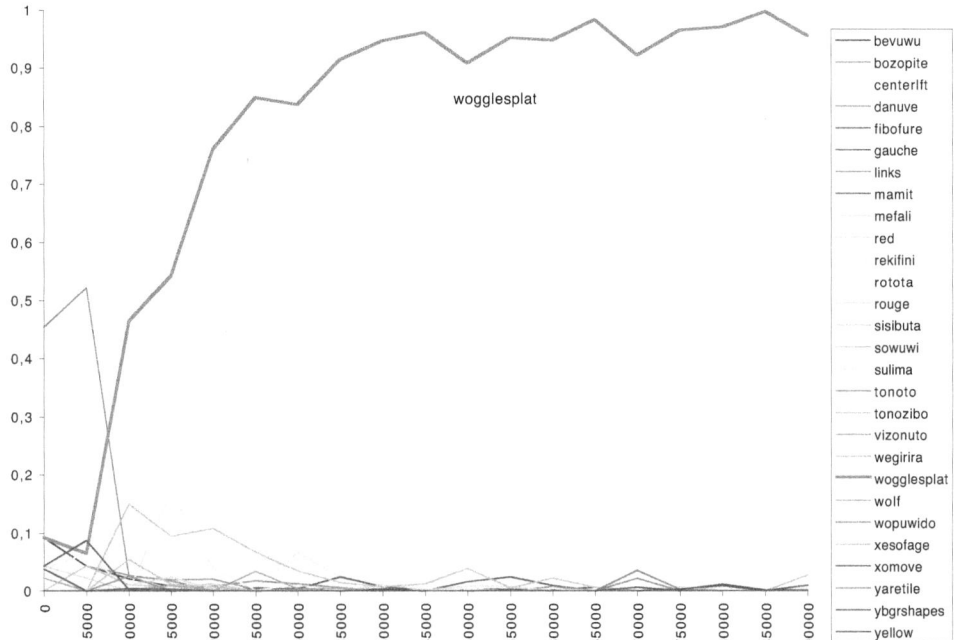

Figure 8.10: Meaning-Form diagram: Different words for expressing the meaning 'left', i.e. horizontal position is less than 0.25 (scaled). New words come up all the time but there is a clear winner-take-all effect with "wogglesplat" winning.

despite a significant scale-up. An enthusiastic user group formed and they actively created agents and sent them out on the network, often also teaching their agents human language words which then propagated in the rest of the population. Users became very attached to their agents, upset when their agents could not get to the sites they had scheduled (because it took almost 1 minute for a complete language game and so other agents had to wait), and trying to figure out how and why they had learned certain words.

Numerous talks were given and various papers published in scientific fora. There were also various talks within the art context.[2] The experiment received wide coverage in the media thanks to its public exposure as part of a major exhibition. The *Süddeutsche Zeitung* called it "Angels with Internet wings". All this led to invitations to show the experiment also in other venues, as discussed in the next chapter. Regrettably, the challenge just to keep the experiment in the air with the available human resources and the pressure for going on with new experiments prevented us from doing more adequate data gathering and analysis. Nevertheless some analyses appeared, particularly as carried out by Frederic Kaplan (Kaplan 2001).

---

[2] Examples are a "gallery talk" as Salon 3 at the Elephant and Castle Centre in London on 2 December 1998, organised by Hans Ulrich Obrist and Molly Nesbit, and a presentation together with Hans-Ulrich Obrist and Rem Koolhaas in Antwerp to launch the Laboratorium book on 3 October 2001.

8 The first series (1999)

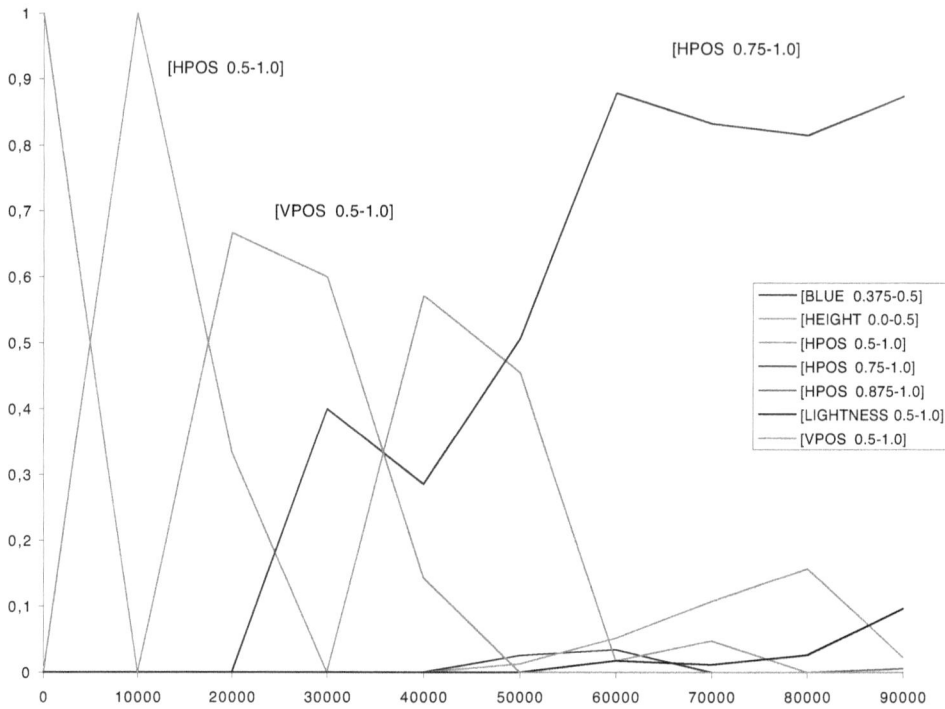

Figure 8.11: Form-Meaning diagram: Different meanings associated with the word *droite*. The dominant meaning is in line with the human use of the word, namely horizontal position (HPOS) to the right of the image.

The field of complex systems science was at that time still in its infancy and adequate tools for analysing language as a complex adaptive system were in the early stages of development.

The experiment ended with the following "tongue-in-cheek" post by Angus McIntyre on the Forum:

```
1999-10-14 15:08:29 Angus McIntyre
Bad news and good news
As the subject says, we have some bad news and some good news.
First, the bad news. The current run of the Talking Heads
experiment will come to an end on the 5th of November. After
that date, access to the system will be closed off, meaning that
you won't be able to create, launch or inspect agents any more.
We realise that this will be a sad day for all of you who've
participated so enthusiastically in the experiment. We will
consider setting up self-help programs for anyone unable to cope
with the pain of 'Talking Heads withdrawal'.
```

8.5 Conclusions

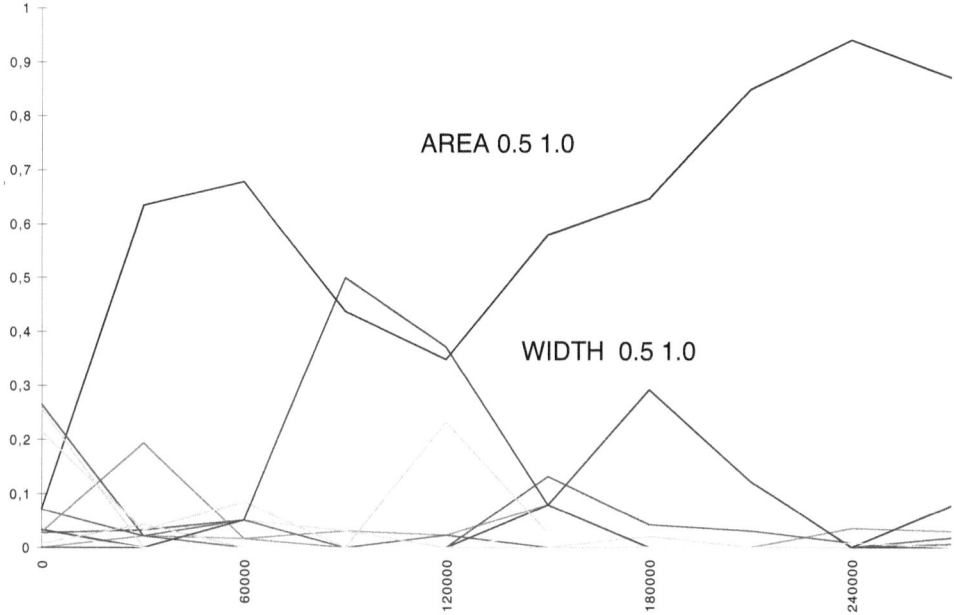

Figure 8.12: Form-Meaning diagram: Different meanings associated with the word *bozo-pite*.

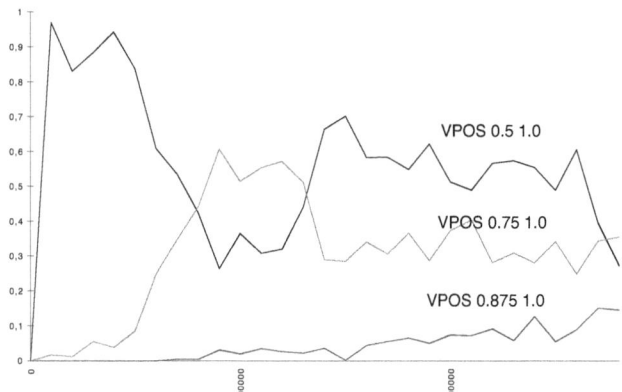

Figure 8.13: Form-Meaning diagram: Different meanings associated with the word *down*. There are in particular two meanings. one is a region on the red-channel and another one a region on the vertical position channel.

8 The first series (1999)

Now the good news. The Talking Heads *will* be back. We
currently expect to launch an improved version of the system
early in 2000, probably late in January. We shall use the
intervening months to try to make our software faster and more
stable. When the system returns, we should also have some new
sites, both public and private. And we're thinking about trying
to find ways to make the system more interesting (i.e. by
giving you greater control over your agents and the way that
they learn and interact with other agents).
If you'd like to comment on your experiences with the Talking
Heads, or suggest ways that the system could be improved, this
forum would be a good place to do that. I can't promise that
we'll implement all your suggestions (we don't have very much
time), but all your messages will certainly be read and
considered.
In the meantime, on behalf of all the Talking Heads team, I'd
just like to say 'thank you' to all of you for taking part and
making the experiment a success.
Angus McIntyre
Agent Public Relations Officer

Here is one commentary of a dedicated user:

1999-10-27 18:52:04 Kampi
RE: Bad news and good news
Are you crazy? Why do you do this at a time where winter with
its long darkness is just ahead. Taking away from me the last
beeings I can realy understand? So, of course I'm very sad about
the bad news. And I insist on a self-help program otherwise I
don't know what will happen to me. I propose to create some kind
of holiday-camp for my agents which I can run on my computer;
for example with some beach scenery, quiet apartment with TV and
pool and only a little bit of teaching abilities, so that they
don't become totaly stupid although they will be able to recover
from all these mad and debile cans in Paris, Brussels and Tokio;
please implement the possibility that it's me who swiches off
the light at night; then, and only then, I can be sure they have
a good time until the restart. But for serious: I hope very
much that the Talking Heads will return as soon as possible.
And I think you should inform those who are interested (me for
example) by e-mail about the re-start. Some wishes for the
improved project: a better performance, especially for the
lexicon. And much, much more information about the scientific
background. How do the agents create their words? Are these
guys on the Web realy part of the 'official'; experiment? Why

8.5 Conclusions

did one of my agents suddenly create a three-part word (was
there a bug in the software, how could it asume, that anyone
would understand this, is it a syntactical genius and therefore
its only natural that noone understands it or is it simply too
stupid to understand the rules of the game? Is it the only agent
who did this, why did it never try this again?... and so on).
Anyway, more explanation for the 'future-heads'; about the
experiment so that I understand why I should teach the agents.
As far as I understood they were created to make sense (develop
language) by their own. Yes, I know, 'stop making sense';. It's
their job, not mine. Therefore at least a very big 'thank you;
for having published the 'talking-heads'; on the net.
A very sad user
P.S.: Please send me the holidy camp including 2 single rooms
and my agents caspar and Leyla as a zipped file by e-mail.

9 The second series (2000–2001)

Shortly after the first Talking Heads exhibition in Antwerp, a new opportunity arose in 2000 to set up and run another large-scale experiment as part of a major exhibition called N01SE, curated by Adam Lowe and Simon Schaffer in Cambridge and London. This was potentially a great occasion because the exhibition was about issues of language origins, coding, replication, and noise. Moreover it would allow the expertise that was built up in the first experiment to be reused, tested again and hopefully yield more data for analysis. So two new installations were set up: one in Cambridge and one in London with additional installations at the VUB Artificial Intelligence Laboratory in Brussels, the Sony Computer Science Laboratory in Paris and in Tokyo, and at the Intelligent Autonomous Systems laboratory of the University of Amsterdam (at the initiative of Ben Kröse). Later on a further opportunity presented itself to add an installation at the Palais de la Découverte, the main science museum of Paris. We also created a mobile version that was shown temporarily in several locations, as parts of other exhibitions, workshops, and conferences. All this further expanded the audience. The Paris exhibition alone was already seen by 300,000 visitors, augmented with hundreds of active participants and many on-lookers through the Internet.

Although all these installations were very instructive from a technological point of view, and certainly spread the word, we were reaching a point where it was no longer of interest from a scientific point of view. The problems of maintaining public sites were overwhelming our scarce resources and the N01SE experiment was invaded by a group of hackers intended on its destruction. This episode, discussed in Section 9.2, was more insightful from the viewpoint of sociology and anthropology than science or engineering.

9.1 The N01SE exhibition

9.1.1 The exhibition

The N01SE exhibition was about information and transformation. Various locations in Cambridge (UK) participated: The Kettle's Yard university gallery, the Cambridge Whipple Museum of the History of Science, the Cambridge University Museum of Archaeology and Anthropology and the Fritzwilliam Museum. The installations ran from 22 January until 26 March 2000. There was also a site in London at the Wellcome Trust Two10 Gallery in Euston Road, which ran from 28 January to 1 May 2000. Apart from the usual press coverage for art exhibitions, articles appeared in Science[1] and the Lancet[2] showing that the exhibition resonated also in the scientific press.

---

[1] http://www.firstpulseprojects.com/sciencerev.html
[2] http://www.garnettmckeen.net/lancet.html

9 *The second series (2000–2001)*

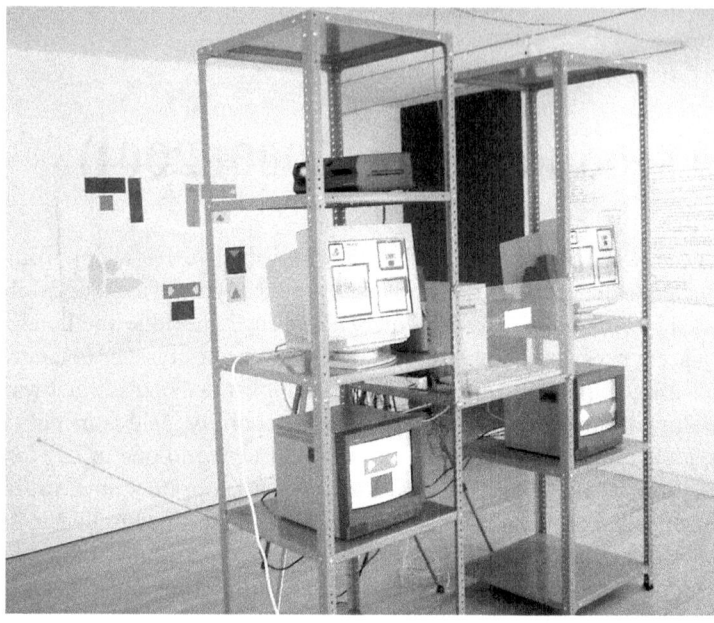

Figure 9.1: View through the street window inside the Kettle's Yard gallery in Cambridge. The cameras are located before the towers. The geometric figures are attached to the wall and explanations of the experiment are located on the right.

The N01SE exhibition was curated by Adam Lowe (see Figure 9.2) and Simon Schaffer. Adam Lowe is an artist and technologist. He is currently the director of Factum arte (Madrid) which is specialised in making life-like replicas of paintings, sculptures and archaeological objects, using laser-scanners and 3d printers. Recent realisations include the sculptures of Giambattista Piranesi (Lowe 2010), the paintings of Caravaggio and the tomb of Tutankhamun. Simon Schaffer is a science historian, professor at the University of Cambridge at the department of History and Philosophy of Science. He wrote extensively about the historical developments in scientific research (Schaffer & Shapin 2011) and animated television and radio programs, including *Light Fantastic* (BBC4).

The exhibition was announced in the following way by its curators:

> A multi-site multimedia exhibition in Cambridge with "realtime" links to London, organised around three key themes in "digitality":
>
> ```
> Universal Language
> Pattern Recognition
> Data Synaesthetics
> ```
>
> N01SE is not limited to electronic media, but traces the digital imagination from such myths as Noah's Ark, through the early modern experiments of Charles

9.1 The N01SE exhibition

Figure 9.2: Adam Lowe (curator of N01SE) during installation of the Talking Heads experiment at the Wellcome Gallery in London. The backwall contained the figures. On the right wall, posters were displayed explaining the experiment.

Babbage's Difference Engine and Morse's Telegraph, up to today's charge coupled devices (CCDs), robotics and beyond ...

Displays highlight digitality in history, technology, art and science, drawing upon a wide range of objects and images from artists and scientists around the globe – everything from 3000BC artefacts to the latest state-of-the-art pictures of the surface of atoms.

Not a virtual reality "hall of mirrors", but a cultural gallery of hard (and fuzzy) fact.

n01se celebrates the world as signal-and-noise – the constant simultaneous creation of content with discontents, as communication society filters "meaningful" messages from background "babble" . . . and back again. Ingenuity, serendipity and excess all play up the sensory wonderment of N01SE: The Digital and Its Discontents.

N01SE is news. It's the nuisance others make, a cacophony which prevents us being heard, or even thinking. Now the big noise is digital, offering us an escape from disorder by arranging, preserving and transmitting information. But is the cloudless noiseless world of digital technology the truth?

N01SE, hazy images and sudden sparks, random mutations and puzzling glitches, can all become the sources of innovation and beauty.

N01SE celebrates the essential excess from which information is drawn. It probes many different ways of seeing and being in the world. Chances are your own sense of order is already someone else's N01SE.

9.1.2 Installation at Kettle's Yard in Cambridge

"The Kettle's Yard Gallery is associated with Cambridge University. It acted as the main site of the N01SE exhibition and showed a variety of historical artefacts (including the brain of Babbage and the original DNA structure built by Watson and Crick) together with new artistic works. The catalogueue published by the Kettle's Yard Gallery [3] featured articles by Brian Smith, Umberto Eco, Bruno Latour, Bruce Sterling, Luc Steels, Peter Weibel and others. Below is my text as it appeared in the catalogue:

> Meanings are not a priori Platonic entities independent of language; meanings are the result of embodied interactions with the world, obtained via the role words play in verbal interactions called "language games". The Talking Heads experiment explores one kind of language game: a guessing game played by two robotic agents about the scene directly in front of them. One agent acts as Speaker and attempts to draw the attention of the Hearer to some object by transmitting a verbal description of it; the Speaker succeeds if the Hearer correctly guesses which object is "meant".
>
> To play the game, the Speaker segments the scene and performs pattern recognition to extract features – area, shape, colour, position – about the segments selected. The Speaker then conceptualises the focus element "topic" as distinct from those of other segments - be it the largest or the furthest to the left or the green one. Next the Speaker verbalises this conceptualisation using descriptive words selected from its lexicon. The Hearer works the other way around; it queries the words transmitted by the Speaker and applies the resultant meanings back to the scene to find what topic the Speaker intended.
>
> To express conceptualisations, agents need a lexicon relating words to meanings. It must function bi-directionally (words-to-meanings and meanings-to-words); it must also store synonyms (more than one word for the same meaning) and ambiguities (more than one meaning for the same word). The agents have not been given a lexicon; they must acquire their own common lexicon as a bi-product of the game.
>
> New words accrue in two ways: either an agent creates its own new words from random combinations of syllables; or it stores transmitted words together with possible-meaning guesses inferred from the scene, then uses a hypothesis-test strategy to render lexicons mutually compatible. Agents keep a running score for every word-meaning pair in their lexicon. When word-topic recognition succeeds the score for that pair goes up, and that of other alternates goes down. This dynamic forces the lexicon of each individual agent to progressively conform,

---

[3] www.kettlesyard.co.uk/noise

and keeps it adapting to any language changes or new meanings that need to be expressed. During the course of the exhibition, a group of robotic agents autonomously constructs a shared language about real world scenes in front of them. Humans can interact with the installation through the Internet; they can teach their agents words and follow the general progress towards the construction of the language.

Intriguing questions: How to bridge the enormous gap between the noisy real world of images and behaviors, and the discrete digital world of symbols and language required for communication and thought? How do language and meaning originate? Why do languages keep changing so as to adapt to the needs of their users? How can a language be transmitted between generations without any central coordination nor telepathy?

The installation consists of two computer-controlled robotic camera heads that capture images from "scenes" in front of them consisting of colored geometric shapes pasted on a magnetic whiteboard. The configurations on the board can be changed at any time, making the robots' world unpredictable and open.

Two robotic structures will be active in this exhibition: one at Kettle's Yard in Cambridge and another one at the Wellcome Institute in London. along with additional installations in Brussels, Paris, Tokyo and elsewhere. A website has also been created for the experiment (http://talking-heads.csl.sony.fr/)[4] allowing anyone to create new agents. People can teach them words, so that elements of human natural languages can sneak into the emerging vocabulary. The agents are autonomous and do not necessarily stick to the words given to them but try to maximally adapt to the behavior of the group and invent their own words. Through the website it is also possible to monitor the progress of the experiment: the lexicon being created, the success rate, the coherence among the agents, the complexity of the language, etc. There is a Hall of Fame listing the best speakers and hearers. This motivates humans to take care of their agents thus ensuring that they move to the top in the Hall of Fame.

The creation of a shared language by a group of autonomous distributed agents is extraordinarily difficult because there are many sources of noise, in the form of disturbances that cause incoherence between the agents:

- Two embodied grounded agents always see the situation from different points of view so that they capture different images. Consequently they may have divergent perceptions and hence great difficulty to arrive at a successful game.
- The word(s) transmitted may not be accurately produced or received. For example, one agent may produce 'wabaku' but the other agent may hear 'mabaku'. This introduces noise in the signal itself and hence possibly confusion among the agents.

---

[4] This website is no longer operational but some remnants can be accessed here: https://ai.vub.ac.be/talking-heads/

- A scene can usually be conceptualised in many different ways, so that there is seldom certainty among the agents whether they share the same meaning. This causes great difficulties in learning the meaning of unknown words.
- The lexicons and conceptual repertoires are never exactly the same as each agent develops them autonomously. This generates in additional sources of confusion.

Any theory claiming to explain the origins of word-meaning must confront the handling of noise head on.

Noise plays yet another role, namely as a motor of language evolution. Indeed natural lexicons evolve - even if there are already perfectly good words in a language. Noise on the word form causes changes in the form which propagate in the remainder of the population. Misunderstandings may destabilise a word and cause its meaning to shift.

Another factor in language evolution is due to changes in the environment. Thus two alternative meanings for a word may be compatible for a while but are then disambiguated when a series of scenes arises in which the two meanings are no longer both applicable. For example, all objects may be both green and small and therefore there may be a word 'sesubipu' which may mean both, until a clear situation arises where a green object is no longer the smallest and a misunderstanding arises.

Semiotic evolution is continually present. Different meanings for a particular word will emerge over over a large number of language games. During specific periods, different words dominate. The word 'droite' (originally introduced by a French speaker) gains the dominant meaning 'to the right', then shifts to 'at the bottom', and then to 'very much to the right'. Particularly the words introduced by humans have a tendency to undergo this kind of strong evolution because human users do not know which meanings their agents employ.

How to bridge the enormous gap between the noisy real world of images and behaviors and the discrete, digital world of symbols and language required for communication and thought? How do language and meaning originate? How do languages keep changing yet remain adapted to the needs of their users? How can a language be transmitted between generations without any central coordination nor telepathy?

What is most remarkable about this experiment, is that the robotic agents do not come with pre-programmed ways of conceptualising reality but have to develop their own concepts.

Each agent has been given a mechanism to 'grow' new distinctions by expanding discrimination trees. Each tree discretises one sensory dimension. For example, there is a tree for the area of a segment (scale with respect to the image) which divides the range of possible values into two discrete regions, which would be named in English 'small' and 'large'. Other trees focus on position (left versus right or top versus bottom), shape (rectangular or oval), color, etc. Trees can go as deep as necessary to carve out smaller and smaller subregions of a continuous space.

The nodes of the discrimination trees grow in a random fashion but the distinctions that are not successful in the game are pruned. This way the conceptual repertoire of an agent can continue to adapt to the needs of the agent.

How do agents manage to reach coherence in their lexicons without a central coordinator and despite all these sources of noise? The answer is self-organisation. Coherence is reached in the same way as an ant society manages to form a coherent path between a food source and the nest, namely by a positive feedback loop. In this case, there is a positive feedback loop between use and success: The more a word is successful, the more it is chosen by the agents, and the more success it will have. This causes the agents to settle in an attractor where they all prefer the same word for the same meaning and vice-versa. We see a damping of synonymy as in the case of natural languages. Noise has the beneficial impact of getting agents out of attractor states (so called local minima) which are not optimal from the viewpoint of the whole although they are a possible solution.

How do agents manage to share their conceptualisation of the world without their concepts being innately given (pre-programmed) nor centrally coordinated? The answer is structural coupling, another concept adopted from biology. Two systems have a structural coupling if one creates a context for the other and vice-versa, so that each system develops to be maximally co-ordinated without any prior design or global control. The conceptual system and the lexicon of each agent is structurally coupled in the sense that agents prune distinctions that are not successful in the language game, and conversely they keep the ones that are useful and successful. This makes the conceptual system progressively well adapted both to the scenes encountered by the agents and the lexicons used in the group. Sources of noise are again beneficial to foster structural coupling. First of all they help the group to push towards the use of categorisations that are robust against noise. Second, they help agents to explore alternatives and avoid them getting stuck in sub-optimal behavior.

A website has been created for the experiment[5]. Through this site, anybody who wants can create new agents and follow their progress. Owners of agents can teach them words, so that words already used in human natural languages sneak into the emerging vocabulary. The agents are autonomous and do not necessarily stick to the words given to them but try to maximally adapt to the behavior of the group and invent their own words. Through the website it is also possible to monitor the progress of the experiment: the lexicon being created, the success rate, the coherence among the agents, the complexity of the language, etc. There is a Hall of Fame listing the best speakers and hearers. This motivates humans to take care of their agents thus ensuring that they move to the top in the Hall of Fame.

---

[5] http://talking-heads.csl.sony.fr/

"To express a conceptualisation, agents need a lexicon relating words with meanings. The lexicon must be consultable in both directions (from words to meanings and from meanings to words). It must be able to store synonyms (more than one word for the same meaning) and ambiguities The agents have not been given a lexicon a priori. They have to acquire their own lexicon as a side effect of the game. New words get into a lexicon in two ways: When an agent has no word to express a particular distinction, the agent can create a new one by a random combination of syllables. When an agent hears a word that he does not know, he stores the new word with his own guess of what the meaning could be in the scene being perceived.

Agents then use a hypothesise-and-test strategy to make their lexicon compatible with the rest of the group. They keep a score for every word-meaning pair in their lexicon. When a word has success in the game, the score goes up, and its competitors go down. When the game fails, the score of the used word(s) goes down. This creates an inhibition-excitation dynamics making the lexicon of the individual agent progressively conform to the most successful lexicon of the group. It also ensures that an agent's lexicon keeps adapting if the language changes or if new meanings need to be expressed." (N01SE exhibition catalogue)

9.1.3 Installation at the Wellcome Gallery in London

The second installation during the N01SE exhibition was installed in the Wellcome Gallery in London (see Figure 9.3) from 22 January until 26 March 2000. This gallery is associated with the Wellcome trust and featured additional art works by Joseph Grigley, Evgen Bavcar, Manuel Franquelo, Garret and Jones, and Giles Revell. The local curator Denna Jones described the exhibition as follows:

"Digitality is transforming traditional ways of thinking about the impact of technology on culture. This exhibition looks at how complex structures can be transformed, translated and transmitted changing the nature of communication. A multimedia multi-site exhibition, N01SE demonstrates how language and our five senses can be changed or enhanced through 'digitality, and introduces visitors to pioneering developments in cross-disciplinary art and science."

The installation itself was similar to the one in Cambridge. There was a wall with geometric figures pasted on it, posters explaining the exhibition, the two pan-tilt cameras mounted on tripods, and the computers driving the software (see Figure 9.4). The London site posed particularly hard problems in the alignment of the cameras. It turned out that a subway was passing under the gallery and causing strong vibrations every few minutes, which caused the cameras to physically shift on the floor. Because the pointing behaviour was sensitive to alignment and prior calibration, this led to growing pointing errors and subsequent errors in feedback, causing a strong decline in the success rate and occasional chaos in the agents' vocabularies. This was partially offset by stable conditions in other sites but nevertheless made the task of reaching coherence virtually impossible.

9.1 The N01SE exhibition

Figure 9.3: Catalogue cover and poster of the N01SE exhibition at the Wellcome Gallery in London.

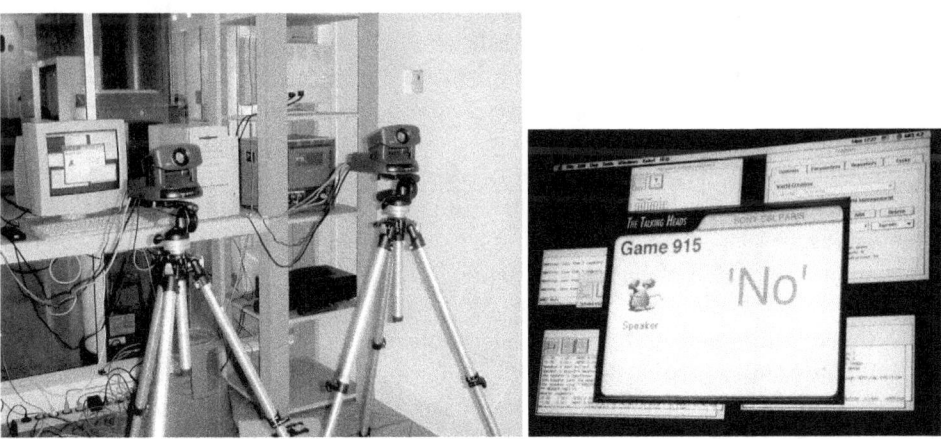

Figure 9.4: Installation at the Wellcome Gallery in London. Left: Talking Heads cameras oriented towards the wall on which geometric figures were pasted. Right: Projection of interaction during ongoing experiment. A game just failed and the speaker says "no".

9 The second series (2000–2001)

The exhibition catalogue, assembled by Denna Jones, contained the following text by Luc Steels:

> "The Talking Heads Experiment is a collective effort of members of the Sony Computer Science Laboratory, Paris and VUB Artificial Intelligence Laboratory Brussels, in particular Luc Steels, Frédéric Kaplan, Angus McIntyre, and Johan Van Looveren. This research has been sponsored by the Sony Computer Science Laboratory in Paris and a GOA grant from the Belgian government to the VUB AI Lab.
>
> 1. How can a cognitive agent bridge the enormous gap between the noisy real world of images and behaviours and the discrete, digital world of symbols and language required for communication and thought?
> 2. How do language and meaning originate? How come languages keep changing and how do they remain adapted to the needs of their users? How can a language be transmitted between generations without any central coordination nor telepathy?

Situated robots and teleports

The installation consists of two robotic heads. These are steerable cameras controlled by a computer that hosts the architecture and knowledge state of each agent. The robots capture images from scenes in front of them. The scenes consist of coloured geometrical shapes pasted on a magnetic white board. The configuration on the board can be changed at any time, making the robots' world unpredictable and open. The robot infrastructure is connected to the Internet, so that an agent may dematerialise from a body and travel over the internet to another body in which it can re-materialise. Two robotic structures will be active as part of the N01SE exhibition: one at Kettles'Yard in Cambridge and another one at the Wellcome Trust Two10 Gallery in London.

There will be additional installations in Brussels, Paris, Tokyo and other places. The agent teleporting facility makes it possible to have thousands of robotic agents and to confront each agent with many different scenes.

Constructing perceptually grounded concepts

What is most remarkable about this experiment is that the robotic agents do not come with pre-programmed ways of conceptualising reality but have to develop their own concepts. Each agent has been given a mechanism to 'grow' new distinctions by expanding discrimination trees. Each tree discretises one sensory dimension. For example, there is a tree for the area of a segment which divides the range of possible values into two discrete regions, which would be named in English 'small' and 'large'. Other trees focus on position (left versus right or top versus bottom), shape (rectangular or oval), colour, etc.

Trees can go as deep as necessary to carve out smaller and smaller subregions of a continuous space. The nodes of the discrimination trees grow in a random fashion but the distinctions that are no successful in the game are pruned. This way the conceptual repertoire of an agent can continue to adapt to the needs of the agent.

Sources of noise
The creation of a shared language by a group of autonomous distributed agents is extraordinarily difficult because there are many sources of noise, in the form of disturbances that cause incoherence between the agents:

- Two embodied grounded agents always see the situation from different points of view so that they capture different images. Consequently they may have divergent perceptions and hence great difficulty to arrive at a successful game.
- The word(s) transmitted may not be accurately produced or received. For example, one agent may produce 'wabaku' but the other agent may hear 'mabakau'. This introduces noise in the signal itself and hence possibly confusion among the agents.
- A scene can usually be conceptualised in many different ways, so that there is seldom certainty among the agents whether they share the same meaning. This causes great difficulties in learning the meaning of unknown words.
- The lexicons and conceptual repertoires are never exactly the same due to the fact that each agent develops them autonomously. This brings in additional sources of confusion.

Any theory claiming to explain the origins of word meaning must confront the handling of noise head on.

Cultural evolution
Noise plays yet another role, namely as a motor of language evolution. Indeed natural lexicons evolve - even if there are already perfectly good words in a language. Noise on the word form causes changes in the form which propagate in the remainder of the population. Misunderstandings may destabilise a word and cause its meaning to shift.

Another factor in language evolution relates to changes in the environment. Thus two alternative meanings for a word may be compatible for a while but are then disambiguated when a series of scenes arises in which the two meanings are no longer both applicable. For example, all objects may be both green and small and therefore there may be a word 'sesubipu' which may mean both, until a clear situation arises where a green object is no longer the smallest and a misunderstanding arises." (Catalogue N01SE exhibition)

9.2 Iconoclasm

The second series of Talking Heads experiments which were part of the N01SE exhibition, featured again a website with which human users could create their own agents, teach them words by going through images of past games, and send them off on the teleportation network. In the first series, a large group of users participated, posting enthusiastic commentaries on the forum, suggesting improvements to the interface, and discussing possible theories of language evolution. Unfortunately, during the second series, a group of students mostly from the University of Hull (UK) evolved from enthusiastic and interested participants into a mob of rude thugs that wanted to destroy the experiment at all cost, stimulated by local curator Denna Jones and insiders at the Wellcome Gallery, who apparently were strongly opposed that the N01SE exhibition took place at their location and somehow had a personal crutch against Adam Lowe, global curator of the N01SE initiative. This iconoclastic event was (in the year 2000) a forerunner of the damage that hackers have been inflicting on the web, destroying the spirit of collaboration and sharing with which the web was founded.

The British hackers realised that they could give dirty names to their agents and, because they could teach their own agents these words, they could also teach their agents dirty words for colours, shapes, or any other concept that agents were using. These words would unavoidably propagate in the population. As these hackers were extremely active, creating many agents, continuously launching them to different sites, and teaching their agents words, the global vocabulary progressively became unacceptable. The installations were in public spaces visited by school children, and so concern grew with the exhibition organisers at other locations (except the London site where those responsable for the exhibition actively encouraged this destructive behaviour). As a response, the experiment was temporarily halted and provisions put in to avoid that a small group would have excessive influence. It was still possible to provide a name to your agent and teach your agents words but some form of decency had to be respected. This change restored order but resulted in an overreaction of the part of the English hacker group who now used all possible means to attack the Talking Heads servers themselves, encouraged by Denna Jones and aided by others at the Wellcome Gallery.

This episode showed a phenomenon that a decade later has become very common. The web is far from an idealistic common ground through which people can exchange ideas and tools. It brings out the worst in some people, particularly if there is a mob effect in which different individuals with unstable ethical values push each other to do things they would otherwise not do.

It is instructive and rather fascinating, particularly from a sociological and anthropological point of view, to follow the dialog on the Talking Heads Website Forum between the main protagonists of the story. It went from enthusiastic interaction and experimentation to aggressive and hateful destruction. The misspellings, grammatical errors and foul language they produced have been left in the text. Only a small fraction of the dialog is reproduced here.

9.2 Iconoclasm

We pick up the dialog on the 25 February 2000. Until that date the forum was very active both with general discussions about the future of intelligence or the origins of language, and with specific questions, mostly why agents were so slow in playing games. Many users were too impatient and did not seem to realise that playing a language game could easily take a minute or two. However the major problem was the deviating alignment of the cameras, which had to guarantee that there was a common frame of reference between the agents, and hence the possibility of sharing attention. The cameras were mounted on tripods. When somebody accidentally moved the tripod, the frame of reference was no longer exact. As mentioned earlier, traffic (particularly subway traffic in London) caused vibrations of the cameras so that they kept shifting and getting out of balance.

A group of University of Hull students (with names like *Trash, yeah8a8y, schedski*) became very much involved. They communicated through the Forum using often slang and sexist language and making a surprising number of spelling errors and grammatical mistakes. The group had been trying to impose their own language by very actively teaching their agents and sending them to the same site, namely Paris, which they had noticed had the most stable operating conditions. This worked (as indeed it was supposed to) at which point they decided to do the same with the London site although the camera alignment was too unreliable to allow the evolution of a stable language.

2000-02-25 21:37:24 Yeah8a8y
Paris
"Hey there peeps... Thanks to the greatness of yeah8a8y, Paris has a great success ratio... Oh yeah with a little help from TRASH.... Ok a lot of help... Heres to Paris!!!
The next server to be conquered is London!!!"

2000-02-25 21:40:13 Yeah8a8y
RE: Paris
And you may notice the succes of a few of our words on the Lexicon.... God the greatness of a couple of wasters from Hull Uni, three days to conquer a server... Didn't think much to those Frenchies anyway!!!!!

2000-02-25 21:52:23 Trash
RE: Paris
"Yeah London being the capital of the greatest country in the world and currently last in the server league well if we can get them frogs to say words the brits WILL CONQUER

2000-02-25 21:55:49 Trash
yellow MK 1 ESCORT
Hey mate nice seeing you around paris !!!! Enjoy the company especially since you know most of our words AND get the Biatches

9 The second series (2000–2001)

```
right... you can have my sister anyday... so then mate see ya
round keep driving the crap car. Have noticed the absence of
fine ass girls in here am i wrong.... hope soooo.
```

At this point, they realised that the London alignment was off and this is the first time that Phlox (as Denna Jones called herself) intervened. She immediately shows a negative attitude towards the experiment triggered by her personal conflict with Adam Lowe. Colleagues of hers (*fish* and *A Londoner*) respond with inside joke remarks that the Hull group does not understand. *Fish* had been trusted with admin passwords because he was responsable for maintaining the London site, but he greatly abused this trust as the experiment proceeded.

2000-02-25 22:02:36 LondonCalling
CALIBratioN OF CAMERAS London
"Can London PLEASE calibrate their cameras???? PLEASE!!!!!

2000-02-26 16:52:32 Yeah8a8y
RE: CALIBratioN OF CAMERAS London
very good.... Absolutely no chance of Domination if the cameras arn't calibrated... SORT IT!!

2000-03-02 15:46:50 phlox
RE: CALIBratioN OF CAMERAS
```
i manage the two10 gallery in which the talking heads display is
currently installed. would that it were so simple to sort it
and keep the cameras correctly calibrated. all equipment was
installed by the brussels group and whenever the cameras need
calibrating - for whatever reason - it means one of the brussels
boffins has to pop over to fix it. they've been over once since
the exhibition opened and decided to move the cameras forward 2
feet. not really an exact science is it? the grand master - luc
steels - is coming to the gallery tomorrow, so perhaps he will
enlighten me as to why the cameras seem to need constant
calibration, and i'll let you know. cheers.
```

2000-03-02 20:04:52 fish
RE: CALIBratioN OF CAMERAS London
that's as maybe, phlox, but i'm guessing you secretly come into the exhibition and kick the cameras when you're in a bad mood, like say when someone has been horrid to you.

2000-03-03 20:08:36 schedski
RE: CALIBratioN OF CAMERAS London
wassup fish?

9.2 Iconoclasm

2000-03-03 23:06:43 fish
RE: CALIBratioN OF CAMERAS London
come on, admit it, you guys there spend all day stomping around
your exhibits, breaking the displays, unplugging the monitors
and generally mucking things up. i'm surprised london's still
got two cameras even working and they haven't already been
flogged down some boozer for a monkey and a couple of jellied
eels

2000-03-07 13:03:46 A Londoner
RE: CALIBratioN OF CAMERAS London
Well, if you people will confuse the poor things with your
outrageous diction, they might know which way to point... One
of them was practically in tears the other day as I watched it
shaking its head in disbelief at the language it was meant to
repeat. What ever happened to 'Adam's a cool bloke'?

Meanwhile the Hull group is pursuing and explaining their particular experiment that they carry out within the Talking Heads framework. The experiment itself is interesting and shows that they understand what is going on and are creative. Also the overall dynamics is working. The group realises that a language can form on its own or that it can be influenced by humans teaching agents their own language. At the same time, there is already one user (called Cheesy) who is pushing to introduce dirty words to the agents. He does not belong to the Hull group but is most probably somebody from the Wellcome Gallery already trying to put the N01SE exhibition in a bad light.

2000-02-25 22:55:28 Norton
Teaching
While participating in this experiment seemed quite interesting
– I'm simply not getting it. When I try to comprehend what is
meant by certain words so that I can teach my agents – I cannot
understand the distinctions made. Does anyone get it?

2000-02-26 16:47:55 Yeah8a8y
RE: teaching
The best thing to do is to leave them for a number of games...
Like the tips say 'bout 50... then start looking at the words
they use, have to be successful tho'... then teach your other
bots this word for that picture! It is a bit hit and miss tho'
coz a lot of words are ambigious (?Sp) and mean different
things... remeber it is actual properties and not usually
shapes... But you can have success! Check out some of mine and
Trash's word in the top 20 lexicon,
Hullcitynutter,eightyfiftyone, msixtytwo, wotsit, mamorys

9 The second series (2000–2001)

(Childish I know, but hey I'm a student) and you'll realise you can actually do it... Helps if your at Paris tho'!

2000-02-26 20:41:20 Trash
RE: teaching / TRIBES
Basically think about it like this... On the Earth there are many different languages spoken by people usually in a specific geographical location. Now myself and yeahbaby looked at this experiment (as we are very interested in AI and have done much work in this field) and decided to test the idea of "Tribes" where all those in that tribe speak the same lingo. We also figured that tribes rarely move out of their "Birth Location" so kept them at one site. As can be seen now ALL our Agents speak the same language and have even taught it to others outside the Tribe (such as the esteemed Yellow Mk 1 Escort and possibly even Anne's little Agent). These agents we considert to be forreigners!! But stilll they can communicate with our Agents... If you have noticed our words in the lexicon as explained by yeahbaby have very few deviations from what was intended unlike others such as "Gumble" which appears to mean Everything!!!!! This I do beleave Validates mine and my colleagues (Yeahbaby) opinion that language can only evolve in the presence of small but tightknit communities.
As the next stage we wish to see what happens when 2 "Tribes" get together Hopefully they become multilingual !!. My theory is thatconfusion of words will be short lived and all will be ironed out after only a few games . Especially if the "tribes" are allowed to consolidate they meanings by once again returning to their own community with little outside influence....
I am sure you will all agree that personel experiments like these improve this and we would be interested to hear any opinion from others ...... are we doing the right thing or just playing gods etc??? Does this prove evolution as a basis or is there a need for gods etc....
Also anyone interested in settingg up a tribe PLEASE talk to us first as we have much experiance in these matters!

2000-02-27 14:39:10 Oisin
RE: teaching / TRIBES
Perhaps tribes could be created by sending agents to a specific server only eg only paris or only brussels and to see what words develop at the separate servers then switch after 2,4,6 months maybe any suggestions?

2000-02-27 19:39:10 Trash
RE: teaching / TRIBES
You mean by not playing god ???? and letting them get on with it

at one site?? .... well yes but the server would have to be
locked down by that tribe otherwise you would get outside
inflences teaching them stupid like gumble which meanbs
everything... it would probably take just 100-300 games each
agent to develop a usable language (Aslong as the server has no
agents from outside the tribe in there)
By teaching them myslef and Yeahbaby got usable language going
in less than 2 days!!!!!!! Just see the success of most of our
words in the lexicon top 20!!
God us 2 are good!!

2000-02-27 19:39:55 smartypants
RE: Collusion Tribes
I think the theories that are starting to surface is the most
interesting part of the experiment for me. I started ignoring
the 'teaching' mails as they seemed concerned with the technical
side but thanks Trash for pointing out you had posted up your
theory (p.s. when you talk about definitions of your words where
are these, or are you just talking about studying the images?).
The bit that I would like more explanation of ('cause
Smartypants is an ironic name) is the bit about the two tribes
coming together, especially as Paris is really the only viable
option at the moment. I noticed that Virtuoso (the only one of
my robots that managed to get into Paris in the last day) was
unranked yesterday, but today has jumped to 140ish as both as
speaker and a hearer - I guess this is because that one 'tribe'
have been forced to cement that language.
The trouble is, without a good interpreter (us I suppose), won't
it just cause confusion in our robots when they go and meet the
other 'dumber' ones? i.e. they teach the others our words, but
the others teach them the wrong words back as well. This means
you would keep playing several iterations of the games.
My thoughts on collusion were centered around this - we could
reduce the iterations by all agreeing on common words to teach
our robots, thus perpetrating more of the 'right' words whilst
eliminating the 'wrong' words...
... any thoughts on my incoherent ramblings??

2000-02-27 19:52:20 Trash
RE: Collusion Tribes
At the minute me and Yeah are off the Paris server (we are
regrouping our thoughts for further action!!!) But yes I did
mean view the pictures when i said definition.
By 2 tribes I mean obviously two who have been taught on the same
server. So say that i train my agents on there this week and you
train your tribe next week on the same server with different
words..... when both tribes are capable of good communication we
then take half of each tribe and place them together in the 3rd
week on the Paris server and see if they become multi lingual.

9 The second series (2000–2001)

We then sned these linguists back to their own tribe and see what happens.
Unfortunately many people have tried to jump on the band wagon of Paris success and send their Agents there with no idea what they are doing ... this has meant that we can not get our tribe to dominate as we would like.....
The problems with organising tribe transfer is immense and it is a shame people don't exp[lain what they are doing on this fprum so that all could help out by say teaching their agents the words being used or even evacuating a site so that two tribes can collide ...
It is a real shame that an experiment into AI and Language is hampered because people are unwilling to communicate with each other ....
Well I guess that those of us who want a proper experiment should just ry their best in difficult circumstances...
About the wrong words being taught !!! If your Tribe is more than 60% of the server then your tribe generallly succeeds in teaching the "foreigners" with little effect on themselves ...
This has more to do with Probability than anything else.

2000-02-27 20:46:29 smartypants
RE: Collusion Tribes
Thanks Trash. I was thinking in different terms...
... seeing as anyone doing anything is on the Paris server, I was imagining that as one 'big' tribe and that any outsiders (stuck on the other servers, or new) are the 'other' tribes so thanks for clearing that up for me.
I'd be interested in working with you and Yeahbaby for a more meaningful experiment, particularly as loads of 'dumber' robots (by that I mean ones not enjoying the Paris success) will soon be unleashed on us.
Just to clarify, my plan up until now was to let my robots learn 40-50 words (as suggested in the tips), I started to teach them the most successful words from the lexicon yesterday (most of which were yours – grrrrrr, jealous!) and then I sent them to Paris. (This was before I started putting stuff up on the forum and saw your theory unfortunately).
The only one that got in was Virtuoso, and even then he didn't really get to play enough games as I was experimenting to see if the number of games you choose has any effect on getting into that server.
Anwyay, let me know if you're interested (I've only created 7 at the moment).
By the way, do I remember seeing somewhere that you're both girls?????
... 'cause I am...

If so it is interesting to see different ways people approach the experiment. If I was running the experiment I reckon I could do research from the forum, as well as the actual experiment.

2000-02-28 14:25:01 Yeah8a8y
RE: Collusion Tribes
At the moment it seems I can't get on the Paris server for love nor money... Never mind... Anyway Trash has good theories!!! Two particlly good tribes at the minute, which also 'collided' (Wait a minute, Frankie goes to Hollywood anyone?) on the Paris server are run by me and Trash. There are some other out there (Cheesy) that are more content teaching obscene word to their bots. Anyway by both me and him filling up Paris (Max. of 16 agents from 20 at one point) a successful dialect has been taught between them. We now rank 5 words in top 10, and 9 overall in top 20. Again Trashs theories ring true.
And the bit about words getting taught wrong is more a case of... well if a french person tuaght you the word for "Tower" and you where listening to someone who understood french, "Tower" would be used in the french wording, but you also retain your interpretation of "Tower" and use this one which you consider more successful in the speaking sense. This is what happened with our own "hullcitynutter" and "lafizana". My agents now understand both, but only seem to say "hullcitynutter" (Thier original word, not the learnt one)
This, of course, all goes out the window when you yourself teachs them... Maybe another bad aspect of this AI programming.

2000-02-28 16:24:47 Yeah8a8y
RE: Collusion Tribes
OK no... I'm no girl!!! But there you go... I'm a bloke

2000-02-28 17:04:23 Yeah8a8y
RE: Collusion Tribes
I'm posed with another problem... As you know Brussels and Paris have been inactive for a bit... do I keep with the project and just send the bots out to Paris... or use this as a change point and educate them in Brussel's...
I'm going to stay with Paris... Teach other people the use of the words carefully set out by me and Trash... and generally gather more success!
I now have 18 bots by the way most are ranked within the top 100.. 1 or 2 exeptions... anyway I have been successful by sending the all to Paris... for top gamage action
It usually takes all night but there you go... even the Earth took an entire week to sculpture.

---

9 The second series (2000–2001)

To deal with the problem of agent congestion, software issues, and camera misalignment at the London and Cambridge sites, maintenance was carried out which led to a temporary unavailability of the experiment. Surprisingly, the reaction of the Hull group was entirely negative as they saw it as a way to prevent them from gaining or keeping control of the language used by the agents, even though Angus McIntyre clearly and patiently explained why maintenance was necessary. Also, Denna Jones (*Phlox*) took it personally as she did not realise that the calibration errors were due to vibrations caused by traffic of the London Underground near and under the Wellcome Gallery.

```
2000-03-01 15:28:10 Angus McIntyre
Performance, problems and fixes
As some of you have noticed, there've been some problems with
this round of the Talking Heads experiment. For one thing,
success rates have generally been very low, because the language
has never properly stabilised. For another, a large backlog of
agents has built up, and there have been considerable delays in
getting certain agents to and from servers.
We are aware of these problems, and are actively working on
fixing them. Part of the problem is that the Talking Heads has
been a victim of its own success - lots of people participating
enthusiastically makes for lots of agents, with new ones being
added every day. Moreover, the Talking Heads is a 'real world'
experiment, with real physical moving parts (the cameras) which
means that each game takes a certain and non-trivial amount of
time. These are just two reasons why things may sometimes move
slowly in the world of the Talking Heads.
Problems have also been caused by the cameras losing calibration
(that evil 'real world' strikes again), so that our agents
sometimes seem to be looking at entirely different parts of the
scene, something which is bound to cause problems. Last but not
least, there turn out to have been some bugs in our software,
particularly in the area of learning. The good news is that
we've identified a number of things that may have an impact on
success, and are currently busy fixing them.
We're about to start applying some fixes and making some changes
to the way things work. We hope that there will be minimal
disruption, but it's possible that the system may be a bit
'up-and-down' over the next few days. We may also start imposing
more limits, for instance on the number of agents that each user
can make, and on the number of agents that can land on a site at
any one time. (When I talk about 'imposing' limits, I don't
mean that we're going to hunt you down and kill you if you make
too many agents, but we might ask you politely to be a little
bit restrained when it comes to creating new agents or sending
them off).
```

We hope that once we've made the changes, things should start to work better. In the meantime, we'd just like to apologise for any frustration or inconvenience, and to thank you all for taking part in the experiment.
Angus McIntyre Talking Heads Current Affairs Correspondent

2000-03-01 16:29:54 Trash
RE: Performance, problems and fixes
Hi Angus, (Are you Threatening me ??? Bunghole!!!! ..... I am Cornholio)
Ok I take the limited number of agents business is directed against my plans for world domination.... Well then its a fight!!! lol...
Yeah take your point but just trying to create order out of anarchy.... strange really when i is an anarchist at heart...
At last you is taking an interest in sorting out the problems/cheats used by people like me to pervert the way the system is run. Well in the best style of Hull University's Electronic Engineering Department you stop the cheats and I'll create new ones!!... only kidding mate ... but world domination is mine...
One request though is if you could have many smaller servers ....
I'm sure this would speed up the learning process.....
May i suggest waterpistols at dawn for the fight???
Bungholio....
Laters mate..
P.S What do the scots know about language??!!!???

2000-03-01 16:09:48 Marvin
Reduced server list
I notice that only Brussels and Paris are now on the server list. Has Cambridge been removed all together ???
I see there have been problems, but reducing the number of server's down to just two, increases the load. Could you not just add more server's, and spread the load around ?
So far I have two agents, waiting since 23rd Feb to get into Brussels."

2000-03-02 22:21:25 Angus McIntyre
RE: Reduced server list
Cambridge and London have been temporarily taken offline because of problems with the alignment of their cameras. If the cameras drift too far out of alignment, the agents end up looking at totally different things, making it impossible for them to agree on a topic of conversation. Under such circumstances, a language can't form and any agent that ends up on such a site will come away deeply confused. While it's true that taking

9 The second series (2000–2001)

sites offline throws a greater load on the remaining sites, in this case it seemed like the lesser of two evils.
We hope to restore service on these sites within the next few days, and to take steps to prevent a recurrence of the problem. We are looking into the possibility of adding some more sites to the network, but this depends not just on the availability of equipment but also on finding generous, public-spirited people who are prepared to find space to set up a Talking Heads installation and devote some of their time to keeping it running smoothly. We do have a few candidates in mind, however (some of whom don't even yet know that they're candidates, he said with a sinister laugh.)
Angus McIntyre
Talking Heads Junior Camera Joggler

2000-03-03 13:46:06 phlox
RE: Reduced server list
so just how do you think the cameras "drift out of alignment"? and what steps do you plan to take to prevent recurrence? ask me to place a cctv camera watching your cameras so we can see what naughty person is touching them?? slap my wrists for not maintaining proper control in the gallery? hmmmm?? (ps - see my posting yesterday in response to yeah8a8y and london calling's messages of 25th and 26th)

2000-03-07 00:56:52 Martin
Nowhere to launch!!!
All my agents are at home and I can launch them...nowhere!!!!!

2000-03-07 13:30:22 Yeah8a8y
RE: Nowhere to launch!!!
Doh!!!... What do you think it says on the server page?
"Due to essential maintance the interactive part of the site will be turned off"
Hence no launching of agents...

2000-03-07 15:08:20 phlox
RE: Nowhere to launch!!!
cant you play nice? do you have to be rude to everyone on the site?

2000-03-07 16:32:44 Yeah8a8y
RE: Nowhere to launch!!!
Yeah... shitface...
Nah anyway... I was pointing out the obvious!!!
How is that message rude???
I dunno, givce a guy the ability to write and he thinks he's a

9.2 Iconoclasm

```
philosopher!!!
Chris
Resident Hull Uni director of derogatory comments
```

The fact that servers went offline was partly a technical matter, because a new site was being linked in from Amsterdam. But this was seen once more as a negative action and it triggered a call to start introducing foul languages both by giving names to agents and teaching obscene words.

```
2000-03-07 20:44:09 Oisin
RE: Nowhere to launch!!!
I agree, our poor agents have no swearwords how arn the
procrastinate against the stupider agents. TEACH YOUR AGENTS
SWEARWORDS NOW!!!!!!!!
```

```
2000-03-07 22:10:09 Yeah8a8y
RE: Nowhere to launch!!!
All hail "cheesyslurpscum"!!! Very good aimed at the
cheesymeister himself... "hullsuckx" indeed!!!
Chris
Resident Hull Uni director of Poonani
```

Once the site came on-line, we began to remove the swearwords based on complaints from the public sites where the experiment was shown (in particular from Cambridge). This was the chance for Denna Jones (alias *phlox*) to stimulate attacks on the experiment's servers by playing on the sentiment of the players that there was a higher authority impinging on their freedom. The Hull hackers then started to divert the php script of the agents so that they could reschedule agents, encouraged by fish who had admin rights to the London site. However they became suspicious of fish (who also had created an agent with the name Francis Crick) because they realised he had these admin rights and therefore should (normally) have been part of the crew that maintained the overall system. Denna Jones tried to quell this suspicion by denying that he was an insider.

```
2000-03-08 13:22:44 phlox
this is rigged
new agents cant be launched because all sites are in the process
of being "flushed' by angus, luc steels et al of the non-lexicon
made up words and theyre now busy re-installing their master
lexicon. this is the real reason no one can launch new agents
from any of the sites. so what is the point of this game? if
```

253

9 The second series (2000–2001)

players cant create their own language - and we can only use the master lexicon - why bother??

2000-03-08 13:39:58 Yeah8a8y
Bahhh!!!
Well if I can't play fair I just might as well tip the board over eh?
If this is the only way they can stabilise AI, I feel sorry for the poor fools that buy a Cyberdog... It'll be in and out of the repair shop more times then a real dog shits in the street!!!
So the big brass can't play eh? Well there's me thinking this was a valid experiement... Yaknow, God playing and that shite...
Well, I'll be going now!!!
Chris
Resident Hull Uni's deluded scientist"

2000-03-08 14:53:31 Trash
RE: this is rigged
Who can't get in to servers ?? There are ways around everything.

2000-03-08 14:57:22 phlox
RE: this is rigged
good. well see to it you stop the powers that be from trying to regulate the game.

2000-03-08 15:23:06 TRASH!!!!!
RE: this is rigged
My good friend ... who you all know has got into this piece of — and made it so we (Me and him) can still launch!!! look for us on the servers and also nice bots called nice things about Angus...
Thats what Mr Scotish bloke gets from messing with a person who has developed his skills instead of working at this esteemed UNI....
Hull remains the forefront of Electronic skill....
Angus and his fellow friends at sony... your good kid but while ever the hull crew is i town you'll always be number 2
As i write this I beleave that sony will once again allow us to launch in the conventional way ... we shall see Until then just watch the best at work

---

2000-03-08 15:33:00 fish
RE: Hull5 Sony 0
big hand to the hull boys. you may be a bit sensitive to personal insults but atleast you can kick ass when it needs it.....
already seen what you're doing in brussels.... and we love it!

9.2 Iconoclasm

2000-03-08 15:50:55 phlox
RE: Hull5 Sony 0
glad to see someones stopping sony's ethnic cleansing of our
bots. excellent.

2000-03-08 15:51:52 Yeah8a8y
In t' kingdon of t' blind, t' 1-eyed man is king
Thanks Fish, been rumbled by Francis Crick tho'... I think he
has administrative capabilities... either
that or he's another of us here HACKDEMONS.... HAHAHAHA
Chris
Resident Hull Uni worshipper of all thing Satanic and Electronic

---

2000-03-08 15:54:17 phlox
RE: In t' kingdon of t' blind, t' 1-eyed man is ki
i know who francis crick is. and as he's good mates with luc and
angus - they probably gave him admin rights. believe me, he's
no hackdemon . . . .

2000-03-08 16:01:19 Trash
Ahhh thats why!!
Oh nice to see that ... I thought that you just hated asomeone
caled adam wasn't aware that adam IS A CUNT... may have to
reopinionate myself with you ... nice on efella you deserve
respect
Hull Uni Coordinator of Total System Breakdown

The story continues as the Hull hackers entice Denna Jones (*Phlox*) to stand in front of one of the talking heads cameras so that they could see her. She actually does, to great acclaim of the hackers – who seem surprised she is a woman. Denna Jones keeps further encouraging the Hull hackers. And from here on, the tone gets increasingly aggressive as loopholes are closed to prevent manipulation of the experiment and attacks on the servers. There are again suspicions against *fish* who clearly has access from the inside using a password only given to trusted collaborators but which he abuses for destroying the experiment. The group is also now beginning to communicate directly instead of through the *Forum* associated with the Talking Heads website.

2000-03-08 17:23:07 Trash
Phloxy Lady
Hey ahhhhhhhhhhhhhh stop the loving start the warring
trash
Dropouts Director of Assault Forces Against Sony Talking Heads

2000-03-08 17:31:27 phlox
RE: Phloxy Lady
too right. do it.

2000-03-08 20:50:28 fish
RE: OK try not to :)
now, i dont think it is angus mucking us all around – it's not his style. it's far more likely to be someone else who's maybe a bit annoyed at having agents being taught certain words....?

2000-03-08 21:03:19 Trash
who is on whos side??
Just a question how you met angus, adam and clive????
Second ques... How you get on?? do you do it the same way as us???
(Please email fire-for-effect@hotmail.com with this one!!)
Finally to get straight to the point are you one of them??? dun dun dunggggggggggggggg
Trash (Hull Uni's Commander of Conspiracy Theories)"

2000-03-08 23:14:10 fish
RE: who is on whos side??
i am most definitely NOT one of them!

2000-03-09 14:26:15 fish
We are continuing to test software fixes...
"yeah, right, and i'm a jelly called Tracy why dont you just admit that you're trying to censor the site and rid it of all unwanted terms? infact, since you're so busy playing with yourselves, why not just take the whole thing offline and carry on in private in your labs?

2000-03-09 15:14:28 Yeah8a8y
Yeah how about it!!
Then Luc and his mates can all go off... With huge wood... Coz they screwed someone off a site for something inoccuous

2000-03-09 15:52:11 Trash
RE: Yeah how about it!!
It matters not who screws who at thsio point the fact remains if they want to run this experiment their way and by their rules they should set it up purely in their own labs .... without us having access if they want us to contribute then they should let us do it our way ..
Hey Luc and all the rest of you get on this forum and have the balls to talk to us"

9.2 Iconoclasm

```
2000-03-09 16:13:23 phlox
we're still waiting. . .
come on sony own up. if youre gonna exercise stalinistic
control at least do it up front; not under the guise of testing
software;. the only agents on site at the mo are owned by luc,
angus, adam and joris. if it's in the public domain - and it is
- then let the public play!
```

The postings on the Forum keep going in crescendo for a while until the exhibition ends March 2000.

Many aspects of this episode are remarkable, not in the least that those responsable for an exhibition (i.c. Denna Jones (i.e. phlox) and "fish") were bent on creating a wave of negative reactions and destructions against one of the exhibition pieces entrusted to them. Apparently this behaviour was triggered through a conflict with Adam Lowe, curator of the N01SE exhibition, but the team behind the Talking Heads experiment had nothing to do with this. Another remarkable fact is that the hacker group became aggressive as soon as they felt they were no longer able to have control the way they wanted to, specifically to introduce disrespectful language or to subvert agent scripts to circumvent the central scheduler so that they could send their agents in priority to the sites of their choosing. This style of behaviour is a personality trait which is commonly recognised as characteristic for hackers, including by members of the hacker community themselves:[6]

> "Hackers have relatively little ability to identify emotionally with other people. ... Unsurprisingly, hackers also tend towards self-absorption, intellectual arrogance, and impatience with people and tasks perceived to be wasting their time. Because of their passionate embrace of (what they consider to be) the Right Thing, hackers can be unfortunately intolerant and bigoted on technical issues, in marked contrast to their general spirit of camaraderie and tolerance of alternative viewpoints otherwise. ... As a result of all the above traits, many hackers have difficulty maintaining stable relationships. At worst, they can produce the classic geek: withdrawn, relationally incompetent, sexually frustrated, and desperately unhappy when not submerged in his or her craft."

Why did we not interfere in what was going on or directly defend our points of view on the Forum? There were two reasons. First, our team was small and engaged with many other activities. The destructive activities of Denna Jones and her friends were not really worth our continuous attention and precious time. Second, this whole episode was yielding significant data about how individuals behave with respect to artificial agents and about the personality traits of those who are most likely to engage with them. The most obvious conclusion from these data is that we should not attempt to launch such experiments in the public domain, not because they are not feasible from a technical point

---

[6] Raymond, E. (2013) The new hackers dictionary. Available as http://www.catb.org/jargon/html/index.html.

of view, particularly today with much more reliable web technologies, but because the way that (some) individuals are likely to behave with respect to these technologies. The job of figuring out how to create artificial societies and cultures that can cooperate with human societies is an unsolved problems and it will require help from anthropologists to figure out how it can be set up. Undoubtedly anonymity is one of the main sources of deviant behaviour (Knight, Dunbar & Power 1999).

9.3 Installation at the Palais de la Découverte in Paris

As the N01SE exhibition was in full swing, the Palais de la découverte, the largest science museum in Paris, took the initiative to integrate the experiment as part of their running exhibition for several months. This lead to the design of a sophisticated framework for housing the computer equipment (see Figure 9.5), additional educational materials explaining what the experiment was about, and a new run in much more relaxed circumstances with therefore much more interesting results. This new installation started its operation during the social dinner for the Evolution Of Language Conference in Paris organised by Jean-Louis Desalles on 5 April 2000. It was seen by an estimated 300,000 visitors during its installment and an article with results of this experiment appeared in the "Revue du Palais de la Découverte" (Steels & Kaplan 2000).

9.4 The portable Talking Heads

As news of the Talking Heads experiment was spreading, more and more inquiries were made to show the experiment live in other locations. So we made a portable version (see Figure 9.6) that could easily be installed and assembled. Initially this version was used to link into the live teleportation infrastructure, but once the N01SE exhibition was finished, it was used to develop focused experiments, in particular on colour language.

Some of the noteworthy locations where the portable installation was used are the following:

1. The *European Conference on Artificial Life* at the EPFL in Lausanne (Switzerland) in September 1999. Papers on computational and robotic models of language evolution were (and still are) greeted with hostility at linguistics conferences (even conferences on computational linguistics) and they are still routinely rejected for linguistics journals, as being irrelevant for understanding more about human language. However the Artificial Life conferences and journals welcomed the approach from the beginning. This is not surprising because agent-base modeling is one of the main tools used in that field and an evolutionary stance is seen as obvious to biologists. The Lausanne conference was organised in line with earlier conferences on artificial life, showing work on life-like robots, computer simulations, and new chemically based forms of life. It also featured a series of live demos. The portable demonstration of the Talking Heads was part of these demonstrations, set

9.4 *The portable Talking Heads*

Figure 9.5: Talking Heads installation at the Palais de la Découverte. It featured new fancy structures that made the installation more attractive visually. Daily explanations were given to visitors by the staff of the Palais de la Découverte.

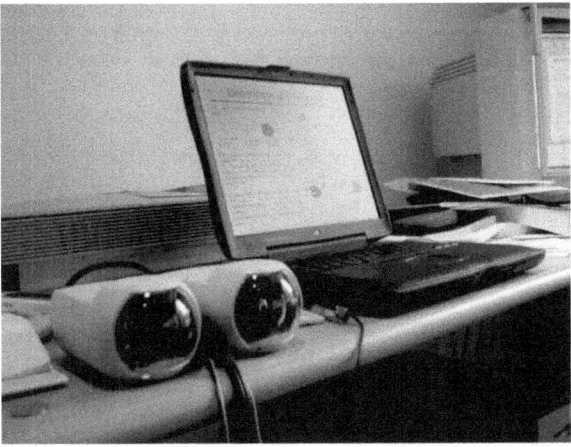

Figure 9.6: Portable installation with two pan-tilt cameras and a portable computer that was able to run the TH software.

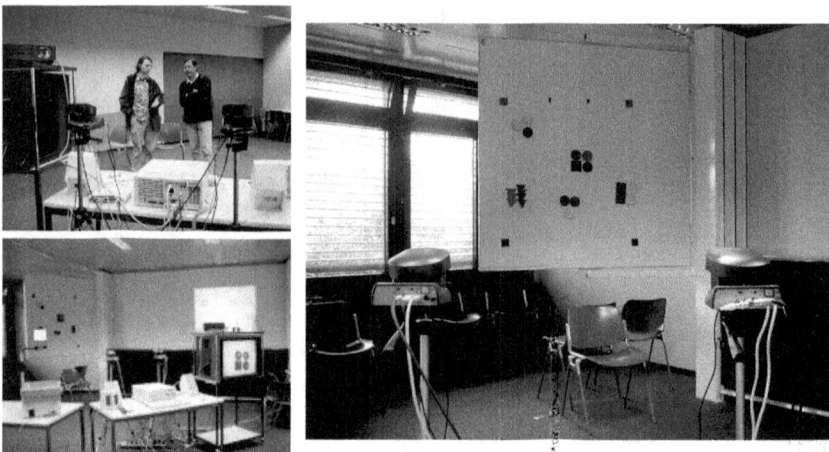

Figure 9.7: Live installation and demonstration of the Talking Heads experiment at the European Conference on Artificial Life in 1999.

up to accompany a presentation at the conference by myself and Frédéric Kaplan[7] It was linked in with the ongoing experiment during Laboratorium in Antwerp.

2. The *Neuer Aachener Kunstverein* in Aachen (Germany) in collaboration with the RWTH (the technical university of Aachen) organised a general exhibition on modelling called Modell-Modell. Within this framework, artist Anne-Mie van Kerckhoven invited me to cooperate in a laboratory on language and colour called "Cyberlabor Chromosophy". As part of this laboratory, the portable Talking Heads experiment was installed and ran from 5 May to 16 June 2000. It featured not only the portable Talking Heads, which was demonstrated live, but also posters, talks about the project and additional art works.

3. The portable Talking Heads was also featured in an exhibition at the *Ludo Mich Gallery* in Antwerp. This exhibition focused on colour again and showed several other pieces related to colour and colour perception. It was accompanied by a very well attended gallery talk.

9.5 Look into the Box

The *Musée d'Art Moderne* in Paris organised a solo exhibition of artist Olafur Eliasson entitled "Chaque matin je me sens différent. Chaque soir je me sens le même" between 22 March and 12 May 2002. (Scherf 2002) Olafur Eliasson is known for his thorough investigations of colour, such as using monochromatic light to create an artificial sun

---

[7] The paper published for this conference is Steels & Kaplan (1999).

9.5 Look into the Box

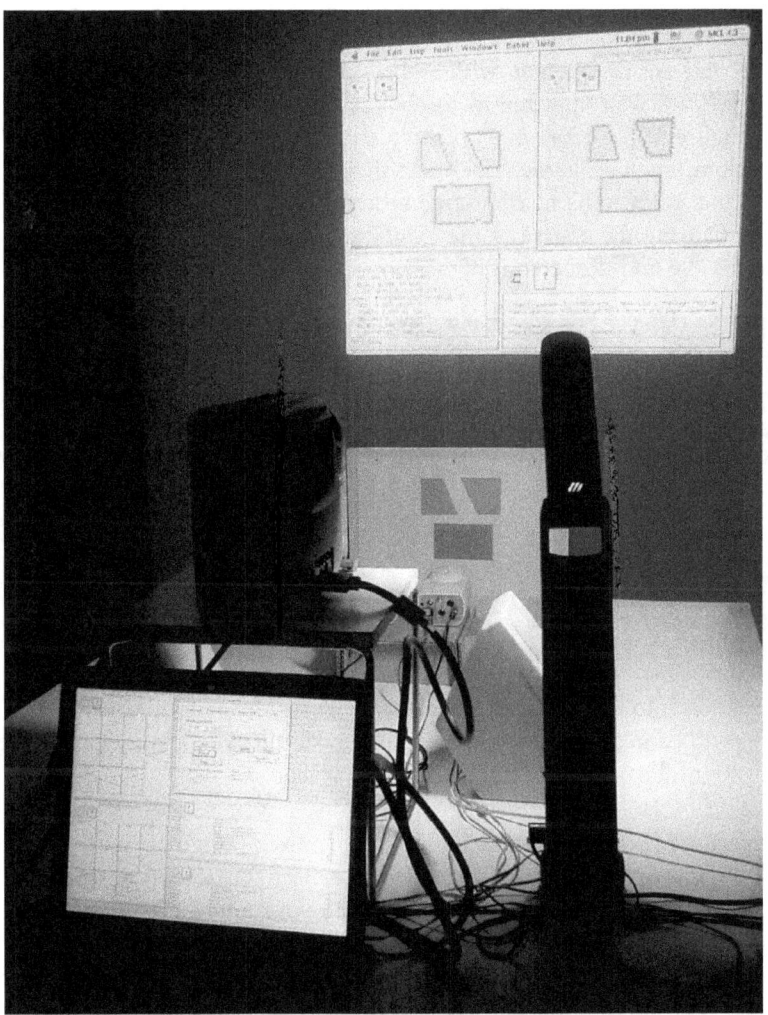

Figure 9.8: Live installation at the gallery of Ludo Mich in Antwerp. There was no white board but different small pancartes with possible scenes (see in the middle of the picture). The game was displayed much larger against the back wall.

9 The second series (2000–2001)

in the Modern Tate Gallery in London (2003). Eliasson invited me to jointly work out a new interpretation of the Talking Heads experiment, which became "Look into the Box". Nicolas Neubauer, a master student working at that time at the Sony Computer Science Laboratory, was the chief implementer together with Angus McIntyre. The set-up and results are described in detail in Steels (2004) and Neubauer (2004).

"Look into the Box" consisted of a box in which a camera was mounted that would take a picture of the eye of a person who looked into the box. The eye was then projected much bigger on a wall opposite to the box, which in itself gave a very strong visual effect (see Figure 9.9). At the same time two artificial agents looked at the eye colour and played a colour language game. Visitors to the exhibition could hear the dialog between the agents and follow on a nearby screen the progression in the emergence of a colour vocabulary. During the course of the exhibition an artificial colour language emerged, reflecting the eye and skin colour of visitors.

Figure 9.9: Look into the Box installation at the Paris Museum of Modern Art. Left: Box with camera inside. A lens would make the eye look bigger for the camera. Right: Projection of the eye on a big screen.

This experiment was fundamentally different from the original Talking Heads experiment because it was no longer a discrimination game but a description game. The agents extracted the main colours from the image of the eye and then described them to another agent. Moreover the domain was now restricted to the colour domain, which had meanwhile become a focal topic of research in the lab (Steels & Belpaeme 2005).

The Look into the Box installation was shown again at several locations. One was in July 2003 in the context of a yearly music festival in Spoleto. In 2003, the theme of semiotic dynamics was chosen and various presentations and discussions were held curated by the Italian semiotician Paolo Fabbri. A new installation of Look into the Box was realised and operated (see Figure 9.11). A system for playing language games with human users, created by Tony Belpaeme of the VUB AI Lab, was also demonstrated. This system was intended to collect data about colour category prototypes and names from human speakers in order to gather more data about colour language in discrimination games.

9.5 *Look into the Box*

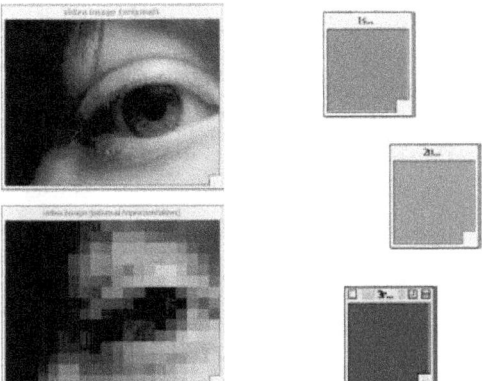

Figure 9.10: Example interaction of the "Look into the Box" art piece. Left: Top and pixelated eye of a spectator. Right: the main colours that were extracted from this image. Agents played language games to describe these eye colours.

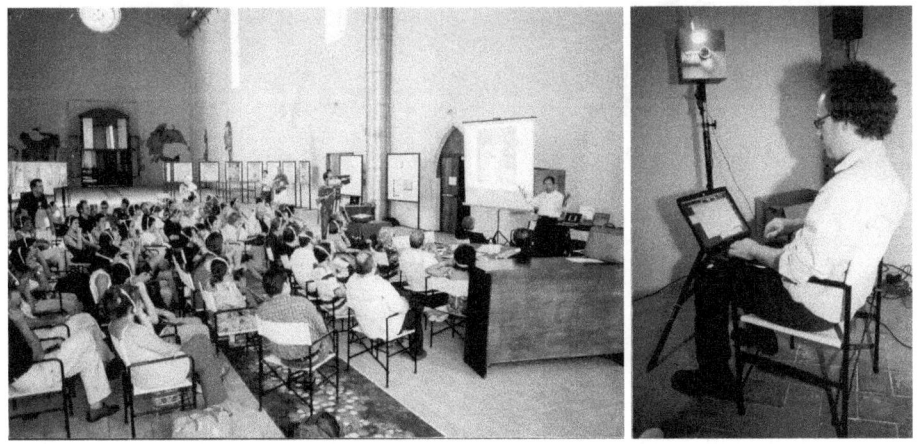

Figure 9.11: Left: My presentation at the Spoleto Science Festival. Right: Nicolas Neubauer debugging the Look into the Box installation.

9 The second series (2000–2001)

The Look into the Box installation was also shown during the "Intensive Science" exhibitions organised in October 2006 on the occasion of the 10th anniversary of the Sony Computer Science Laboratory. It was first shown in Paris at the exhibition space "La Maison Rouge" near the Bastille in Paris, which featured science/art installations and collaborations involving members of the Sony Computer Science Laboratory, including work by Atau Tanaka, Francois Pachet in collaboration with Jazz pianist Albert van Veendaal, Peter Hanappe in collaboration with photographer Armin Linke, Frederic Kaplan in collaboration with the Design School of EPFL in Lausanne. The same exhibition traveled to Tokyo where it was shown in the Sony Explorascience museum from 22 December 2006 to 12 February 2007 (see Figure 9.12).

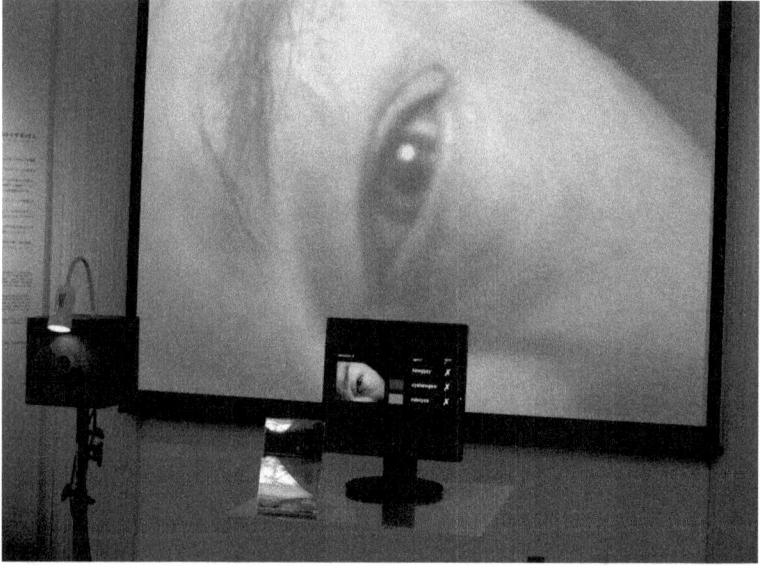

Figure 9.12: Installation at the Tokyo Explorascience Museum. The box is in the left corner. The eye is projected on a big screen. A smaller screen shows the image captured by the camera, the colours recognised, and the words used by the agents.

9.6 Conclusions

The many installations and experiments taught us a lot about how it was possible to technically set up and maintain a distributed network of agents grounding their activities in the real world through cameras. These pioneering experiments happened at a time when the Internet was not as common as today and not as stable. It was before up- and down-loading and apps became widespread and sufficient bandwidth was available even in private homes. The experiments were stopped around 2002 because they took a lot of

9.6 Conclusions

time and not much more could be learned from a technical and scientific point of view.

The installations were also one of the pioneering attempts to develop a strong interaction between art and science, which today are more common and more recognised than they were in the late 1990s. They were conceived to be part of exhibitions and well established artists, such as Olafur Eliasson, took great interest and collaborated to give them a twist to function better within an art context. The context of an exhibition is a very effective way to reach an audience that has normally no access to ongoing scientific experiments. It also generated a stream of newspaper articles, and contributions to radio and television programs, which normally pay only little attention to what goes in science.

The experiments also taught us a lot about the interaction between humans and artificial agents. The idea that a benign symbiosis between artificial agents and humans was possible proved to be naive. There are too many people around with sufficient computer skill but without any ethical consciousness. They see no problem in destroying computational infrastructure simply for their own joy. More recent examples show that these hackers go much further, using their power to do harm or widespread theft. As artificial systems will never be immune to this behaviour, it is probably not possible to imagine a future in which there are autonomous robotic agents, not because the robots would be harmful in themselves but because of the use some individuals will most likely make of them.

Finally, the experiments taught us that the proposed mechanisms for lexicon and concept formation and for reaching coherence worked out. The lateral inhibition learning dynamics and the structural coupling between lexicon formation and concept formation used by the agents proved later not only relevant for lexicon formation but also for grammar. On the other hand this dynamics is not robust enough in the face of extreme uncertainty coming from embodiment (i.e. camera disalignment), high population flux, uncertain environmental conditions or destructive human user interventions. Presumably in such conditions child language and concept learning would also be heavily compromised and perhaps impossible. Anthropologists have argued that the origins of language required a strong form of sociality which is not found in other primate species (Knight & Lewis 2014). The experiment indeed confirms that without empathy, respect and a common purpose, a shared language will not come off the ground.

Part III

Beyond the Talking Heads

10 Beyond the Talking Heads experiment

The Talking Heads experiments were obviously not an end point, but only the beginning. They confirmed the results that had been obtained with earlier theoretical models and computer simulations but did not push these models towards greater complexity. But subsequent work did expand the envelope of our understanding and modelling way beyond these boundaries, thanks to the work of many researchers who have since joined the research programme. The expansion has happened along several dimensions: increased sophistication of the robots, a deeper theoretical understanding of semiotic dynamics, growth in the complexity of semantics and grammar, and new breakthroughs by studying the emergence and evolution of language strategies. An exhaustive survey of these exciting profound developments is beyond the scope of the present book. Instead, I will highlight here only some of the key language game experiments that used real physical robots and were direct variations or further extensions of the environments, game scripts and strategies used in the Talking Heads experiment. This chapter focuses on experiments in the period before 2005, particularly work with the AIBO robots and the first attempts towards the emergence of grammar.[1] The next chapters focus on experiments after 2005.

10.1 Experiments with the AIBO robots

From 1996, even before the first Talking Heads experiment was started, experiments were already conducted in our laboratory, primarily by Paul Vogt, exploring language games on the cybernetic mobile robots that we were able to build ourselves at the time. These robots were constructed from Lego bricks and used a basic processing board for linking directly simple sensors (touch sensors, infrared sensors) and actuators (left and right motors) using an adaptive dynamical system (see Figure 1.3). They were however too unreliable for long-term repeatable experimentation and the sensori-motor experiences were too restricted to hope for the development of interesting languages. The use of pan-tilt cameras, as in the Talking Heads experiment, was an attempt to have an experimental set-up at relatively low cost that was reliable and used vision as the source of information about the world. Of course this came at the price of less mobility and no true physical interaction with the real world. Nevertheless, many further fruitful experiments were done using the same set-up, particularly to explore in much greater depth the domain of

---

[1] An overview of these experiments is also given in: Steels & Belpaeme (2005).

colour lexicons[2] and multi-word naming games.[3] A Talking Heads simulator was also built by Paul Vogt in order to speed up such experiments and prepare the way for more advances with real robots (Vogt 2003).

10.1.1 AIBO's first words

Meanwhile significant developments started to happen in the world of robotics that pushed the state of the art in fully-embodied mobile robots forward. Around the year 2000, a new generation of robots was becoming available, built by industrial companies which mastered the technology to manufacture very robust machines, and these robots could therefore be used continuously without constant breakdown. Because of experience and contacts in the field of robotics, our team was able to move language game experiments to a new level of sophistication. The first platform we could use was the Sony AIBO robot.

The AIBO is a fully autonomous 4-legged mobile robot, inspired by a small dog. It is fully autonomous with more than a thousand behaviours coordinated through a complex behaviour-based motivational system.[4] The robot was pioneered by Toshi Doi and designed by Masahiro Fujita and his team at the Sony Corporation in Tokyo at the end of the nineties (Fujita & Kitano 1998). In all 150,000 AIBO's were sold to customers. The AIBO featured 4-legged locomotion, a camera for visual input, two microphones, a wide range of body sensors, on-board batteries and the necessary computing power. This robot was the most complex reliable robot available in the early 2000's. The AIBO was also the first robot that was explicitly designed for human interaction so that basic useful components (for example for face recognition) were available. Language game research could therefore focus entirely on the linguistic and conceptual aspects of the semiotic cycle, even though we still had to program the physical interaction patterns and behaviours necessary for language games.

Language Game experiments started on the AIBO when the Talking Heads experiment was still going on, namely in 2000. Frédéric Kaplan was the main developer.[5]

These experiments extended the Talking Heads experiment in several directions:

1. **Vision.** The pan-tilt cameras and the flat white board with geometric figures ensured that the vision system of the Talking Heads was relatively reliable, although light conditions and camera misalignment could occasionally cause havoc. The AIBO experiments now used 3d objects in the real world that were seen from many

---

[2] Colour became a focal point of research because there is an extensive literature in cognitive science that has been gathering empirical data about colour and its evolution and because it is relatively straightforward to do colour naming games. One of the main papers on our colour naming research is Steels & Belpaeme (2005).

[3] Multi-word games were the focus of the Ph.D research by Joris Van Looveren, with a thesis defended in 2004.

[4] This robot was entirely based on a series of design principles that I had pioneered together with Rodney Brooks in the mid-nineties under the label 'behaviour-based AI'. See: Steels & Brooks (1995), Steels & McDermott (1994).

[5] A paper summarising the AIBO experiment was published as Steels (2001). Kaplan wrote his Ph.D thesis on the subject which is published (in French) as Kaplan (2001).

different angles and in different light conditions (see Figure 10.1, right). This obviously pushed up the difficulty of visual perception enormously and it also made it much more difficult to acquire stable categories for reliably recognising the objects in the environment.

2. **Speech.** The interaction with the robot used spoken language, which implied that the robot needed speech synthesis and a speech recognition system that could acquire new words. These components were available on the robot and could therefore be easily integrated.

3. **Flexible scripts.** The Talking Heads experiments used a single very streamlined interaction scenario whereby the robots played a Guessing Game with a clear turn-taking script. The AIBO experiments targeted different kinds of interactions with humans and therefore the robot needed not only a way to represent and execute these different scripts but also a much more flexible way to move from one step to another within a script and to move between scripts. Moreover the scripts had to be integrated intimately with the physical behaviours that were steering the robot itself, which could in many cases not be overridden or directly controlled.

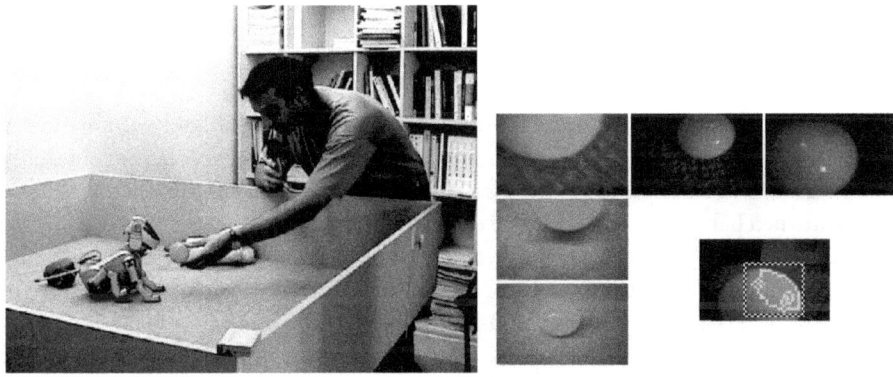

Figure 10.1: Left: Frédéric Kaplan interacts with the AIBO robot in an experiment for the social learning of lexicons. Right: View of the ball through the eye of the robot. As the same object is now seen from many different viewpoints it becomes much more challenging to consistently recognise it.

The first AIBO experiments did not involve a population of agents but rather a single agent that was interacting directly with a human experimenter. The agent had to learn the lexicon of the human through social interaction within the context of situated language games. The 2001 paper "AIBO's first words" by Steels and Kaplan described experiments in which an AIBO robot learned words about objects in the environment, such as *ball* or *smiley*, as well as words for actions, such as *sit down* or *stand up*.

A typical example of a game is the DO game, used to learn the names of behaviours. The robot is programmed with a repertoire of behaviours, such as walk, sit down, stand up, look left/right/up/down, push ball, etc. When the human utters a word, the hearing robot looks up the word in its own memory and performs that behaviour. If it does not know the word, it performs one of the behaviours for which it does not have a word yet. If this behaviour is the wrong one, the robot receives feedback and correction, thus learning (i) that the behaviour is not associated with the word and (ii) what the right word is for the behaviour just performed. When the right behaviour was chosen, the association between this behaviour and the word can be stored if the association was not yet in memory, or reinforced if it was using the lateral inhibition learning strategy. Games therefore always come with two variant scripts. There is one with a successful interaction, which then leads to a reinforcement of the existing lexicon, and one with a non-successful interaction, where the robot gets corrected and learns a new word. Here are the two variants for the DO Game:

Reinforcement script	Correction script
Human: Listen, Walk.	H: Listen, Walk.
R: Walk?	R: Walk?
(walks)	(sits)
H: Yes	H: No, this is 'sit'.
	R: Sit ?
	H: Yes.

The scripts of the agents are represented internally using probabilistic finite state machines with temporal annotations. This computational formalism (pioneered by Rodney Brooks) was also used to program the physical behaviour of the robots (Figure 10.2).[6]

Each state in a behaviour network represents a decision point. A transition is an event happening in the real world or a condition in the internal memory of the agent. Occasionally there is more than one possible continuation from a state and a transition is then decided purely based on a probabilistic basis. When waiting for events in the environment, the transitions have a timer, so that the robot can recover when an expected event is not occurring. In the subsumption architecture networks are stacked and one network may overtake another one. For example, an obstacle avoidance behaviour will become active when touch, vision or infrared sensing has detected an object, whatever other network is governing at that time the robot behaviour.

The main conclusion of these experiments was that the state of the art in robotics and language game research was sufficiently advanced at that time (i.e. in 2001) to implement these more complex games. Moreover several experiments were done to compare different learning methods and interaction patterns, comparing social, situated learning with observational learning. In social situated learning, the learner maximally uses information from the context, the interaction, and the existing state of his language system, to make the best possible guess about the meaning of unknown utterances. He gets help

---

[6] This architecture was first described in Brooks (1986). For the experiments I implemented a LISP-based Behaviour Language that ran also on the AIBO.

10.1 Experiments with the AIBO robots

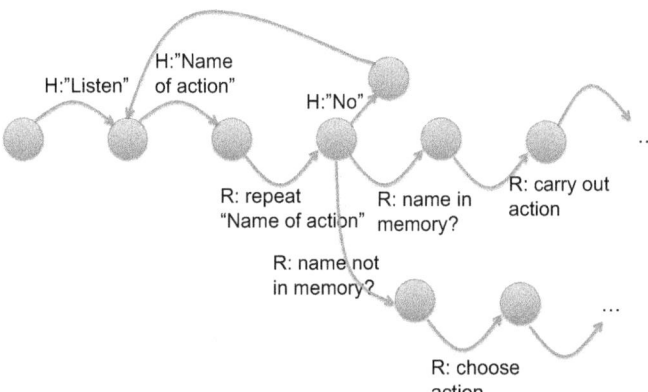

Figure 10.2: The behaviour on the AIBO, including the language game scripts, are programmed using probabilistic finite state machines that bring the robot from one internal state to another one depending on internal or external conditions.

from the speaker which is acting as a tutor and gives useful feedback to constrain the uncertainty as much as possible. An utterance is seen as purposeful and the hearer assumes that the speaker conceptualises and expresses what is relevant to achieve communicative success. In observational learning, the learner is passively observing interactions of others and stores them as data. When there is a sufficiently big corpus he can employ cross-situational learning to grasp the meaning of each word by scanning through the data to find the commonalities between situations using the same word. This approach works also to some extend but experiments showed that it was much slower and not so easily made incremental (De Beule, De Vylder & Belpaeme 2006).

The AIBO experiments were the first robotic experiments demonstrating social, situated learning in action. They were highly relevant for discovering the subtle interaction patterns that would work and could be realistically implemented in human-robot scenarios. The goal of these experiments was not to address the question of the origins of a new language in a population of agents. However, another experiment, still with the AIBO robots, did substantially advance the state of the art: the Perspective Reversal experiment carried out by Martin Loetzsch and Luc Steels in 2004–2005.[7]

10.1.2 The Perspective Reversal experiment

The Perspective Reversal experiment focused on the question how a spatial language could emerge that employed perspective reversal. It was the first experiment to system-

---

[7] Very little was published about this experiment, partly because reviewers had the greatest difficulty to grasp its underlying rationale or understand the technical details. The main paper is Steels & Loetzsch (2008). Subsequent work by Michael Spranger significantly scaled up the experiment, as discussed in the next chapter.

atically compare different language strategies, thus introducing for the first time the COMPARATIVE METHOD that would inform all later language game experiments.

A LANGUAGE STRATEGY prescribes how some aspect of meaning needs to be conceptualised, expressed, and acquired. The Talking Heads experiment used a single strategy: find a discriminating category for the topic and employ a word for that category. But languages use a variety of strategies all intermixed. For example, speakers might have a strategy for expressing argument structure using cases (as in Latin or German) or a strategy for expressing tense and aspect using morphological markers on the verb (as in Spanish). Each strategy gives rise to a particular feature of a language and in order to demonstrate why languages exhibit this feature it is therefore possible to compare a language with the feature to one without the feature by doing an experiment where agents are endowed with a strategy that generates this feature and another one where they employ a different strategy that does not. The performance of the resulting system, for example, its average communicative success, the time to reach linguistic convergence, the amount of cognitive effort involved, can be measured and thus the adaptive value of one strategy (and hence one feature of language) can be compared with another.

The comparative method fits within the larger framework of selectionist theories of language origins, which argue that language users are able to configure strategies by recruiting and configuring cognitive mechanisms (such as sequence detection, categorisation, perspective reversal, etc.) and that those strategies that make a positive contribution to the language are retained.[8] The strategies being compared have to form a chain where one strategy is a slight variation on the previous one, typically an additional component is begin recruited and linked into the strategy, so that we can begin to imagine an evolutionary trajectory in which strategies progressively complexify (see Section 11.1.2)

The Perspective Reversal experiment applied this methodology to explain a remarkable universal feature of human languages, namely, that speakers may use a different perspective on the scene than their own when conceptualising what to say, and that they may explicitly mark perspective switching, using lexical or grammatical means. Suppose a speaker is facing a hearer, then it indeed makes a big difference whether she says *the door to your left* or *the door to my left*. If the speaker says *the door to my left* she expects the hearer to perform an egocentric perspective transformation and see the situation from her own point of view. Perspective switching is here signalled by explicitly expressing which perspective is used: *your* left versus *my* left. The German prepositions *herein* and *hinein*, both meaning 'into' are another example of perspective marking. They distinguish whether the direction of movement is towards the speaker *herein* or away from the speaker *hinein*, analogous to English *come* (to where I am) versus *go* (to another location). Although there are obvious differences in how languages express perspective, there can be no doubt that perspective marking is pervasive across languages and language families, and that speakers make abundant use of it.

The Perspective Reversal experiment worked as follows. A population of AIBO robots roam around freely in an unconstrained in-door environment. As soon as one sees the ball, it comes to a stop and searches for another robot nearby, which also looks for the

---

[8] More on the recruitment theory of language origins in Steels (2007). And on the selectionist framework in general in Steels (2012).

10.1 *Experiments with the* AIBO *robots*

Figure 10.3: Luc Steels demonstrates live the Perspective Reversal experiment in Tokyo, April 2005. AIBO robots track the movement of a ball and the robot acting as speaker describes to the hearer an observed movement, possibly taking into account the perspective of the hearer. For example, the speaker might say *the ball rolls from my left to your right.*

ball and stops when it sees it. Then the human experimenter pushes the ball with a stick so that it rolls a short distance (see Figure 10.3). The two robots next play a description game. One robot (acting as the "speaker") describes the ball-moving event to the other robot (the "hearer"), going through the same semiotic cycle as the Talking Heads agents. The game is a success if the meaning conveyed by the speaker is compatible with the hearer's own perception of the scene.

The robots start without any prior lexicon or ontology and have to come up with their own purely based on the feedback in the game and without any human intervention. They have been programmed to achieve autonomous locomotion and vision-based obstacle avoidance, and maintain a real-time analogue model of their immediate surroundings based on visual input. Using this vision-based world model, the robots are able to detect and track other robots as well as orange balls using standard image processing algorithms (see Figure 10.4). Furthermore, the robots have been endowed with mechanisms to segment the flow of data into distinct events and they have a short term memory in which they can store a number of past events.

Within this experimental setting three different strategies were tried in a long-term experiment where a new strategy was injected at certain stages and performance monitored:

- In stage I, agents use the Discrimination Game strategy and the Naming Game strategy discussed in chapters 4 and 5. A lexicon is emerging and there are some successful games (those for which the speaker and the hearer see the situation from the same perspective). But the lexicon keeps expanding and success is very limited as games where robots have a different perspective on the rolling ball all fail.

- In stage II, agents have an extended strategy where agents can geometrically transform a model of the scene, based on their own perspective, into a model of the scene as seen from the perspective of the hearer. They can then conceptualise the scene from that perspective. Communicative success significantly increases and the lexicon starts to decrease. However there is ambiguity because the hearer cannot know whether the speaker has conceptualised the scene from his own viewpoint or performed a perspective reversal, leading to a large number of failed communications (more than 50 %).

- In stage III, a more elaborate strategy is used. The speaker now expresses whether he has performed perspective reversal (as in to YOUR *left* vs. simply *left*). Only with this strategy are agents able to reach high communicative success with a stable inventory.

The Perspective Reversal experiment was significant in many ways. Not only did it use for the first time mobile robots in a sophisticated open real world set-up, but it also pioneered the use of perspective reversal that was the basis of later experiments in spatial language games with the QRIO robot by Michael Spranger and it was the first convincing example of the comparative method that now underlies all advanced language game

10.1 Experiments with the AIBO robots

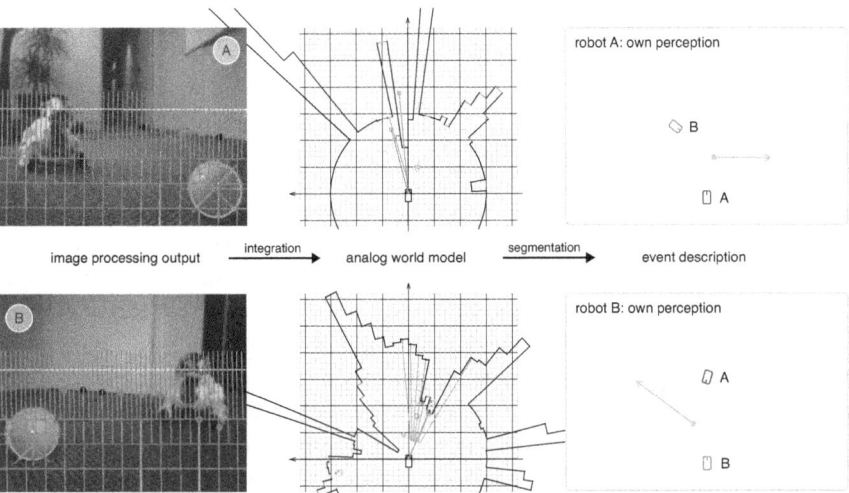

Figure 10.4: Chain from visual image (left) to an analogue world model (middle) and a discrete event description that is the topic of the language game (right). The top row shows this chain for robot A and the bottom row the chain for robot B, both looking at the same ball.

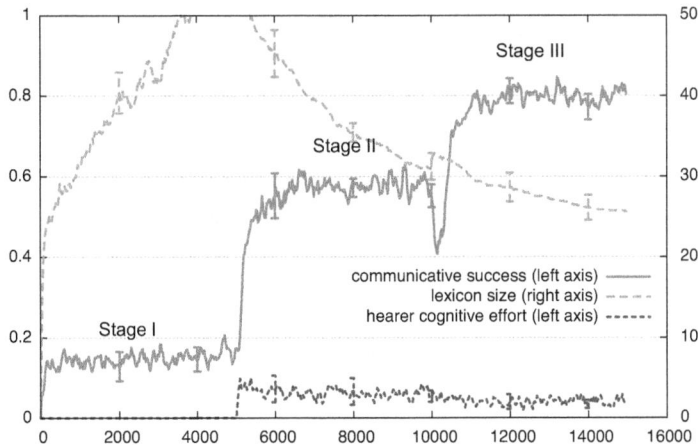

Figure 10.5: Three strategies are compared. In Stage I (left) agents categorise the event from their own perspective. In Stage II (middle) they conceptualise the scene from the viewpoint of the other agent as well. In Stage III (right) they express that they performed a perspective reversal. Only the third strategy leads to successful performance.

277

research. What this experiment did not address was how agents could come up with new strategies themselves and how more adapted strategies could propagate and become shared in the population.

10.2 Scaling up to grammar

We now look at other dimensions in which language game research moved beyond the original Talking Heads experiment. The original experiments focused exclusively on the question how a vocabulary of grounded concepts could arise in a population of agents. Agents could already use multiple word utterances but without any notion of grammar. The obvious next question was how all this could scale up towards grammar. This is of course an extremely difficult challenge that required significant advances both for the representation of the linguistic inventory available to the agents and how meaning is expressed and interpreted. As common in scientific and engineering research, we moved step by step, systematically adding more complexity but testing out each step before moving to the next one, and this progressive complexification is still on the way today.

10.2.1 Early syntax experiments

The earliest attempts to investigate the emergence of syntax date back to 1997, in other words even before the first Talking Heads experiment started. The first report appeared as a paper in the Artificial Intelligence journal as Steels (1998). It was described by the journal editors (Dan Bobrow and Mike Brady) as "obviously in an early stage, but very provocative and suggestive." The paper was based on my keynote lecture at IJCAI 1997 in Nagoya and used a precursor of the pan-tilt cameras built by Tony Belpaeme. (see Figure 1.6).

The paper describes the grammar formalism as follows:

> The grammar is seen as a natural continuation of the lexicon, in the sense that it consists also of associations between forms and meanings. Use and success are monitored for each association so that the same type of self-organised coherence arises in the group, as seen in the lexicon. The form is now a more complex structure, defined as a syntactic schema. The meaning is a semantic schema. The schemas circumscribe a feature-set in terms of a set of slots, restrictions on the fillers of each slot, and constraints on the combination of the fillers to form the total covered by the schema.
>
> Syntactic schemas describe word groups. They have an associated category which corresponds in linguistic terms to grouping categories like noun-group, verb-group, sentence. The slots in syntactic schemas correspond to syntactic functions (also called grammatical relations) such as subject, object, modifier, complement. They name the roles that certain words or word groups play in the group. The categories

used to restrict possible slot-fillers correspond in linguistic terms to syntactic categories like noun, verb, adjective, etc. An example of a syntactic schema is the following:

```
Schema-541
  SLOTS: (syn-slot-51 syn-slot-50)
  DESCRIPTION-SET:
      ([syn-slot-50 syn-cat-751]
       [syn-slot-51 syn-cat-761])
  CONSTRAINTS:
      ((PRECEEDS (>> syn-slot-50) (>> syn-slot-51)))
  CATEGORY: syn-cat-77
  USE: 10
  SUCCESS: 3
```

Of course, instead of noun, noun-group, subject, etc. computer-generated symbols are used such as syn-cat-77, syn-slot-50, etc. The constraints on the schema are represented in terms of a constraint system. Each constraint has a dual procedural function: to enforce the constraint when re-enacting the situation described by a schema or to test the constraint when determining whether a schema fits with a situation. In the present case only a precedence relation is recorded as a constraint. Agreement, intonation, or morphological endings, are some other possible constraints on syntactic schemas.

The categories restricting slot-fillers are either themselves defined in terms of schemas (for example, syn-cat-77 could be the restriction on a slot-filler in another schema), or they are defined as rules that are applied in a forward-chaining fashion during matching. Two examples of rules related to the above schema are:

```
rule 101: ([WORD (W U)]) => ([MEMBER syn-cat-761])
rule 99:  ([WORD (W O)]) => ([MEMBER Syn-Cat-751])
```

Semantic schemas describe the language-specific semantic structures underlying the meanings of complete word groups. The closest linguistic correspondent to a semantic schema is the notion of a case-frame. The constraints indicate how the total meaning is constructed/decomposed into the meaning of the parts. During interpretation such constraints therefore perform the same role as Montague style semantic interpretation functions. The slots correspond to cases such as agent, patient, time, distance, or arguments of semantic functions. The categories used to constrain what can fill a slot correspond in linguistic terms to selection restrictions like animate, human, edible, future, etc. The schema has also an associated category for the whole so that hierarchical combination is possible. An example of a semantic schema is:

```
Schema-542
  SLOTS: (sem-slot-51 sem-slot-50)
  DESCRIPTION-SET:
     ([sem-slot-50 sem-cat-751] [sem-slot-51 sem-cat-761])
  CONSTRAINTS:
     ((CONJUNCTION (>> sem-slot-50) (>> sem-slot-51)))
  CATEGORY: sem-cat-77
  USE: 10
  SUCCESS: 3
```

Inference rules such as the following define the selection restrictions:

```
rule 102: ([VISIB v-4111) => ([MEMBER sem-cat-761)
rule 100: ([VER v-4311) => ([MEMBER sem-cat-751)
```

Each association in the grammar couples a syntactic schema with a semantic schema. The association can be used in two directions. If a syntactic schema is recognised, i.e., all its constraints are satisfied by the input utterance, the semantic schema is used to reconstruct its meaning. If a semantic schema is recognised, the syntactic schema is used to reconstruct the form. The association contains a mapping of the slots in order to enable this reconstruction. For example, the association combining the above two schemas is:

```
Association-271
  MEANING: Schema-542
  FORM  : Schema-541
  MAPPING : ((syn-slot-51 sem-slot-51)
             (syn-slot-50 sem-slot-50))
  USE: 10
  SUCCESS: 3"
```

An application of these schemas in producing the utterance *(W O) (W U)* is represented in Figure 10.6 and shown here:

```
127 ++> Speaker: head-40 Topic: 2 Context: 6 5 4 3 1 0
Categorial Perception:
  ([VISIB v-4111] [VER v-431])
  ([VER v-4311] [AREA v-4061])
Lexicon lookup: (Association-259 Association-234)
Syntactic structure:
  (syn-cat-77
    (syn-slot-50 (syn-cat-75 |(W O)|))
    (syn-slot-51 (syr-cat-76 |(W U)|)))
Semantic structure:
```

10.2 Scaling up to grammar

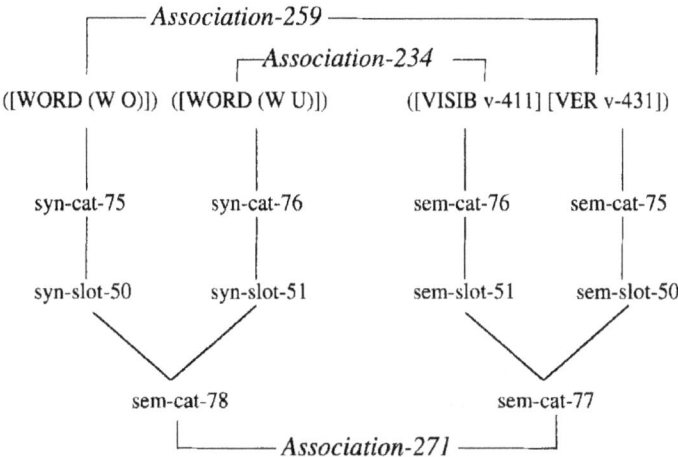

Figure 10.6: Top: Two lexical associations have become active (association-259 and association-234) to cover the distinctive feature-set ([VISIB v-411] [VER v-431]) resulting from discrimination and perception. Bottom: The group of words and the meanings match with schemas forming part of a grammatical association that combines the words.

```
(sem-cat-78
    (sem-slot-50 (sem-cat-75 (VER v-431)))
    (sem-slot-51 (sem-cat-76 (VISIB v-411))))
Meaning:
    ([VISIB v-4111] [VER v-4311)
Expression: ((W O) (W U))
```

So this experiment already contained several kernel ideas that would become the basis of further developments towards computational formalisms that could handle evolutionary language game experiments, such as the representation of the grammar in terms of form-meaning pairs – similar to the lexicon – , the use of schemas to represent the syntactic and semantic pole of a coupled feature structure, and the use of constraints to specify the properties of each pole, so that the grammar can be used in a bi-directional fashion. The relationship to construction grammar, which came to the foreground in linguistics around 1995, was not yet clear at the time.

The paper also briefly described the mechanisms by which such a grammar emerged in the experiment in terms of a cognitive memory system:

> "The cognitive memory system acts in a first instant purely as a device that records a particular way in which language has been produced so that it can later be reproduced in the same way. Also the hearer can perform this recording operation. He is presented with a specific set of word forms from which he can abstract a

syntactic schema. He derives meaning from the definition of the words in the lexicon and the distinctive feature-set coming out of perception. From this, a semantic schema can be extracted. More interesting grammars emerge when additional operations to restructure the set of grammatical associations are used. For example, in the case of a partial match, substructures may be recategorised so that they nevertheless fit, two partially overlapping schemes with common fillers may lead to a new schema that integrates both, etc."

10.2.2 The Case Grammar experiments

The first of these efforts started around 2001 and focused on case grammar, i.e. on how grammatical constructions for expressing the arguments of a predicate describing a relation or event could emerge and convergence in a population of grounded agents. Case grammar is one of the core functions of grammar and focusing on this domain would guarantee that we are addressing empirically attested core phenomena of human language. The first wave of work on case grammar took place from 2001 to 2003. It required the construction of a more sophisticated vision system (accomplished by Jean-Christophe Baillie) and the design and implementation of a more sophisticated grammar formalism (accomplished by Luc Steels and Nicolas Neubauer), although this was still only one step on the way towards later developments in Fluid Construction Grammar.

Based on these components, I implemented an initial experiment with two agents.[9] In 2005 Remi van Trijp picked up this line of research again and worked out the experiment further with great skill and sophistication. He extended the 2-agent simulation to a multi-agent simulation and could finally report a complete running system in his 2008 Ph.D thesis (van Trijp 2014b). Here I give only a brief account of the first attempts towards case grammar and how this pushed the state of the art in language game research.

But first we need a clearer idea on what case grammar is. In the sentence *John gave Mary a book*, John plays the role of agent, the giver of the book, Mary that of recipient or beneficiary and the book is the "patient" or object of the action. Languages differ in terms of the strategies that they use to express these participant roles. Some of them, like German, have an elaborate system of morphological markers attached to constituents of the noun phrase. These markers signal that the phrase is nominative, accusative, dative, etc., and these cases then map in complex ways onto semantic roles such as agent and patient. Other languages, like English, use a strategy based on word order and prepositions. For example, *Mary gave John a book* contains the same participants as *John gave Mary a book* but now Mary is the agent and John the recipient. Still other languages, like Japanese, use a strategy based on particles following the noun, as in the Japanese sentence *Tanaka-san wa Tokyo de o-to-san ni atta* meaning 'Tanaka met his father in Tokyo'. *Tanaka-san* is the name of a person, *oto-san* means 'father' and *atta* means 'met'. The markers are *wa* for the topic, *de* for location and *ni* for another sense of location which

---

[9] These experiments were first reported at the Harvard Evolution of Language conference in 2002 with a paper by Luc Steels entitled "Computer Simulations of the origins of Case grammar". The paper was later deemed "too incomprehensible for the Evolution of Language community" to be acceptable for the conference proceedings edited by Maggie Tallerman.

can also function as possessive. The case grammar experiments focused on modelling the latter strategy.

It used the comparative method again to compare three progressively more complex strategies:

1. **Lexical strategy.** The experiment starts from a purely lexical language that is predefined in all agents. The lexicon contained words for expressing properties of objects (such as *smooth, red,* etc.) as well as actions involving objects (such as *move-away-from, move-towards* or *push*). English words were chosen to make the experiment easier to follow. Agents form multi-word utterances using straightforward lexicon lookup, producing utterances like *move-towards red jill* (Jill moves towards the red object) or *push jack jill green* (Jack pushes the green block to Jill). There is no syntax at all. Agents can nevertheless already achieve communicative success when they use the real world as a way to figure out the participant roles, even though the utterance does not provide any information. For example, to detect whether Jack pushes the green block to Jill or Jill pushes the green block to Jack.

2. **Specific marker strategy.** The second strategy introduces markers in the form of particles added to words referring to objects, in order to specify what argument the object fills in the predicate describing the event. For example, there could be two markers: *pi* and *pa* specifying that the referent plays the role respectively of giver and gift in a give event, as in *pi jill pa block give*. The markers are entirely specific for each event in the sense that there is no generalisation yet to *agent, patient* or other more abstract semantic roles. This already yields a more effective communication system because the complexity of seeking an interpretation matching with the world model is heavily reduced and residual ambiguity (i.e. there is still more than one way in which the meaning matches with the world model) is also avoided.

3. **Role strategy.** The third strategy introduces generalisations of the markers, so that fewer markers are needed. This decreases the size of the inventory and thus makes the language more efficient to process and easier to learn. There are many strategies that could be used for generalisation. Our experiments have explored the use of analogy: When arguments need to be expressed for an event e, agents no longer create new specific markers for each argument of e but look for analogies between this event e and other events for which markers already exist. If a good analogy can be found they reuse it and generalise the argument-specific marker.

This analogy-based method of generalisation is explained in some more detail later in this section, but first we look briefly at other advances that were needed: What world was made available to the agents for their language games? How did the vision system work? And what grammatical formalism was devised to handle case grammar?

We used a similar set-up as the Talking Heads experiment (see Figure 10.7), but the world had to be made more complex, involving dynamical scenes in which different

10 Beyond the Talking Heads experiment

Figure 10.7: The installation for the case grammar experiments used a more sophisticated vision system and objects that could be moved around. We see the two Talking Heads cameras in the background. They are oriented towards objects on the table or situations in the environment. The monitors show the camera images and the states of image processing, just as for the original Talking Heads experiment.

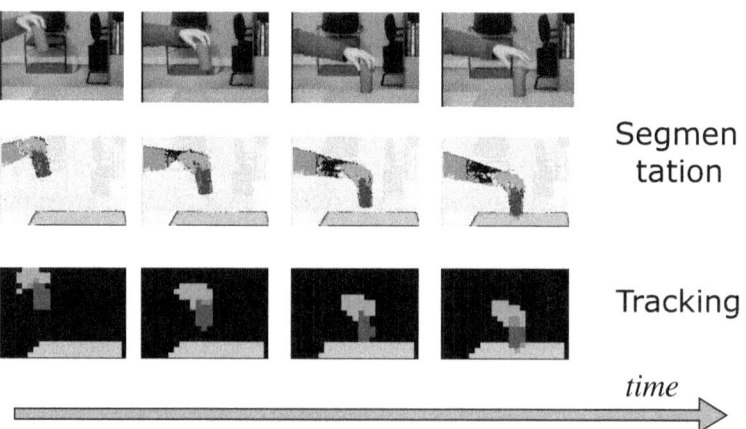

Figure 10.8: Top: Some of the images recorded during the action of picking up a cylinder. Middle: Results of segmentation algorithms. Bottom: The spatio-temporal continuity of objects is tracked.

284

10.2 Scaling up to grammar

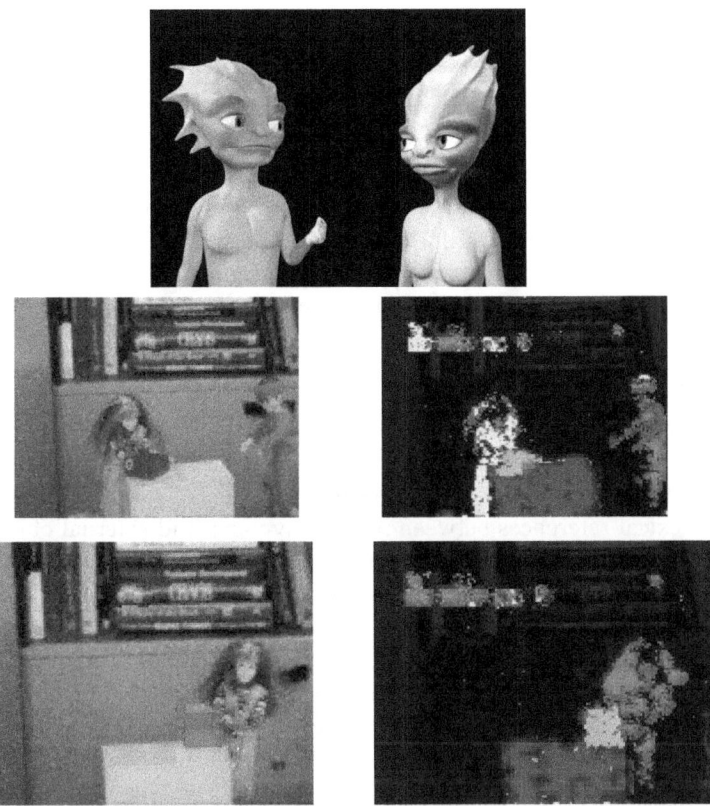

Figure 10.9: Top: Computer animation of the speaking and hearing agent used in public demonstrations of the case experiment. Middle: Example of a puppet scene, where Jill gives a block to Jack. It shows the source image (left) and a (partial) result of image processing (right). Bottom: Another example of a puppet scene where Jill pushes the block.

animate objects performed actions. So I decided to use puppets and enacted little scenes before the cameras (see Figure 10.9 middle and bottom). There were two puppets, named Jack and Jill. They were actually sold at that time as puppet versions of Harry Potter and Hermione Granger inspired by the famous Harry Potter book series. The puppets appeared and disappeared within the field of view of the cameras. They manipulated small objects, for example pushing a green cube, picking it up, sliding the cube towards the other puppet, putting it in a box, etc. To make the simulation more lively and easier to follow for a lay public, the agents engaging in a language game were also visually animated (see Figure 10.9 top).[10]

---

[10] The animations were developed by Veronique Caraux in Paris.

10.2.2.1 Scaling up the vision system

The vision system of the Talking Heads only dealt with static scenes. This had to be scaled up to deal with dynamical scenes and event recognition. It was the focal work of Jean-Christophe Baillie at the Sony Computer Science Laboratory in Paris, who built a vision system called PERACT inspired by an event-recognition developed by Jeffrey Siskind.[11] The vision system was decomposed into three subsystems with information flowing both in a bottom-up (from image to world model) and top-down way (from world model and predictions to image): the subsystems achieved object identification, event identification, and derivation of qualitative descriptors.

10.2.2.2 Object identification

The first subsystem attempts to detect and track visual units at different hierarchical levels. It detects and "latches onto" regions in the image that are generated by objects of interest in the environment. This results in deictic pointers or "anchors" that establish and monitor indexical references between internal symbols and external objects. Tracking not only takes place for a single object, but for an open-ended set of objects at different hierarchical levels, as long as they are part of the same spatio-temporal context.

The detection and tracking of units at different hierarchical levels starts in a bottom-up manner from the images captured by the camera, and goes through various processing steps: figure/ground separation based on colour perception, creation of a cellular occupancy grid, spatial region growing to identify spatial regions, and construction of spatio-temporal continuities based on color histograms of the objects (Figure 10.8).

10.2.2.3 Event identification

The second subsystem detects and tracks events, again at different hierarchical levels. The task is similar to that of detecting objects but the grouping is based on changes in properties of objects rather than on invariances. Event detection is organised in three steps:

1. Detect change by computing qualitative descriptions for the movement of an object, the contact between two objects, the approaching of two objects, the positioning of an object with respect to another one, etc.

2. Detect micro-events by grouping image subsequences during which the same configuration of qualitative descriptors holds.

3. Detect events which are defined as sequences of micro-events recognised using probabilistic state machines. For example a pick-up event (as in Figure 10.8) involves three micro-events: (1) the hand moves towards the object, (2) the hand touches the object, and (3) both move away together. Processes concerned with

---

[11] The vision system is described in the Ph.D thesis of J-C Baillie. A summary is found here: Steels & Baillie (2003). Inspiration for the event recognition system came primarily from the paper by Siskind (2000).

10.2 Scaling up to grammar

recovering such events use a library of event definitions which is matched against the stream of micro-events.

An example of output from this subsystem is shown below. Each event has an index (e.g. 77), a time period (e.g. from 780 to 803), other events or properties that have played a role in recognising this event, a label (e.g. Appear}), and information of the status (like ongoing or finished).

```
...
(77 780 803 ((780 2) (783 20)) Appear 5 ONGOING)
(89 784 810 ((784 5) (790 20)) Halt 5 ONGOING)
(87 780 919 ((780 118) (899 20)) Appear 1 ONGOING)
(87 780 924 ((780 123) (904 20)) Appear 0 ONGOING)
(82 904 928 ((904 20) (925 3)) Halt 0 FINISHED)
(95 900 933 ((900 12) (913 20))
    Approach_Resttogether 1 5 ONGOING)
(93 904 933 ((904 8) (913 20)) Put 1 0 5 ONGOING)
(92 780 937 ((780 123) (904 33)) Appear 0 FINISHED)
(74 924 937 ((924 3) (930 7))
    Resttogether_Moveawayfrom 0 1 FINISHED)
(97 900 944 ((900 23) (924 20)) Halt 1 ONGOING)
(93 929 958 ((929 8) (938 20)) Halt 0 ONGOING)
(80 929 1017 ((929 8) (938 79)) Halt 0 FINISHED)
(91 938 1038 ((938 79) (1018 20)) Appear 0 ONGOING)
...
```

10.2.2.4 Qualitative descriptors

The third subsystem consists of feature detectors that attempt to find qualitative descriptions for units at different levels of the object or event hierarchy. The result of all these processes is a set of streams, reporting objects and their properties dynamically in response to a changing world as well as the roles these different objects play in the events. A (short term) memory of these streams is kept as events unfold. It is used by the semantic system to construct or interpret the semantic structures that have to be expressed. Here is a small snapshot of the state of this visual memory with time stamps when the states occurred.

```
...
(CAUSE-MOVE-INSIDE ev-7 TRUE) <15:50:2>
(CAUSE-MOVE-INSIDE-TARGET ev-7 obj-1) <15:50:2>
(CAUSE-MOVE-INSIDE-PATIENT ev-7 obj-2) <15:50:2>
(CAUSE-MOVE-INSIDE-AGENT ev-7 YOU) <15:50:2>
(HALT ev-3 TRUE) <15:49:41>
(HALT-ARG ev-3 obj-1) <15:49:41>
(MOVE ev-1 TRUE) <15:49:24>
```

10 Beyond the Talking Heads experiment

```
(MOVE-ARG ev-1 obj-1) <15:49:24>
(STRIPED obj-2) <15:48:42>
(HUGE obj-2) <15:48:42>
(BALL obj-2) <15:48:42>
(WHITE obj-2) <15:48:42>
(OBJECT obj-2) <15:48:42>
(STRIPED obj-1) <15:48:42>
(BIG obj-1) <15:48:42>
(PYRAMID obj-1) <15:48:42>
(\textsc{yellow} obj-1) <15:48:42>
(OBJECT obj-1) <15:48:42>
...
```

Since this pioneering vision work, subsequent language game experiments on robots have all been using similarly sophisticated vision systems and currently such systems are standard components on commercially available robots.

10.2.2.5 Scaling up the language system

Not only the vision system, but also the language system had to be scaled up significantly to do these experiments. Together with Nicolas Neubauer, I built upon the formalism I had developed for the early syntax experiments, designing and implementing a next generation system, called COGAR, which stands for Cognitive Grammar Architecture.[12] Here is a brief description of this formalism.

COGAR represents syntactic and semantic structures as frames with units, slots and constraints on the slots. The frames are in many ways similar to the feature structures used in feature-structure based grammars such as HPSG, although there are many important differences. For example, each unit has a unique name so that it becomes possible to refer back to units in defining constraints. COGAR also used logic variables (denoted by a symbol with a question mark in front) as opposed to path descriptions, which lead to the adoption of techniques from logic programming. The syntactic and semantic structure of a particular utterance are coupled together as a coupled feature structure by making the unit-names shared. Often both are combined when the coupled feature structure needs to be displayed as in this example below.

```
((unit-15
   (scope utterance)
   (subunits (unit-17 unit-18 unit-16))
   (ordering (unit-17 unit-18 unit-16)))
 (unit-17
   (form (smooth))
   (meaning ((smooth ?source-object1)))
```

---

[12] No official publication of the COGAR system exists. Such technical papers are virtually impossible to get published in journals or conferences. There was however a technical report: Steels (2001).

```
    (referent ?source-object1)
    (gramcat (takes-marker-1))))
  (unit-18 (form (po)))
  (unit-16
    (form (move-away-from))
    (meaning
      ((move-away-from ?event ?state)
       (move-away-from-1 ?event ?object)
       (move-away-from-2 ?event ?source-object1)))))
```

This example could have been constructed, either in parsing or producing, for the utterance *po smooth move-away-from*. Syntactic properties such as the form of the word, the ordering of the units, or the grammatical categories of a unit are represented explicitly on the syntactic side and the meaning and referent are represented on the semantic side. In general, COGAR allows the representation of any kind of information at whatever level of linguistic analysis as part of a feature structure.

Notice that the arguments for a predicate describing an event are decomposed into separate predicates, one for each argument. For example move-away-from (?event, ?object, ?source-object) has three arguments and this is decomposed into three expressions:

```
  (move-away-from ?event ?state)
  (move-away-from-1 ?event ?object)
  (move-away-from-2 ?event ?source-object)
```

?state is bound to true, false or unknown.

The lexicon and grammar in COGAR takes the form of a set of bi-directional rules. The rules have two poles which are typically the semantic and syntactic pole, although there could be rules that work only on the syntactic level and others that work on the semantic level. The rules are applied from right to left in production and from left to right in parsing. The rules can have variables at any position and in any of the two poles. In order to be applicable, one pole of the rule has to match, which means that the structure defined in the pole had to have correspondents within the target structure, possibly after binding the variables to concrete symbols in the coupled feature structure. If a complete match is found, the other pole is merged with the target, which means that all variables get instantiated and every element which is not yet in the target is added. The underlying computational model of COGAR is therefore similar to a rule-based inference system, with an inference engine that cycles through the rules until no more rules can be applied. The variables are logic variables and hence the matching and merging is similar to the process of unification as used in PROLOG or other logic programming languages.

Here is an example of a lexical rule that defines the meaning of the word for an event *move-away-from*. The referent is the object that is referred to by the word, in this case it is the event itself.

10 Beyond the Talking Heads experiment

```
((?unit
   (meaning
      (== (move-away-from ?event ?state)
          (move-away-from-1 ?event ?object)
          (move-away-from-2 ?event ?source)))
   (referent ?event))
<-->
((?unit
   (form (== move-away-from)))))
```

Next, here is an example of a rule for the marker *po*. On the semantic side it ensures that the referent of one unit whose referent is ?source is equal to the object filling the argument move-away-from-2 in a move-away-from event. On the syntactic side, it triggers when there is a word that has the grammatical category *takes-marker-1* and is preceded by the marker *po*. (<< stands for 'precedes')

```
((?predicate
   (meaning
      (== (move-away-from ?evnt)
          (move-away-from-1 ?evnt ?patient)
          (move-away-from-2 ?evnt ?source))))
 (?argument
   (referent ?source)))
<--->
((?argument
   (gramcat (== takes-marker-1)))
 (?marker-unit
   (form (== po)))
 (<< ?marker-unit ?argument))))
```

There are additional rules that specify which word takes which marker, by assigning them to a particular grammatical category. For example, the word *smooth* has the category *takes-marker-1*:

```
((?unit
   (gramcat (== takes-marker-1))
   (form (== smooth))))
<--->
((?unit (form (== smooth)))))
```

The marker *po* in the above example is entirely specific for one argument of the move-away-from predicate, as would be the case when the second strategy is enacted. To implement the third strategy (to achieve more abstract semantic roles) requires that the markers become generic, which implies that we get additional rules that recategorise the arguments of a predicate in terms of semantic roles like: agent, patient, source, etc. Here is an example of a rule that has this effect. role-1 is an example of a semantic role created by the agent as an abstraction of the move-away-from-2 argument.

```
((?predicate
    (meaning
      (== (move-away-from ?evnt)
          (move-away-from-1 ?evnt ?patient)
          (move-away-from-2 ?evnt ?source)))))
<--->
  ((?predicate
      (meaning
        (== (move-away-from ?evnt)
            (move-away-from-1 ?evnt ?patient)
            (move-away-from-2 ?evnt ?source))))
   (expanded-meaning (== (role-1 ?evnt ?source))))
```

And the rules that click everything together now operate over semantic roles as shown in the following example:

```
((?predicate
    (expanded-meaning (== (role-1 ?event ?source))))
  (?unit (referent ?source)))
<--->
  ((?unit (gramcat (== takes-marker-1)))
   (?marker-unit (form (== po)))
   (<< ?marker-unit ?unit))
```

Recall that all rules must be reversible and that the conditional part must match and the concluding part must unify.

10.2.2.6 Analogy as the driver of generalisation

There is of course a lot more to say about how all this works computationally and about how these rules are built during learning. The reader is referred to the references given earlier. But let us here just focus only on the very non-trivial question where role-abstractions like agent, patient, or source come from. Analogy, which is clearly a basic feature of human cognition in general, is proposed as the key mechanism. When agents have to express which argument an object fills in an event, they first try to see whether there is already a marker that expresses an argument in an analogous event. When this is the case, the marker is first generalised to express a new semantic role (if it was not yet a role) and then the unexpressed event-argument is categorised in terms of this role. If the hearer encounters a new use of a marker, he will also use analogy to find the connection between the event used earlier on and the newly encountered event.

Operationalising analogy is extremely difficult because humans tend to incorporate almost anything in how they make analogical inferences and inferences are heuristic as opposed to rigid logical derivations. The analogical mapping used in the case grammar experiment starts from two events, further called the source-event, for which some relations have already been expressed, and the target event for which a marker needs to be constructed. The first step in analogy-making consists in decomposing both events into the primitive micro-events that the vision system is using to recognise the event. The second step is to find a mapping between them.

Here is an example showing how the argument walk-to-1 is mapped onto the argument move-inside-1. The walk-to event features two arguments, walk-to-1 (the agent walking) and walk-to-2 (the target towards which the agent is walking). It consists of four micro-events: The agent does not move, the target does not move, then the agent approaches the target, and then the agent touches the target. This means that the event

```
(WALK-TO-2 ev-100 JILL)  (WALK-TO-1 ev-100 JACK)
(WALK-TO ev-100 TRUE)
```

expands into:

```
(MOVE ev-165641 TRUE)    (MOVE-1 ev-165641 JACK)
(MOVE ev-165419 FALSE)   (MOVE-1 ev-165419 JILL)
(APPROACH ev-165486 TRUE) (APPROACH-2 ev-165486 JILL)
(APPROACH-1 ev-165486 JACK)
(TOUCH ev-165633 TRUE)   (TOUCH-2 ev-165633 JACK)
(TOUCH-1 ev-165633 JILL)
```

The move-inside event has also two arguments: move-inside-1 (the agent moving) and move-inside-2 (the location in which the agent is moving). It consists of eight micro-events: The agent is visible, the location is visible, the distance between the agent and the location decreases, the location does not move, the agent does not touch the location, then the agent touches the location, and then the agent becomes invisible. The following description of a move-inside event

```
(MOVE-INSIDE ev-163190 TRUE)
(MOVE-INSIDE-2 ev-163190 HOUSE-1)
(MOVE-INSIDE-1 ev-163190 JILL)
```

therefore expands into the following micro-events:

```
(VISIBLE ev-161997 TRUE)  (VISIBLE-1 ev-161997 JILL)
(DISTANCE-DECREASING ev-162441 TRUE)
   (DISTANCE-DECREASING-2 ev-162441 HOUSE-1)
(DISTANCE-DECREASING-1 ev-162441 JILL)
(MOVE ev-161794 FALSE)   (MOVE-1 ev-161794 HOUSE-1)
(TOUCH ev-161801 FALSE)  (TOUCH-2 ev-161801 HOUSE-1)
   (TOUCH-1 ev-161801 JILL)
(TOUCH ev-162493 TRUE)   (TOUCH-2 ev-162493 HOUSE-1)
   (TOUCH-1 ev-162493 JILL)
```

10.2 Scaling up to grammar

```
(VISIBLE ev-161791 TRUE)   (VISIBLE-1 ev-161791 HOUSE-1)
(VISIBLE ev-162665 FALSE)  (VISIBLE-1 ev-162665 JILL)
```

Next each micro-event in the target-event is paired with all micro-events in the source-event which use the same predicate. Micro-events which cannot be mapped this way are ignored. The temporal information which is part of the hierarchical event description is not used either. For the mapping from the move-inside event to the walk-to event, we get the following result:

```
 move-inside event => walk-to event
(TOUCH ev-162689 TRUE)     => (TOUCH ev-165633 TRUE)
(TOUCH-1 ev-162689 JACK)   => (TOUCH-1 ev-165633 JILL)
(TOUCH-2 ev-162689 HOUSE-1) => (TOUCH-2 ev-165633 JACK)
(TOUCH ev-161796 FALSE)    => (TOUCH ev-165633 TRUE)
(TOUCH-1 ev-161796 JACK)   => (TOUCH-1 ev-165633 JILL)
(TOUCH-2 ev-161796 HOUSE-1) => (TOUCH-2 ev-165633 JACK)
(MOVE ev-161794 FALSE)     => (MOVE ev-165419 FALSE)
(MOVE ev-165641 TRUE) (MOVE-1 ev-161794 HOUSE-1) =>
        (MOVE-1 ev-165419 JILL) (MOVE-1 ev-165641 JACK)
```

A good mapping is such that the filler of the argument of interest (in this case Jack, which fills the move-inside-1 argument in the move-inside event) always maps onto the same object in the source-event. This is indeed the case here because Jill, which fills the role of move-inside-1 in the walk-to event, always plays the same role in all source micro-events as Jack in the matching target micro-events. Note that walk-to-2 would not extend by analogy to move-inside-2 because the object house-1 (which fills the role of move-inside-2) maps onto different object roles in the source-event. Once the analogy established, the marker already available for the walk-to-1 event-object relation is re-used for marking the move-inside-1 relation.

Here are some results from comparative experiments using real world data. The graph in Figure 10.10 compares the number of markers that have been derived by the agents for two experiments, each using data from the same series of 1300 language games. The first experiment (top graph) does not use analogy, hence new markers are created for every argument in every predicate that needs to be expressed. The grammars basically stabilise after about 700 games with 28 markers. In the second experiment (the two bottom graphs) the strategy with analogy has been used. There is a graph showing the growth in the number of role markers and another one in the number of argument markers. Agents generated 4 role markers in the second experiment, covering a wide range of events, and 7 more specific argument markers, which might still be generalised later. The grammars of the agents stabilised much earlier after 200 games, which proves the point that the use of analogy not only results in a more compact grammar with more expressive power, but also in a grammar that is faster to emerge and easier to learn.

This first case experiment was only the beginning of more thorough and systematic research by Remi van Trijp who scaled up the experiment to multi-agent simulations and made several additional discoveries, such as the necessity to use multi-level alignment

(Steels, van Trijp & Wellens 2007). But the early experiment was already of huge importance to open the path towards realistic grammars. In parallel, other areas of grammars began to be tackled, particularly grammars for tense and aspect.[13]

10.3 Conclusions

This chapter described a first batch of language game experiments, happening at the same time or right after the Talking Heads experiment. They were beginning to climb slowly up on the long and winding path towards languages that are similar in complexity from the viewpoint of interaction, perception, conceptualisation and grammar to human natural languages. The research landscape was becoming clearer but at the same time the enormity of the challenges that remained became obvious. There is clearly not a single simple mechanism that can explain all of language. Instead we have to do concrete case studies to advance the state of the art step by step, both for the explanation of concrete language phenomena such as perspective reversal or case grammar, and for finding the general theory that underlies the emergence and evolution of language.

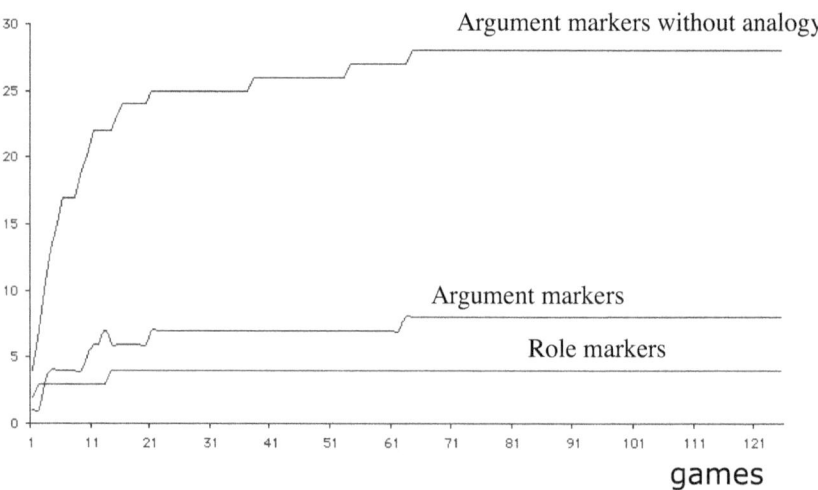

Figure 10.10: Comparison between two different strategies: The top-graph shows the growth in the average number of markers for the event-specific marker strategy. The bottom two graphs show the average size of the set of markers when analogy is used. As usual, the y-axis shows the number of games played. Overall, fewer markers are needed, making the case marking system more efficient and thus explaining why we get abstract semantic roles.

---

[13] Work on tense and aspect was first carried out by Joachim De Beule and reported in: De Beule (2004), De Beule, De Vylder & Belpaeme (2006). It was then continued in (Gerasymova, Spranger & Beuls 2012), although this domain still remains in an exploratory phase today.

11 Language strategies for humanoid robots

This chapter discusses additional language game experiments directly inspired by the Talking Heads experiment, set up after 2005. Major breakthroughs along several dimensions have been achieved. Robots became hugely more complex, with humanoid shapes, and going from a few degrees of sensing and actuation to close to a hundred. The grammar formalisms developed for language game experiments matured, specifically the Fluid Construction Grammar formalism, developed as a successor of the COGAR formalism reported in the previous chapter.[1] Semantics was scaled up from propositional and predicate logic to fully open-ended procedural semantics. And last but not least the theory of semiotic dynamics received a major impetus when statistical physicists became seriously involved, applying techniques and methods from complex systems science to study language game dynamics, Loreto & Steels (2007). A large number of contributions were made by Loreto's Statistical Physics group at the University of Rome (La Sapienza), see in particular: Dall'Asta et al. (2006) and Baronchelli, Loreto & Tria (2012). A full overview of all these developments is beyond the scope of this book. Instead we only look here at developments that directly pertain to language game experiments with robots.

While introducing these experiments I will highlight two conceptual breakthroughs: semiotic networks and language strategies.

- A SEMIOTIC NETWORK consists of a weighted network that links words to concepts, concepts to prototypes, and prototypes to sensory experiences. Each agent constructs his own semiotic network but through consecutive interactions these networks become progressively similar. From this perspective, setting up a language game requires a definition and operationalisation how new nodes are created in this network, how new links are made between the nodes, and how the weights between nodes are adjusted.

- A LANGUAGE STRATEGY is helpful to think about how we can go beyond individual words and towards more complex grammatical expressions. It was already introduced in the previous chapter. A language strategy is a particular way to deal syntactically and semantically with one domain of meaning. It includes ways for conceptualising, expressing, acquiring and expanding a specific domain. For example, the colour domain requires not only strategies for basic colour terms

---

[1] A full introduction into Fluid Construction Grammar is beyond the scope of this book. The interested reader is referred to the following two paper collections: Steels (2011) and Steels (2012).

(like 'blue'), but also for graded membership expressions ('very blue'), composite colours, ('greenish blue'), analogical colours ('sky blue'), a.o. The Talking Heads experiments used a single strategy that was entirely hard-coded: discrimination trees for categorisation and words without syntax to express distinctive categories. Research efforts moved towards the study of other strategies, and to the question how such strategies may arise (discussed in the next chapter).

The remainder of the present chapter illustrates these two notions through different language game experiments: The Proper Naming Game and the Action Naming Game illustrate the use of semiotic networks. The Colour Description Game and the Spatial Language Game illustrate the use of language strategies. These experiments also show how the focus of research progressively moved towards the emergence of grammar in co-evolution with more complex compositional, but still grounded, semantics.

11.1 The Proper Naming Game

Around 2005, the same team that had built the AIBO robot at the Sony Corporation central laboratories, managed to make another enormous leap forward by building the QRIO humanoid robot. This robot is about 60 cm tall and weighs 7.3 kg. Its sensors include two cameras in the head, a microphone, and sensors in each motor joint to monitor posture and movement. The robot has enough computing power and battery to autonomously walk around on its two legs and perform various actions in the world. The QRIO never made it to a commercial product for economical reasons. However, we were able to use QRIO robots to carry out a series of ground-breaking experiments that without doubt pushed the state of the art in language games forward considerably. The teleportation infrastructure developed for the original Talking Heads experiment was used again to allow experiments with populations of agents, despite having only a few robotic bodies available. For every game, two agents were downloaded into the on-board memory and processors of the QRIO robot and after a game, the state of the agent was uploaded back to a central server. Agents never interacted without being physically instantiated in the world.

Initially the experiments were very close to the Talking Heads experiments but progressively they tackled more and more challenging semantic domains including action description, spatial expressions, and quantifiers, and consequently the complexity of the grammar increased. This section discusses one of the first experiments, namely for the emergence of a vocabulary of proper names, i.e. names for individuals.

In January 2007, Luc Steels, Martin Loetzsch, and Michael Spranger travelled to the Sony Computer Science Laboratory in Tokyo to do the first experiments with the QRIO robots. We decided to redo the Talking Heads experiment, but focusing on proper names for individual objects, rather than the emergence of generic terms such as colours, shapes or positions.[2]

---

[2] The first paper on the Proper Naming Game is: Steels & Wellens (2007) It also discusses the concept of a semiotic network. A more recent paper is: Steels et al. (2012). A more in-depth discussion of the experiment is included in the Ph.D thesis of Martin Loetzsch, defended in 2014 at Humboldt University.

We also introduced games with multiple turns: While the agents were looking, we changed the environment for them, for example putting down a standing block so that agents could learn the appearance of object from different perspectives and in different positions. Not many changes were made to the Naming Strategy itself. The lateral inhibition strategy of the Talking Heads experiment was entirely adequate. The big issue was how to identify and consistently recognise objects as individuals and to figure out how language could help agents to do so.

The general set-up for the Proper Naming Game experiment is shown in Figure 11.1. We see two QRIO robots and an environment consisting of objects of various sizes and shapes. At any time a new object can be added or the position of an object can be changed. So the world is entirely open and robots do not know how many individuals there are. Importantly, the robots had to recognise an object as an individual, independently of its position. If a specific object disappeared from the world and was put back later, the same name would still have to be used.

Figure 11.1: Set-up for the Grounded Proper Naming Game. Two Qrio robots are playing a game of reference about individual objects in their environment. They are using proper names and hence have to recognise objects as individuals.

11.1.1 Challenges

It is useful to emphasise how extraordinary difficult this task is, even though the Talking Heads experiment and earlier experiments with the AIBO already provided a good foundation. These difficulties are encountered for communication within any group of autonomous physically embodied agents and hence also humans. First of all it is extremely challenging to set up joint-attention frames with free roaming robots, which may explain why no other animals except humans can self-organise shared symbolic systems. For the Proper Naming Game experiment, a robot moves around until another robot comes into view and remains sufficiently stationary. Both robots follow this strategy and so sooner or later a pair of robots find each other and a game becomes possible. Next the robots both scan their immediate environment and build up an initial world model. They keep tracking the environment because it may change as games are being played. Because the robots can detect each other, they can reconstruct what the scene looks like from the other's point of view, which is particularly relevant for experiments on spatial language discussed later. Moreover the speaker could provide a correction in case of communicative failure by physically pointing to the topic, although the resolution of the vision system of the QRIO was not fine-grained enough to actually detect pointing gestures, so the direction of pointing was transmitted directly, although this is still a noisy communication channel because the observer has to interpret this direction in terms of his own perception of what the other agent might be seeing.

Second, it is non-trivial to identify physical objects based on visual sensations, particularly if both the objects and the robot move around. The robot cameras yield images at a rate of 30 images/sec. Each image must be analysed in quasi-real time to detect regions that may correspond to objects and track them over time. Once object regions are found, feature detectors can compute values for colour, brightness, position, width, size, texture, speed of movement, direction of movement, etc., but these will always be very noisy (see Figure 11.2).

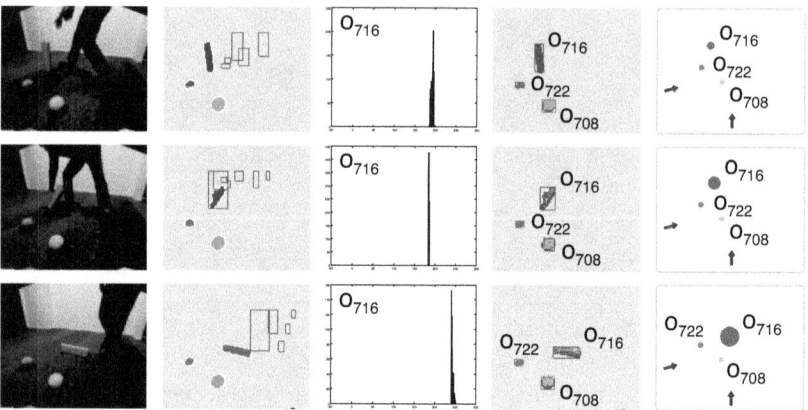

Figure 11.2: A robot is looking at consecutive scenes (from top to bottom) and tracking the objects in the scene. One object (labelled O_{716}) is moved by a human experimenter. We see from left to right: the original source image, results of region detection and colour segmentation, the (average) value for one dimension of one object (O_{716}), the segmented and labelled objects, and the world model, including the position of the other robot (indicated by a pointing arrow).

We call the feature vector for each object a SENSORY EXPERIENCE. It is represented using a spiking diagram, with a spike for each dimension and the value on that dimension marked (see Figure 11.3, left-most column). Real world vision is difficult enough, but because the robots look at the scene from different points of view, they often do not carve out the same regions and they will certainly see different views of the objects and locate them in different positions within their own egocentric reference frame. So sensory experiences of the same scene are always going to be different. This makes coordination and hence successful communication very challenging.

Third, it is very difficult to establish which individual is associated with a particular sensory experience because the appearance of an object changes, depending on its posture, its position with respect to the viewer, and the changing light conditions in the environment. A standard method in object recognition, for which there is also evidence in human subjects, is to capture the invariant properties of a particular view of an object in terms of prototypes. A prototype has for each sensory dimension a typical value and a tolerated variance within which the certainty of recognising the prototype decreases. Prototypes are also displayed using a spiking diagram, with a spike for each dimension and an indication of the best value as well as the minimum and maximum (see Figure 11.3). Internally, agents store a set of cases and compute the mean value for each dimension as the typical value and the variance as a way to determine minimum and maximum cut-off points. So the learning and adjustment of categories is statistical in nature.

The best matching prototype for a given sensory experience is found by a weighted sum of the match for each dimension. Many neural network models exist that perform this kind of computation, such as Radial Basis Function networks, and their behaviour is well understood. But the difficulty here is that robots do not have access to a clear data set of examples and counter examples from which they can learn how a prototype should be defined. Moreover clusters found through unsupervised learning (such as through Kohonen nets) may not necessarily correspond to the prototypical views of an object. In addition, each agent independently and autonomously develops his own repertoire of prototypes based on his history of interactions with the world and others. Hence it is totally unlikely that the agents have exactly the same set of prototypes, which further aggravates the coordination and communication problem.

Fourth, although an individual may have some notion of the invariant properties of an object, usually there are significant differences between different views of the same object. So reliable object recognition requires the acquisition of different (prototypical) views and this raises the question how the robots can know whether two quite different views (for example a front view of an object standing up and a back view of the same object laying down) belong to the same object.

Finally, the robots must build up a lexicon associating names with individuals. When no name exists yet, the robots can baptise the object with a newly invented name that will spread in the population through consecutive games because hearers can acquire the meaning of an unknown name based on feedback from the speaker after a game. But since a language game is always a local interaction between only two agents, it is

11 Language strategies for humanoid robots

possible that another agent has invented a different name for the same object which also has propagated to some extent, and so synonymy (different names for the same object) is unavoidable. Moreover because of the inherent noise and unreliability of visual perception and recognition of pointing gestures as well as different prototype boundaries for different agents, it is possible that one agent makes an incorrect guess about the meaning of an unknown name or misinterprets feedback and thus acquires a different meaning for a name. So homonymy (different objects for the same name) is unavoidable as well. This raises the critical question how a shared optimal vocabulary can be reached at the level of the population without central control or telepathy, which will require mechanisms for damping synonymy and homonymy at the individual and population level.

11.1.2 Semiotic networks

We have already seen from earlier experiments that the solution to these various issues lies in setting up the right kind of "semiotic dynamics". In the present case, this dynamics should gradually coordinate sensory experiences, prototypical views, individuals, and names, both within a single individual and across the population. This led to the notion of a SEMIOTIC NETWORK, which was a significant conceptual advance in the methodology of conceiving and carrying out language game experiments.

A semiotic network of an agent a is defined as $S_a = O_a \times V_a \times I_a \times N_a$ where O_a is the set of sensory experiences of the agent grouped per scene, V_a the set of prototypical

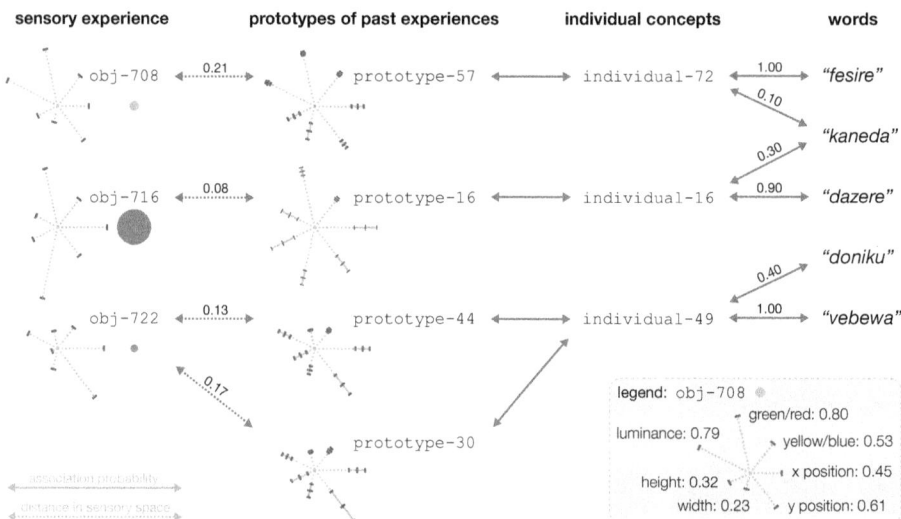

Figure 11.3: In the Proper Naming Game experiment the memory of the agents is conceived in terms of a semiotic network that spans the full semiotic cycle from sensory experience and conceptualisation to naming.

views maintained by a, I_a the set of individuals known to a, and N_a the set of names in a's vocabulary (see Figure 11.3). Each link in the network is weighted (with a real number between 0.0 and 1.0). The weight of the link between a sensory experience and a prototypical view is based on nearest neighbour computation. The other weights are stored in memory and reflect the confidence of the agent in the use of that link based on past experience.

A semiotic network is bidirectional and dynamic in the sense that new nodes can be added or removed as a side effect of a language game and the weights between nodes change based on the outcome of a game. In order to decide which name to use for a chosen topic, the speaker traces pathways in his private semiotic network. He starts from the set of sensory experiences perceived in the current scene, activates the best matching prototypical views, activates the individuals linked to these prototypical views, and then looks up the names for these objects. The pathway that has the highest cumulative score, which is the sum of all weights of the links involved, is considered to be the winner and the name occurring at the endpoint of this path is the name transmitted by the speaker to the hearer.

Conversely, in order to decide which physical object to point at given a name, the hearer traces pathways in his own semiotic network but in the other direction. He starts from the name, looks up the individuals associated with this name, then the possible prototypical views associated with this individual, and then the sensory experiences belonging to the object regions in the current scene which are the best matches with these prototypical views. The pathway with the highest cumulative score is the winner and the object occurring at the endpoint of that path is considered by the hearer to be the topic to which he should point. The speaker then interprets the pointing gesture and gives non-linguistic feedback about success or failure.

Given this notion of a network, the key question for designing an effective strategy for playing the language game becomes: What are the operators that are building and changing the semiotic networks in each agent? We focus first on the vocabulary, i.e. the links between nodes for individual objects m_i and their names f_i. We use a variant of the strategy used in the Talking Heads experiment. Only the hearer changes the score after a game. In the case of a successful game, the score σ_{f_i,m_i} of the used association is increased and its competitors are decreased according to the following equations with the alignment rate $\gamma = 0.2$:

$$\sigma_{m_i,f_i} \leftarrow \sigma_{m_i,f_i}(1-\gamma) + \gamma \tag{11.1}$$

$$\sigma_{m_j,f_i} \leftarrow \sigma_{m_j,f_i}(1-\gamma) j \neq i \tag{11.2}$$

$$\sigma_{m_i,f_k} \leftarrow \sigma_{m_i,f_k}(1-\gamma) k \neq i \tag{11.3}$$

A competitor is another individual m_j stored in the hearer's memory for the name f_i or another name f_k for the individual m_i. When the speaker is using a name which is not linked in the network of the hearer to any individual, then the hearer adds a new

11 Language strategies for humanoid robots

relation between the recognised individual (after pointing by the speaker) and this new name. This alternative then competes from now on with existing associations through the lateral inhibition dynamics. We already know from many other experiments that this strategy, when used collectively in consecutive games between randomly chosen members of the population, leads to the self-organisation of a shared lexicon due to positive feedback.[3]

When an agent sees a scene in which there are different segments, each yielding their own sensory experience, he can safely assume that these segments belong to different individuals and therefore must match best with different prototypes. If this condition is violated, the agent can use the sensory experiences without a unique match as seeds for new prototypical views and link them to newly introduced individuals. Prototypes are later adjusted to better reflect invariant properties by updating their mean value and variance.

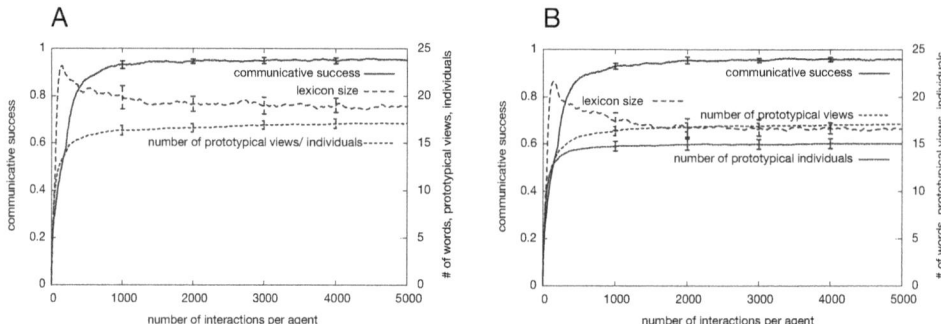

Figure 11.4: *Left:* Results for Proper Naming games in a population of 10 agents that have to name 15 individual objects. We see that a vocabulary establishes itself after agents have played a few hundred games. There is again the typical peak until alignment kicks in. The number of individuals is larger than 15, implying that agents name prototypical views rather than individuals. *Right:* Results after the addition of a heuristic based on tracking an object over time. We see that there are fewer individuals than stored prototypical views, which means that agents have improved their ability to recognise object identity.

With these mechanisms, the population reaches a high level of communicative success (above 90 %). However the average number of individuals in the agents' semiotic networks is much larger than the number of distinctive objects introduced in the experiment (see Figure 11.4, left). Apparently, agents are naming prototypical views of individual objects instead of the individuals themselves. So we did not adequately address how a robot learns to interrelate different views. To do this, various heuristics need to be added.

---

[3] The semiotic dynamics of lateral inhibition has been studied thoroughly by Bart de Vylder as reported in his Ph.D thesis (2007 at the VUB AI Lab) and summarised in this paper: De Vylder & Tuyls (2006).

11.1 The Proper Naming Game

We have operationalised just one example of such a heuristic. When an object is moving or being moved, its appearance may change but the observer tracking the object still knows that he is dealing with the same object and so he can exploit this information to fine-tune his semiotic networks. Because the vision system we used on the QRIO robots, developed by Michael Spranger,[4] is able to track an object, it can align object regions across different images, enriched with top-down predictions of how an object region will change over time based on Recursive Bayesian estimation using Kalman filters. The object being moved by the experimenter in Figure 11.2 yields two quite different sensory experiences when standing up or lying down which match with two different prototypes, but thanks to the tracking heuristic, the semiotic network can be rearranged to reflect that they are two views of the same object (see Figure 11.5).

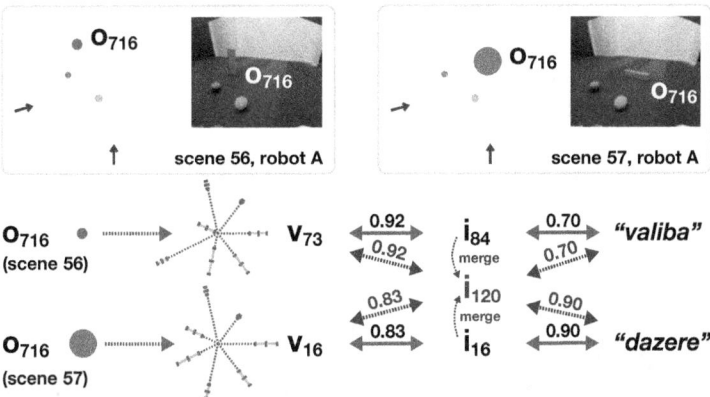

Figure 11.5: When the identity of two objects is discovered (because two prototypical views have been established as belonging to the same individual object), the former nodes for identities can be merged while keeping the links to their names intact.

Figure 11.4, right shows what happens when the robots use this heuristic. The population exhibits still the same capacity to achieve communicative success as in Figure 11.4, left, but now the number of individuals has significantly lowered, becoming equal to the number of distinct objects that were introduced (i.e. 15). So the heuristic has done its work.

Clearly humans use many additional heuristics. For example, if we see somebody walking into a building with a refrigerator and we later see the same person on the top floor handling a refrigerator we assume it is the same refrigerator, even if we could not track this object. Or if we know that a particular person is going to come and visit, and next we hear the bell and open the door, we expect and recognise this particular person even if clothes or hair have changed drastically. The point of the present experiment was not to operationalise all imaginable heuristics but to show that heuristics help to

---

[4] This system is described in-depth in: Spranger, Loetzsch & Steels (2012).

optimise and coordinate semiotic networks and thus further increase the ability of a population to develop internal shared representations anchored in the world.

11.2 Action Games

As a second example of how thinking in terms of semiotic networks is useful, we turn to an experiment building further on the work on action-word learning using the AIBO reported in the previous chapter. It was first designed and carried out with the QRIO robot in 2007/2008 by Luc Steels and Michael Spranger with considerable help from Martin Loetzsch[5] and then ported in 2010 to the MYON, a robot developed by Manfred Hild and his team at the Humboldt University in Berlin (see Figure 11.6) (Steels et al. (2012)). A BBC video clip of the experiment can be seen at: https://youtu.be/lmoXByLkK14. The porting exercise showed that once we discover how to do a certain type of language game on one robot we can relatively easily transfer it to another one, after adapting the lowest level sensing and actuation routines.

Figure 11.6: Two Myon robots playing an action game. One robot (the speaker) names an action and the other robot (the hearer) has to perform the action. When the hearer performs the right action the speaker signals success by nodding the head, otherwise he performs the action himself so that the hearer can adjust his semiotic network accordingly. *Left:* the speaker requests an action. *Middle:* the hearer interprets this as moving up both arms. *Right:* correction by the speaker.

The basic goal of the experiment is to simulate the emergence of a repertoire of actions and action terms, such as 'move up your left arm', or 'stretch out both arms'. As often, a seemingly straightforward semantic domain generates a set of fundamental subproblems that need to be solved and integrated so that the solutions work together:

1. The robots need a REPERTOIRE OF ACTIONS. So they need a sensori-motor system that allows them to carry out repeatedly and reliably an action. They can themselves observe the action both in the visual domain, looking at their own body or looking at their body in the mirror, or through proprioception, using sensors attached to the motors and joints on the body. There are many ways in which an action repertoire can be built up. One

---

[5] Papers describing this experiment more fully are: Steels & Loetzsch (2008) and Steels & Spranger (2008a).

way is through motor babbling: The robot makes random movements and thus explores the sensori-motor space in order to find possible coherent actions. In the experiments reported here, the motor actions are acquired by kinesthetic learning: The experimenter moves parts of the body of the robot. These movements are recorded by the robot and he can then play the movement back.

2. The robots need to be able to recognise actions carried out by others. This can be accomplished again with a prototype-based approach, as in the Proper Naming Game described in the previous subsection. Each individual action is always slightly different from another instance of the same action and so totally accurate matching would not work. For example, two instances of the same 'moving up both hands' gesture will always look slightly different because of the position of the hands and arms and the exact starting body posture of the robots or the perspective from which the gesture is perceived.

The features used in the experiment focus on the upper torso of the robot and are based on a binary version of the original image. They rely on a standard pattern recognition technique, known as Normalised Centralised Moments (Hu (1962)). Moments are a global description of shape, capturing the statistical regularities of its pixels for area, centre of mass, and orientation. Centralised moments are invariant to translation and normalised moments are invariant to translation and scale. Here we use seven moments, so that an image schema of the upper torso is captured in terms of a feature vector with seven data points, represented as a graph, although it could also be represented using the spike diagram used in the Proper Naming Game (Figure 11.7, right). These feature vectors are then classified using the same prototype-based approach as in the Proper Naming Game. A prototype of a posture consists of typical points for the seven moments, as well as a minimum and maximum deviation from each point. The best matching prototype is found by nearest neighbour computation. New prototypes are created when there is no prototype that matches distinctively with the sensory experience of a body posture and matching prototypes are slightly adjusted to integrate new instances, so that the prototype progressively and adaptively reflects the body postures observed in the world.

3. The robots need a *mirror system* that relates perceived actions carried out by others to their own actions. The topic of mirror systems has received a lot of attention the past decade because cells were discovered in the brain that serve this purpose.[6] However the fact that such cells are discovered in the brain does not yet tell us how mirror systems are being learned or how they operate. For the action language game, we tried several approaches.

In one of them, the robot stands before the mirror (Figure 11.8) and observes its own postures, which generates the data for learning the association between body postures and prototypes. The robot selects a posture, and activates the corresponding motor behaviour. This motor behaviour generates a sensory image and hence a sensory experience categorised with a particular prototype. Through standard Hebbian learning (which enforces the connection between nodes that are simultaneously active) the link between the posture prototype and the motor action gets established and progressively enforced.

---

[6] An overview of mirror system research and its relevance to the question of the origins of language is given here: Rizzolatti & Arbib (1998).

Because all robots have the same body shape, a robot can use visual posture prototypes of himself in order to categorise the body image of another robot, after perspective reversal. Perspective reversal means that the robot is able to detect the position of the other robot and is able to perform a geometric transformation to map the visual image of the other robot onto the canonical body position of itself.

4. Once the robots have a reliable mapping between image schemata of postures and body movements, the lateral inhibition dynamics used in the Proper Naming Game can easily solve the task of evolving a shared vocabulary. The score of the association between a word and a posture prototype is increased in a successful game and synonyms decreased. In an unsuccessful game, the score of the used association is decreased. Figure 11.9 shows the global behaviour of a population of 10 agents after each individual has coordinated motor behaviour and visual body-image through the mirror for 10 postures. 100 % success is reached easily after about 2000 games. After 1000 games, which means 200 games/agent, there is already more than 90 % success. The graph shows the typical overshoot of the lexicon in the early stage as new words are invented in a distributed fashion followed by a phase of alignment as the agents converge on an optimal lexicon.

This experiment shows that other language games, which do not rely on feedback through pointing, can be set up easily. Here the feedback happens through the actions of the hearer. The experiment also shows that the same technique of setting up a semiotic network can be applied to other domains. The network used here is shown in Figure 11.10. Compared to the Proper Naming Game, we see the same relation between sensory experiences, visual prototypes, postures (instead of nodes for individuals), and words. But now there is an extra dimension because motor behaviours achieving a posture are also linked with the posture nodes. This suggests also another approach besides the use of a mirror for coordinating the relationships between perception and motor action: When the hearer has learned to associate a word with a particular posture node through the visual prototype of this posture, he can later get feedback on which motor behaviour should be associated with the same posture node, or, vice-versa, he can first learn the association between a motor behaviour and a word (when the speaker asks to perform the posture) and then learn what visual prototype corresponds to that. Experiments show that this method indeed also works to achieve a coherent mirror system, Steels & Spranger (2008b).

11.3 The Colour Description Game

Already from 2001, as a direct follow up of the Talking Heads experiment, in-depth experiments were started on the emergence of colour vocabularies. This topic was chosen because there is a substantial body of research on colour in the cognitive sciences, with detailed analysis of its underlying biology, psychological experiments on colour perception and categorisation and extensive work, often building further on the studies of Berlin and Kay, on colour language. It is also relatively easy to carry out colour naming game experiments, because it does not require complex feature extraction and pattern recognition. Moreover the grammar for colour descriptions is highly restricted and so

11.3 The Colour Description Game

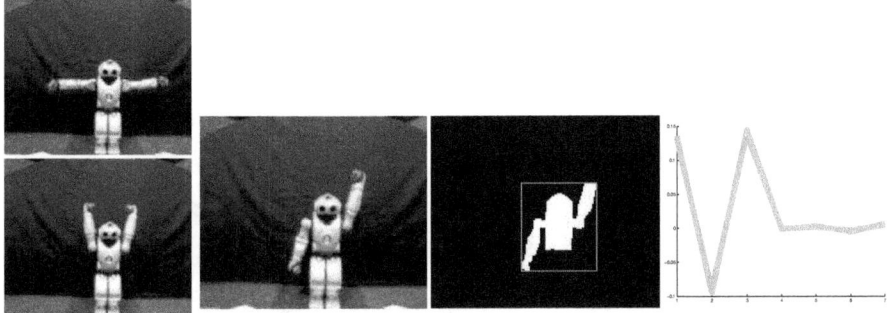

Figure 11.7: *Left:* Example postures of the robot (which is the QRIO in this case). *Right:* Visual analysis. From left to right we see the source image, the foreground/background distinction and object segmentation (focusing on the upper torso), and the feature signature of this posture represented as a graph connecting the values (on the y-axis) of the seven centralised normalised moments (on the x-axis).

Figure 11.8: The QRIO humanoid robot stands before a mirror and performs various motor behaviours thus observing what visual body-images these behaviours generate.

11 Language strategies for humanoid robots

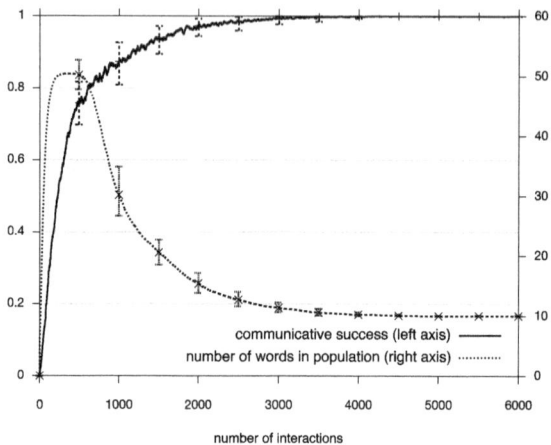

Figure 11.9: Results of the Action Game played by a population of 10 agents for 10 postures after coordinating image schemata and motor control through a mirror. The x-axis plots the number of language games. The y-axis shows the running average of communicative success and average lexicon size.

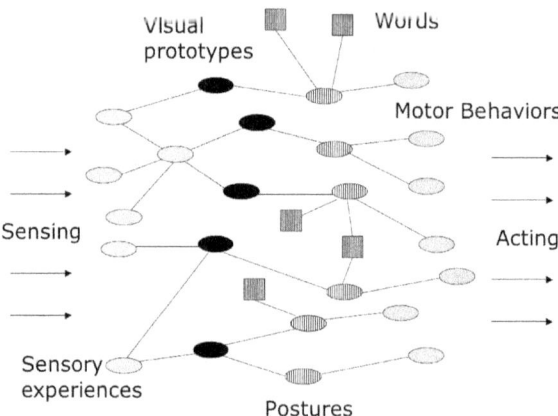

Figure 11.10: Semiotic network linking sensory experiences, visual prototypes of postures, nodes for postures acting as mirror neurons, and nodes triggering the motor behaviour that achieves the posture. Nodes for words (shown as squares) are associated with the posture nodes.

it is a good micro-domain for advancing not only research in the interaction between categorisation and naming but also in grammar.

In our group, Tony Belpaeme became the main Ph.D researcher for Colour Naming, finishing his thesis in 2005.[7] This work was then continued by Joris Bleys, who managed to scale up from colour naming to colour description with a thesis defended in 2010.[8] The colour domain has attracted several other language game researchers, attempting to explain universal trends in colour categorisation.[9]

Figure 11.11: Set-up with two QRIO humanoids, similar to Munsell chip tests used in psychology. The same game as the Talking Heads was used, but only colour chips were provided as input and the robots use pointing and head movements to provide feedback.

When the QRIO humanoid robots became available, we decided to use this existing work for pushing forward the state of the art in colour language research in two ways:

- To use more realistic circumstances of object perception. Because robots are moving around in three dimensions and see the situation from different points of view, the reflection of light changes and is different for speaker and hearer (see Table 11.1). This difference did not play a role in earlier experiments but it certainly plays an important role in the stabilisation and choice of colour prototypes.

- To focus on colour descriptions beyond basic colour terms, i.e. descriptions like *slightly blue, blue-green, bluish green, very bright, shiny yellow, dark red, sky blue, very dark bluish red*, etc. Indeed, it turns out that basic colour terms are used only in about 10 to 15 % of the occurrences of colour descriptions. The rest are

---

[7] The first extensive paper on this research appeared as: Steels & Belpaeme (2005).
[8] This thesis is published as another volume in the present series as: Bleys (2015).
[9] Most notably: Puglisi, Baronchelli & Loreto (2008), Baronchelli et al. (2010).

11 Language strategies for humanoid robots

more complex expressions. Complex colour descriptions require scaling up the semantics and introducing grammar, they also require the introduction of language strategies as a layer of abstraction above lexical and grammatical constructions.

Table 11.1: Colour perceptions of two robots for the same scene. The robots see the yellow duck (obj-17 for the left robot and obj-15 for the right robot) from different sides and distances and thus perceive very different colour values on the a^* and b^* colour dimensions for the same object.

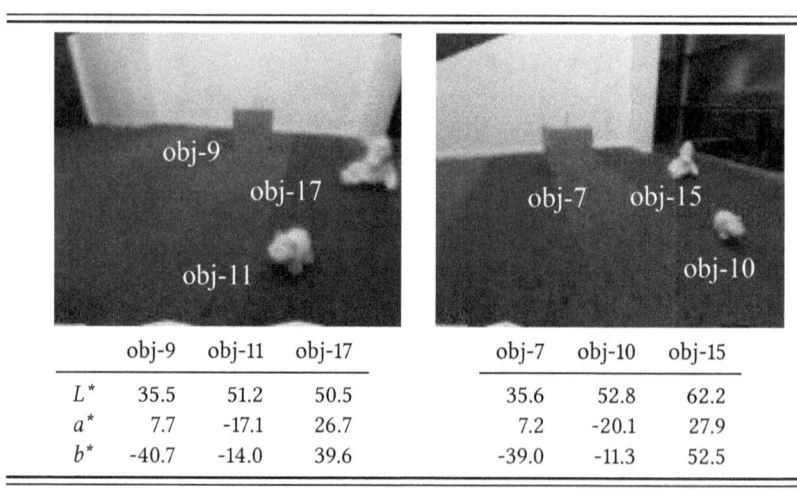

	obj-9	obj-11	obj-17	obj-7	obj-10	obj-15
L^*	35.5	51.2	50.5	35.6	52.8	62.2
a^*	7.7	-17.1	26.7	7.2	-20.1	27.9
b^*	-40.7	-14.0	39.6	-39.0	-11.3	52.5

Together with Joris Bleys and using the vision system developed by Michael Spranger, we performed language game experiments both for the same set-up as shown in Figure 11.1, i.e. geometric objects in an environment but now ignoring all dimensions except those related to colour, and from a set-up that was similar to the Munsell chips used in psychological experiments (see Figure 11.11). The colour space used by the agents was the CIE L*a*b* space, where L stands for lightness and a* and b* are the two opponent channel dimensions (yellow-blue and red-green).

A language strategy has two components: (i) a particular way of conceptualising reality (and learning the categories involved in this conceptualisation) and (ii) a particular grammatical pattern that suggests to the listener what strategy is intended and provides the contents to execute the strategy. For example, in the phrase *very green*, the combination of an adverb *very* and a basic colour adjective *green* suggests a "graded membership strategy" where not only a basic colour prototype (*green*) is introduced but also how close the sample is to this prototype (*very*). I will now introduce first how the conceptual aspect of a language strategy is defined using a procedural semantics system called IRL and then how the linguistic aspect is defined, using Fluid Construction Grammar.

11.3.1 Compositional procedural semantics with IRL

Procedural semantics, dating back to research on natural language understanding in the early seventies by Philip Johnson-Laird, Terry Winograd and Bill Woods, argues that the meaning of an utterance is equal to a program.[10] This approach is very amenable to grounded language understanding, because programs can be physical actions that the robot executes or operations over the internal states in memory, such as retrieving information from the visual data, performing perspective reversal, storing information, etc. Procedural semantics contrasts with a logic-based approach to semantics which assumes that facts are available in a fact base and semantics operates by matching queries against this database. The problem for a logic-based approach is that there is an infinite amount of information that can be computed about the world and so it is not possible to get a complete set of facts. Instead, language actively constrains what facts are collected about the world. For example, if we say "the red ball", the hearer knows that he has to focus on the shape and colour of the objects in front of him, and so attention and processing resources can be targeted to those feature dimensions.

To work out the procedural semantics hypothesis, we need to address the question what the primitives are of these semantic programs, and what computational formalism is most suited to combine them. Already in 2000, I reported a representation system for computational semantics, called IRL.[11] IRL stands for Incremental Recruitment Language, for reasons that will become clear soon. IRL uses a constraint language approach. Constraint programming languages were pioneered in the seventies by Borning, Steele, and others. It is a very active field with its own conferences, organisations and journals[12] with wide applications in user interfaces, scheduling problems, design, games, etc.

The basic idea of a constraint language is that only data flow is expressed explicitly, not control flow. There is a set of slots (variables) and a constraint attempts to reduce the set of possible fillers (bindings) for a slot. Constraints are combined in a constraint network, based on sharing slots. A solution is found when every slot in the network has unique bindings. Usually it requires looping several times through the constraints and often even a rewiring of the constraints to find a solution. A numerical example of a set of constraints on natural numbers could be:

```
x = y + z with 2<y<5 and 0<x<5
```

The constraints expressed here form a network because the same variables x and y (which are the slots of the network) appear in different constraints (the sum constraint and two instances of the <-constraint). Given this network, constraint propagation can compute easily that x = 4, y = 3, and z = 1.

IRL formalises constraints using prefix notation in the following way. Slots are symbols preceded by question marks. Constraints are defined with a list with the first argument the name of the constraint and the remaining arguments the slots:

```
(<constraint> <arg1> ... <arg-n>)
```

---

[10] See for the early research in particular: Winograd (1971), Woods (1981), Johnson-Laird (1977).
[11] The earliest paper introducing IRL is: Steels (2000). A more recent description of a new implementation is reported as: Spranger et al. (2012).
[12] see http://www.informatik.uni-trier.de/ley/db/journals/constraints/.

The first argument is called the target of the constraint because it is the most logical "outcome" of applying a constraint, but as shown in the example above, data may flow in all directions. The numerical example given earlier translates into the following IRL program.

```
(sum ?x ?y ?z)
(between ?y 2 5)
(between ?x 0 5)
```

How are constraints defined? We need to specify for every possible case how the constraint can help to constrain the possible values of its slots. Just focusing on the sum constraint, we have the following cases:

- If ?x and ?y are filled (i.e. bound) we can compute ?z by ?z = ?x - ?y.
- If ?y and ?z are filled we can compute ?x by ?x = ?y + ?z.
- If ?x and ?z are filled we can compute ?y by ?y = ?z - ?x.
- If all three are filled we can test whether the constraint relation holds.
- If only ?x or ?y or ?z is filled, then it is not really possible to compute any of the others directly, but we can start to enumerate all possibilities if this is a finite set.

The latter is not always possible because any number from the infinite set of numbers can be a filler and so it is better to wait until perhaps other constraints are able to limit the set of possibilities further. But for finite domains it might be conceivable to generate a set of possibilities. Concretely, for the above example the between-constraint could easily generate the list of possible numbers between the two given values.

IRL is a general language for defining constraints and constraint networks. The IRL system includes a constraint engine (which propagates constraints) as well as a constraint network planner, which finds a possible constraint network, given available information and a goal. Because a constraint network is a structure, it can also be matched against other constraint networks, for example, to complete a partial network or to find a network that is similar to another one.

Constraint networks are an obvious choice for grounded (natural) language processing. For example, to interpret the sentence *the ball behind the block*, it is possible that there are many blocks, many balls, but only one ball that is behind a block. So the unique referent of *the ball*, *the block* and of the total noun phrase only become clear when all constraints have been applied. Natural languages clearly do not supply control information but assume that the interpreter is smart enough to interpret constraints based on data flow. The other properties of constraint programming are also important. The constraint network planner can be used for conceptualising what to say and the constraint network matcher is highly useful in parsing an incomplete language fragment or in learning the meaning of a new grammatical construction.

11.3 The Colour Description Game

11.3.2 Building blocks for natural language semantics

What is the nature of the constraints that we will need for the semantics of natural language? Take a phrase like *the ball behind the block*. It invokes the following constraints, also called semantic operations:

- *the ball* evokes a constraint to use a prototype [BALL] to find a referent in the current scene.
- The same holds for *the block* which uses another prototype [BLOCK].
- The preposition *behind* implies another constraint, namely to use the spatial relation [BEHIND] to filter a set of objects (namely those found by using the [BALL] prototype) and retain only those that satisfy the behind-relation to an object in another set.

In IRL notation we get the following. There are first variables for the semantic entities (prototypes and relations) involved:

```
(bind prototype ?prototype-1 [BALL])
(bind prototype ?prototype-2 [BLOCK])
(bind relation ?relation-1 [BEHIND])
```

Next there are four constraints: to get the context, come up with the set of blocks (bound to ?object-set-1), the set of balls (bound to ?object-set-2), and then pick out the object that is a member of both sets and satisfies the behind-relation (bound to ?referent):

```
(get-context ?context)
(filter-using-prototype
   ?object-set-1 ?prototype-1 ?context)
(filter-using-prototype
   ?object-set-2 ?prototype-2 ?context)
(select-object-using-relation ?referent ?object-set-1
   ?object-set-2 ?relation-1)
```

Note how the different semantic operations are linked together because they share slots. ?referent is the final result of the network, which would be the topic of the language game.

It should be possible for the filter-using-prototype operation to either apply a filler for ?prototype-1 and ?context and then compute ?object-set-1, or provide ?object-set-1 and ?context and obtain a filler for ?prototype-1. The 'normal' use is the first one, but the second use is just as important in planning what to say (as speaker) or in guessing a possible prototype while learning the meaning of some unknown word. Moreover the "identify-set-using-prototype" operation can be made smart enough that it can actually come up with a new prototype, when there isn't one yet that does the job. Hence learning can be integrated directly into the constraint network itself.

So IRL is in fact a way to integrate the broad set of mechanisms used in pattern recognition (including neural networks) and AI (including machine learning). For example, an operation could implement a radial-basis-function network for doing categorisation and use the network to identify an object in a set. It could not only use the network but also adapt the weights in the network. Another operation could implement categorisation based on discrimination trees (as discussed in Chapter 4) and would not only do it, but also expand the discrimination trees when necessary. Other operations could implement set-theoretic operations, for the semantics of connectives like *and, or,* and *not,* by carrying out UNION, INTERSECTION and COMPLEMENT operations over sets. There is no limit to the possible semantic operations, except that they have to terminate in finite time, possibly giving up when they cannot reach a valid result. IRL just provides a framework to define these operations and make them available to be recruited by the constraint network planner. IRL uses LISP as the host language, which means that all the computational machinery of LISP is available to implement semantic operations and associated learning algorithms.

The constraint network planner works on an evolutionary basis, similar to genetic algorithms. Starting from the goal (for example identifying a particular object in the environment), it will generate possible networks by recruiting existing primitive operations, linking them in, and checking whether the computation makes progress towards reaching the goal. The slots of a constraint are typed to limit what semantic operations will be tried next. Networks that perform useful functions are "chunked" into higher order units that then can be used as units in their own right, thus scaling up complexity. These chunked networks become associated with stereotyped grammatical expression, so that there is a very fast retrieval and semantic execution.

11.3.3 Strategies for colour

Let us now look at concrete examples from the colour domain as worked out by Joris Bleys, studying the following strategies:

1. The first strategy is the BASIC COLOUR STRATEGY which implements a prototype-based approach to the basic colour categories. This approach is similar to the one used in the Proper Naming Game, except that only the three colour-dimensions are profiled (the opponent channels red-green, yellow-blue and the brightness channel). The strategy is similar to the one shown earlier.

```
(equal-to-context ?s1)
(profile-colour-dimensions ?s2 ?s1)
(filter-by-colour-lenient ?s3 ?s2 ?cc)
(select-most-activated ?t ?s3)
```

When the speaker says *green*, this network is used together with a specific binding of ?cc to the prototype for green (denoted as [green]).

```
(bind colour-category ?cc [green])
```

11.3 The Colour Description Game

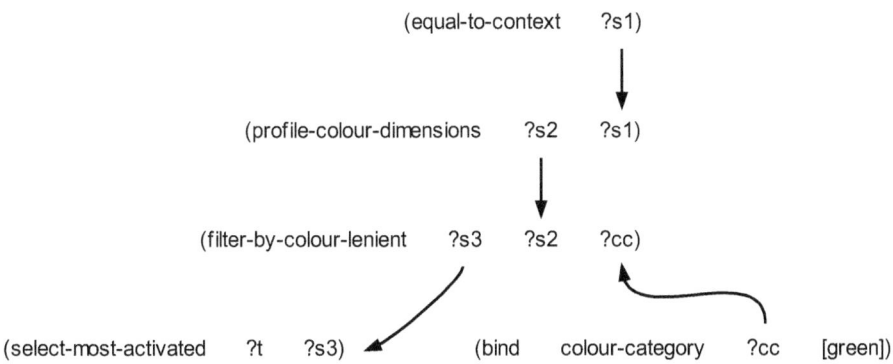

Figure 11.12: Constraint network for the Basic Colour strategy. The colours of each object in the context are retrieved, their similarity to the prototype computed, and the one with the highest similarity is chosen.

A graphical representation of this network is shown in Figure 11.12.

2. The second strategy is the GRADED MEMBERSHIP STRATEGY which categorises the topic first using a basic colour but then qualifies how well its colour fits with the prototype. For example, we can say *greenish* or *very green*. Some languages (such as Tarahumara spoken in Northern Mexico) obligatory mark graded membership using suffixes. The core of the constraint network is defined as follows. A graphical representation of the network is shown in Figure 11.13.

```
(equal-to-context ?s1)
(profile-colour-dimensions ?s2 ?s1)
(filter-by-colour ?s3 ?s2 ?cc)
(filter-by-membership ?s4 ?s3 ?mc)
(select-most-activated ?t ?s4)
```

This network grabs the objects in the context and binds them to ?s1 using the equal-to-context operation. The profile-colour-dimensions operation picks out the colour properties of the various objects in ?s1 resulting in a new set ?s2. The filter-by-colour operation computes for each object in the set ?s2 how well they match with the prototype bound to ?cc, constructing a new set ?s3. The filter-by-membership operation then computes how well each object in ?s3 satisfies the graded membership qualification bound to ?mc, constructing ?s4. And then the select-most-activated operation picks out the best candidate and binds it to ?t. Other data flows within the same network are possible, for example to find the bindings of ?mc and ?cc given a context and a referent ?t that needs to be identified.

The network is entirely general for all expressions that use graded membership and gets instantiated for a particular case by specifying the semantic entities involved using the bind operation. For example, Tarahumara has the word *sita* for a particular colour prototype and *kame* for one type of graded membership:

11 Language strategies for humanoid robots

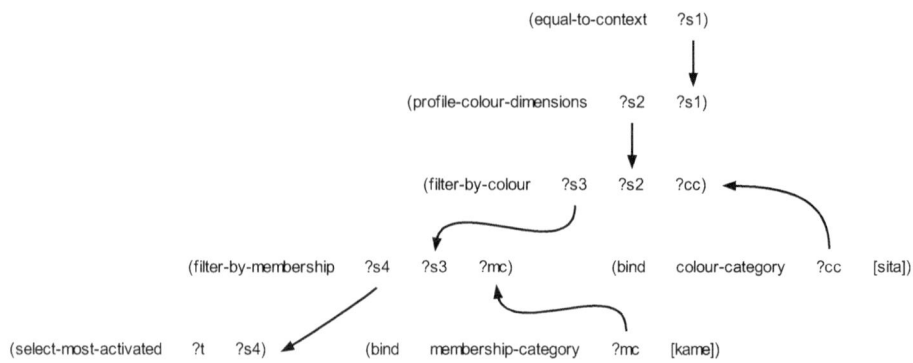

Figure 11.13: Constraint network implementing the Graded Membership Strategy. It builds further on the network for Basic Colour Categorisation but adds a constraint to handle graded membership.

```
(bind colour-category ?cc [sita])
(bind membership-category ?mc [kame])
```

3. The third strategy is the CATEGORY COMBINATION STRATEGY which compounds a category into two new ones, in expressions like *greenish blue* or *red orange*. This compounding is not a simple intersection. The set of objects that are *greenish blue* is not found by taking all the ones that are green and all the ones that are blue and then the intersection of the two. Rather, it appears that the discretisation of the colour landscape is scaled with respect to the colour which appears as head of the phrase and then categorisation is done. This is achieved with the IRL network shown in Figure 11.14.

4. The next strategy is the BASIC MODIFICATION STRATEGY which modifies a colour along the brightness dimension, as in *light green, dull yellow*, etc. It is implemented by projecting the modifying dimension onto the basic colour space whereby the colour being modified lies on the projecting vector and a new discretisation of the colour space can be performed. The network for this strategy is shown in Figure 11.15.

Many other strategies for colour can be imagined and some of them are found in human languages (although not necessarily in English). These strategies always involve operations over the colour space (such as rescaling, dimensionality reduction, etc.) alongside additional operations (such as getting the context, picking out a referent, computing the intersection of two sets, etc.).

11.3.4 Translation to grammar

The Colour Description Game used the Fluid Construction Grammar (FCG) formalism which was meanwhile being developed by our group with the explicit aim of supporting experiments in language emergence and evolution. A full exposition of this formalism

11.3 The Colour Description Game

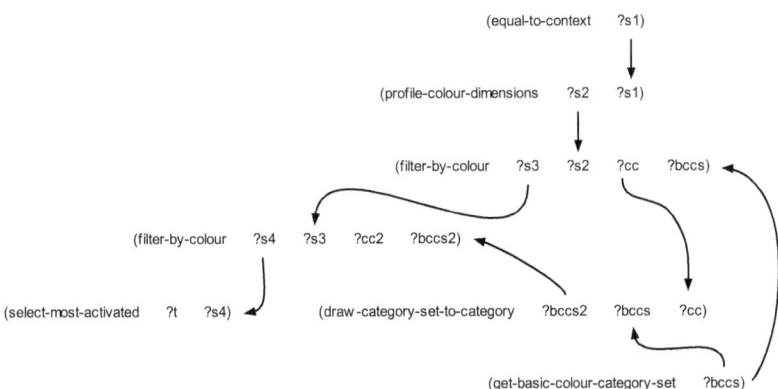

Figure 11.14: Constraint network implementing the Colour Combination strategy leading to expressions like *greenish blue*. The filter-by-colour operation now has an extra argument, namely category-sets, and there is a draw-category-set-to-category operation that rescales the basic colour category set.

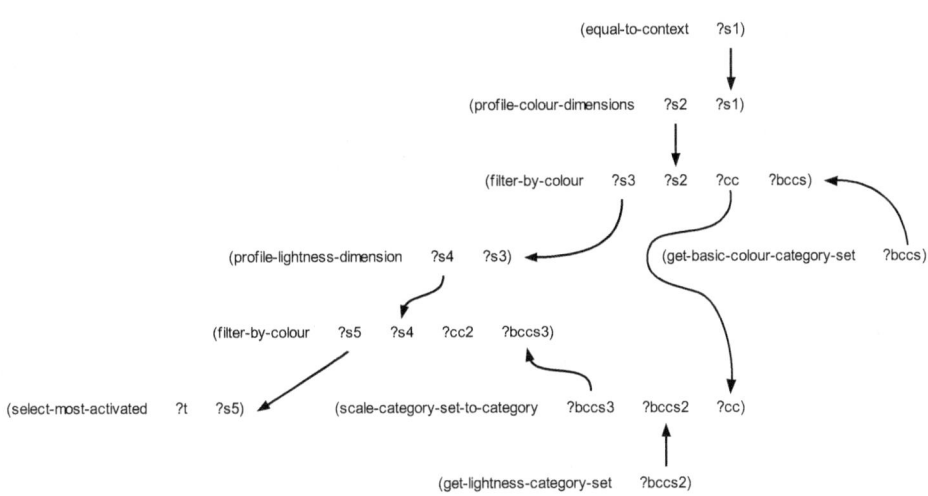

Figure 11.15: Constraint network for the basic modification strategy, for expressions like *light green*.

falls outside the scope of the present book, but there is now a considerable literature for the interested reader (Steels (2011)). Here we just look briefly at the basic principles by which IRL expressions are translated into utterances.

FCG represents syntactic and semantic structure in terms of units which have a set of features and values for these features. The features can be about any layer of linguistic analysis, from phonetics and morphology to various forms of syntactic description (constituent structure, functional structure, argument structure, information structure), semantic categorisations or meaning. The syntactic structure to express the basic colour strategy involves three levels of hierarchy. Units are built and expanded by three types of constructions (see for example Figure 11.16, left, which is an instantiation of the Basic Colour strategy in Figure 11.12).

1. There are first LEXICAL CONSTRUCTIONS that associate a word with the introduction of a semantic entity such as a colour category or a qualifier for indicating graded membership. So the meaning for the word *yellow* introduces a BIND-operation, as in:

```
((bind colour-category ?c [yellow]))
```

When the word *yellow* is encountered, a unit for this word is created with this BIND-operation as meaning and the word-string itself as the form. It is the unit called Yellow-unit in Figure 11.16. The construction also introduces a lexical category (part of speech) for the word (in this case the lexical category is colour-category) and specifies which variables in the meaning can be linked with other variables in other units. The variables are typed. In this case there is one variable ?c which is of type colour-category.

2. Next there are FUNCTIONAL CONSTRUCTIONS that determine in which semantic operation the meaning of a word will play a role. It is necessary to have this layer above lexical categories because the same word/category can have many different functions. The choice is determined by the lexical category, and the syntactic and semantic context as defined in functional and phrasal constructions. For example, an adjective can appear both in an adjectival function (as in *the red block*) and as a predicate (as in *the block is red*) but it can also be coerced into a nominal function (as in *red is a beautiful colour*). The same word can also belong to more than one lexical category, for example, *walk* can be a verb (*He walks home*) as well as a noun (*I take a walk*).

Functional constructions create a unit on top of the word. For example, in the Basic Colour Strategy, the colour-category is used in the filter-by-colour-lenient operation (see Figure 11.12). The new unit is called colour-unit in Figure 11.16, left. The meaning specifies the operations to be added to the network, which is in this case:

```
((filter-by-colour-lenient ?s3 ?s2 ?c))
```

There are two variables that can be linked to other operations with this meaning: ?s3 and ?s2 both of type object-set. On the syntactic side, the unit is categorised as a constituent named colour-category.

3. Finally there are PHRASAL CONSTRUCTIONS that pull together the functional units in order to create a phrase. The phrase usually has additional semantic operations as well. Figure 11.16,left shows an example. The ColourPhrase-Unit is constructed on-top of the Colour-Unit. It adds three additional operations to the meaning:

11.3 The Colour Description Game

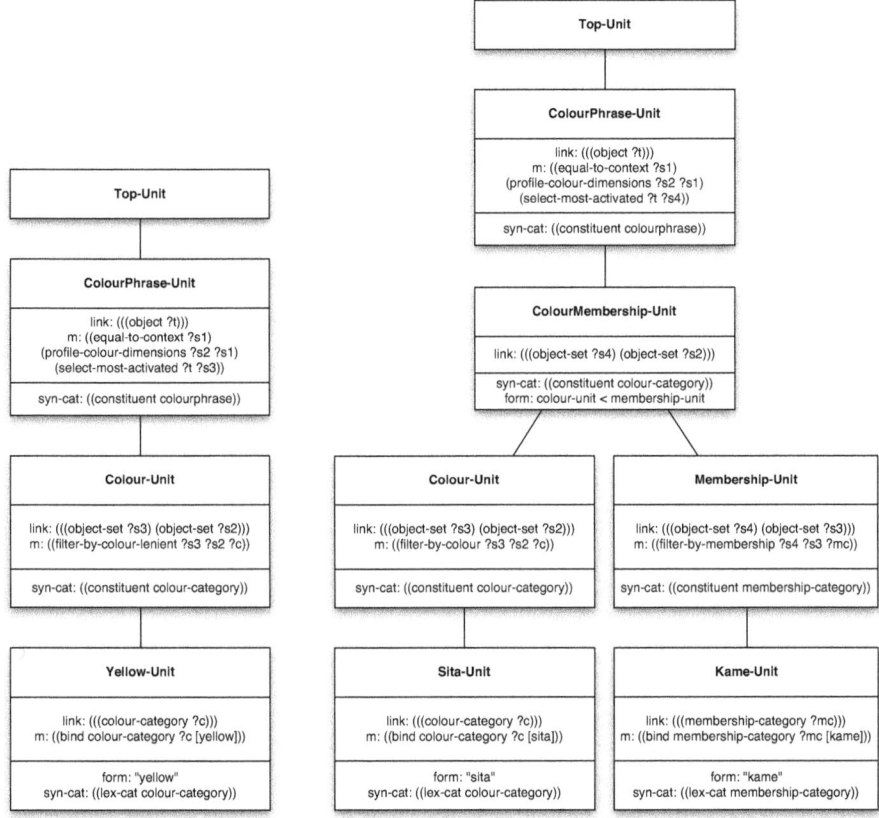

Figure 11.16: *Left:* Example of structure for the Basic Colour strategy. It involves three levels of hierarchy: for the word itself, the function of the word, and the combination of the different functions into a Colour-Phrase. Each box shows the name of the unit, and some of the key features of the syntactic and semantic pole. *Right:* Example of structure for the graded colour strategy.

```
((equal-to-context ?s1)
 (profile-colour-dimensions ?s2 ?s1)
 (select-most-activated ?t ?s3))
```

It links to the variables supplied by Colour-unit (namely ?s3 and ?s2) and the unit itself has a variable that can be linked further, namely ?t, which is the topic of the whole utterance. The constituent is called Colour-Phrase.

Figure 11.16, right shows another example, namely the structure for an instantiation of the graded-membership strategy for the Tarahumara utterance *sita kame*. It is again a Colour-Phrase. We see that there are now 4 levels of hierarchy. The ColourMembership-Unit pulls together a colour-category and a membership-category to form a new colour-category which then becomes a ColourPhrase-Unit again.

11.3.5 Influence of embodiment

Bleys conducted two types of experiments for each of these strategies, both in computer simulations and on real robots. The first type of experiment demonstrated that an agent could learn the colour vocabulary of another agent, given a language strategy. One agent was provided with an existing human colour system (for example the basic colours of English, the graded-membership terms of Tarahumara, etc.) and the other agent had to learn this colour system through situated interactions. The second type of experiment demonstrated that a population of agents could form a new vocabulary from scratch, according to the templates provided by a language strategy which was given to all agents. The details of these experiments are published in the Ph.D dissertation of Joris Bleys (Bleys (2015)).

I report here just briefly one additional experiment, relevant for understanding the impact of embodiment on language. The experiment compares three conditions (see Figure 11.17): (i) simulated perception (left column), (ii) shared grounded perception (middle column), meaning that both robots are given the same perception, and (iii) individual grounded perception (right column). The latter is the normal case when two robots are looking at the scene. It furthermore compares results for the Basic Naming Strategy (implemented with the IRL constraint network in Figure 11.15) for four experimental conditions:

1. There is a BASELINE experiment which starts out with the basic English colour categories provided by design to the agents.

2. An ACQUISITION experiment, where one agent (the tutor) is initialised with a set of basic colour categories and the other agent (the learning) has to acquire them.

3. A FORMATION experiment which involves a population of ten agents which develop a colour ontology and lexicon from scratch.

4. And an ADAPTATION experiment that starts with agents that are initialised with the English categories but then are allowed to further adapt their lexicons depending on the challenges of the situations they encounter.

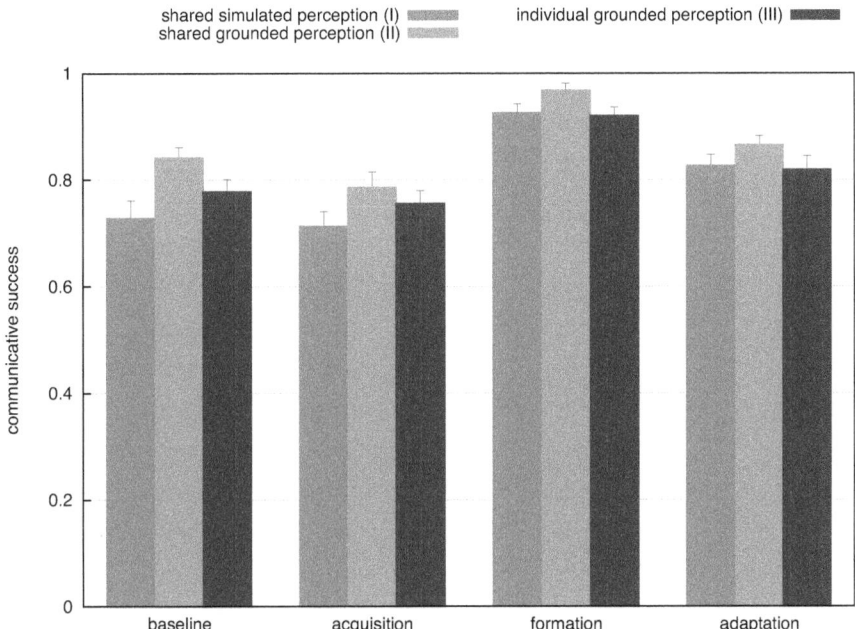

Figure 11.17: Comparison of three different environmental set-ups (left, right, and middle columns) and four different learning conditions. Communicative success is shown on the y-axis.

Interestingly, the best results in terms of communicative success are obtained when the agents are allowed to evolve their own colour language, partly because there was no limit on the number of prototypes they could introduce. This was better than using the set of basic colour prototypes for English, simply because English would turn to more complex expressions (such as *bluish green*) when the basic colour categories are not effective. Moreover, agents still achieve better results compared to the English colour system when they do not need to stick dogmatically to it. Indeed this shows why alignment, which is widely observed in human dialogues,[13] is a good strategy for achieving more successful communication.

11.4 Conclusion

This chapter has introduced two major advances with respect to the original Talking Heads experiment: the use of semiotic networks to build a more sophisticated mapping between sensory experiences and words, and the introduction of language strategies. Each language strategy pairs a particular way of conceptualising reality with a particular method to express it using lexicon or grammar. These developments were illustrated

---

[13] See: Garrod & Anderson (1987) and Galantucci (2005).

through several experiments with humanoid robots. Each of these experiments was a major step forward in terms of the use of highly sophisticated humanoid robots with many degrees of freedom and sophisticated visual processing, grounded compositional semantics for the meaning of utterances, and a full-fledged formalism for grammar.

12 Language evolution

The previous chapters have shown that huge advances have been made in the decade after the original Talking Heads experiment. It is now realistic to do experiments with physical humanoid robots, which was unthinkable in the late nineties. Whereas categorisation using basic perceptually grounded categories was a big achievement at the end of the nineties, experiments now routinely use complex compositional semantics. Another big boost has come from the development of a grammar formalism (Fluid Construction Grammar) that is adequate from the viewpoint of linguistic complexity and allows at the same time sophisticated experiments in grammar emergence. We now have several in-depth studies of language strategies for several domains although much more work obviously needs to be done to map out the vast landscape of language strategies found in human languages. This work is difficult and time consuming because each semantic domain generates its own set of fundamental problems in perception and action, conceptual representation, grammar, and language game interaction.

But the sceptical observer will argue that most of these experiments are about language emergence rather than language evolution per se. Agents are given a certain set of strategies, which thus constitutes their innate Language Acquisition Device, and it is then demonstrated by computer simulations or robotic experiments (i) how these strategies are effective to ACQUIRE an existing language system in a population, (ii) how they are effective to EXTEND a language system so that it remains adaptive to the needs and environments of its user, and (iii) how a population can INVENT AND COORDINATE a new language system from scratch by using the strategy.

Although long-term change is possible given a particular language strategy (for example, new colour categories and colour terms might emerge when needed to cope with new situations in the environment), this change does not alter the set of language strategies available to the agent. Therefore - the critical observer would say - all this does still not address the question yet where the strategies come from.

12.1 Culture-driven language evolution

To clarify these issues, let us first define a distinction between emergence, language change, and evolution:

- LANGUAGE EMERGENCE is the phenomenon whereby a language system, i.e. a set of conventions and conceptualisations for a particular semantic domain, for example tense-aspect, colour, space or determination, arises in a population and becomes shared, based on a particular strategy (or a set of strategies) that is shared by all agents.

- LANGUAGE CHANGE happens when the components of a language system and its conceptualisations shift, but the change remains within the bounds of a particular strategy. For example, the boundaries how different cases are used may shift (as is happening with the dative and genitive at the moment in German) or a new basic colour category and colour word may arise and claim a region within the colour space (as happened with the word 'orange' which started to be used as a basic colour word in 16th century Middle English to occupy a distinctive region between yellow and red).

- LANGUAGE EVOLUTION occurs when new strategies arise. There is plenty of evidence from creole languages and from historical linguistics that this happens at a cultural time scale. Here are three examples:

    1. Phrase structure (in the sense of strict word order based on abstract hierarchical patterns) emerged gradually in proto-Indo European, from a stage with largely free word order but a strong inflectional system (Van de Velde 2011).
    2. Word order and prepositions became the dominant strategy instead of morphological cases for expressing argument structure in the late Old English period (Van Kemenade 1987).
    3. There is currently an evolution going on in Spanish clitics ('le', 'la', 'lo') whereby the etymological system of Standard Spanish, which uses clitics to express different cases (nominative, dative, accusative), is shifting to a referential system (expressing gender and number). Case differentiation is lost, but existing forms are recruited for the new functions implied by a referential strategy (Fernandez-Ordonez 1999).

It is not always obvious from the observation of language facts whether we are dealing with change (within the boundaries of a strategy) or with a new strategy. However, this becomes entirely clear when we try to computationally model the processes of acquisition, expansion or invention of the language strategy involved. We always try to understand change first using existing strategies until we are forced to introduce a new strategy because the differences at the conceptual or linguistic level are too profound to computationally handle them.

The distinctions made here map to similar ones in biology. Biological strategies encoded in the genome govern the construction of phenotypes which include the form of organisms and their behaviours ensuring survival issues such as predator avoidance, food gathering, navigation, mate finding, nest building, etc. When we see a swarm of birds in the sky, or a path formed by ants, or a beaver dam, we see an example of *emergence*: A large-scale macroscopic structure emerges from the individual activities of the agents (i.e. animals) without central control, similar to the way a language system emerges as a macroscopic shared structure through the individual activities of the linguistic agents.

12.1 Culture-driven language evolution

The activities of the ants or the beavers are all governed by the same innate strategy. For example, to achieve path formation, ants put down pheromone when returning from the nest and they follow pheromone gradients to find a path.

Living organisms are ADAPTIVE to their environment and so even within the bounds of a given set of innate strategies there may still be significant changes observed in appearance, behaviour or internal functioning. For example, beavers may start using rocks for dams when mud and branches are not available, birds use plastics or other waste products, a goat may start to walk on two hind legs when it did not grow the forelegs (Jablonka & Lamb 2013). Nevertheless true EVOLUTION is only said to happen if there are new innate strategies, i.e. genetically coded strategies, that arise, for example if a fish species genetically speciates into subspecies where one continues to bread eggs deposited on the bottom of the sea whereas the new variant does mouthbrooding, meaning that eggs are bred within the mouth of a parent. Also in biology it is not always clear whether we are dealing with adaptive change (without genomic change) or evolution (with genomic change). Some variants that were thought to be a different species at one point of time turned out to be ecotypes of the same species, i.e. variants that have the same genetics but a different appearance or behaviour due to adaptation to the environment. However today these debates can be entirely settled when a genetic analysis is performed.

For biological organisms, the standard approach to find out how (innate) strategies evolved is through the framework of genetic evolution by natural selection and it is logically possible that language strategies are also innate, in which case we should be able to figure out how they are genetically coded and evolved. There are indeed several researchers who strongly favour this hypothesis and they group their work under the banner of biolinguistics (Boeckx & Grohmann 2013).

But it is also possible that language strategies are the outcome of cognitive development and cultural evolution, just like humans have developed a multitude of non-innate strategies in a wide range of domains: strategies for finding your way in cities, for building shelters, for preparing food, for playing Jazz piano, for fixing technical equipment, for organising trade, composing music, negotiating a contract, finding a partner, etc. This is the idea behind the RECRUITMENT THEORY of language evolution, which postulates that cognition and cultural evolution are the primary motors for the origins and propagation of new language strategies, even though of course they require the necessary neurobiological capacities that make each strategy possible. Once a strategy culturally evolved, it exerts a pull effect on genetic evolution, because genetic variants are favoured that can carry out a strategy more easily. So this hypothesis implies CULTURE-DRIVEN GENE EVOLUTION rather than gene-driven cultural evolution (Fisher & Ridley 2013).

It is this recruitment hypothesis that has been driving our experiments in language evolution and this chapter discusses very briefly some of the experiments that explore this hypothesis with the same rigor and computational backing as the experiments in language emergence and change discussed in the previous chapters. Much remains to be done before an experiment can be set up for evolving new strategies in some domain. We need to understand fully all the cognitive mechanisms required (both the semantic and the syntactic aspects). But since we now have at least a good technical basis and several concrete case studies, as shown in the previous chapters, the study of language evolution, in the sense of the emergence and propagation of novel language strategies and their selectionist competition is within reach.

What could a theory of cultural evolution look like? There is certainly no consensus on this.[1] But the most obvious choice is to view cultural evolution as another instance of a Darwinian evolutionary dynamics, happening at the cultural and cognitive level rather than at the genetic level. This idea has been suggested by many researchers, including Richard Dawkins in his theory of memes (Dawkins 1976). The basic principle underlying Darwinian dynamics is to split the process of coming up with a design in three subprocesses:

1. There is a process of GENERATING possible variants, often by making changes to existing variants or by information transfer between variants, for example through cross-over.

2. There is a separate process of TESTING whether these variants satisfy desired selection criteria. This happens usually in a kind of competition where different variants compete for available resources.

3. There is a SELF-ENFORCING CAUSAL LOOP between the outcome of selection and the frequency with which a variant is maintained and hence used to generate new variants.

The last step makes Darwinian dynamics cumulative: Partly working solutions can be built upon further and lead the way to even better ones.

Today, Darwinian evolutionary dynamics is recognised as a general principle that can and has been applied to many different types of systems, in chemistry, neurobiology or economics.[2] It has also been used successfully to come up with new artificial systems, for example to evolve controllers for robots using genetic algorithms (Nolfi & Floreano 2001). It is therefore not so surprising that selectionism can also be mapped to the cultural and more specifically to the linguistic domain in the following way:

1. Speakers generate variants, either accidentally through errors in their speech production, or deliberately, for example, when they try to express a novel idea by inventing new forms or appropriating existing forms for new purposes, for example, by coercing a word or grammatical construction into a new usage.

2. Which variants will survive in the communal language depends on selectionist criteria. I will discuss them shortly in more detail. They include for example whether the speaker is understood by the hearer, or whether it reduces the cognitive complexity of parsing and producing and hence allows larger sentences to be understood.

---

[1] See the debate in: Richerson & Boyd (2005).
[2] See Arthur (1996), Edelman (1987) and Luisi & Oberholzer (2001).

12.1 Culture-driven language evolution

3. The self-enforcing causal loop happens when variants created by one speaker start to propagate in the population and begin to replace their competitors. For example, a particular word to express a given meaning gets out of fashion and is taken over by another one. Some of these developments are simply fashion trends, but the more profound ones, in particular the ones that involve grammar, are related to critical selectionist criteria.

This Darwinian dynamic is already active in the operation of language strategies, since a strategy regulates the creation and selection of variants, determines how feedback has to be handled, and implies a self-enforcing causal loop through lateral inhibition so that variants satisfying the selection criteria become dominant in the population.

The key argument of this chapter is that the Darwinian evolutionary dynamics also applies to the evolution of new strategies, which implies that (i) speakers and hearers have to be able to come up with new language strategies, (ii) selection operates not only on the level of choices given a strategy, but also at the level of the strategies themselves, and (iii) there is competition between strategies and a self-enforcing causal loop based on the success that language users have with the language system they created with a particular strategy, so that some strategies survive and become dominant and others fade away.

Linguists are often reticent to use a selectionist approach because they believe that language is maladapted (Boeckx & Piattelli-Palmarini 2005). However we have to keep in mind that: (i) An evolutionary process seldom comes up with the perfect solution, even though it is remarkable effective given that there is no enlightened intelligent designer. (ii) There are conflicting criteria so that there is no optimal solution. For example, the speaker may want to minimise the effort needed for producing and pronouncing a sentence but this may make it harder for the hearer to reconstruct an interpretation of the meaning. (iii) Some of the selectionist criteria have to do with processing. A linguistic theory that only focuses on competence has nothing to say about processing and therefore cannot lay bare how processing issues play a role in language evolution. (iv) It is often possible to maintain communicative success with a simpler system (even a purely lexical language without any grammar at all) and then gradually optimise semantic interpretation by the progressive introduction of more grammar - as we see indeed in the emergence of creole languages which regenerate syntactic complexity from a lexical language (Mufwene 2008).

What kind of selectionist forces are relevant in the case of language? Clearly, the bottom line is that language users want to achieve COMMUNICATIVE SUCCESS. Communicative success means that the speaker achieves his or her non-linguistic goal. For example, if a speaker wants a hearer to perform some action (such as 'Can you get me the car keys?'), there is communicative success if the hearer indeed performs the requested action. Speakers and hearers generally do not care whether their sentences are perfectly grammatical or complete or semantically accurate. Speakers assume that hearers are intelligent enough to infer the missing information and that they can fill in the required details from the context. In normal spoken dialogue, communicative success is immediately obvious, either from the actions that the hearer performs as a consequence of an utterance or by gestural cues whereby the hearer informs the speaker that he or she is being understood.

Communicative success rests on a number of features of a language which thus act as key selection criteria:

- EXPRESSIVE ADEQUACY: The language systems available to the speaker and the hearer must have the necessary expressive adequacy to reach communicative success. The available conceptual systems must include the needed conceptual distinctions and the available linguistic systems must be able to express these distinctions. Expressive adequacy depends not only on the goals of the speaker and the available embodiment but also on the environment. For example, if only black-and-white pictures are available, a strategy based on hue is entirely inadequate. On the other hand, if one of the dialogue partners is colour blind, a hue-based strategy would not work for coloured pictures.

- COGNITIVE EFFORT: In order to cope with the incredible speed of normal language production and comprehension, reducing cognitive effort is of primordial importance. Cognitive effort is expended at all levels of language: How much time and memory needs to be spent in coming up with adequate conceptualisations? How complex is the process of constructing a sentence? How difficult is it to articulate the speech sounds? How efficiently can the sentence be parsed? How complicated is the interpretation of the sentence? If sentences are too complex to comprehend, for example because they trigger a large amount of combinatorial search, then hearers give up. Or if sentences are too hard to produce, the production process will be too slow to maintain the hearer's attention. Optimisations of cognitive effort are often in conflict for speaker and hearer. What requires less effort for the speaker might mean more effort for the hearer and vice versa.

- LEARNABILITY: Speakers must occasionally expand their language systems to express novel meanings or better capture the attention of hearers with a "fresh" way of saying something. But these innovations will lead nowhere if they cannot be acquired by hearers. They will lead to communicative failure and the innovation will not propagate in the population and therefore it has no chance to survive in the shared language. Learnability depends on whether speaker and hearer share the same language strategies, how much additional context is available, and how far the speaker has stretched established conventions to achieve his communicative goal.

- SOCIAL CONFORMITY: Speakers and hearers can greatly optimise their language production and comprehension by making their language systems as similar as possible. Moreover, details of language use, such as pronunciation, signal to which group a speaker belongs, and speakers often seek social conformity with the language use of their peers in order to belong to the group. Or they mimic the language systems of the most prestigious group in order to show they belong to that.

The opposite happens as well. Speakers may try to mark themselves as linguistically different from a group to which they do not want to belong.

Language users certainly cannot consciously construct their language to satisfy these selectionist criteria, even if they would want to. They can have no foresight about all the possible distinctions that are going to be relevant in their world because new objects, new artefacts, new types of interactions always come up. They have no obvious way to know consciously how much cognitive effort a particular sentence is going to require from the hearer. They cannot know in advance whether a metaphorical extension will be understood or whether the coercion of a word into a new grammatical function is going to be grasped by the hearer. And they cannot know for sure what the norm is in the group because they have no general overview, but can gain evidence only from local interactions with others whom they might not even be sure of whether they belong to the same group. The only thing they know for sure (and not even always or immediately) is whether a communicative interaction was successful. This is why language evolution has to be a selectionist process. Language users are able to generate or reuse certain variants but they can never be absolutely sure whether these variants satisfy the linguistic selection criteria that would lead to more adapted persistent communicative success.

12.2 Fitness landscapes

Organisms use a variety of strategies for survival and offspring production: bodily shape and appearance, specific sensors and actuators, metabolism, innate behaviours. Biologists call the ecological area that a particular organism occupies thanks to its physiological and behavioural strategies its ecological NICHE. A niche is defined through the ecological conditions (temperature, altitude, habitat type, food availability, presence of predators, etc.) for which the organism's strategies are appropriate and hence within which the species reaches a sufficiently high fitness to survive and fend off predators. Organisms may also have strategies to alter their environment so that some of their strategies become more possible or more optimal, a process called NICHE CONSTRUCTION (Odling-Smee, Laland & Feldman 2003)

Niche analysis is performed by defining a multi-dimensional space, further called the NICHE SPACE. Each dimension or NICHE FACTOR has to be dealt with by the species in order to remain viable. There is consequently a direct relation between the dimensions of the niche space and the selectionist pressures on the organisms trying to flourish within that niche which form a fitness landscape. Niche analysis typically examines how the different species within a delineated geological area are located within the niche space. It is then possible to see how species overlap, how they compete, how they are complementary, or whether some species are beginning to occupy a niche left open by others. Usually the dimensions of the niche space are not known but have to be inferred through multi-variate analysis from empirical observations of species occurrence and detailed descriptions of environmental factors (Elith & Leathwick 2009). But it is also possible to operate in a top-down manner, based on prior analysis of what might be niche factors, and to manipulate the environment to detect under what conditions the members of a species will thrive or not (Nosil & Sandoval 2008).

By analogy with biology, we can apply the concept of a niche to the evolutionary study of language systems and language strategies. To investigate linguistic niches in a systematic way, we need to identify first what factors are relevant. Some of these factors have to do with external conditions, for example, if the language games require expressing fine-grained hue distinctions or temporal and aspectual distinctions. Others relate to internal conditions, for example, how big is the search space during parsing, how much does a model of the situation need to be consulted. Next we can examine the performance of different systems and strategies for these factors, and map performance as points or regions in the niche space. Then we can study whether these points move towards greater or lesser optimality over time, how different systems or strategies compete when occupying the same niche, or how language systems and language strategies adapt to changes in the ecological conditions and hence the dimensions or critical values of the niche space. The factors relevant for a linguistic niche include the selectionist criteria discussed earlier, and they can be analysed by identifying a fitness landscape, where each dimension is a selection component. I discuss first examples of this kind of analysis for language systems and then for language strategies.

12.2.1 Fitness landscapes of language systems

To illustrate this approach let us look at a first example, using a fascinating study conducted by Remi van Trijp of change in the German article system as historically observed over the past 10 centuries.[3] The change is puzzling, because the article system started from a rather clean design in old High German to retain only a few forms in contemporary German. This contemporary system seems to be maladapted because the same forms are now used for many different purposes (syncretism) causing uncertainty and hence combinatorial search in parsing. For example, in Old High German there was a three-way gender distinction between masculine, neuter, and feminine for both nominative and accusative plurals, but in New High German only one form 'die' is left. Many linguists have argued that these changes are just random, caused by phonological erosion and confusion of closely related word-forms. But van Trijp hypothesised that the changes were actually Optimisations, whereby speakers optimised their own cognitive effort at the cost of that of hearers, even though the reduction in system complexity stopped at a critical point to preserve the disambiguation power of the system. See Figure 12.1.

Van Trijp initialised three populations of agents: with the Old High German system, the Middle High German system, or the New High German System. He then defined the following four dimensions for the fitness landscape:

1. SEARCH EFFORT, which is the amount of search that is needed, scaled between minimum (when there is one marker for every of the 18 possible configurations and so no search is needed) and maximum (when there are no markers at all).

---

[3] This section draws on the following publications: van Trijp (2013) and van Trijp (2014a).

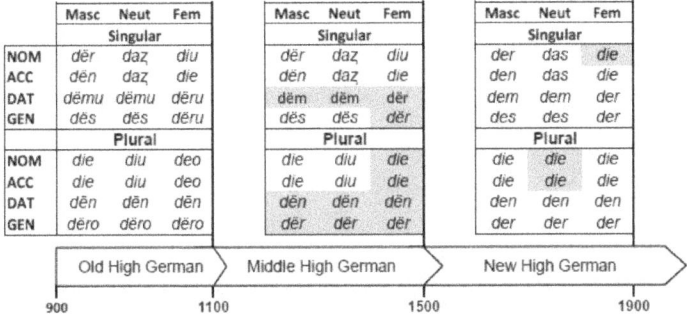

Figure 12.1: The German article system has morphological marking for case (nominative, accusative, dative, genitive), number (singular, plural) and gender (masculine, feminine, neuter). The system simplified from a well-structured clear system in old-high German to a system with more syncretism (the same form used for multiple purposes.)

2. DISAMBIGUATION POWER, which is based on the number of possible interpretations left after application of the grammar. The disambiguation power is also scaled with maximum power for 12 markers and minimum for 0 markers (not counting the genitive).

3. ARTICULATORY EFFORT, which is calculated in terms of the number of movements that articulators such as the lips and tongue have to make when pronouncing the different phonemes that make up each article.

4. ACOUSTIC PRECISION, which is based on the phonological distance between words.

Criteria (1), (2) and (4) pertain to the hearer and (1) and (3) to the speaker. They are calculated for each utterance in a corpus and the weighted average gives a value for the performance of the language system for each of these dimensions. The global performance can be assessed by taking a (weighted) average of each of the values for all dimensions. As expected, Old High German scores the highest for disambiguation power and acoustic precision and the lowest for articulatory effort and processing effort, thus being an advantage for the hearer but not for the speaker (see Figure 12.2).

On the other hand, the New High German system manages to become equally effective for disambiguation while requiring less search effort and articulatory effort, if other complementary cues are made available to the hearer by additional grammatical strategies, namely grammatical agreement between the article and the noun within a noun phrase, so that features of the article can be deduced from the noun, and syntactic valence of the verb, because that suggests which cases noun-phrases and hence their articles may have. This demonstrates that we should not always focus on a single strategy alone but have to take other relevant strategies into account. Moreover some forms, which are not

12 Language evolution

very distinctive from an acoustic point of view (such as 'der', 'den' and 'dem'), and therefore risk being collapsed into a single form, are nevertheless maintained because they are needed to resolve ambiguities that are not mitigated by other syntactic devices. This shows how an evolutionary point of view helps us to formulate explanatory hypotheses about language.

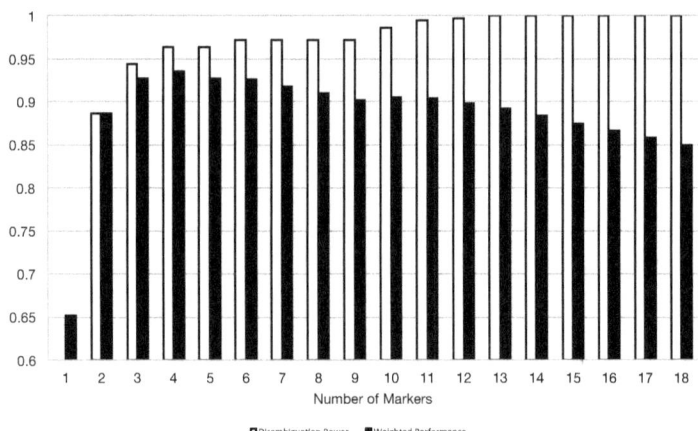

Figure 12.2: Fitness landscape for the German marker system. When the number of markers increases (x-axis), the disambiguation power (y-axis) (which takes into account not only the markers themselves but also the other cues available for distinguishing gender and number) goes up. However the total performance for all four dimensions (y-axis) (which includes articulatory effort and search goes down). The optimal performance is reached for 4 markers (New High German has 5 markers whereas old High German had 9.

This example shows how it is possible to analyse the fitness landscape for stages of a language system at different points in time. The same analysis can also be done for different regional variants that are currently competing to become dominant in the standard language. An example of the latter is the currently ongoing evolution from the etymological Spanish pronoun system to the referential pronoun systems, which has three different possible regional variants: 'leísmo', 'laísmo' and 'loísmo'. Van Trijp showed how each of these variants could equally arise with the same referential strategy and how it is a matter of historical contingency which one becomes dominant. Indeed we see that different regions of Spain have chosen different variants (van Trijp 2010).

Here is another example of a fitness landscape from the domain of space, developed by Michael Spranger.[4] It focuses on understanding the role of grammar for optimising spatial language. The experiment involves QRIO humanoids (see Figure 12.3) and uses a sophisticated vision system developed by Spranger, together with IRL and Fluid Construction Grammar (in the previous chapter). A variety of spatial language strategies were operationalised, in particular:

---

[4] These results are documented at length in: Spranger (2015).

1. The use of PROJECTIVE RELATIONS such as front/back, above/below, left/right. This requires imposing a coordinate system on the world model and name areas within this coordinate system. A common coordinate system is to take an object, such as the human body of the speaker as reference point and project vectors emanating from the body.

2. The use of PROXIMAL RELATIONS such as far/near. This requires that the distances of objects with respect to the reference point are computed and categorised.

3. The use of ABSOLUTE RELATIONS, such as North/West/East/South, related to global directions.

4. The use of an ALLOCENTRIC LANDMARK (as opposed to an egocentric one) from which the situation is conceptualised. For example, in the phrase 'the block in front of the box', the box is acting as a landmark and the projective spatial relations are computed as emanating from that object. Another example is 'the block on your left' where the landmark is the hearer.

Spranger analysed the fitness landscape for grammatical strategies. He compared one population of agents that was initialised with a pidgin German, i.e. only a vocabulary for objects and spatial relations but no grammar, and another population initialised with a full locative grammar of German. He investigated three external factors:

Figure 12.3: Set-up for the spatial language game experiments. Two robots are looking at a scene with a few blocks, a bigger box with tags indicating front, back or left and right side, and a global landmark in the form of a large tag pasted on the wall. *Top left and right:* World as seen through the camera of the robot. *Bottom left and right:* The internal world model as perceived by the left and right robot.

12 Language evolution

1. Scenes with many objects distributed around a landmark.

2. Scenes with several objects but no landmark that can be used as a spatial vantage point.

3. Scenes with an allocentric and without an allocentric landmark but more complex with respect to number of objects and distribution of objects compared to (1).

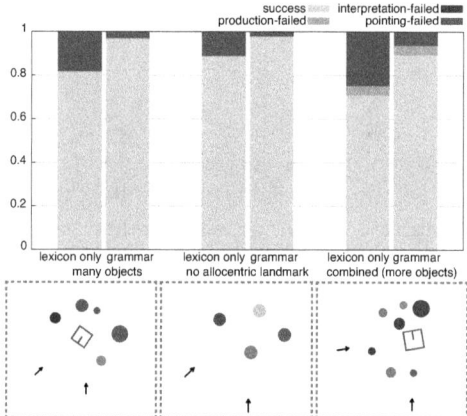

Figure 12.4: Investigation how the two language systems (lexical or grammatical) are performing with respect to the communicative success dimension and for each of the three ecological conditions. A purely lexical system in itself has already considerable success, but grammar becomes more and more relevant when the situation becomes more complex. The bottom images show examples for the three ecological conditions being examined.

Spranger used the following additional internal factors:

1. COMMUNICATIVE SUCCESS, including whether production failed, interpretation failed, or the hearer pointed to the wrong object (pragmatic failure). We see (Figure 12.4) that the more complex a situation becomes, the more grammar becomes relevant.

2. SEMANTIC AMBIGUITY, being the number of semantic structures that remain after syntactic analysis and have to be mapped onto the perceived world in order to be disambiguated (See Figure 12.5, left). Without grammar there is a lot more semantic ambiguity and hence more cognitive effort to consult the world model.

3. INTERPRETATION SHARING, which takes place when the semantic structure derived by the hearer is equal to that originally intended by the speaker (See Figure 12.5, right). Interpretation sharing is important in cases of displaced communication when agents do not have access to a shared world. We see that without grammar, interpretation sharing is heavily compromised.

12.2 Fitness landscapes

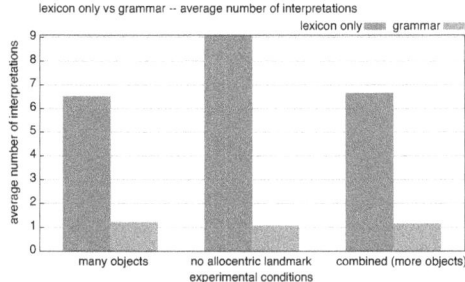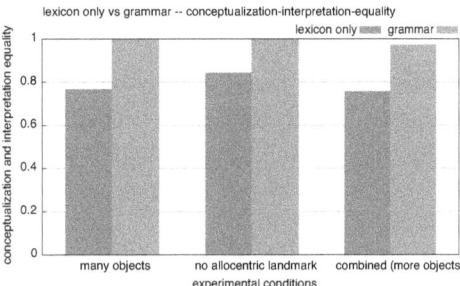

figure 12.5: Left: performance for semantic ambiguity for the same three ecological conditions. We see that without grammar the world model needs to be consulted heavily to weed out potential interpretations. And Right: Performance for interpretation sharing. Only with grammar are agents able to share the same semantic structure, ensuring a higher degree of communicative success.

12.2.2 The fitness landscape of language strategies

We now move one level up, and show how a fitness landscape can be identified at the level of strategies as well. Rather than supplying agents with language systems, we initialise them with specific strategies, let them build language systems, and then examine the performance of these language systems for the different dimensions of the fitness landscape, so as to understand which niche the strategy occupies. Here is one example of this approach from the domain of color (developed by Joris Bleys).[5]

The previous chapter already showed that there are different strategies for colour language: basic colour terms, graded membership ('very green'), compounds ('sky blue'), brightness qualification ('light green'), etc. All these strategies use a particular colour space, more specifically the CIE L*u*v* space where the L* dimension represents brightness (ranging from black to white), the u* dimension represents the red-green opponent channel, and the v* dimension the yellow-blue channel. This space was chosen because the distance between two colours in the L*u*v* space accurately represents the psychological distances between these colours as perceived by human subjects.

Let us focus on a family of strategies that all use a prototype-based approach, i.e. they perform categorisation using a standard nearest neighbour classification algorithm operating over an inventory of prototypical points, as also used in the Proper Naming Game and the Basic Colour Naming Game discussed in the previous chapter. Three variant strategies are imaginable (and can be found in human languages):

1. The BRIGHTNESS-ONLY STRATEGY which uses only the L* dimension (dark, grey, bright, etc.).

2. The HUE-ONLY STRATEGY which uses only the hue dimension (blue, yellow, green, etc.).

3. And the FULL-COLOUR STRATEGY which uses all dimensions.

---

[5] These results are documented at length in: Bleys (2015).

12 Language evolution

In order to understand the niche of each strategy, Bleys has set up experiments where the context is controlled with respect to the importance of hue. For example, agents can be presented with contexts with samples where the hue is the same but brightness is different on the one hand versus contexts with samples where the brightness is the same but hue is different. In between we get a mixed importance of hue.

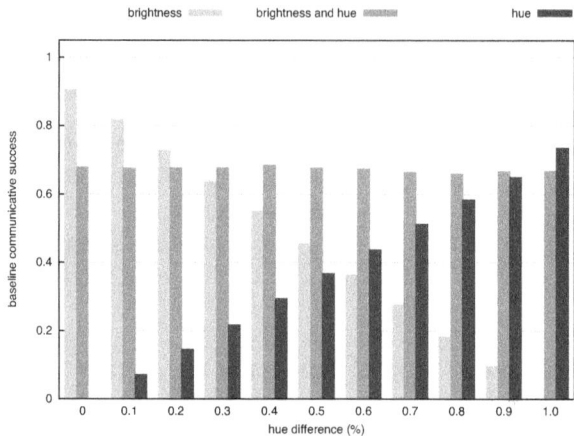

Figure 12.6: Niche analysis for three different colour strategies: brightness-only, brightness-hue, and hue-only. The properties of the context vary on the x-axis and the y-axis shows performance of each strategy. Only one niche dimension is examined, namely communicative success. We see that each strategy has its own niche for which it is optimal, but the full-colour strategy is globally performing the best across contexts, which may explain why it has become preferred in most language families.

Bleys initialised the three populations with the three different strategies and let them first learn an interpretation of the Spanish focal colours (with prototypes in brightness-only, hue-only, and full-colour spaces). Then he measured performance for communicative success for the varying ecological conditions. Not unexpectedly, he found that depending on the percentage of the importance of hue differences in the context, a different strategy is more optimal (see Figure 12.6). Not surprisingly, a hue-only strategy fails completely when the samples in each context have equal hue but different brightness, whereas a brightness-only strategy fails when the samples have equal brightness but different hue.

Another very useful type of experiment investigates in how far a particular strategy indeed makes a difference with respect to certain factors. Here is an example. It is again in the domain of spatial language discussed earlier and was conducted by Michael Spranger.

Recall that three internal factors were used for the fitness landscape in this domain: communicative success, semantic ambiguity and interpretation sharing. Spranger began with a population without any grammar but just a lexicon for expressing spatial relations and properties of objects. The agents were then initialised with a strategy that would build a grammar consisting of hierarchical constructions which group all the components of a spatial relation, put them in a particular sequential order, and add a marker to them. For example, a construction could arise that groups a spatial relation (like 'front'), a determiner acting as selector (like 'the'), and a noun introducing an object class (e.g. 'box'), puts them in the order: spatial relation - determiner - noun, and adds a marker to them (e.g. '-bo').

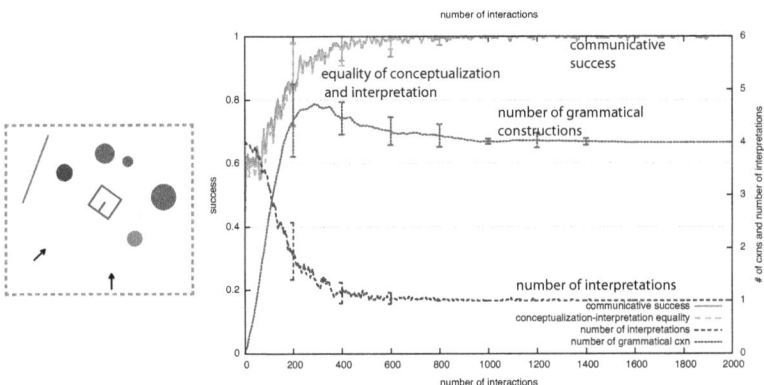

Figure 12.7: Agents have been given a grammatical strategy that introduces constructions to signal which conceptualisation strategy has been used and what its elements are. We see that communicative success and interpretation sharing go up to the maximum and semantic ambiguity (number of interpretations) goes down to 1, as the number of constructions built by the strategy increases.

A series of language games were played using contexts (such as the one shown in Figure 12.7, left) that contained a wide range of objects and also a landmark stimulating the need for perspective reversal. As shown in the niche analysis earlier (see Figure 12.5 and 12.4) a language without a grammatical expression supporting how spatial relations need to be analysed will reach a communicative success rate of only 70 %. So the question is whether the agents will increase this success rate when they exercise this grammatical strategy. The same question can be posed for the other two niche factors (disambiguation and semantic sharing). Experimental results are shown in Figure 12.7. They confirm that as the language system is getting built up, key factors (communicative success, semantic sharing, and disambiguation) indeed get optimised, demonstrating that the strategy "does its job".

12.3 Selection and alignment of language strategies

It is only one step now to achieve the selection and alignment of language strategies. Basically, two mechanisms needs to be added:

1. Agents need to track the performance of their strategies by tracking the performance of the language systems that were built based on their strategies. In other words, not only lexical or grammatical constructions but also strategies need to have a score. These STRATEGY SCORES should be updated using the same lateral inhibition dynamics that we have been using at the level of word-meaning associations or more generally constructions.

2. It is also necessary that the conceptualisations and the lexical and grammatical constructions that are implicated within a particular strategy are tagged with that strategy, so that if their score is updated, the score of the strategy can be updated as well (Figure 12.8). This is necessary for implementing a proper credit assignment mechanism and also for ensuring that a word becomes unambiguously used with a particular strategy.

The same word may be tagged with more than one strategy because a learning agent does not know which strategy has been used by the speaker and so this may lead to different hypotheses. But in the end, agents strive for convergence so that they all use the same word with the same meaning. For example, a hearer cannot know whether a particular word (e.g. 'yellow') is to be interpreted using the brightness-based or the full-colour-based strategy, particularly because both strategies could work in similar circumstances. For example, yellow colour chips are often the most bright ones and hence both strategies would work. Consequently it is unavoidable that different strategies compete to recruit the same words, and this explains that we see this phenomenon indeed in the historically attested evolution of language. Indeed, many of today's hue words like 'yellow', 'brown' or 'blue' were all expressing brightness-based distinctions in Old English before they became used as part of the Basic Colour Strategy in the late Middle English period (1350–1500).[6]

We now look at an experiment, developed by Joris Bleys, which puts this evolutionary dynamics to work. This is very challenging because language users must reach agreement about a dominant strategy without central coordination and while keeping communicative success intact. The application domain is colour.

The Bleys experiment concerns the brightness-based and the full-colour strategy. Both use a prototype-based nearest neighbour categorisation. We know from earlier experiments with the Proper Naming Game and the Action Naming Game that this strategy enables a population of agents to self-organise a colour lexicon from scratch. Figure 12.9 illustrates (on the left) how communicative success increases and the lexicon becomes more coherent, and (on the right) how the prototypes of the different agents gradually expand and become similar to be almost identical after 1200 games per agent, when the system has stabilised to 6 basic colours.

---

[6] See MacLaury (1992) and Casson (1997).

12.3 Selection and alignment of language strategies

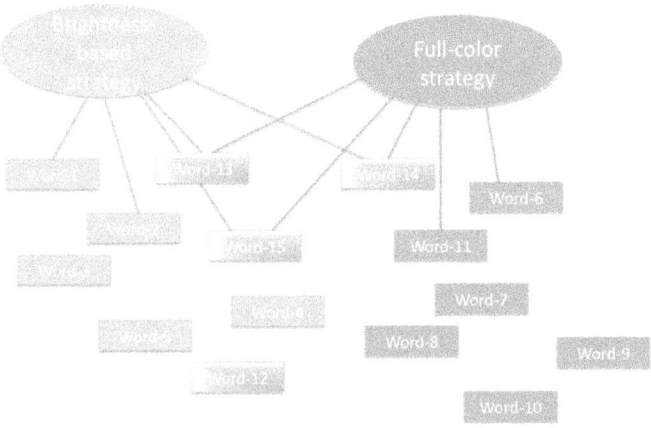

Figure 12.8: Different words are tagged with the strategy with which they should be interpreted. This allows the operationalisation of a 2-level selectionist dynamics, operating at the level of strategies and at the level of the language system built with each strategy.

The BRIGHTNESS PROTOTYPE STRATEGY is similar to the Basic Colour Strategy, but instead of taking all three dimensions into account, only the L* dimension of both the stimuli in the context and the prototypes of the colour categories are compared. While learning, the prototype of the used colour category is shifted on the L* axis towards the L* value of the topic. During invention, only the L* value of the topic is considered relevant. Figure 12.3 shows that this strategy is also adequate to allow a population of agents to self-organise and coordinate a colour lexicon from scratch. The resulting colour lexicon now consists of different shades of grey. The set of prototypes also expands and becomes similar across agents.

We now turn to the main issue here: the selectionist dynamics between both strategies. The following selectionist process has been implemented:

- In speaking, agents handle a communicative problem with the solution that had most success in the past and this solution implies a particular strategy. When the problem cannot be handled, the speaker has to expand his set of meanings and his lexicon and he uses the default strategy, i.e. the strategy that had most success in the past, which translates into having the highest strategy-score. It is only when this strategy does not work that other alternative strategies are tried out in decreasing order of their scores.

- In listening, the hearer first applies his own stored solution to interpret the utterance, which again implies the use of a language strategy associated with this solution. When the hearer is confronted with an unknown word or with a situation in which his interpretation of the word does not work for the present context

12 Language evolution

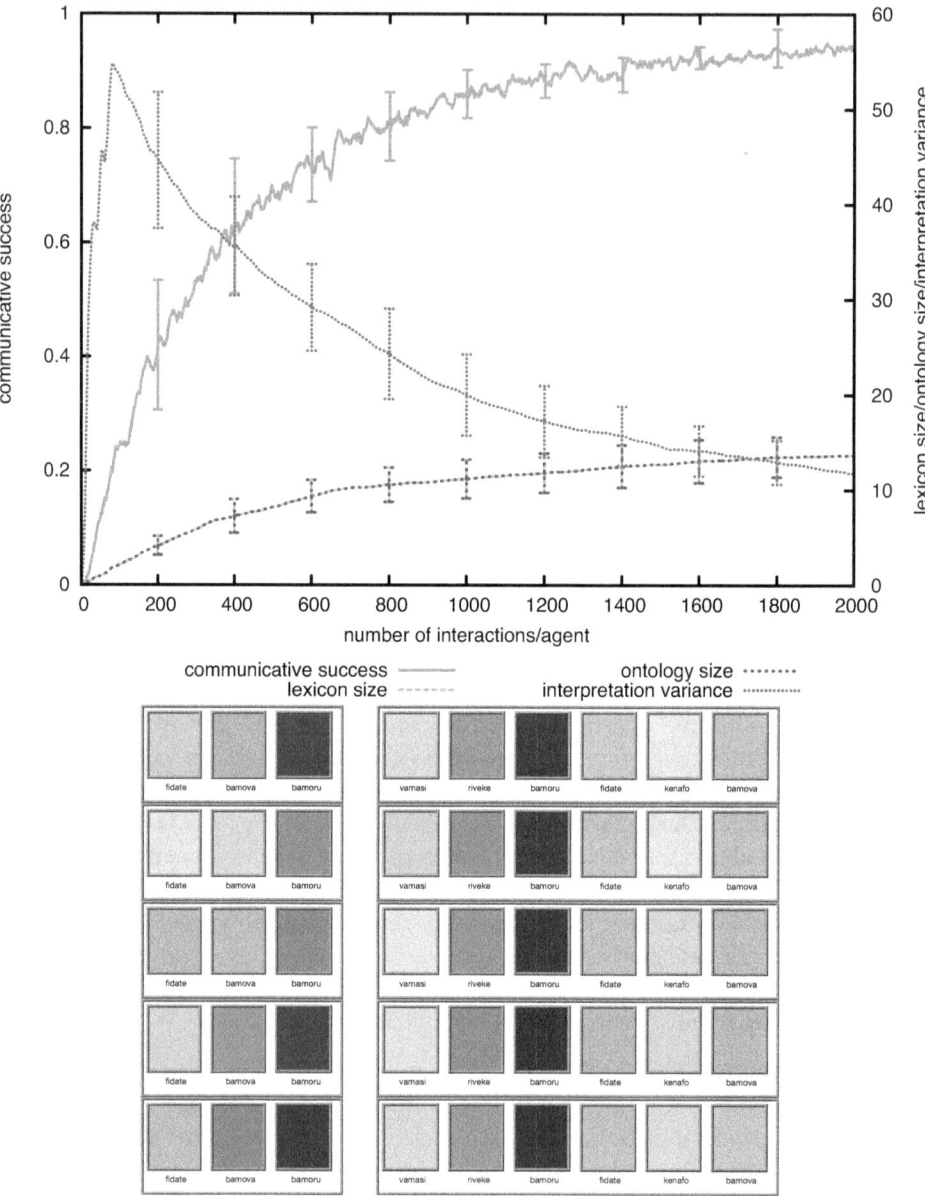

Figure 12.9: The BASIC COLOUR STRATEGY allows a population of agents (in this case 10) to self-organise a colour lexicon from scratch. The graph shows that high communicative success is reached with a lexicon of about 15 colour words (top). The evolution of a typical lexicon in a smaller population (5 agents), is shown after 400 (bottom left) and 1200 (bottom right) games per agent. Each row represents the lexicon of one agent.

12.3 Selection and alignment of language strategies

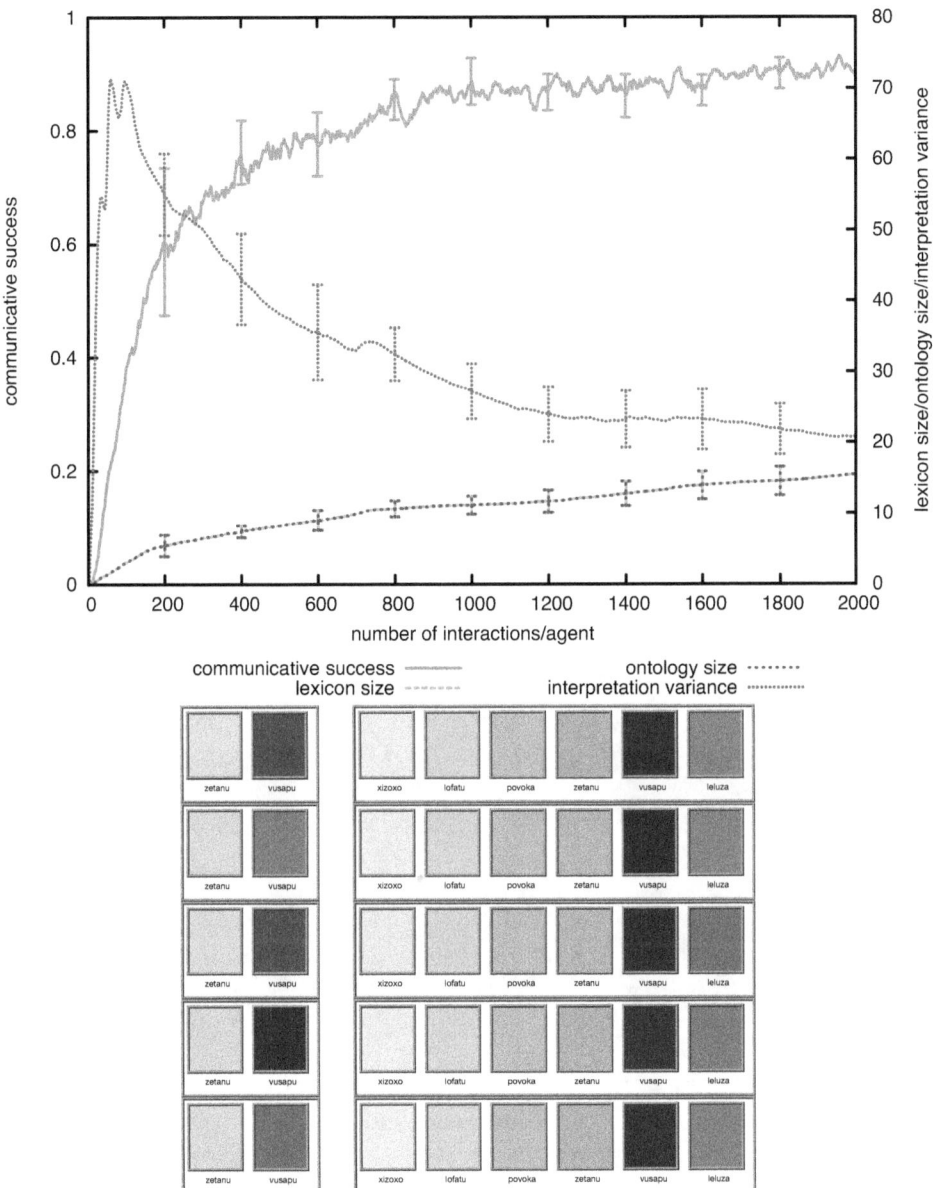

Figure 12.10: The BRIGHTNESS COLOUR STRATEGY also allows a population of agents (in this case 10) to evolve an adequate colour lexicon (top). The evolution of a typical lexicon in a smaller population (5 agents), is shown after 400 (bottom left) and 1600 (bottom right) games per agent. Each row represents the lexicon of one agent.

12 Language evolution

(because apparently the speaker used another strategy for this word), he uses first his own default strategy to figure out the meaning of the unknown word, and, if that does not work, he tries out alternative strategies, again in decreasing order of their scores.

Rich and complex dynamics results from this general system. In the results shown in Figure 12.11, the set of prototypes is kept fixed, namely equal to the focal colours underlying the Spanish colour system, which can be used either for the Full-Colour strategy or for the Brightness strategy. For example, the word *morado* ('purple') can both be interpreted in the full-colour space and in the brightness space.

Agents are initialised with a random value for the strategy-score for the Brightness-based versus Full-colour based strategy. When the dynamics described here takes its course (which includes the shifting of prototypes by speakers and hearers to be maximally adapted to the contexts that are presented), we observe several possibilities. In one simulation run (see Figure 12.11), the brightness-based strategy becomes and remains dominant. It could have been the brightness or the full-colour strategy, depending on small fluctuations in the early stages. In another simulation run we see that one strat-

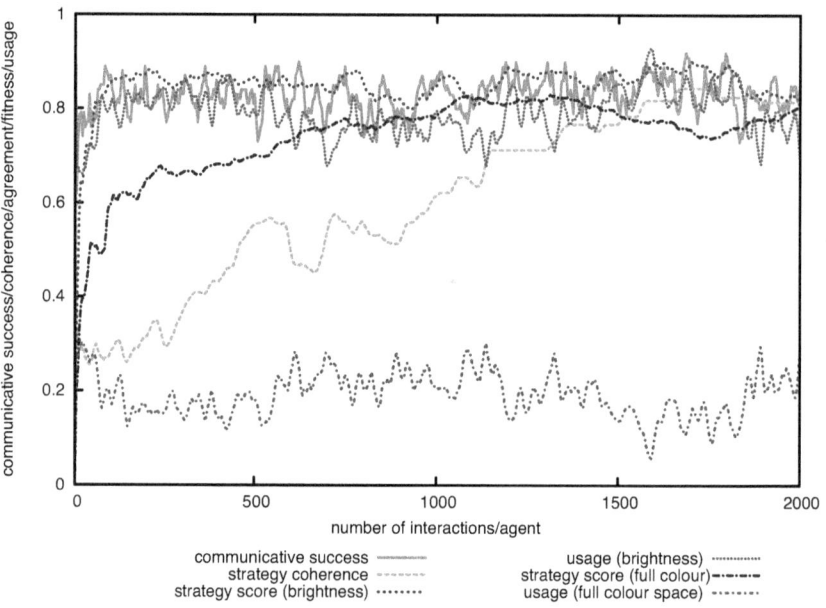

Figure 12.11: Communicative success stays constant. The Brightness Colour Strategy becomes dominant very early due to random fluctuations. It stays dominant but barely. The strategy coherence (i.e. whether agents agree on the default strategy) increases gradually. The Full Colour Strategy remains still in use for cases where it is needed.

12.4 Generation of new strategies

egy becomes dominant first (in this case the brightness strategy) to be overtaken later by another strategy (i.c. the full-colour strategy), as attested in the history of English colour terms (see Figure 12.12). The two strategies continue to co-exist. Brightness is still used in circumstances where this gives a higher chance of communicative success, for example when colour chips are close in hue but distinct in brightness or when there is a word which has most of its success in the brightness dimension.

12.4 Generation of new strategies

The previous section showed how there can be competition or cooperation between strategies, fought out through the performance of the language systems against the niche factors in which the language strategies operate. But a Darwinian evolutionary framework requires that there is not only selection and a self-enforcing causal feedback loop but also that new elements get generated, in this case new strategies, which can then be subjected to a selectionist dynamics. How can we explain that new strategies arise? This is the most challenging difficult question of evolutionary linguistics research and very much an open question. We basically have to move up to a meta-level where we have strategies for building strategies, further called meta-strategies. It is unclear

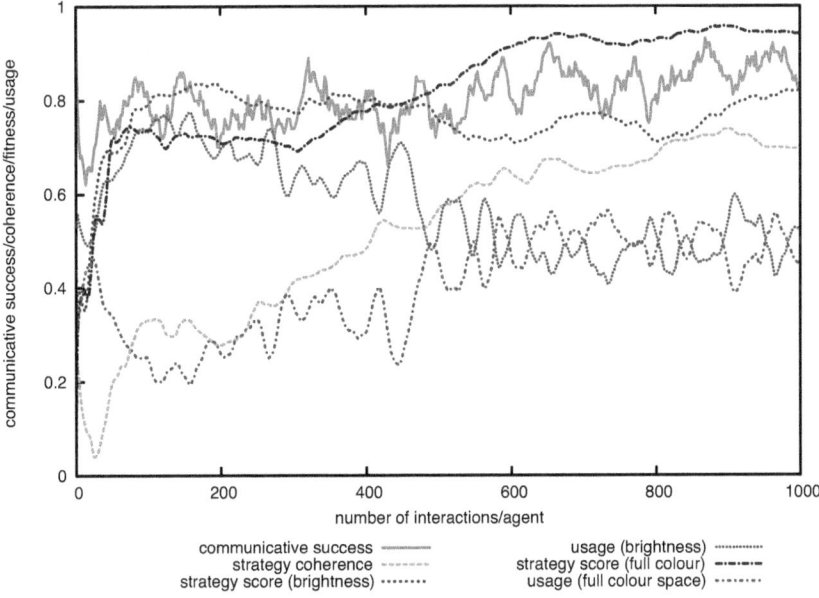

Figure 12.12: Initially the brightness strategy is dominant, but then the full-colour strategy gradually takes over and becomes dominant around 400 games/agents. Strategy coherence within the population progressively increases.

whether they have to be innately given or whether they are themselves also the result of developmental processes and a cultural dynamics. There are two aspects to a strategy: a conceptual side and a linguistic side. For the conceptual side, solid results have been achieved using IRL, which was from the beginning developed to allow the generation of new conceptualisation strategies. So far a single meta-strategy has proven to be quite successful in this case. The linguistic side however is still to a large extent in a stage of fundamental research, and here there appear to be several different meta-strategies, used by different language communities. Each of these two aspects is now discussed.

12.4.1 A meta-strategy for generating new conceptualisation strategies

As explained in the previous chapter, the conceptualisation of grounded meaning takes the form of programs which perform operations over the world model. For example, for the spatial domain, this amounts to cognitive operations such as filtering the objects in the context with a particular prototype, geometric transformations to re-interpret the scene from a particular perspective, execute set operations, etc. We have seen that these programs can be formulated in terms of constraint networks. Each cognitive operation helps to determine or constrain the value of slots and computation terminates successfully when all slots could be filled.

We will use the domain of spatial language again as a source of examples, based on experiments carried out by Michael Spranger. It uses the QRIO humanoid robots and scenes like the one shown in Figure 12.3. An example of a constraint network from this domain is shown in Figure 12.13. It is the network for the phrase 'near the box'. 'Near' is a proximal relation which categorises objects in terms of how near they are to a landmark (in this case the box). In a list form the network looks like this:

```
1. (get-context ?ctx-1)
2. (construct-region-proximal
     ?region ?ctx-1 ?landmark ?cat)
3. (bind proximal-category ?cat NEAR)
4. (apply-selection ?landmark ?landmarks ?selector-2)
5. (apply-class ?landmarks ?ctx ?landmark-class)
6. (bind selector ?selector-2 UNIQUE)
7. (get-context ?ctx)
8. (bind object-class ?landmark-class BOX)
```

The order of these operations does not matter as values propagate and constraints become active until no further progress can be made. Operations in 4, 5, 6, 7 and 8 provide the referent of 'the box'. The following contributions can be made by each of the cognitive operations: The predicate BOX gets bound to ?landmark-class in operation 8. Object-class is the type of ?landmark-class. The context, i.e. all objects in the present situation, gets bound to ?ctx in operation 7. The selector UNIQUE gets bound to ?selector-2 in operation 6. Then the operation apply-class is applied to all the objects in ?ctx (the context) to find the possible landmarks which get bound to ?landmarks using the ?landmark-class (BOX). This set is assumed to be a singleton and so in operation 4 the unique element in the set of ?landmarks can be selected and bound to ?landmark.

12.4 Generation of new strategies

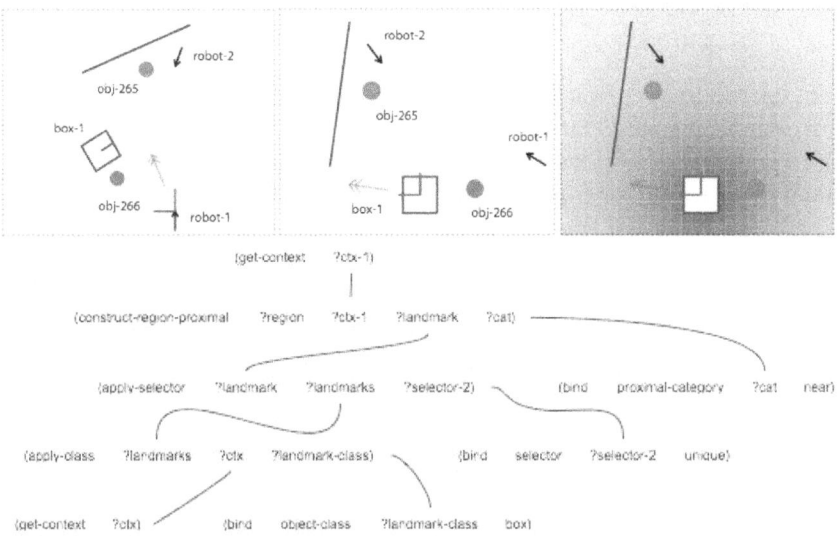

Figure 12.13: Example of a conceptualisation for the phrase *near to the box*. *Top:* Leftmost: The situation as perceived by the robot. Middle: situation after a geometric transform where the box is made the central perspective. Right: Area around the box which reflects (in terms of darkness of the colour) how near objects are to the box. *Bottom:* IRL constraint network for this conceptualisation.

The remaining three operations apply the proximal relation. In operation 3 ?cat is bound to the proximal-category NEAR. In operation 1, ?ctx-1 gets bound to the context. And finally in operation 2, the region around the landmark, which satisfies the category ?cat (NEAR), can be computed and bound to ?region by "construct-region-proximal". The construction-region-proximal constraint has to perform first a geometric transformation on the scene, constructing a world model from the viewpoint of the landmark, i.e. the box.

A CONCEPTUALISATION STRATEGY is an abstraction of such a concrete conceptualisation network. It consists of a network that acts as a useful chunk and is therefore a modular unit that can be linked into a larger network. The chunk has a set of open variables with which the network can be linked to other networks. For example, the network shown in Figure 12.13 can be made more abstract to handle many instances of proximal relations, not only *near the box*, but also *far from the box, close to the box, near the boxes, near the table, very far from the wall*, etc. The open variables are ?cat, ?selector-2, and ?landmark-class, which have to be supplied by lexical items or phrases. The network is then as follows, with operations at 3, 6 and 8 removed:

1. `(get-context ?ctx-1)`
2. `(construct-region-proximal ?region ?ctx-1 ?landmark ?cat)`
4. `(apply-selection ?landmark ?landmarks ?selector-2)`

345

12 Language evolution

```
5. (apply-class ?landmarks ?ctx ?landmark-class)
7. (get-context ?ctx)
```

The network has to be completed with bindings for the open variables, but all the other variables can be computed through the network itself. Network-chunks are expressed through a grammatical construction, which expresses which chunk is involved and how the initial values of the slots are to be expressed. In this case it is a noun-phrase construction, syntactically of the form [noun preposition article noun] and semantically constrained as [proximal-category selector object-class].

Spranger demonstrated how new spatial conceptualisation strategies can be derived. The process uses the regular way in which the speaker agent finds possible conceptualisations, namely through a search process (Figure 12.14).

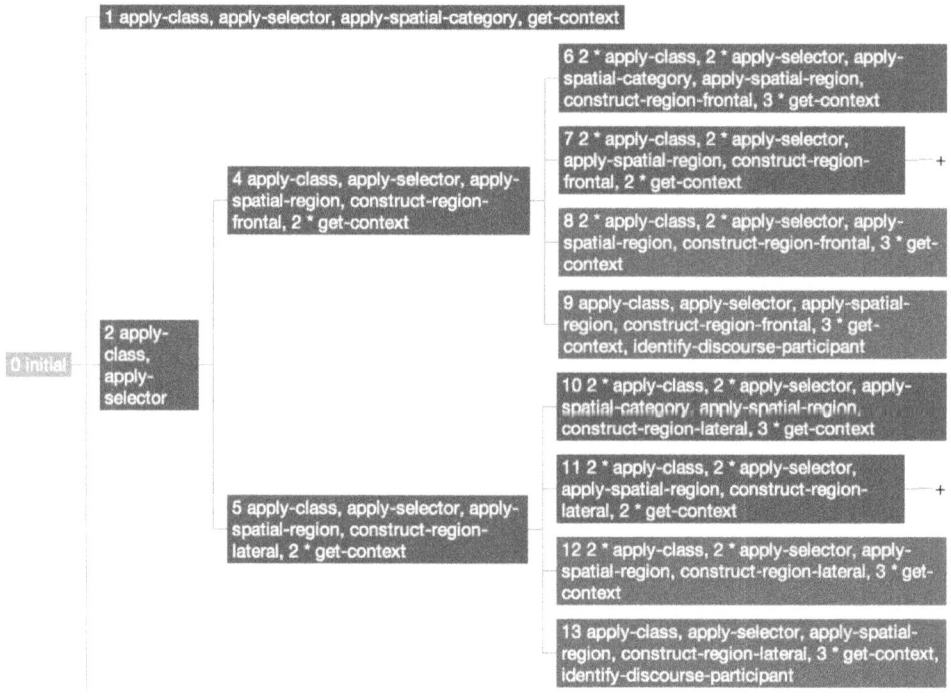

Figure 12.14: The meaning of an utterance is found through a search process, starting from an empty network, progressively more constraints are added until a solution network is found that, when executed, yields the topic chosen by the speaker.

As explained in the previous chapter, the speaker starts from a particular communicative goal (the topic) within a specific context. Each step in the search process adds progressively more nodes and at each step, the network is tried out to see whether it is able to compute anything in the present context and whether it brings the speaker closer to a possible effective conceptualisation. The end-nodes of the search tree contain either networks that do not yield a solution or a network that is a possible conceptualisation offered for translation into an utterance.

Often there is more than one solution. (There are already four solutions in the tree in Figure 12.14 and more solutions would turn up if some of the nodes are worked out further.) Solutions are ranked based on various criteria such as their complexity, the score of the prototypes involved, or how well they can be translated into an utterance.

Once an adequate conceptualisation is found and it leads to a successful game, modular sections of the network can be abstracted and used as the basis of reusable conceptualisation strategies in the future. Each conceptualisation strategy has its own score which is updated using the lateral inhibition dynamics as used for the lexical or grammatical constructions as explained in earlier chapters. The frequency of use and success of a strategy depends partly on whether the "niche" in which a strategy is most effective occurs frequently, partly on what is preferred by the rest of the population, and other criteria such as complexity.

Figure 12.15 shows an example experiment in which all the aspects discussed in this section are brought together. A population of 10 agents is developing new conceptualisation strategies for a niche that encourages preference for a particular strategy, namely a projective strategy with possible perspective reversal, as in *the box in front of the wall*. We see that communicative success steadily rises and that the number of spatial categories increases. The bottom graph zooms in on the conceptualisation strategies. We see that agents reach a consensus about a dominant strategy after a period in which new strategies are invented and tried out.

12.4.2 Meta-strategies for generating new lexicogrammatical strategies

Are there general meta-strategies that can be used to generate the kind of lexicogrammatical strategies that can in turn generate all the language systems we observe in today's languages? This is a very profound question, related to the ongoing debate in linguistics on the existence of a universal language acquisition device. A lot of ink has been spilled but we need to do profound computational modelling of meta-strategies and thorough experiments to find out.

Generally speaking, a lexico-grammatical strategy has two components: DIAGNOSTICS which monitor how language processing is going and REPAIRS which add new constructions to the agent's inventory.

For LEXICAL STRATEGIES, the diagnostics consist in checking whether there is part of the meaning that is not yet covered by any lexical item. The repair then consists in introducing a (possibly new) word and introducing a new lexical construction for this word. This strategy is already used by the Talking Heads. When part of a meaning cannot be covered, a new word form is randomly generated and used from then on for this meaning, but possibly in competition with other words that were later acquired for the same meaning.

12 Language evolution

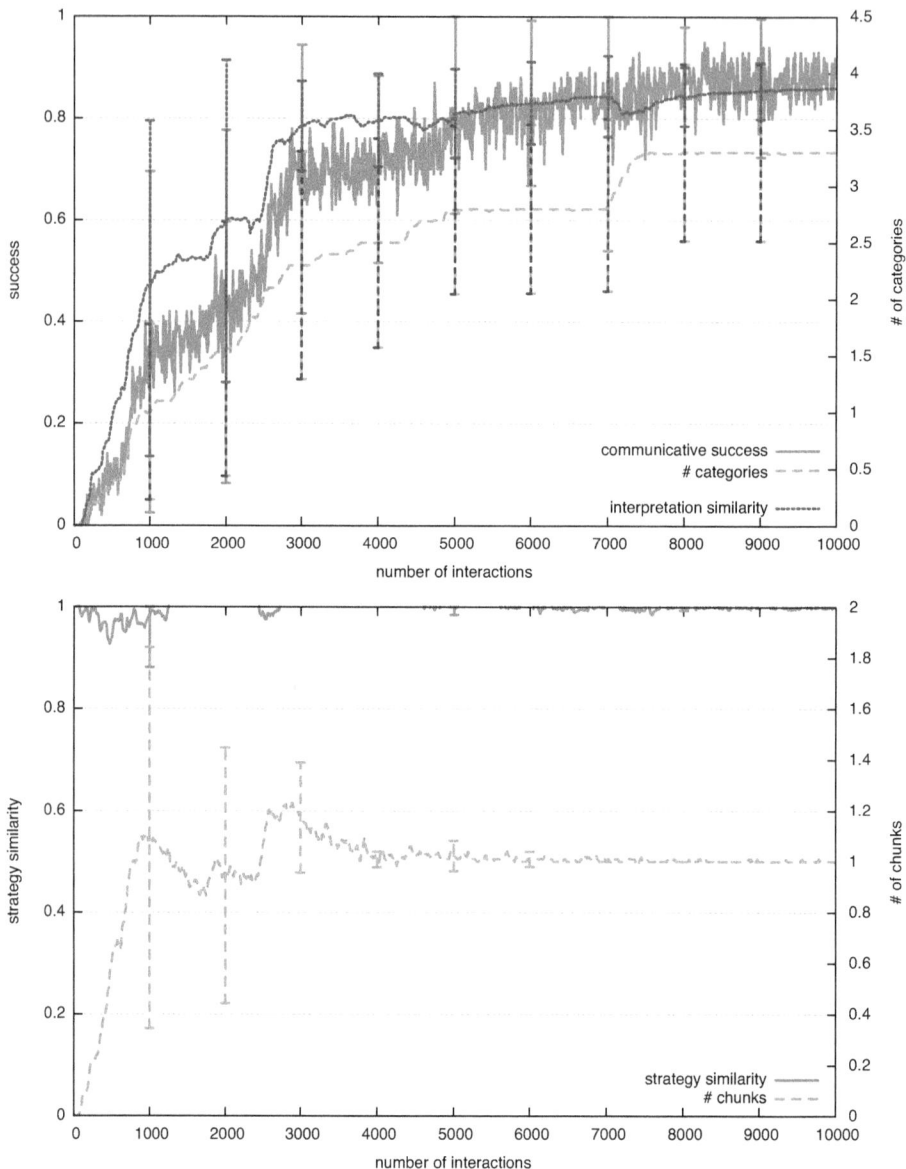

Figure 12.15: This experiment combines strategy invention, alignment, and category development by each strategy. The top figure shows language games on the x-axis, and communicative success, average number of categories, and interpretation similarity on the y-axis. The bottom figure shows the similarity between strategies and the average number of strategies in the population. One strategy becomes dominant.

12.4 Generation of new strategies

A study of ongoing change in the vocabularies of human speakers shows that the invention of a brand new word form happens seldom. Usually an existing wordform is recruited to express an uncovered meaning. The meaning of the already existing word form expresses aspects of the novel meaning to be expressed but there is not an exact overlap. However, the existing word is sufficiently suggestive so that the hearer can guess what meaning is intended by the speaker. For example, the word 'mouse' becomes adopted for computer mouse based on its appearance. Often a compound of several words is used, each of them suggesting other aspects of the meaning, such as *bitcoin*, which suggests digital (*bit*) and currency (*coin*). There are several other strategies, for example, an abbreviation of a long word becomes itself a single new word, such as *MOOC*, meaning 'massively open on-line course' and now standing for a course made available through the internet. There are also playful variations created with existing words, as for example *wackadoo* which means 'bizarre person' and probably originally came from the word *wacky*.

It is not really possible to capture the enormous creativity of human word creation in computational simulations because that would involve components for common sense inference and access to massive cultural knowledge. However we can do experiments to understand how new words may arise by analogy with existing words and how the meaning of words can develop further, for example by abandoning some of the aspects of the original meaning or gaining new meanings. Such experiments have been carried out in particular by Wellens, Loetzsch & Steels (2008).

In their "adaptive, flexible word meaning strategy", Wellens and Loetzsch assumed that the association between a word and the different components of the meaning (called its features) is flexible. Each component feature has a score and not all features have to be present in order to use a word. The scores of the features are updated depending on the success of the word and whether they were relevant in the situation in which the word was used. As a consequence we get a much more fine-grained dynamics in which the meanings of words may flexibly shift and a word may come to be used for another constellation of features that is only partially matching. Figure 12.16 shows examples of how these features evolve over time. They show the kinds of progressive shifts in meaning that we also observe in human lexicon evolution and demonstrate how words can come to be used for quite different meanings than their rigid original sense would demand.

Grammatical strategies come in two types. There are first of all strategies that express additional meaning using syntax. The syntax can either take the form of ordering of the words, as in the distinction between an affirmative sentence and a question, signalled by the use of the auxiliary *do* and inversion of the main verb and the subject (as in *Does he come?* versus *he comes*), or by the use of syntactic structure and function words, as in the verb phrase. For example, a phrase like *will have been coming* involves a future perfective using the auxiliary *will*, the infinitive auxiliary (*have*), the past participle auxiliary (*been*), and the present participle main verb (*coming*).

There are also strategies that focus on minimising the cognitive effort of the listener by signalling how words in the sentence need to be semantically grouped together. This happens generally in two ways:

12 Language evolution

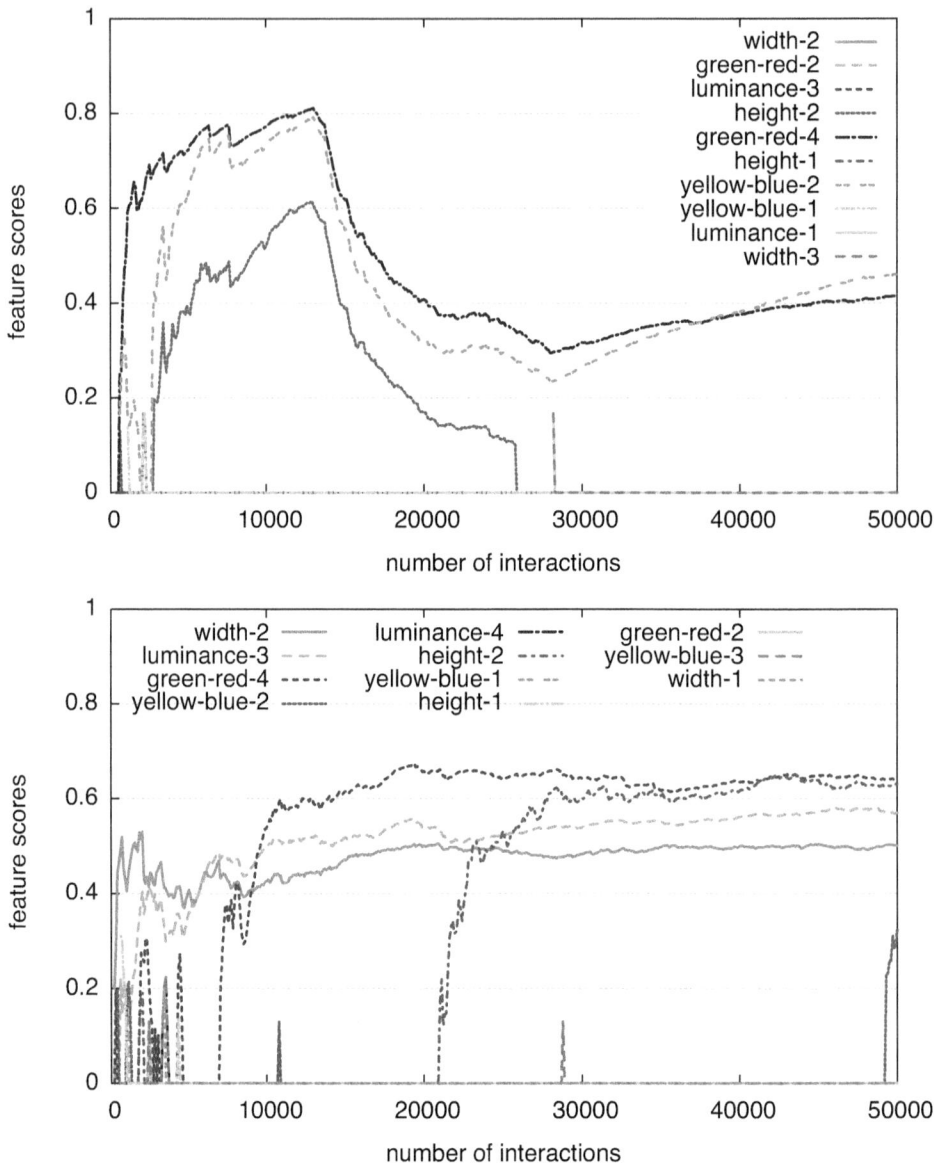

Figure 12.16: Two examples of the meaning of words in terms of a set of component features whose weight can change over time.

12.4 Generation of new strategies

- Language-dependent markers for various syntactico-semantic features, such as number, gender, case, are introduced and the different words which need to be grouped are all marked for the same features. An example of this kind of grammatical agreement is 'la belle fille' (French: the beautiful girl) where the article 'la' and the adjective 'belle' are both marked as singular feminine.

- The second strategy is phrase structure. Words are grouped together that are about the same object, a sequential order is imposed on these words, and patterns of orderings based on syntactic and semantic categories are introduced.

Extensive empirical work on grammaticalisation has given us a wealth of data how these strategies play out in the history of human languages.[7] And the key challenge for evolutionary linguistics is to model these processes, the same way evolutionary biologists model speciation or species evolution.

I here just point to one series of experiments, I conducted with Katrien Beuls, on the origins of agreement systems, which follow the latter strategy Beuls & Steels (2013). The challenge was to discover by what kind of language strategies an agreement system could arise and to identify the basic building blocks with which evolutionary experiments could be set up.

Historical linguists have researched many concrete examples of how agreement systems arise.[8] There are invariably the following phases:

1. Agreement markers derive from reusing existing words, such as pronouns or classifiers.

2. The markers derived from independent words become shorter, they lose part of their form, then become clitics and later affixes. For example, the Dyirbal (Australian aboriginal) agreement marker *m-* evolved from the classifier *mayi*, which means 'non-flesh food'.

3. The features that agreement markers express, which are initially semantically grounded, invariably become more abstract and get to be used in a purely conventional manner. For example, the masculine/feminine gender distinction has its basis in male/female sex, but is then arbitrarily applied to inanimate objects, so that table might be masculine in one language (German: *der Tisch*) but feminine in another (French: *la table*).

Starting from a game of reference, similar to the Talking Heads experiment, populations of agents were programmed first to build a "formal" agreement system, i.e. a system based on formal markers without any meaning, and then a meaningful grammatical system, with grammatical markers that express semantic features. The experiment was then extended with further strategies that optimise three niche factors:

---

[7] See for example: Heine & Kuteva (2007), Hopper & Traugott (1993), Lehmann (1982), Traugott & Trousdale (2013).
[8] See for example: Lehmann (1988), Luraghi (2011).

12 Language evolution

1. The recruitment of existing words as markers makes the acquisition of new markers more accurate because it is based on existing words and so the meaning can be guessed more easily. This helps to propagate the markers faster in the population.

2. The phonological reduction of word forms leads to less articulatory effort, as we have already seen with the German article system.

3. Conventionalisation leads to a smaller inventory, and hence less memory requirements and better preservation of the language system.

Here I just show results for one example, the phonological reduction strategy. Although sophisticated models of speech articulation exist and they predict the kind of errors and variations that speakers tend to introduce and how they influence sound change, we have used a simpler model that nevertheless brings out the language dynamics clearly. Speakers optimise articulation by leaving out the last consonant or vowel of a marker with a certain probability $\epsilon = 0.1$. Hearers are flexible enough in their parsing of markers to recognise that a truncated form is a variant of an existing marker, as long as it deviates for only one consonant or vowel. When an agent produces or encounters a truncated marker, he stores it in his inventory as a new variant of the original marker, and later uses the original or the truncated form with equal chance. However, as soon as an agent encounters the truncated marker for a second time, he adopts it as the new norm and the old form is discarded. It is possible that the agent encounters again the previous older form which may then be re-adopted and reused if it is encountered more than once. However, at some point, there are enough agents using the new variant so that the whole population shifts in a phase transition.

Figure 12.17 shows the outcome of a computer simulation of this phonological reduction strategy. An agreement system based on meaningful markers is emerging using the meaningful marker strategy. But after agents reach a stable level of performance (in the experiment this is typically after 200 games per agent), they occasionally introduce phonological reductions with probability $\epsilon = 0.1$ and this leads to the erosion of the original markers. Figure 12.17 top) shows that the average marker length is decreasing from an average of 7 to 4 consonants and vowels, without affecting performance. There is greater variation V_g in the population because there are always different variants of the same marker in use, but this generally does not have an impact on communicative success because agents are able to recognise them as a variant of their own norm. Figure 12.17 bottom) shows a typical example how a marker (in this case -*uinbui*) erodes. At the beginning there is still competition for two meanings for this marker but soon the second meaning dominates. The form gets phonologically reduced in the sequence -*uinbui* → -*uinbu* → -*uinb* → -*uin* → -*ui* → -*u*. At this point reduction stops because speakers are able to detect that otherwise the function of the marker would get lost.

These results are significant from a language dynamics point of view because they show, for the first time, how phonological reduction carried out by individual agents can lead to marker erosion, without destroying the functioning of the agreement system as a whole and even though there is no central control to ensure that shared norms are maintained.

12.4 Generation of new strategies

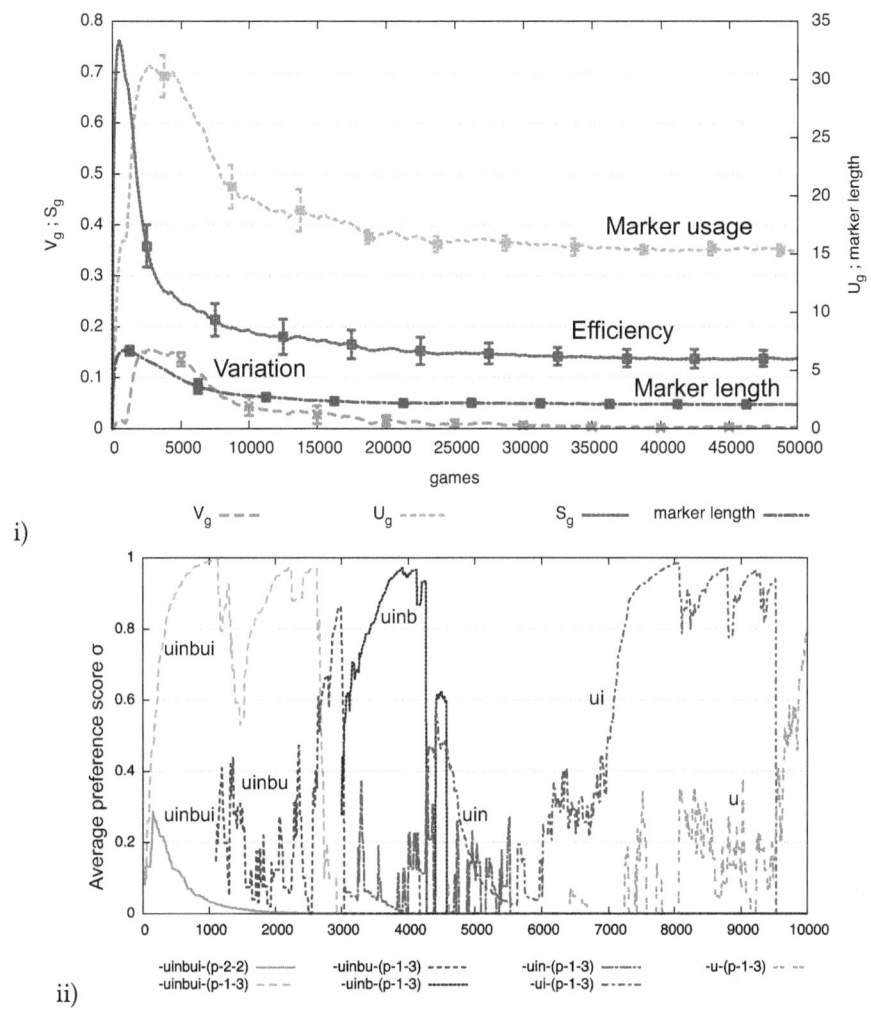

Figure 12.17: Performance of the phonological reduction strategy. i) Average performance values for 50 game series for a total of 50,000 games (average of 10,000 per agent). We see that the length of the markers progressively diminishes, thus reducing articulatory effort, but variation V_g does not increase, implying that the system is stable. The marker inventory size remains constant as well. ii) Trace of the changes to a marker in a single experiment. The marker -*uinbui* erodes progressively to -*u*. A truncated variant is typically present for a while in the population until a phase transition happens and it becomes dominant.

353

12.5 Conclusions

This section reported on experiments in the 2010–2015 time period that have tried to scale up language dynamics from a single strategy (as in the Talking Heads) to multiple strategies. This led to the discovery that we need a dual dynamics: on the level of language systems governed by one or more strategies, and on the level of language strategies. We have applied a cultural Darwinian dynamics on both levels. How that works for language systems is quite clear now, but many questions remain and much more work needs to be done to see how it would work on the level of language strategies. This chapter reported some of the progress made recently. It introduced three steps: niche analysis as a way to understand the evolutionary landscape, selection and alignment of language strategies, and the generation of new language strategies.

It is now time to come to a general conclusion of this book. The intellectual adventure that has been described here is not over yet. Here are some of the many lines for further research remaining.

First we need much more work along the paths of which we have seen many examples:

1. The study of more language systems, based on firm empirical data. For example, the study of the verbal system of Italian or the determiner system of Dutch.

2. A study of the language strategies that underly these systems. A language strategy should define how a particular type of language system operates, how it is learned, and how it is expanded and aligned.

3. A study of the niche occupied by the language systems governed by a particular language strategy.

4. Evolutionary experiments to show how new strategies may arise.

Then there are also several deep open questions which have not been addressed extensively so far. Here are a few examples:

1. What are implications of the models presented here for the neurobiology of language? Right now it remains largely a mystery how the human brain is processing language and current neural network models are entirely insufficient from a representational and computational point of view to handle the structures and processes that we have been using in the various experiments reported in this book.

2. How to orchestrate long-term evolution, both within the individual and in a population? Some suggestions have been made based on the autotelic principle which allows agents to control the communicative challenges in relation to their level of skill (Steels & Wellens 2007). But these suggestions need to be tested more seriously in large-scale long term experiments.

3. What is the interaction between cultural evolution and genetic evolution? I have argued in favour of culture-driven genetic evolution but what kind of genetic

change is necessary to support the processes that we have been found to be operating at the cultural level? Clearly, flexible recruitment and huge amounts of memory are key demands on the human brain, but there are undoubtedly others.

4. What is the interaction between social evolution, cultural evolution and biological evolution? The language games which we have studied all required honest communication. Agents do their best to play the game as well as they can and agents are fully cooperative. This is not the default condition in the natural world and it is not so easy to explain how human sociality arose, and how human language may have fostered it (Dor, Knight & Lewis 2014).

These questions can only be properly addressed by bringing up and working out hypotheses and doing detailed computational analysis and computational experiments. The field of evolutionary linguistics is still in its infancy and so far too few researchers are contributing through the kind of computational simulations that were discussed in this book. This is not surprising given the technical complexity and the breadth of knowledge needed to work in this area. It takes Ph.D students on average 5 years of training and experimentation to carry a research thread to fruition, assuming that the student starts with considerable background in computational linguistics or Artificial Intelligence. Let us hope that in the future the resources will be available so that younger generations can pursue this exciting path. Many discoveries are waiting to be made!

Bibliography

Anastacio, Thomas J. & David A. Robinson. 1989. Distributed parallel processing in the vestibulo-oculomotor system. *Neural Computation* 1. 230–241.

Arkin, Ronald. C. 1998. *Behavior-based robotics*. MIT Press.

Arthur, Brian (ed.). 1996. *The economy as a complex adaptive system* (Santa Fe Institute Series on Complexity). Menlo Park: Addison-Wesley.

Babloyantz, Agnes. 1986. *Molecules, dynamics and life. An introduction to self-organization of matter*. New York: John Wiley.

Badii, Remo & Antonio Politi. 1997. *Complexity. Hierarchical structures scaling in physics*. Cambridge: Cambridge University Press.

Ballard, Dana H. & Christopher M. Brown. 1982. *Computer vision*. Englewood Cliffs: Prentice Hall.

Baronchelli, Andrea, Vittorio Loreto & Francesca Tria. 2012. Language dynamics. *Advances in Complex Systems* 15(3–4).

Baronchelli, Andrea, Tao Gong, Andrea Puglisi & Vitorrio Loreto. 2010. Modeling the emergence of universality in color naming patterns. *Proceedings of the National Academy of Sciences* 107(2403).

Bates, Elisabeth, Inge Bretherton & Lynn Snyder. 1988. *From first words to grammar*. Cambridge: Cambridge University Press.

Belpaeme, Tony, Luc Steels & Joris van Looveren. 1998. The construction and acquisition of visual categories. In Andreas Birk & Yiannis Demiris (eds.), *Proceedings of the 6th European Workshop on Learning Robots* (Lecture Notes on Artificial Intelligence 1545), 1–12. Berlin: Springer.

Beuls, Katrien & Luc Steels. 2013. Agent-based models of strategies for the emergence and evolution of grammatical agreement. *PLoS ONE* 8(3). e58960. http://dx.doi.org/10.1371%2Fjournal.pone.0058960.

Bickerton, Derek. 1999. *Language and species*. Chicago: Chicago University Press.

Billard, Aude & Kerstin Dautenhahn. 1999. Experiments in learning by imitation - grounding and use of communication in robotic agents. *Adaptive behavior* 7(3/4). 415–438.

Bleys, Joris. 2015. *Language strategies for the domain of colour* (Computational Models of Language Evolution 3). Berlin: Language Science Press.

Boeckx, Cedric & Kleanthes Grohmann. 2013. *The Cambridge handbook of biolinguistics*. Cambridge: Cambridge University Press.

Boeckx, Cedric & Massimo Piattelli-Palmarini. 2005. Language as a natural object, linguistics as a natural science. *The Linguistic Review* 22. 447–466.

de Boer, Bart. 2000. Emergence of vowel systems through self-organisation. *AI Communications* 13. 27–39.

Bowerman, Melissa. 1996. Learning how to structure space for language: A crosslinguistic perspective. In Paul Bloom, Merrill A. Peterson, Lynn Nadel & Mary F. Garrett (eds.), *Language and space* (Language, Speech and Communication), 385–436. Cambdrige: The MIT Press.

Braitenberg, Valentino. 1984. *Vehicles: Experiments in synthetic psychology.* Cambridge: The MIT Press.

Briscoe, Ted. 1999. *Linguistic evolution through language acquisition: Formal and computational models.* Cambridge: Cambridge University Press.

Brooks, Rodney A. 1986. A robust layered control system for a mobile robot. *IEEE Journal of Robotics and Automation* 2(1). 14–23.

Brooks, Rodney A. 1991. Intelligence without reason. In *Proceedings of the 1991 International Joint Conference on Artificial Intelligence*, 569–595. San Mateo: Morgan Kaufmann.

Brown, Roger. 1973. *A first language: The early stages.* Cambridge: Harvard University Press.

Bybee, Joan, Revere D. Perkins & William Pagliuca. 1994. *The evolution of grammar.* Chicago: University of Chicago Press.

Byrne, Alex & David R. Hilbert. 1997. *Readings on colour.* Cambridge: The MIT Press.

Cangelosi, Angelo & Domenico Parisi. 1996. *The emergence of 'language' in an evolving population of neural networks.* Technical Report, NSAL-96-004, Institute of Psychology, National.

Carnap, Rudolf. 1928. *The logical structure of the world.* London: Paul Kegan.

Casson, Ronald W. 1997. Color shift: Evolution of English color terms from brightness to hue. In Clyde L. Hardin & Luisa Maffi (eds.), *Color categories in thought and language*, 224–240. Cambridge: Cambridge University Press.

Cavalli-Sforza, Luigi Luca, Francesco Cavalli-Sforza & Sarah Thorne. 1996. *The great human diasporas: The history of diversity and evolution.* Basic Books.

Changeux, Jean-Pierre. 1997. *Neuronal man. The biology of mind.* Princeton: Princeton University Press.

Chomsky, Noam. 1986. *Knowledge of language: Its nature, origins, and use.* New York: Praeger.

Chomsky, Noam. 1987. Language in a psychological setting. *Sophia Linguistica* 22. 1–73.

Churchland, Patricia S. & Terrence J. Sejnowski. 1992. *The computational brain.* Cambridge: The MIT Press.

Clancey, William J. 1997. *Situated cognition: On human knowledge and computer representations.* Cambridge: Cambridge University Press.

Clark, Eve V. 1993. *The ontogensis of meaning.* Wiesbaden: Akademische Verlagsgesellschaft Athenaion.

Clark, John & Colin Yallop. 1995. *An introduction to phonetics and phonology.* Oxford: Blackwell.

Dall'Asta, Luca, Andrea Baronchelli, Alain Barrat & Vittorio Loreto. 2006. Nonequilibrium dynamics of language games on complex networks. *Physical Review E* 74(3). 36105.

Dawkins, Richard. 1976. *The selfish gene*. Oxford: Oxford University Press.

De Beule, Joachim. 2004. Creating temporal categories for an ontology of time. In *Proceedings of the 16th Belgium-Netherlands Conference on Artificial Intelligence (BNAIC '04)*. Groningen.

De Beule, Joachim, Bart De Vylder & Tony Belpaeme. 2006. A cross-situational learning algorithm for damping homonymy in the guessing game. In Luis M. Rocha, Larry S. Yaeger, Mark A. Bedau, Dario Floreano, Robert L. Goldstone & Alessandro Vespignani (eds.), *Artificial life X*, 466–472. MIT Press.

De Jong, Edwin D. & Luc Steels. 1999. Generation and selection of sensory channels. In Ricardo Poli, Hans-Michael Voigt, Stefano Cagnoni, David Corne, George Smith & Terrence Fogarty (eds.), *Proceedings of Evolutionary Image Analysis, Signal Processing and Telecommunications. First European workshops, EvoIASP'99 and EuroEcTel'99* (Lecture Notes in Computer Science 1596), 90–100. Berlin: Springer.

De Vylder, Bart & Karl Tuyls. 2006. How to reach linguistic consensus: A proof of convergence for the naming game. *Journal of Theoretical Biology* 242(4). 818–831.

Deacon, Terrence W. 1997. *The symbolic species: The co-evolution of language and the brain*. New York: W. W. Norton.

Dor, Daniel, Chris Knight & Jerome Lewis. 2014. *The social origins of language*. Oxford: Oxford University Press.

Eco, Umberto. 1997. *The search for the perfect language*. Oxford: Blackwell Publishing.

Edelman, Gerald M. 1987. *Neural Darwinism: The theory of neuronal group selection*. New York: Basic Books.

Elith, Jane & John R. Leathwick. 2009. Species distribution models: Ecological explanation and prediction across space and time. *Annual Review of Ecology, Evolution and Systematics* 40. 677–697.

Elman, Jeffrey L., Elizabeth A. Bates, Mark H. Johnson, Annette Karmiloff-Smith, Domenico Parisi & Kim Plunkett. 1996. *Rethinking innateness: A connectionist perspective on development*. Cambridge: The MIT Press.

Fauconnier, Gilles. 1994. *Mental spaces: Aspects of meaning construction in natural language*. Cambridge: Cambridge University Press.

Ferber, Jacques. 1998. *Multi-agent systems: An introduction to distributed artificial intelligence*. Reading: Addison-Wesley.

Fernandez-Ordonez, Ines. 1999. Leismo, laismo, loismo: Estado de la cuestión. In *Gramática descriptiva de la lengua española*, 1319–1390. Madrid, Spain: Real Academia Española.

Fischler, Martin A. & Oscar Firchein. 1987. *Readings in computer vision: Issues, problems, principles and paradigms*. Los Altos: Morgan Kaufmann.

Fisher, Simon & Matt Ridley. 2013. Culture, genes, and the human revolution. *Science* 340. 920–930.

Fodor, Jerry A. 1983. *The modularity of mind*. Cambridge.: MIT Press.

Fujita, Masahiro & Hiroaki Kitano. 1998. Development of an autonomous quadruped robot for robot entertainment. *Autonomous Robots* 5(1). 7–18.

Galantucci, Bruno. 2005. An experimental study of the emergence of human communication systems. *Cognitive Science* 29(5). 737–767.

Garrod, Simon & Anthony Anderson. 1987. Saying what you mean in dialogue: A study in conceptual and semantic co-ordination. *Cognition* 27(2). 181–218.
Gazdar, Gerald & Chris Mellish. 1989. *Natural language processing in LISP. An introduction to Computational Linguistics.* Reading: Addison-Wesley.
Gerasymova, Kateryna, Michael Spranger & Katrien Beuls. 2012. A language strategy for aspect: Encoding aktionsarten through morphology. In Luc Steels (ed.), *Experiments in cultural language evolution* (Advances in Interaction Studies 3), 257–276. John Benjamins.
Gleitman, Lila & Barbara Landau. 1994. *The acquisition of the lexicon.* Boston: MIT Press.
Goldberg, David E. 1989. *Genetic algorithms in search, optimization and machine learning.* Reading: Addison-Wesley.
Gärdenfors, Peter. 2000. *Conceptual spaces: The geometry of thought.* MIT Press.
Halliday, Michael Alexander Kirkwood. 1987. *Learning how to mean.* Cambridge: Cambridge University Press.
Harnad, Stevan. 1990. The symbol grounding problem. *Physica D* 42. 335–346.
Hauser, Marc D. 1996. *The evolution of communication.* Cambridge: The MIT Press.
Hawkins, John A. 1992. Innateness and function in language universals. In John A. Hawkins & Murray Gell-Mann (eds.), *The evolution of human languages* (Santa Fe Institute, Studies in the Sciences of Complexity), 87–120. Addison-Wesley.
Heine, Bernd. 1997. *The cognitive foundations of grammar.* Oxford: Oxford University Press.
Heine, Bernd & Tania Kuteva. 2007. *The genesis of grammar* (Oxford Studies in the Evolution of Language). Oxford: Oxford University Press.
Hintikka, Jaakko. 1998. *Paradigms for language theory and other essays.* Norwell: Kluwer.
Hopper, Paul & Elizabeth C. Traugott. 1993. *Grammaticalization.* Cambridge: Cambridge University Press.
Hu, Ming-Kuei. 1962. Visual pattern recognition by moment invariants. *IRE Transactions on Information Theory* IT-8. 179–187.
Hurford, James R. 1989. Biological evolution of the Saussurean sign as a component of the language acquisition device. *Lingua* 77. 187–222.
Hurford, James R., Michael Studdert-Kennedy & Chris Knight (eds.). 1998. *Approaches to the evolution of language: Social and cognitive bases.* Cambridge: Cambridge University Press.
Hutchins, Edwin L. & Brian Hazlehurst. 1995. How to invent a lexicon: The development of shared symbols in interaction. In Nigel Gilbert & Rosaria Conte (eds.), *Artificial societies: The computer simulation of social life*, 157–189. London: UCL Press.
Ikegami, Takashi. 1994. Genetic evolution to emergence of game strategies. *Physica D* 75. 292–309.
Jablonka, Eva & Marion Lamb. 2013. *Evolution in four dimensions. Genetic, epigenetic, behavioral, and symbolic variation in the history of life.* Cambridge: The MIT Press.
Jackendoff, Ray. 1997. *The architecture of the language faculty.* Boston: MIT Press.
Johnson, Mark. 1987. *The body in the mind. The bodily basis of meaning, imagination and reason.* Chicago: The University of Chicago Press.

Johnson-Laird, Philip N. 1977. Procedural semantics. *Cognition* 5(3). 189–214.
Kaiser, Peter K. & Robert M. Boynton. 1996. *Human colour vision*. Washington, DC.: Optical Society of America.
Kaneko, Kuni. 1996. Chaos as a source of complexity and diversity in evolution. In Christopher Langton (ed.), *Artificial life*, 163–177. Cambridge: The MIT Press.
Kaplan, Frédéric. 1999. Dynamiques de l'auto-organisation lexicale: Simulations multi-agents et têtes parlantes. *In Cognito : Revue internationale francophone en Sciences Cognitives* 15. 3–23.
Kaplan, Frédéric. 2001. *La naissance d'une langue chez les robots*. Hermes Science.
Kauffman, Stuart. 1993. *The origins of order: Self-organization and selection in evolution*. Oxford: Oxford University Press.
Kirby, Simon. 1999. *Function, selection and innateness: The emergence of language universals*. Oxford: Oxford University Press.
Knight, Chris, Robert Dunbar & Camila Power. 1999. *The evolution of culture*. Edinburgh: Edinburgh University Press.
Knight, Chris & Jerome Lewis. 2014. Hunter-gatherer egalitarianism enabled grammar to evolve. In Daniel Dor, Chris Knight & Jerome Lewis (eds.), *Social origins of language*. Oxford: Oxford University Press.
Koza, John R., David E. Goldberg & David B. Fogel (eds.). 1996. *Genetic programming 1996: Proceedings of the First Annual Conference, July 28–31, 1996*. (Complex Adaptive Systems). Cambridge: The MIT Press.
Labov, William. 2000. *Principles of linguistic change. Volume 2: Social factors*. Oxford: Basil Blackwell.
Langacker, Ronald W. 1987. *Foundations of Cognitive Grammar*. Vol. 1. Stanford: Stanford University Press.
Langton, Christopher G. (ed.). 1995. *Artificial life: An overview*. Cambridge: The MIT Press.
Lee, Penny. 1996. *The Whorf theory complex: A critical reconstruction* (Studies in the history of the language sciences 81). Philadelphia: John Benjamins.
Lehmann, Christian. 1982. Thoughts on grammaticalization. *Arbeiten des Kölner Universalienprojekts* 48(1).
Lehmann, Christian. 1988. On the function of agreement. In Michael Barlow & Charles Ferguson (eds.), *Agreement in natural language: Approaches, theories, descriptions*. 55–65. Stanford: Center for the Study of Language & Information.
Levelt, Willem J. M. 1989. *Speaking: From intention to articulation*. Boston: MIT Press.
Levinson, Stephen C. & David Wilkins (eds.). 2006. *Grammars of space. Explorations in cognitive diversity* (Language, Culture and Cognition). Cambridge: Cambridge University Press.
Liljencrants, Johan & Bjorn Lindblom. 1972. Numerical simulations of vowel quality systems. *Language* 48. 839–862.
Linsker, Ralph. 1990. Perceptual neural organization: Some approaches based on network models and information theory. *Annual Review of Neuroscience* 13. 257–281.
Lorenz, Edward N. 1993. *The essence of chaos*. Seattle: University of Washington Press.

Loreto, Vittorio & Luc Steels. 2007. Social dynamics: Emergence of language. *Nature Physics* 3(11). 758–760.
Lowe, Adam. 2010. Sei oggetti in cerca di artigiano. Na contaminazione del gusto: Appunti su sei ri-creazioni piranesiane realizzate da Factum Arte. In Giuseppe Pavanello (ed.), *Le arti di Piranesi. Architetto, incisore, antiquario, vedutista, designer*, 170–204. Venice: Marsilio.
Luger, George F. 1994. *Cognitive science. The science of intelligent systems*. San Diego: Academic Press.
Luisi, Luigi & Thomas Oberholzer. 2001. Origin of life on earth: Molecular biology as an approach to the minimal cell. In Franco Giovanelli (ed.), *The bridge between the Big Bang and Biology*, 345–355. CNR Press.
Luraghi, Silvia. 2011. The origin of the Proto-Indo-European gender system: Typological considerations. *Folia Linguistic* 45(2). 435–464.
MacLaury, Robert E. 1992. From brightness to hue: An explanatory model of color-category evolution. *Current Anthropology* 33(2). 137–186.
MacLennan, Bruce J. & Gordon M. Burghardt. 1993. Synthetic ethology and the evolution of cooperative communication. *Adaptive Behavior* 2(2). 161–188.
Margulis, Lynn. 1991. *Symbiosis in cell evolution*. San Francisco: W. H. Freeman.
Marr, David. 1982. *Vision*. San Francisco: Freeman.
Maturana, Humberto & Francisco Varela. 1998. *The tree of knowledge (revised edition)*. Boston: Shambhala Press.
May, Robert M. 1976. Simple mathematical models with complicated dynamical behavior. *Nature* 261. 25–44.
Maynard Smith, John. 1982. *Evolution and the theory of games*. Cambridge: Cambridge University Press.
Maynard Smith, John. 1989. *Evolutionary genetics*. Oxford: Oxford University Press.
McCarthy, John. 2008. The well-designed child. *Artificial Intelligence* 172(18). 2003–2014. http://dx.doi.org/10.1016/j.artint.2008.10.001.
McIntyre, Angus. 1998. Babel: A testbed for research in origins of language. In *Proceedings of Coling-ACL '98*. Montreal, August.
McIntyre, Angus, Luc Steels & Frédéric Kaplan. 1999. Net-mobile embodied agents. In *Proceedings of Sony Research Forum 1999*.
McMahon, April. 1994. *Understanding language change*. Cambridge: Cambridge University Press.
Meinhardt, Hans. 1982. *Models of biological pattern formation*. London: Academic Press.
Minsky, Marvin. 1986. *The society of mind*. New York: Simon & Schuster.
Minsky, Marvin & Seymour Papert. 1969. *Perceptrons*. Cambridge: The MIT Press.
Montague, Richard. 1974. The proper treatment of quantification in Ordinary English. In Richard Montague (ed.), *Formal philosophy. Selected papers*. New Haven: Yale University Press.
Moravec, Hans P. 1995. *Mind. Children. The future of robot and human intelligence*. Cambridge: Harvard University Press.

Mufwene, Salikoko. 2008. *Language evolution: Contact, competition and change*. New York: Continuum.
Neubauer, Nicolas. 2004. Emergent compositionality in language through negotiation. In *Proceedings of EvoLang V*. Leipzig.
Newborn, Monty. 1996. *Kasparov versus Deep Blue: Computer chess comes of age*. Berlin: Springer.
Newell, Allen & Herbert A. Simon. 1976. Computer science as empirical inquiry: Symbols and search. *Communications of the ACM* 19(13). 113–126.
Nichols, Johanna. 1992. *Linguistic diversity in space and time*. Chicago & London: The University of Chicago Press.
Nicolis, Grégoire & Ilya Prigogine. 1989. *Exploring complexity: An introduction*. New York: W. H. Freeman.
Nilsson, Nils J. (ed.). 1998. *Artificial intelligence*. Menlo Park: Morgan Kaufmann.
Nolfi, Stefano & Dario Floreano. 2001. *Evolutionary robotics. The biology, intelligence, and technology of self-organizing machines*. Cambridge: MA: MIT Press.
Norvig, Peter. 1992. *Paradigms of AI: Case studies in Common Lisp*. PWS.
Nosil, Patrik & Cristina P. Sandoval. 2008. Ecological niche dimensionality and the evolutionary diversification of stick insects. *PLoS ONE* 3(4). e1907. http://dx.plos.org/10.1371%2Fjournal.pone.0001907.
Obrist, Hans Ulrich. 2003. Interview with Luc Steels. In *Interviews*, 858–877. Milano, Italia: Edizioni Charta.
Obrist, Hans Ulrich & Barbara Vanderlinden. 1999. *Laboratorium*. Cologne: Dumont Verlag.
Odling-Smee, John, Kevin Laland & Marcus Feldman. 2003. What is not niche construction? In *Niche construction: The neglected process in evolution* (Monographs in Population Biology 37). New Jersey: Princeton University Press.
Ogden, Charles Kay & Ivor Armstrong Richards. 1935. *The meaning of meaning: A study of the influence of language upon thought and of the science of symbolism*. London: Routledge.
Oliphant, Mike. 1996. The dilemma of Saussurean communication. *Biosystems* 37(1–2). 31–38.
Oliphant, Mike. 1997. *Formal approaches to innate and learned communicaton: Laying the foundation for language*. University of California, San Diego PhD thesis.
Osherton, Daniel M. (ed.). 1995. *An invitation to cognitive science* (An Invitation to Cognitive Science). Cambridge: The MIT Press.
Pasteels, Jacques M. & Jean-Louis Deneuborg. 1987. *From individual to collective behaviour in social insects*. Basel: Birkhauser.
Peitgen, Heinz-Otto, Hartmut Jurgens & Dietmar Saupe. 1992. *Chaos and fractals. New frontiers of science*. Berlin: Springer.
Piaget, Jean. 1985. *The equilibration of cognitive structures: The central problem of intellectual development*. Chicago: University of Chicago Press.
Piattelli-Palmarini, Massimo (ed.). 1980. *Language and learning. The debate between Jean Piaget and Noam Chomsky*. London: Routledge.

Pinker, Steven. 1994. *The language instinct: How the mind creates language*. New York: W. Morrow.
Port, Robert F. & Tim van Gelder. 1995. *Mind as motion: Exploration in the dynamics of cognition*. Cambridge: The MIT Press.
Puglisi, Andrea, Andrea Baronchelli & Vittorio Loreto. 2008. Cultural route to the emergence of linguistic categories. *Proceedings of the National Academy of Sciences* 105(23). 7936–7940.
Quartz, Steven R. & Terrence J. Sejnowski. 1997. The neural basis of cognitive development: A constructivist manifesto. *Behavioral and Brain Sciences* 20. 537–596.
Quine, Willard Van Orman. 1960. *Word and object*. Cambridge: The MIT Press.
Regier, Terry. 1996. *The human semantic potential: Spatial language and constrained connectionism* (Neural Network Modelling and Connectionism). Boston: MIT Press.
Richerson, Peter & Robert Boyd. 2005. *Not by genes alone. How culture transformed human evolution*. Chicago: University of Chicago press.
Rizzolatti, Giacomo & Michael A. Arbib. 1998. Language within our grasp. *Trends in neurosciences* 21(5). 188–194.
Romaine, Suzanne. 1988. *Pidgin and creole languages*. London.: Longman.
Rousseau, Jean-Jacques. 1781. *Essai sur l'origine des langues*. English Version. Chicago: University of Chicago Press.
Ruhlen, Merritt. 1994. *On the origin of languages. Studies in linguistic taxonomy*. Stanford: Stanford University Press.
Rumelhart, David E. & James L. McClelland. 1986. *Parallel distributed processing: Exploration in the microstructure of cognition*. Volume 1 and 2. Cambridge: The MIT Press.
Russell, Stuart J. & Peter Norvig. 2003. *Artificial intelligence: A modern approach*. Upper Saddle River: Prentice Hall, Inc.
Schaffer, Simon & Steven Shapin. 2011. *Leviathan and the air-pump: Hobbes, Boyle and the experimental life*. Princeton: Princeton University Press.
Scherf, Angeline. 2002. *Olafur Eliasson: Chaque matin je me sens différent, chaque soir je me sens le même*. Musée d'Art Moderne de la Ville de Paris (Artist's Book/Exhibition Catalogue).
Sipper, Moshe, Daniel Mange & Perez-Uribe Andres. 1998. *Evolvable systems: From biology to hardware*. Berlin: Springer.
Siskind, Jeffrey Mark. 2000. Visual event classification via force dynamics. In *Proceedings of the national conference on artificial intelligence (AAAI)*, 149–155.
Spranger, Michael. 2015. *The evolution of grounded spatial language* (Computational Models of Language Evolution 5). Berlin: Language Science Press.
Spranger, Michael, Martin Loetzsch & Luc Steels. 2012. A perceptual system for language game experiments. In Luc Steels & Manfred Hild (eds.), *Language grounding in robots*, 89–110. Springer.
Spranger, Michael, Simon Pauw, Martin Loetzsch & Luc Steels. 2012. Open-ended procedural semantics. In Luc Steels & Manfred Hild (eds.), *Language Grounding in Robots*, 153–172. Springer.

Steels, Luc. 1995. A self-organizing spatial vocabulary. *Artificial Life Journal* 2(3). 319–332.

Steels, Luc. 1996. Self-organizing vocabularies. In Cristopher G. Langton (ed.), *Proceedings of the conference on artificial life V (Alife V) (Nara, Japan)*.

Steels, Luc. 1997a. Self-organizing vocabularies. In Christopher Langton & Katsunori Shimohara (eds.), *Artificial life V: Proceedings of the Fifth International Workshop on the Synthesis and Simulation of Living Systems*, 179–184. Cambridge: The MIT Press.

Steels, Luc. 1997b. The synthetic modeling of language origins. *Evolution of Communication* 1(1). 1–34.

Steels, Luc. 1998. The origins of syntax in visually grounded robotic agents. *Artificial Intelligence* 103(1–2). 133–156. http://dx.doi.org/10.1016/S0004--3702(98)00066--6.

Steels, Luc. 1999. Cognitive teleportation and situated embodiment. In Dario Floreano, Jean-Daniel Nicoud & Francesco Mondada (eds.), *Advances in artificial life* (Lecture Notes in Computer Science 1674), 7. Berlin: Springer.

Steels, Luc. 2000. The emergence of grammar in communicating autonomous robotic agents. In Werner Horn (ed.), *ECAI 2000: Proceedings of the 14th European Conference on Artificial Intelligence*, 764–769. IOS Publishing.

Steels, Luc. 2001. *COGAR A formalism for Cognitive Grammar*. Technical Report 2001-17, Sony CSL Paris.

Steels, Luc. 2004. The color of your eyes. In Richard Torkiae (ed.), *Olafur Eliasson: Your colour memory*. Glenside: Arcadia University Art Gallery.

Steels, Luc. 2007. The recruitment theory of language origins. In Caroline Lyon, Chrystopher L. Nehaniv & Angelo Cangelosi (eds.), *The emergence of communication and language*, 129–151. Berlin: Springer Verlag.

Steels, Luc (ed.). 2011. *Design patterns in Fluid Construction Grammar*. John Benjamins.

Steels, Luc. 2012. Self-organization and selection in language evolution. In Luc Steels (ed.), *Experiments in cultural language evolution*, 1–37. Amsterdam: John Benjamins.

Steels, Luc & Jean-Christophe Baillie. 2003. Shared grounding of event descriptions by autonomous robots. *Robotics and Autonomous Systems* 43(2–3). 163–173.

Steels, Luc & Tony Belpaeme. 2005. Coordinating perceptually grounded categories through language: A case study for colour. *Behavioral and Brain Sciences* 28(4). 469–529.

Steels, Luc & Rodney A. Brooks (eds.). 1995. *The 'artificial life' route to artificial intelligence: Building embodied, situated agents*. New Haven: Lawrence Erlbaum Ass.

Steels, Luc & Frédéric Kaplan. 1999. Collective learning and semiotic dynamics. In Dario Floreano, Jean-Daniel Nicoud & Francesco Mondada (eds.), *Advances in artificial life (ecal 99)* (Lecture Notes in Artificial Intelligence 1674), 679–688. Berlin: Springer.

Steels, Luc & Frédéric Kaplan. 2000. Origine et évolution du langage : Expériences robotiques. *Revue du Palais de la Découverte* 278. 63–67.

Steels, Luc & Frédéric Kaplan. 2001. Aibo's first words: The social learning of language and meaning. *Evolution of Communication* 4(1). 3–32.

Steels, Luc & Martin Loetzsch. 2008. Perspective alignment in spatial language. In Kenny R. Coventry, Thora Tenbrink & John. A Bateman (eds.), *Spatial language and dialogue*. Oxford University Press.

Steels, Luc & John McDermott. 1994. *The knowledge level in expert systems: Conversations and commentary* (Perpectives in Artificial Intelligence 10). New Haven: Academic Press.

Steels, Luc & Michael Spranger. 2008a. Can body language shape body image? In Seth Bullock, Jason Noble, Richard Watson & Mark A. Bedau (eds.), *Artificial life XI: Proceedings of the eleventh international conference on the simulation and synthesis of living systems*, 577–584. The MIT Press.

Steels, Luc & Michael Spranger. 2008b. The robot in the mirror. *Connection Science* 20(4). 337–358.

Steels, Luc, Remi van Trijp & Pieter Wellens. 2007. Multi-Level Selection in the Emergence of Language Systematicity. In Fernando Almeida e Costa, Luis M. Rocha, Ernesto Costa & Inman Harvey (eds.), *Proceedings of the Ninth European Conference on Artificial Life* (LNAI 4648). Springer.

Steels, Luc & Paul Vogt. 1997. Ancrage de jeux de langage adaptatifs dans des agents robotiques. In Arab Ali Cherif & Jacqueline Signorini (eds.), *Intelligence artificielle et complexité*, 27–39. Paris.

Steels, Luc & Pieter Wellens. 2007. Scaffolding language emergence using the autotelic principle. In *IEEE symposium on artificial life 2007 (Alife'07)*, 325–332. Honolulu: Wiley – IEEE Press.

Steels, Luc, Michael Spranger, Remi van Trijp, Sebastian Höfer & Manfred Hild. 2012. Emergent action language on real robots. In Luc Steels & Manfred Hild (eds.), *Language grounding in robots*, 255–276. Springer.

Tager-Flusberg, Helen. 1994. *Constraints on language acquisition. Studies of atypical children*. Hillsdale: Lawrence Erlbaum.

Taylor, John R. 1995. *Linguistic categorization: Prototypes in linguistic theory*. Second edition. Oxford: Oxford University Press.

Thelen, Esther & Linda B. Smith. 1994. *A dynamic systems approach to the development of cognition and action*. Boston: MIT Press.

Thomason, Sarah G. & Terrence Kaufman. 1988. *Language contact, creolization, and genetic linguistics*. Berkeley: University of California Press.

Tomasello, Michael. 1992. *First verbs: A case study of early grammatical development*. Cambridge: Cambridge University Press.

Traugott, Elizabeth C. & Bernd Heine (eds.). 1991. *Approaches to grammaticalization*. Vol. 1 & 2. John Benjamins.

Traugott, Elizabeth C. & Graeme Trousdale. 2013. *Constructionalization and constructional changes*. Oxford: Oxford University Press.

Turing, Alan. 1950. Computing machinery and intelligence. *Mind* 59. 433–460.

Ullman, Shimon. 1996. *High-level vision: Object recognition and visual cognition*. Boston: MIT Press.

Van Kemenade, Ans. 1987. *Syntactic case and morphological case in the history of English*. Dordrecht: Foris.

van Trijp, Remi. 2010. Strategy competition in the evolution of pronouns: A case-study of spanish leísmo, laísmo and loísmo. In Andrew D. M. Smith, Marieke Schouwstra,

Bart de Boer & Kenny Smith (eds.), *The evolution of language (EVOLANG 8)*, 336–343. Singapore: World Scientific.
van Trijp, Remi. 2013. Linguistic assessment criteria for explaining language change: A case study on syncretism in German definite articles. *Language Dynamics and Change* 3. 105–132.
van Trijp, Remi. 2014a. Fitness landscapes in cultural language evolution: A case study on German definite articles. In *The evolution of language (Evolang-X)*. Singapore: World Scientific.
van Trijp, Remi. 2014b. *The evolution of case grammar*. Berlin: Language Science Press.
Van Valin jr, Robert D. & Randy J. LaPolla. 1997. *Syntax: Structure, meaning and function*. Cambridge: Cambridge university press.
Varela, Francisco J., Evan Thomson & Eleanor Rosch. 1991. *The embodied mind. Cognitive science and human experience*. Cambridge: The MIT Press.
Varela, Francisco J., Antonio Coutinho, Bruno Duprie & Nelson Vaz. 1988. Cognitive networks: Immune, neural and otherwise. In Alan Perelson (ed.), *Theoretical immunology* (Science of Complexity 2). Englewood Cliffs: Addison-Wesley.
Van de Velde, Freek. 2011. Left-peripheral expansion of the English NP. *English Language and Linguistics* 15. 387–415.
Velichkovsky, Boris M. & Duane M. Rumbaugh. 1996. *Communicating meaning. The evolution and development of language*. Mahwah: Lawrence Erlbaum Associates.
Vogt, Paul. 2003. The talking heads simulation tool. In Wolfgang Banzhaf, Thomas Christaller, Peter Dittrich, Jan Kim & Jens Ziegler (eds.), *Advances in artificial life - Proceedings of the 7th European Conference on Artificial Life (ECAL)*. Berlin, Heidelberg: Springer.
Waddington, Conrad Hal. 1975. *The evolution of an evolutionist*. Ithaca: Cornell University Press.
Wellens, Pieter, Martin Loetzsch & Luc Steels. 2008. Flexible word meaning in embodied agents. *Connection Science* 20(2). 173–191.
Werner, Gregory M. & Michael G. Dyer. 1991. Evolution of communication in artificial organisms. In Christopher G. Langton, Charles Taylor, J. Doyne Farmer & Steen Rassmussen (eds.), *Artificial life II, vol. X of SFI studies in the sciences of complexity*. Redwood City: Addison-Wesley.
Whorf, Benjamin Lee. 1956. *Language, thought and reality: Selected writings of Benjamin Lee Whorf*. John. B. Carrol (ed.). Cambridge: The MIT Press.
Wierzbicka, Anna. 1992. *Semantics, culture and cognition. Universal human concepts in culture-specific configurations*. Oxford.: Oxford.
Winograd, Terry. 1971. *Procedures as a Representation for Data in a Computer Program for Understanding Natural Language*. Massachusetts Institute of Technology PhD thesis.
Wittgenstein, Ludwig. 1922. *Tractatus logico-philosophicus*. London: Kegan Paul, Trench, Trubner.
Wittgenstein, Ludwig. 1953. *Philosophical investigations*. New York: Macmillan.

Woods, William Aaron. 1981. Procedural semantics as a theory of meaning. In Aravind Joshi, Bonnie Weber & Ivan Sag (eds.), *Elements of discourse understanding*. Cambridge: Cambridge University Press.

Worden, Robert. 1995. A speed limit for evolution. *Journal of Theoretical Biology* 176. 137–152.

Wunsch, Susi. 1998. *The adventures of sojourner: The mission to mars that thrilled the world*. New York: Mikaya Publishing.

Zeki, Semir. 1993. *A vision of the brain*. Oxford: Blackwell Scientific Publications.

Name index

Anastacio, Thomas J., 69
Anderson, Anthony, 321
Andres, Perez-Uribe, 81
Arbib, Michael A., 305
Arkin, Ronald. C., 11, 52
Arthur, Brian, 125, 326

Babloyantz, Agnes, 123
Badii, Remo, 183
Baillie, Jean-Christophe, 286
Ballard, Dana H., 34
Baronchelli, Andrea, 295, 309
Bates, Elisabeth, 37
Belpaeme, Tony, 60, 262, 269, 270, 273, 294, 309
Beuls, Katrien, 294, 351
Bickerton, Derek, 37
Billard, Aude, 14
Bleys, Joris, 309, 320, 335
Boeckx, Cedric, 325, 327
Boer, Bart de, 32
Bowerman, Melissa, 37
Boyd, Robert, 326
Boynton, Robert M., 51
Braitenberg, Valentino, 51, 53
Bretherton, Inge, 37
Briscoe, Ted, 13
Brooks, Rodney A., 11, 52, 53, 88, 270, 272
Brown, Christopher M., 34
Brown, Roger, 26
Burghardt, Gordon M., 28, 119
Bybee, Joan, 44
Byrne, Alex, 51

Cangelosi, Angelo, 108
Carnap, Rudolf, 167

Casson, Ronald W., 338
Cavalli-Sforza, Francesco, 80
Cavalli-Sforza, Luigi Luca, 80
Changeux, Jean-Pierre, 83
Chomsky, Noam, 8, 195
Churchland, Patricia S., 50, 77
Clancey, William J., 12
Clark, Eve V., 37
Clark, John, 32

Dall'Asta, Luca, 295
Dautenhahn, Kerstin, 14
Dawkins, Richard, 81, 326
Deacon, Terrence W., 8, 78
Deneuborg, Jean-Louis, 124
De Beule, Joachim, 273, 294
De Jong, Edwin D., 84
De Vylder, Bart, 273, 294, 302
Dor, Daniel, 355
Dunbar, Robert, 258
Dyer, Michael G., 106

Eco, Umberto, 188
Edelman, Gerald M., 57, 79, 83, 326
Elith, Jane, 329
Elman, Jeffrey L., 76, 79

Fauconnier, Gilles, 59
Feldman, Marcus, 329
Ferber, Jacques, 20
Fernandez-Ordonez, Ines, 324
Firchein, Oscar, 34
Fischler, Martin A., 34
Fisher, Simon, 325
Floreano, Dario, 326
Fodor, Jerry A., 57, 78
Fogel, David B., 81

Name index

Fujita, Masahiro, 270

Galantucci, Bruno, 321
Garrod, Simon, 321
Gazdar, Gerald, 46
Gelder, Tim van, 60
Gerasymova, Kateryna, 294
Gleitman, Lila, 37
Goldberg, David E., 81
Grohmann, Kleanthes, 325
Gärdenfors, Peter, 59, 90

Halliday, Michael Alexander Kirkwood, 26
Harnad, Stevan, 53
Hauser, Marc D., 28, 106
Hawkins, John A., 5
Hazlehurst, Brian, 106
Heine, Bernd, 44, 351
Hilbert, David R., 51
Hintikka, Jaakko, 168
Hopper, Paul, 351
Hu, Ming-Kuei, 305
Hurford, James R., 5, 106
Hutchins, Edwin L., 106

Ikegami, Takashi, 28

Jablonka, Eva, 325
Jackendoff, Ray, 30
Johnson, Mark, 91
Johnson-Laird, Philip N., 311
Jurgens, Hartmut, 98

Kaiser, Peter K., 51
Kaneko, Kuni, 126
Kaplan, Frédéric, 20, 69, 189, 225, 258, 260, 270
Kauffman, Stuart, 183
Kaufman, Terrence, 37
Kirby, Simon, 164, 187
Kitano, Hiroaki, 270
Knight, Chris, 5, 258, 265, 355
Koza, John R., 81

Kuteva, Tania, 351

Labov, William, 46
Laland, Kevin, 329
Lamb, Marion, 325
Landau, Barbara, 37
Langacker, Ronald W., 46
Langton, Christopher G., 13
LaPolla, Randy J., 29
Leathwick, John R., 329
Lee, Penny, 196
Lehmann, Christian, 351
Levelt, Willem J. M., 30
Levinson, Stephen C., 196
Lewis, Jerome, 265, 355
Liljencrants, Johan, 32
Lindblom, Bjorn, 32
Linsker, Ralph, 84
Loetzsch, Martin, 273, 303, 304, 349
Looveren, Joris van, 60
Lorenz, Edward N., 42
Loreto, Vittorio, 295, 309
Lowe, Adam, 232
Luger, George F., 5
Luisi, Luigi, 326
Luraghi, Silvia, 351

MacLaury, Robert E., 338
MacLennan, Bruce J., 28, 119
Mange, Daniel, 81
Margulis, Lynn, 187
Marr, David, 53
Maturana, Humberto, 90
May, Robert M., 113
Maynard Smith, John, 27, 183
McCarthy, John, 78
McClelland, James L., 77
McDermott, John, 78, 270
McIntyre, Angus, 20, 23
McMahon, April, 46, 113
Meinhardt, Hans, 124
Mellish, Chris, 46
Minsky, Marvin, 57, 77
Montague, Richard, 29, 46

Name index

Moravec, Hans P., 20
Mufwene, Salikoko, 327

Neubauer, Nicolas, 262
Newborn, Monty, 9
Newell, Allen, 8
Nichols, Johanna, 127
Nicolis, Grégoire, 13
Nilsson, Nils J., 11
Nolfi, Stefano, 326
Norvig, Peter, 11, 23
Nosil, Patrik, 330

Oberholzer, Thomas, 326
Obrist, Hans Ulrich, 16, 203, 204
Odling-Smee, John, 329
Ogden, Charles Kay, 29
Oliphant, Mike, 106, 108
Osherton, Daniel M., 5

Pagliuca, William, 44
Papert, Seymour, 77
Parisi, Domenico, 108
Pasteels, Jacques M., 124
Peitgen, Heinz-Otto, 98
Perkins, Revere D., 44
Piaget, Jean, 81
Piattelli-Palmarini, Massimo, 46, 327
Pinker, Steven, 9
Politi, Antonio, 183
Port, Robert F., 60
Power, Camila, 258
Prigogine, Ilya, 13
Puglisi, Andrea, 309

Quartz, Steven R., 80
Quine, Willard Van Orman, 105

Regier, Terry, 106
Richards, Ivor Armstrong, 29
Richerson, Peter, 326
Ridley, Matt, 325
Rizzolatti, Giacomo, 305
Robinson, David A., 69

Romaine, Suzanne, 127
Rosch, Eleanor, 12, 61, 76, 86, 91
Rousseau, Jean-Jacques, 76
Ruhlen, Merritt, 119
Rumbaugh, Duane M., 5
Rumelhart, David E., 77
Russell, Sturart J., 11

Sandoval, Cristina P., 330
Saupe, Dietmar, 98
Schaffer, Simon, 232
Scherf, Angeline, 260
Sejnowski, Terrence J., 50, 77, 80
Shapin, Steven, 232
Simon, Herbert A., 8
Sipper, Moshe, 81
Siskind, Jeffrey Mark, 286
Smith, Linda B., 81
Snyder, Lynn, 37
Spranger, Michael, 294, 303, 304, 306, 311, 332
Steels, Luc, 11, 13, 14, 20, 52, 60, 78, 84, 88, 106, 189, 205, 258, 260, 262, 269, 270, 273, 274, 278, 286, 288, 294–296, 303, 304, 306, 309, 311, 318, 349, 351, 354
Studdert-Kennedy, Michael, 5

Tager-Flusberg, Helen, 19
Taylor, John R., 36, 91
Thelen, Esther, 81
Thomason, Sarah G., 37
Thomson, Evan, 12, 61, 76, 86, 91
Thorne, Sarah, 80
Tomasello, Michael, 37
Traugott, Elizabeth C., 44, 351
Tria, Francesca, 295
Trousdale, Graeme, 351
Turing, Alan, 15
Tuyls, Karl, 302

Ullman, Shimon, 28, 53

van Trijp, Remi, 282, 294, 330, 332

Name index

Van Valin jr, Robert D., 29
Vanderlinden, Barbara, 16, 203
Van Kemenade, Ans, 324
Varela, Francisco, 90
Varela, Francisco J., 12, 61, 76, 82, 86, 91
Velde, Freek Van de, 324
Velichkovsky, Boris M., 5
Vogt, Paul, 14, 270

Waddington, Conrad Hal, 81
Wellens, Pieter, 294, 296, 349, 354
Werner, Gregory M., 106
Whorf, Benjamin Lee, 196
Wierzbicka, Anna, 78
Wilkins, David, 196
Winograd, Terry, 311
Wittgenstein, Ludwig, 8, 167
Woods, William Aaron, 311
Worden, Robert, 80
Wunsch, Susi, 10

Yallop, Colin, 32

Zeki, Semir, 21, 50, 61

Subject index

AIBO, 270
COGAR (cognitive grammar architecture), 288
GEOM world, 70
PERACT vision system, 286

action game, 304
actuators, 50
agent, 5, 23
ambiguity, 149, 188
analogy of semantic roles, 291
artificial life, 10
autocatalysis, 123

behaviour network, 272
behaviour-based robots, 11
behaviours, 52
bottom-up approach, 9
bounding box, 53

Case Grammar experiment, 282
categorial adaptivity, 100
cognitive effort, 328
Color Description Game, 335
Colour Description Game, 309
colour strategies, 314
communicative success, 113
comparative method, 274
competition diagram, 185
conceptual spaces, 59
conceptualisation strategy, 345
constraint network, 312
Constraint Programming, 311
context-sensitivity, 61
culture-driven language evolution, 323

Darwinian evolutionary dynamics, 326

Discrimination Game, 88
discrimination tree, 35
discriminatory success, 98
divergent perception, 56
DO game, 271

empiricism, 77
environmental influence, 174
expressive adequacy, 328

feature extraction, 54
fitness landscape, 329
flexible word meaning, 349
Fluid Construction Grammar, 295*
FM-diagram, 185
functional constructions, 318

game theory, 27*
German article system, 330
grammar emergence, 278
grammatical agreement, 351
grammaticalisation, 351
Guessing Game, 26, 134

iconoclasm, 242
ideal language, 187
image segmentation, 33
increasing returns economics, 125
influence of embodiment, 320
innate categories, 78
instructionism, 81
Intensive Science exhibition, 264
interactionism, 81
IRL, 311

Laboratorium exhibition, 16, 203
language contact, 129

Subject index

language grounding, 168
language strategy, 274
lateral inhibition, 108
learnability, 328
lexical coherence, 115
lexical memory, 107
lexical self-organisation, 122
linguistic relativism, 195

meta-strategy, 343
Montague grammar, 29*
multi-level alignment, 294
Museum of Modern Art installation, 262

N01SE exhibition, 231
Naming Game, 106
non-monotonicity, 44
Normalised Centralised Moments, 305

ontological coherence, 197

Pachinko machine, 89
perceptual anomalies, 179
perceptual constancy, 60
Perspective Reversal, 273
phonological reduction strategy, 352
phrasal construction, 318
population change, 120
portable Talking Heads, 258
positive feedback, 90
prisoners dilemma game, 28
procedural semantics, 311
Proper Naming Game, 296
proto-language, 37
prototype, 299

rationalism, 78
re-entrance, 140
recruitment hypothesis, 325
RF-diagram, 185
RMF-coherence, 186
Rousseau's paradox, 195

S-shape curve, 113
saliency, 62

scaffolds, 66
scaling, 61
score, 107
segmentation, 53
selectionism, 81
selectionist forces, 327
semiotic dynamics, 183, 295
semiotic landscape, 183
semiotic network, 301
semiotic square, 28
sensors, 50
sensory channels, 34, 58
sensory experience, 299
sieve architecture, 56
situated grounded semantics, 43
social conformity, 329
social situated learning, 272
Spatial Language Game, 332
Spatially Distributed Naming Games, 127
strategy generation, 343
strategy selection, 338
synonymy, 144

Talking Heads website, 208
teleportation, 20
Turing test, 15

verbalisation, 37

Wittgenstein, 8

Subject index

www.ingramcontent.com/pod-product-compliance
Lightning Source LLC
Chambersburg PA
CBHW060303010526
44108CB00042B/2619